April 18/1997

To My Son
Jeremiah

Love
Dad.

Learn This & beat Me Ha Ha.!!

Contact Purvis

The Complete Chess Course

Also by Fred Reinfeld

HOW TO GET MORE OUT OF CHESS
HOW TO PLAY CHESS LIKE A CHAMPION
HOW TO BE A WINNER AT CHESS
CHESS IN A NUTSHELL
A NEW APPROACH TO CHESS MASTERY

The Complete Chess Course

by Fred Reinfeld

Doubleday & Company, Inc.
Garden City, New York

ISBN: 0-385-00464-8

Library of Congress Catalog Card Number 59-13043
Copyright © 1953, 1954, 1955, 1956, 1957, 1959 by Sterling Publishing Co., Inc.
Printed in the United States of America

30   29   28   27   26

Table of Contents

Introduction

Although seven of the eight sections of this book were originally published as separate volumes, they were written with their co-ordination as a complete chess course in mind. Conveniently prefaced now by a new summarized review of the basic elements of chess, the resulting comprehensive whole provides the instruction that any chessplayer needs to develop a respectable degree of skill.

The interrelated progression of subjects is treated in the following order. A player who knows the elements but little more about chess may not need the introductory steps revealed in Book One, but he does need to be warned about the types of mistakes—neglected development and the like—that beginning and intermediate players make so frequently. He can then go on to study opening play in its larger aspects, and examine its consequences in the ensuing middle game. From this point he proceeds to study the endgame stage, which evolves out of the middle game previously studied. And finally, having seen the logical relationship which binds together opening, middle game, and ending, the student is now ready to go back to the initial stage and study the chief openings in rewarding detail.

With this over-all scheme in mind, the reader is in a better position to appreciate the detailed treatment in each section.

Book One is a summary of chess fundamentals that provides the first springboard into the "royal" game for beginners, and also serves as a refresher for the more advanced player.

Book Two is a study of the nine most common mistakes made by chessplayers. These include such typical errors as failing to guard against hostile captures, underestimating the opponent's threats, and making Pawn moves that weaken the castled position. Many examples are given to show how these and other mistakes prove disastrous in the opening and middle game.

Now that the reader has been made aware of the kinds of mistakes that he must avoid, he is ready to study the problem of planning the opening so as to get a promising middle-game position. First the subject is treated from White's point of view (Book Three), dealing with such problems as control of the center, how to exploit superior development and mobility, and the like. But it is at least equally important to deal with opening problems from Black's point of view, and this brings us to Book Four; here problems of counterattack and defense are emphasized.

These studies of middle-game play lead logically to a treatment of the endgame stage, for whatever happens in this final part of the game is the consequence of what happened earlier in the opening and middle game. As a rule, the chief practical problem of endgame play is how to win with a material advantage which has been obtained in the middle game. In Book Five the different types of endings are classified and studied; many practical examples are explained, and the reader acquires an excellent grasp of the vital problem of converting a material advantage into victory.

But to know how to make use of advantages is not enough; so in Book Six we go on to the related problem of how to make the most of disadvantageous positions. This section contains many valuable pointers that will help the reader to salvage many an apparently lost game.

Now that opening, middle game, and endgame have been surveyed, what remains? It is now time to survey the chess openings in some detail, paying particular attention to the way in which opening moves are intertwined with the ensuing middle-game play. This material appears in Book Seven and Eight. Each opening is presented with explanations of its *basic ideas*—the plans of each player, their middle-game goals, the clash that follows their attempts to enforce their disparate conceptions.

Throughout, my aim has been to give the reader a better idea of the fine points of chess as it is played by the masters. The appreciative comments I have had from readers encourage me to believe that a much wider circle of new readers will enjoy this material and apply it profitably in their own games.

The
Basic Rules
of
Chess

Book One

THE BASIC RULES OF CHESS

CHESS is played by two opponents, "White" and "Black," who take turns making their moves. White always makes the first move. The chessboard (Diagram 1) has 8 horizontal rows ("ranks") and 8 vertical rows ("files"). Each row is therefore made up of eight squares.

All 64 squares are used in the play, and in order to make it easier to tell them apart, they are alternately light-colored ("white squares") and dark-colored ("black squares").

THE OPENING POSITION

At the beginning of a game, each player has 16 chess-men, always placed as in Diagram 2.

1 *The Chessboard*

2 *The Opening Position*

White always takes the light-colored chessmen; Black has the dark-colored chessmen. The names of the forces shown in Diagram 2 are:

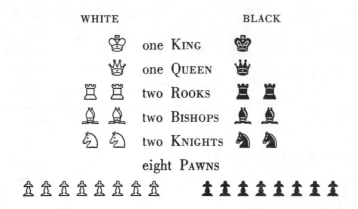

WHITE			BLACK
	one	KING	
	one	QUEEN	
	two	ROOKS	
	two	BISHOPS	
	two	KNIGHTS	
	eight	PAWNS	

An important point to remember is that in the opening position the right-hand corner square nearest to White must be a white square.

Another important point about the opening position: the two Queens face each other along the same vertical row ("the Queen file"). Each Queen is placed on a square of its own color, the White Queen on a white square, the Black Queen on a black square.

Both Kings likewise face each other across the King file.

The *King Bishop* is placed next to the King, on the King Bishop file.

The *King Knight* is placed next to the King Bishop, on the King Knight file.

The *King Rook* is placed next to the King Knight, on the King Rook file.

The *Queen Bishop* is placed next to the Queen, on the Queen Bishop file.

The *Queen Knight* is placed next to the Queen Bishop, on the Queen Knight file.

The *Queen Rook* is placed next to the Queen Knight, on the Queen Rook file.

The *Pawns* are set out in the second row, in front of the pieces just named. Each Pawn is named for the piece it stands in front of — or, to put it another way, for the file on which it stands.

Thus, the Pawn on the King file — in front of the King — is the *King Pawn*.

HOW THE PIECES MOVE

Each of the men moves in a different way. In describing the moves it is necessary to refer to ranks, files, and also to diagonals. (A diagonal is a row of squares of the same color all going in the same direction. In Diagram 2 the row of white squares from White's King Rook to Black's Queen Rook is a diagonal.)

The King

The King (subject to limitations that are described later on) moves one square in any direction (Diagram 3). It cannot displace or leap over any of its forces.

The King captures the same way it moves (Diagram 4). When it captures an enemy piece it displaces that piece (occupies the square of the captured unit).

3 *White's King has 8 possible moves, indicated by crosses.*

4 *White's King can capture any one of the Black men.*

6

The Queen

The Queen is the most powerful of all the chess forces. Like the King, the Queen can move in any direction — but with this important difference: the Queen can move the whole length of any available line, as long as there is no obstacle in its way (Diagram 5).

There are two possible obstacles: friendly pieces, which the Queen cannot displace or leap over; or enemy pieces, which can be captured by displacement (Diagram 6).

5 *The Queen can move to any of the squares indicated by an arrow; it moves in only one direction at a time.*

6 *The White Queen can capture the Black Rook or Bishop or either Black Knight.*

7

The Rook

The Rook (next most powerful piece after the Queen), moves horizontally *or* vertically — one direction at a time.

The Rook captures hostile pieces by displacement, but it cannot displace or leap over its own forces. The Rook captures in the same way it moves.

(Some players call the Rook a "Castle," but "Rook" is the proper term.)

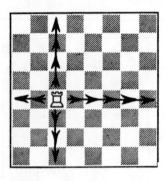

7 *The Rook can move to any square indicated by an arrow.*

8 *The Rook can capture the Bishop or Knight; but not the Pawn.*

The Bishop

The Bishop, moving in one direction at a time, moves and captures *diagonally*.

The Bishop captures hostile pieces by displacement. It cannot displace or leap over its own forces.

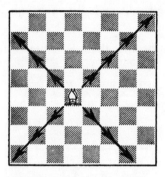 

9 *The Bishop can move to any of the squares indicated by an arrow.*

10 *The Bishop can capture either of the Black Pawns.*

The Knight

The Knight is the only piece that can leap over other units — his own or the opponent's.

The Knight is also the only piece that has a move of fixed length. It moves a total of three squares — in either one of two ways:

(a) one square forward *or* backward; then two squares to the right *or* left.

(b) one square to the right *or* left; then two squares forward *or* backward.

The Knight captures only on the terminal square of his move, displacing the piece it captures.

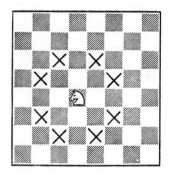

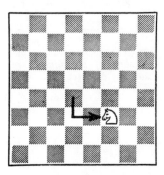

11 *The Knight has the option of moving to any square indicated by a cross.*

12 *This is one of the eight possible moves available to the Knight in Diagram 11.*

Note that the Knight changes the color of its square each time it moves. It goes from a white square to a black square; or from a black square to a white square.

13 *The White Knight can capture Black's Bishop.*

14 *The Knight leaps over two Pawns to capture the most distant Pawn.*

11

The Pawn

The Pawn is the only unit that is limited to moving in only one direction: straight ahead.

With one exception (to be noted shortly), a Pawn moves one square forward unless its path is blocked by one of its own units or by a hostile unit.

The path for White Pawns (as seen in Diagram 2) is directly forward from the opening position. How a White Pawn moves is shown in detail on Diagrams 15 and 16.

15 *The White Pawn is about to move.*

16 *The White Pawn has moved.*

The path for Black Pawns (likewise seen in Diagram 2) is also directly forward from the opening position. How a Black Pawn moves is shown in detail in Diagrams 17 and 18.

17 *The Black Pawn is about to move.*

18 *The Black Pawn has moved.*

The Pawn has one important option. When any Pawn is moved from its opening position — even if this occurs at a late stage of the game — that Pawn on its first move has the option of moving one square or two. Thus, in Diagram 2 (the opening position) all the Pawns, while on their second rank, have the option of moving one square or two.

19 *White has accepted his option by advancing his King Pawn two squares. Black has done likewise.*

20 *White has accepted the option by advancing his King two squares. Black, however, has advanced his Queen Pawn one square.*

The Pawn's capturing methods differ from the way it moves.

The Pawn moves by advancing straight along a file. In capturing, however, the Pawn can take a hostile unit only if it is located on either of the *diagonally-forward adjoining squares* — that is, one square forward to the right or left (Diagram 21). The Pawn *cannot* capture a hostile unit which is directly in front of it.

21 *The White Pawn can capture the Black Bishop.*

22 *The White Pawn cannot capture the Black Bishop.*

CHECK AND CHECKMATE

The King is the most important piece in chess.

The basic method of winning a game of chess is *to attack the hostile King in such a way that it cannot escape.* This is called "checkmate." (The King is actually not captured; its inability to escape from attack is what constitutes the checkmate.)

Any attack by a piece or Pawn directly on a King is called a "check." When a King is checked, it must *immediately* get out of check. The King cannot be allowed to remain in check.

If it is a player's turn to move and his King is *not* in check, he cannot make any move that exposes the King to check. The King must never come within the capturing range of hostile pieces.

There are three ways to get out of check:

(1) to capture the unit that is giving the check;

(2) to move the King out of the line of attack — but not into the line of attack of some other hostile unit;

(3) To interpose one of your own units between the King and the hostile unit that is giving check.

If none of these three methods can be applied, then the King is checkmated.

In Diagrams 23 and 24 the Black King was in check, but it was possible to get out of check. In Diagram 25 the attacked King is able to escape; but in Diagram 26 the attacked King is checkmated.

23 White's Queen is checking the Black King. Black has a choice of three different ways of getting his King out of check.

24 Black has captured the White Queen, getting his King out of check. Black could also have moved his King, or interposed his Rook.

25 Black's King is in check from White's Rook but it has a "loophole." By playing his King diagonally forward to the right, Black escapes from the check.

26 Black's King is in check from White's Rook and has no escape, as its own Pawns block the exit. This is an example of checkmate.

The positions in Diagrams 26, 27 and 28 are all examples of checkmate. In each case the checking piece cannot be captured; the attacked King cannot move out of the capturing range of the hostile forces; and no friendly unit can be interposed on the line of attack between the checking unit and the checked King.

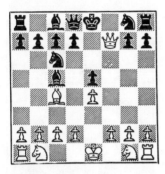 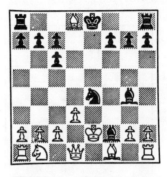

27 *Black's King is check-mated. White's Queen is giving check and Black's King cannot capture the White Queen, which is protected by a White Bishop. Having no flight square, or way of interposing a friendly unit, Black's King is trapped.*

28 *White's King is check-mated. White has no escape from the Black Bishop's check. Note that Black's Knight and Bishops command all the possible squares available to White's King, and White cannot interpose any of his own units.*

Discovered Check

This is a special kind of check, caused by removing a unit to unmask a line of attack by another unit. For example, in Diagram 29 White's Bishop can give check without moving; the check is "discovered" by moving the White Rook which has been blocking the diagonal. The result appears in Diagram 30.

29 *White can give a discovered check with his Bishop by moving his Rook.*

30 *By moving his Rook, White has opened up an attacking line for a discovered check by his Bishop.*

Double Check

This is a discovered check with an added feature: the piece that unmasks an attacking line for the discovered check also gives check.

31 *By moving his Bishop to give check, White can give double check with his Queen.*

32 *As Black's King cannot move out of check, he is checkmated. The double check was devastating.*

The double check is the most difficult kind of check to meet, as capture or interposition is impossible. For if either checking unit is captured, the other unit continues to give check. Similarly, an interposition to one check still leaves the other check functioning.

The only possible reply to a double check, then, is to move the attacked King. Where this is not feasible, the King is checkmated.

CASTLING

We have seen what happens when the King is exposed to attack. The special move known as "Castling" offers a valuable method for safeguarding the King against attack.

Castling is the only move in chess which is really two separate moves — a King move and a Rook move. Castling, as well, is the only move that each player can carry out only once during a game.

It is possible to Castle with the King and King Rook (King-side Castling); or with the King and Queen Rook (Queen-side Castling). Diagrams 33 and 34 show how King-side Castling is accomplished.

33 *Before King-side Castling (King and King Rook)*   **34** *After King-side Castling (King and King Rook)*

To Castle King-side, a player moves his King two squares, landing next to the King Rook.

He then moves his Rook to the other side of the King. When Castling is completed, the Castled King and Rook are on adjacent squares, as in Diagram 34.

Queen-side Castling is illustrated in Diagrams 35 and 36.

20

35 *Before Queen-side Castling (King and Queen Rook)*

36 *After Queen-side Castling (King and Queen Rook)*

Requirements for Castling

Castling is permanently impossible if:

1. The King has already moved (Diagram 37);

or 2. The Rook intended for Castling has already moved (Diagram 38).

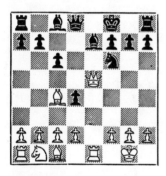

37 *Black cannot now Castle because his King has moved from its original square.*

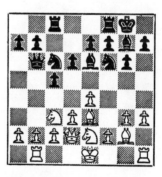

38 *White can Castle King-side, but not Queen-side. (His King Rook is still on its original square.)*

21

Castling is impossible for the time being when:

1. The squares between the King and Rook are not all vacant (Diagram 39).

2. A player's King is in check (Diagram 40).

3. The King has to pass over a square controlled by an enemy unit (Diagram 41).

4. The King will land on a square commanded by an enemy unit (Diagram 42).

While Castling is impossible as long as any of these conditions applies, Castling becomes feasible as soon as all limiting conditions are removed.

 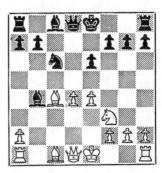

39 *White cannot Castle because one of the squares between his King and King Rook is still occupied.*

40 *White cannot Castle because his King is at the moment being checked by the Black Bishop.*

 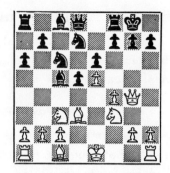

41 *Black cannot Castle because in order to do so his King would have to pass over a square controlled by White's black-squared Bishop.*

42 *White cannot Castle because the square on which his King would land is controlled by Black's black-squared Bishop.*

ADDITIONAL POWERS OF THE PAWN

The Pawn is the least valuable of all the chess units, yet it has one power which enhances its value considerably in special situations.

Pawn Promotion

If a Pawn reaches the last square in a file, it is promoted — must be promoted — to a Queen or a Rook or a Bishop or a Knight. While the player has an option here, he usually chooses a new Queen, as this is the most powerful of all the chess units. This process, known as "promoting" or "queening" a Pawn, is illustrated in Diagrams 43 and 44.

43 *White's Pawn is about to advance to the eighth rank and be promoted. White has decided to take a new Queen, giving check at the same time.*

44 *White has queened his Pawn, giving check and forcing the Black King to move. White will then capture the Black Rook.*

Pawn Captures en Passant ("in passing")

This is a special capturing option which a player can exercise when any of his Pawns has reached advanced rank. This is possible only if *all* the following conditions are present:

1. The Pawn that will do the capturing must be on its fifth rank.

2. The Pawns involved must be on adjacent files.

3. The Pawn that will ultimately be captured must still be on its second (original) rank.

4. The Pawn that is to be captured advances two squares (Diagram 46).

5. In reply, the opposing Pawn captures the first Pawn as if it had advanced only one square (Diagram 47).

Remember that only a Pawn can capture in passing, and only a Pawn can be captured in passing.

45 *Here is a situation in which only Pawns are involved; they are on adjacent files; one Pawn is on its second rank (still in opening position); the other Pawn has reached its fifth rank.*

46 *Black exercises his option and advances his Pawn two squares. White can now capture Black's Pawn "in passing," producing Diagram 47.*

47 *White has captured in passing as if the Black Pawn had only advanced one square and had been captured in the normal manner.*

As a rule, capturing in passing is optional. However, if a player does not make the capture in passing at the first opportunity, he loses his option.

There are two cases when capturing or not capturing in passing is compulsory. If the only way to get out of check is by means of an *en passant* capture, then the capture must be made. Likewise, if capturing in passing would expose one's King to attack, then the capture cannot be made.

Each chessman has a name and each square on the chessboard has a name derived from the placement of the chessmen in the opening position.

48 *The opening position*

The pieces (White or Black) are named as follows — reading from left to right on the diagram:

1. Queen Rook (QR)
2. Queen Knight (QN)
3. Queen Bishop (QB)
4. Queen (Q)
5. King (K)
6. King Bishop (KB)
7. King Knight (KN)
8. King Rook (KR)

The first three pieces get their names from the fact that they are placed to the left of the Queen. The last three pieces get their names because they are placed to the right of the King.

Each Pawn is named for the piece in front of which it stands, and the files (vertical rows) are likewise named for the piece. Thus, the file on which both Kings are placed at the beginning of the game is the King file. The names of the files are permanent; they are retained throughout even when the piece involved moves to a different file.

The names of the Pawns (Diagram 48, and still reading from left to right) are:

1. Queen Rook Pawn (QRP)
2. Queen Knight Pawn (QNP)
3. Queen Bishop Pawn (QBP)
4. Queen Pawn (QP)
5. King Pawn (KP)
6. King Bishop Pawn (KBP)
7. King Knight Pawn (KNP)
8. King Rook Pawn (KRP)

The names of the files (see Diagram 49) are as follows:

1. Queen Rook file
2. Queen Knight file
3. Queen Bishop file
4. Queen file
5. King file
6. King Bishop file
7. King Knight file
8. King Rook file

The ranks (horizontal rows) have two names — one name for recording White's moves, and another name for recording Black's moves. Diagrams 50 and 51 illustrate this set-up:

28

QUEEN-ROOK'S FILE	QUEEN-KNIGHT'S FILE	QUEEN-BISHOP'S FILE	QUEEN'S FILE	KING'S FILE	KING-BISHOP'S FILE	KING-KNIGHT'S FILE	KING-ROOK'S FILE

49 *The names of the files*

8 WHITE'S EIGHTH RANK
7
6
5
4
3
2
1 WHITE'S FIRST RANK

1 BLACK'S FIRST RANK
2
3
4
5
6
7
8 BLACK'S 8TH RANK

50 *The ranks from White's side of the board*

51 *The same ranks from Black's side of the board*

Because the ranks are numbered differently from each side of the board, each square has two names, depending on whether White or Black is moving. The two names of each square, reading from White's side and from Black's side, are shown in Diagram 52.

BLACK

QR1 / QR8	QN1 / QN8	QB1 / QB8	Q1 / Q8	K1 / K8	KB1 / KB8	KN1 / KN8	KR1 / KR8
QR2 / QR7	QN2 / QN7	QB2 / QB7	Q2 / Q7	K2 / K7	KB2 / KB7	KN2 / KN7	KR2 / KR7
QR3 / QR6	QN3 / QN6	QB3 / QB6	Q3 / Q6	K3 / K6	KB3 / KB6	KN3 / KN6	KR3 / KR6
QR4 / QR5	QN4 / QN5	QB4 / QB5	Q4 / Q5	K4 / K5	KB4 / KB5	KN4 / KN5	KR4 / KR5
QR5 / QR4	QN5 / QN4	QB5 / QB4	Q5 / Q4	K5 / K4	KB5 / KB4	KN5 / KN4	KR5 / KR4
QR6 / QR3	QN6 / QN3	QB6 / QB3	Q6 / Q3	K6 / K3	KB6 / KB3	KN6 / KN3	KR6 / KR3
QR7 / QR2	QN7 / QN2	QB7 / QB2	Q7 / Q2	K7 / K2	KB7 / KB2	KN7 / KN2	KR7 / KR2
QR8 / QR1	QN8 / QN1	QB8 / QB1	Q8 / Q1	K8 / K1	KB8 / KB1	KN8 / KN1	KR8 / KR1

WHITE

52 *The names of all the squares on the chess-* board

For purposes of recording moves it is necessary to learn these names. In stating a move, we first name the chessman that is moving, and then name the square to which it is moving. Thus, if the King Pawn moves from its opening position one square up to the third rank, we write "P—K3." If the Queen Pawn advances two squares up to the fourth rank, we write "P—Q4."

The moves of a game are recorded in two vertical columns. The first column is for White's moves; the second column is for Black's moves.

Here is a list of the abbreviations and symbols used in chess notation:

King	K	
Queen	Q	
Rook	R	
Bishop	B	
Knight	N	
Pawn	P	
captures	x	
moves to	—	
check	ch	
discovered check		dis ch
double check		dbl ch
en passant (in passing)		*e.p.*
a good move		!
a very good move		!!
a bad move		?
a very bad move		??
from, at		/
promotes to a Queen		/Q

31

RELATIVE VALUES OF THE CHESS FORCES

It is essential to know the values of the chess units to avoid giving up a unit of greater value in return for a unit of less value.

In addition, you will discover that when you have an advantage in the values of your units (a material advantage), it is generally possible to force checkmate or the queening of a Pawn. Consequently you have to understand clearly the nature of your material advantage if you capture a hostile unit without giving up one of your own in exchange.

Here are the relative values of the chess units:

Queen	9 points
Rook	5 points
Bishop	3 points
Knight	3 points
Pawn	1 point

(The King is not included in this table, as it cannot be captured.)

The Queen is clearly the most valuable piece by far.

Bishop and Knight are of equal value. Giving up a Knight for a Bishop (or the reverse) is considered an equal exchange.

If a player captures a Rook in return for a Knight (or Bishop), he is said to "win *the* Exchange." If he captures a Knight (or Bishop) in return for a Rook, he is said to "lose *the* Exchange."

HOW GAMES ARE DRAWN

Most chess games end decisively — victory for one player, defeat for his opponent.

But there are times when the result is indecisive; neither side wins; the game is a "draw." There are several ways in which a drawn result may be arrived at.

Perpetual Check

This is the term for an endless series of checks which the opponent cannot avoid. Many a player has escaped from a lost game by giving a perpetual check. Thus, in Diagram 53 White, who is so far behind in material that he would lose under normal circumstances, can ward off defeat by resorting to a perpetual check.

53 *White plays for perpetual check:*

1	Q–K8ch!	K–R2
2	Q–R5ch	...

See Diagram 54

54 *Black's King cannot escape from the checks:*

2	...	K–N1
3	Q–K8ch	K–R2
4	Q–R5ch etc.	

In Diagram 54 it is clear that Black's King is limited to seesawing between two squares with no support from the other Black pieces. Under the circumstances White's Queen can maintain the checks indefinitely — any other course would lose for him. So the game is abandoned as a draw.

Stalemate

In the description of *checkmate*, it was stated that a player is checkmated when his King is in check (under attack) and when there is no possibility of getting the King out of check.

In the case of *stalemate*, the following conditions have to be present:

1.   It is a player's turn to move.

2.   His King is *not* in check.

3.   The only moves he can make would place his King within the attacking range of an enemy unit.

This is stalemate, and the game is a draw. Diagrams 55 and 56 are cases in point.

55   *White (to move) is stalemated.*   **56**   *White (to move) is stalemated.*

In both cases it is White's turn to move. In both cases his King is *not* in check. In both cases he is limited to moves that would place his King within the range of an enemy unit.

Inadequate Checkmating Material

Toward the end of a game a player may be left with a material advantage which is not great enough to force checkmate. As it is impossible to checkmate with a Knight or with a Bishop, the positions in Diagrams 57 and 58 are drawn.

57 *Drawn position*

58 *Drawn position*

Other Drawing Methods

A game can be called a draw by mutual agreement.

If fifty moves have been made on each side without a capture or a Pawn move, either player can claim a draw.

If a player whose turn it is to play is about to make a move that will bring about the same position for the third time, he can claim a draw.

The
Nine
Bad
Moves

Book Two

NEGLECTING DEVELOPMENT
OF YOUR PIECES

IN THE ORIGINAL starting position of a game of chess, the pieces are not ready for action. The process by which we advance them to squares on which they can attack and defend and maneuver freely is called "development."

If we develop the pieces slowly or ineffectively, their action is limited. Their attacking ability is slight, and the initiative passes into the hands of our opponent.

If we move one piece repeatedly, it follows that other pieces are being neglected, still left on their original squares where they accomplish nothing. Lagging or ineffective development accounts for many a stinging defeat on the chessboard.

While each opening presents its special problems, there are some practical rules that are helpful guides. Always start by playing out a center Pawn, as this creates a line for developing a Bishop. Bring out the King Knight very early—preferably to KB3. By playing out the King Knight and King Bishop quickly, you make early castling possible and thus get your King out of any immediate danger.

Try to avoid placing your Bishops on diagonals where they are blocked by your own Pawns. Avoid, too, an excessive number of Pawn moves—they contribute little or nothing to development.

39

Play over your games to see whether you are achieving the following minimum in the first ten moves: both center Pawns advanced; both Knights developed; both Bishops developed; castling completed. This is an ideal goal which you may not always achieve, but it will help you to guard against moving the same piece repeatedly.

Managing the Queen is a different matter. If you develop her too soon you will only expose her to harrying by enemy pieces of lesser value. A later chapter will treat this point in detail.

DISASTROUS PAWN MOVES

King's Knight's Opening

WHITE	BLACK
1 P—K4	P—K4
2 N—KB3	N—QB3
3 B—B4	P—B3 ? ?

Black's 3rd move should have been *3 . . . B—B4 or 3 . . . N—B3*—useful developing moves that prepare for castling.

Instead, the move actually played, 3 . . . P—B3 ? ?, is damaging in a number of ways. It is basically bad because it opens up a line of attack on the Black King. (The further play will illustrate the dangers involved.)

Secondly, 3 . . . P—B3 ? ? has the great defect of making it very difficult for Black to castle. The Pawn move extends the diagonal of White's Bishop at QB4 so that the Bishop controls KN8—the square the Black King would occupy in castling.

There might be some point to 3 . . . P—B3 ? ? if the move had good qualities to set off its defects. But it not only has no advantageous features—it even has a fourth defect! —it deprives the Black King Knight of its best square at KB3.

                4 N—R4   . . . .

White wants to exploit 3 . . . P—B3 ? ? by playing Q—R5ch.

                4 . . . .   P—KN4 ? ? ?

Suicide. Now White's Queen check will lead to checkmate.

                5 Q—R5ch   K—K2
                6 N—B5 mate

Of the five moves that Black made, three were Pawn moves and one a King move. Aside from contributing nothing to the development of his pieces, the Pawn moves were definitely harmful in opening the gates to the enemy.

POOR DEVELOPMENT, POOR DEFENSE
Ruy Lopez

WHITE	BLACK
1 P—K4	P—K4
2 N—KB3	N—QB3
3 B—N5	N—B3
4 Castles	N x P
5 P—Q4	N—Q3
6 B x N	NP x B
7 P x P	N—N2

Out of his first seven moves, Black moves the Knight four times and winds up on a bad square toward the side of the board. Even with best play from now on, Black will have to make at least one more move with the Knight to get him into active play.

As the game goes, the Knight never gets into play.

8 N—Q4	B—K2
9 N—B5	B—B1

More loss of time. The Bishop makes two moves and lands on his original square. All that Black has to show for nine moves is a Knight at the wretched square QN2. Such faulty "development" must lead to disaster.

10 R—K1	P—N3

Black's anxiety to be rid of the encroaching Knight is understandable. He succeeds in driving off the Knight, but his success is a very costly one. In any event, it no longer seems possible for Black to make up for previous lost time.

11 N—Q6ch !	. . . .

42

11 . . . .   B x N

Or 11 . . . P x N; 12 P x P dis ch, B—K2; 13 R x Bch winning easily.

And if 11 . . . K—K2; 12 B—N5ch leading to a quick mate (*12 . . . K—K3; 13 Q—N4ch*, etc.).

12 P x B dis ch	K—B1
13 B—R6ch	K—N1
14 Q—Q4	. . . .

Threatens mate.

14	P—B3
15 Q—B4 mate !	

Black's lack of development plagues him to the very end. Bad development plus King in the center—a fatal combination of weaknesses.

WHITE NEGLECTS HIS KING'S WELFARE
King's Gambit Declined

WHITE	BLACK
1 P—K4	P—K4
2 N—QB3	N—QB3
3 P—B4	B—B4
4 N—B3	P—Q3

White should now continue developing his pieces by playing *5 B—B4.*

5 P—B5 ?	. . . .

Not good. He wastes time by moving the Pawn again.

5	N—B3

Note how Black keeps developing his pieces.

6 P—KR3 ?	. . . .

Another time-killer.

6	P—Q4 !

True, Black loses time by moving the Queen Pawn a second time, but he is opening up the game to his advantage.

7 N x KP ?	. . . .

White expects 7 . . . N x N—which he will answer with 8 P—Q4, winning back the piece.

But Black has other plans.

7	N x P !

Threatening immediate destruction with . . . Q—R5ch. White's King, stranded in the center, is exposed to a devastating attack. In fact, even at this early stage White is lost.

44

The game is opened up, his King is subject to assault by four Black pieces, his lagging development leaves him without the means to fight back.

           8 N—B3   . . . .

A shamefaced retreat: he wants to prevent . . . Q—R5ch.

           8 . . . .   Q—R5ch ! ! !

Black gives short shrift to the unfortunate White King stranded in the center.

           9 N x Q   B—B7ch
          10 K—K2   N—Q5ch

Black sacrificed his Queen to make this move possible.

          11 K—Q3   N—B4 mate !

The brilliant attack has exacted a brutal penalty for White's foolish policy of neglecting the development of his pieces and the safety of his King.

HOW TO LOSE IN NINE MOVES
Bird's Opening

WHITE	BLACK
1 P—KB4	N—KB3
2 P—B4	. . . .

White's first two moves are unfortunate. He should begin by moving center Pawns (King Pawn and Queen Pawn), which would create lines of development for his Bishops and gain control of important squares in the center.

2	P—Q4
3 P x P	N x P
4 P—Q3	P—K4

Black sacrifices a Pawn to seize the initiative.

5 P x P	B—N5ch
6 B—Q2	N—K6

This attack on White's Queen cannot be met by B x N, as White's Bishop at Q2 is pinned. White's only chance now is *7 Q—B1.*

7 Q—R4ch ? ?	. . . .

After this plausible (?) move White's Queen is lost!—
a clear indication that he has botched his development.

7 . . . .   P—QN4 ! !

This is the move that traps the Queen. White belatedly
realizes he cannot play *8 Q x B*, for the reply *8 . . .
N—B7ch* forks King and Queen.

8 Q x NPch   B—Q2
9 Q—N7   B—B3
Resigns

White's Queen is still trapped: again, if *10 Q x KB, N—
B7ch!*

The pitiable situation in which White finds himself underlines the serious mistake he made in neglecting his
development.

The chief moral for you to derive from the game is that
playing out the *center* Pawns at an early stage gives you
your best chance of achieving a quick, normal development. Neglecting the center Pawns may create lasting difficulties in getting your pieces out and in finding a safe
refuge for your King. And, of course, your chances of
successful attack or defense are ruined by poor development. Your pieces cannot function effectively if they are
badly developed, or undeveloped.

WH...

1 P—K4	P—K4
2 N—KB3	N—QB3
3 B—N5	P—QR3
4 B—R4	P—QN4
5 B—N3	N—R4 ?

This move does not lose material, for if *6 N x P, N x B; 7 RP x N, Q—N4* and Black recovers his Pawn. But Black moves the Knight *three times* and then exchanges it for White's Bishop. Naturally Black's development suffers sadly.

6 Castles	N x B
7 RP x N	P—Q3
8 P—Q4	B—N5

Previously Black neglected his development; here he makes a thoughtless developing move. As you will see next move, Black must exchange . . . *B x N*, thus speeding up White's development.

9 P x P	. . . .

Now if *9 . . . P x P; 10 Q x Qch and 11 N x P* winning a Pawn for White. This forces Black's reply.

9	B x N
10 Q x B	P x P
11 R—Q1	. . . .

Let's take stock. As a result of Black's unsatisfactory development, he has parted with the two pieces he developed —his Queen Knight and Queen Bishop. White meanwhile has castled, placed both Rooks on open files and developed his Queen aggressively. All Black's forces are still on the back rank, his King helplessly exposed. *11 . . . B—Q3* is his best chance to catch up in development.

11	Q—B3
12 Q—Q3	Q—B3

If *12 . . . B—Q3* White has a brilliant reply in *13 R x P !, R x R; 14 Q x Pch* winning the Black Rook.

13 R x P ! !	Resigns

A pretty conclusion. *If 13 . . . R x R; 14 Q—Q8 mate. If 13 . . . Q x R; 14 Q—Q7 mate.* White made admirable use of the open lines that Black presented to him.

GOOD DEVELOPMENT TROUNCES POOR DEVELOPMENT

Scotch Gambit

WHITE	BLACK
1 P—K4	P—K4
2 N—KB3	N—QB3
3 P—Q4	P x P
4 B—B4	B—B4
5 Castles	P—Q3
6 P—B3	B—KN5

So far both players have consistently devoted themselves to good development.

7 Q—N3	B x N
8 B x Pch	K—B1
9 B x N	R x B
10 P x B	P—KN4 !

Black's King has lost the castling privilege, but he is in no danger. The foregoing exchanges have left White with only one piece developed—his Queen.

On the other hand, White's King-side is broken up, and this is a source of danger. Another difficulty, as far as White is concerned, is that all three Queen-side pieces are still roosting on their home squares.

11 Q—K6	N—K4 !
12 Q—B5ch	K—N2 !

Black does not fear *13 B x P*, for after *13 . . . K—R1 !* the Bishop is pinned and lost (*14 P—KR4, P—KR3 etc.*).

Incidentally, the seemingly exposed position of the Black King is deceptive. Since White is playing a one-piece attack, Black's King has nothing to fear and will be tucked away safely in the corner. Actually it is the White King, menaced by several Black pieces, that is in danger.

13 K—R1	K—R1
14 R—N1	P—N5 !
15 P—KB4	N—B6
16 R x P	Q—R5 ! !

This brilliant move threatens . . . *Q x RP mate*. White is lost.

17 R—N2	Q x RPch !
18 R x Q	R—N8 mate !

Very pretty play, made possible by the efficient cooperation of Black's aggressively developed pieces. Note that White's Queen-side pieces are still on their original squares.

HOW EXCHANGES MAY INFLUENCE DEVELOPMENT

King's Gambit

WHITE	BLACK
1 P—K4	P—K4
2 P—KB4	P x P
3 N—KB3	P—KN4

This Pawn advance often weakens Black's King-side formation.

4 P—KR4	P—N5
5 N—K5	N—KB3
6 N x NP	N x P
7 Q—K2	P—Q4
8 P—Q3	. . . .

Threatening to win the pinned Knight and thereby forcing Black's reply. The exchange that follows is the first of a series of exchanges that greatly increase White's lead in development. Although Black does not commit any clear error, he finds that his arrears in development keep increasing all the time.

8	B x N
9 Q x B	N—N6
10 R—R3	B—Q3
11 B x P	Q—K2ch
12 K—B2	B x B
13 Q x B	N x B

An instructive moment: the Knight, which has made four moves, is exchanged for White's Bishop which is still on its original square. This involves a colossal loss of time for Black.

14 N—B3 . . . .

As Black's Knight cannot escape, White keeps hammering away at development.

14 . . . . Castles

Naturally he cannot allow his Queen to be pinned by R—K1. However, castling is anything but safe, in view of the gap left in the castled position by the disappearance of Black's King Knight Pawn.

15 K x N   P—QB3
16 R—K1   Q—Q1

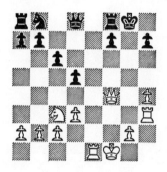

The upshot of the exchanges is that White has all his pieces out, while Black's forces are all on the back row. Add to this the exposed position of Black's King, and you have the elements of a brilliant finish.

17 R—N3ch   K—R1
18 Q—R6   . . . .

Threatens 19 Q—N7 mate.

18 . . . .   R—N1
19 R—K8 ! !   . . . .

Beautiful play. Naturally Black cannot play *19 . . . R x R*, while *19 . . . Q x R* also allows mate.

19	Q x R
20 Q—B6ch	R—N2
21 Q x R mate	

White clearly owed his victory to his overwhelming lead in development. Had Black developed his Queen Knight, that would have been enough to make the winning combination impossible!

EXPOSING YOUR KING TO ATTACK

THE KING is unlike any other piece. In every game of chess, the object, direct or potential, is to checkmate your opponent's King. No matter how the game proceeds, no matter what your plans may be, you must guard your King and look for opportunities to menace your opponent's King.

Since the King's safety controls the fate of the game, you take unnecessary risks whenever you expose your King to attack. One of the most common ways to endanger the King is to leave him on his original square in the middle of the back rank. The other chess pieces are most active in the center and exert their greatest power in that area. Consequently, the King is most vulnerable at his original square.

Leaving the King in the center is particularly dangerous in "open" positions—those in which there are open files. Such open lines are highways along which the Queen and Rooks can operate to menace the hostile King. (In "closed" positions—those in which the Pawn position is locked—a King *may* be fairly safe in the center.)

Leaving the King in the center sometimes leads to ferocious "King-hunts." In the course of such a savage drive on a hostile King, he may be hounded all the way from his original square to the other side of the board. The King-hunt is the extreme example of the helplessness of a King stranded in the center and exposed to the fury of the hostile pieces.

WHITE TO MOVE

Here is a good example of the dangers confronting a King in the center in an open position. After 1 Q x Pch ! ! Black resigns, for *if 1 . . . N x Q; 2 B x P mate.*

Knowing that it is bad policy to leave the King exposed to attack in the center, how are we to avoid such dangers? The safest course is to castle fairly early in the game—say no later than the tenth move. Once the King is castled on one side or the other, he is much less vulnerable than in the center.

BLACK TO MOVE

Though White is three Pawns up, his position is disorganized, his development chaotic, his King endangered in the center. It is interesting to see how Black drives the White King to his doom by a series of smashing moves. White is in no position to resist as his King steadily gives ground.

To break up White's position, Black must remove the Bishop at QB6 and the Knight at K2.

1	R x B !
2 P x R	B x N
3 R x B	. . . .

Mission accomplished. Now Black can begin the King-hunt.

3	Q x QPch
4 K—K1	Q—N8ch
5 K—Q2	R—Q1ch
6 K—B3	. . . .

Now 6 . . . Q x Q would win easily. However, the continuation Black chooses shows that he has a sense of humor.

6	Q—B4ch
7 K—N2	N—R5ch !
Resigns	

For if 8 P x N, Q—N5 mate.

The amusing alternative is *8 K—N1, N—B6ch; 9 K—N2, N x Qch; 10 K—N1, N—B6ch followed by 11 . . . N x R.*

57

BLACK PROVOKES A KING-HUNT
Evans Gambit

WHITE	BLACK
1 P—K4	P—K4
2 N—KB3	N—QB3
3 B—B4	B—B4
4 P—QN4	B x NP
5 P—B3	B—R4
6 P—Q4	P x P
7 Castles	N—B3
8 B—R3	. . . .

White sacrifices a Pawn in this opening to gain time and open up lines for attack.

8	B—N3

Four of Black's moves have been made with this Bishop. Such loss of time is bound to lead to disaster.

9 Q—N3	P—Q4
10 KP x P	N—QR4
11 R—K1ch	B—K3

11 . . . K—Q2 is refuted by 12 B—N5ch, P—B3; 13 P x Pch and 14 Q x Pch.

58

White can now win a piece with *12 Q—R4ch.* Instead, he decides to sacrifice his Queen to bring about a murderous King-hunt.

12 P x B ! !	N x Q
13 P x P dbl ch	K—Q2
14 B—K6ch	K—B3

Black's King gets no support from the other Black pieces.

15 N—K5ch	K—N4
16 B—B4ch	K—R4
17 B—N4ch	K—R5
18 P x N mate	

The King has met a gruesome fate deep in enemy territory.

WHITE NEGLECTS CASTLING
Giuoco Piano

WHITE	BLACK
1 P—K4	P—K4
2 N—KB3	N—QB3
3 B—B4	B—B4
4 P—B3	B—N3
5 P—Q4	Q—K2
6 P—Q5	. . . .

A questionable move; it closes the diagonal of White's Bishop at QB4 and opens the diagonal of Black's Bishop at QN3.

6	N—Q1

This is a good point for White to castle his King into safety.

7 B—K2 ?	. . . .

Incomprehensible. Not only does White neglect to castle; he loses time by moving the already developed Bishop.

7	P—Q3
8 P—KR3 ?	. . . .

Again neglecting castling and again wasting time; besides, the Pawn move may turn out to have a weakening effect on White's position.

8	P—KB4
9 B—KN5	N—KB3
10 QN—Q2	Castles
11 N—R4 ?	. . . .

Once more he misses castling, and once more he fritters away precious time by moving an already developed piece.

11	P x P
12 N x P	. . . .

Calmly relying on the pin on Black's King Knight. But White's numerous violations of chess theory allow Black to violate chess theory too! Black now sacrifices his Queen for a piece of considerably lesser value.

12	N x N ! !

13 B x Q	B x BPch
14 K—B1	N—N6 mate

What are the technical factors that made this mate possible? First, 7 B—K2 ? deprived the King of a possible flight square. Secondly, 8 P—KR3 ? weakened the Kingside (allowing the eventual . . . N—N6 mate). Finally, 11 N—R4 ? resulted in the complete opening of the King Bishop file.

Thus we see that Black's brilliancy was grounded in the shortcomings of White's faulty play. Yet the crowning mistake was White's *failure to castle*.

Black's King is in the center and, what is even worse, he lags considerably in development. The position of Black's King is an invitation to attack. The aggressive disposition of White's forces gives him the means of sacrificing successfully.

The lack of communication among Black's forces is likely to be disastrous for him. Reckoning on this favorable factor, White plays:

1 N—B7ch ! . . . .

This leaves Black no choice. If he refuses to capture the Knight, he loses a whole Rook. But why shouldn't he capture the Knight?

1 . . . .   B x N
2 R x B   . . . .

This is why! White menaces the Black Queen and also threatens 3 Q x P mate.

2 . . . .   Q x R
3 Q x Rch   K—K2

Forced. But now he loses the other Rook, leaving him with a hopeless disadvantage in material.

4 Q x R   Resigns

It was the vulnerable *position of Black's King in the center* that made White's brilliant combination possible. Had Black's King been castled, White's position would still have been vastly superior; but no immediate win would have been in sight.

WHITE TO MOVE

The position of Black's King is
ominous. Both center files are
open, but Black is not yet ready
to castle. In all such cases the
attacker must proceed incisively.
If he fails to press his advantage
energetically, he will give the
hostile King time to escape.
Thus time is of the essence.

     1 R—K1ch   . . . .

Black's vulnerable King must submit to a disagreeable
pin. *If 1 . . . N—K2; 2 N—B3*, and White has lasting
pressure on the King file, as Black's castling is postponed
indefinitely.

     1 . . . .   B—K2

Hoping to gain time to castle. Everything hinges on the
question of *time*.

     2 N x B   . . . .

The simplest way to dispose of his menaced Knight.

     2 . . . .   N x N
     3 B—N5 ! !   . . . .

A surprise stroke which *gains time* to develop his Queen
Rook with decisive effect. *If 3 . . . P—KB3; 4 B x P ! ,
P x B; 5 QR—Q1 ! , Q—B1; 6 Q x BP wins at once.*

     3 . . . .   R x B
     4 QR—Q1 !   Q—B1

*If 4 . . . R—Q4; 5 R x R and Black cannot retake the
Rook because of the pin.*

     5 Q—K3 !   Castles

He cannot save his Rook *and* stop the mate too.

     6 Q x R   Resigns

With the Exchange ahead, White wins easily.

All the elements in this picture are familiar to you by now. Black's King is in the center and has little cooperation from the Black pieces. Particularly bad is the indifferent position of Black's Queen, which is "out of the battle" and offers no support to the menaced King.

White has sacrificed a piece to get this position—a good investment, for the Black pieces have left their King to a miserable fate. White's astounding first move is the key to a fantastic winning process:

1 Q x KPch ! ! !   K x Q

He must capture.

2 B—B4ch   K—B3

Again Black has no choice. Yet his King is so critically threatened that his enormous material advantage is useless.

3 R(Q1)—Q6ch ! ! B x R

And again he has no choice.

4 R—B7 mate

An extraordinarily impressive finish. White's enormous material disadvantage underlines the tragic split in the placement of the Black pieces. Given the *scattered formation* of Black's men, catastrophe was bound to come.

WHITE TO MOVE

Black failed to castle and his battered King has been driven from the center. His King-side Pawns are gone. One Rook is bottled up; the other has little value. Momentarily White has two pieces under attack, but this is of little importance; with *1 R—K3* he avoids loss of material.

As you have seen from the discussion of the diagramed position, White can play 1 R—K3 with satisfactory results. But the exposed position of Black's King is tantalizing: there ought to be some rapid, sensational, conclusive method of putting an end to the Black King's sufferings. And there is!

1 R—K8ch ! ! !

To find such a winning line requires imagination of the highest order. But remember this: without the previous weakening of the Black King's position, all the imagination in the world would be useless. Perfectly sound positions are safe from sudden, startling demolition.

1 . . . . R x R
2 Q—N4ch ! ! ! . . . .

White's amazing first move was merely the preparation for the even more amazing Queen sacrifice.

2 . . . . Q x Q

Now that Black's Queen is out of the way, White achieves his objective.

3 N—B6 mate !

MAKING TOO MANY QUEEN
MOVES IN THE OPENING

REPEATED MOVES with the same piece in the opening are a form of neglected development. While the same piece is moving again and again, the other pieces remain undeveloped. Always a serious fault, it becomes even more serious when the Queen is the piece which is being moved repeatedly. There are a number of reasons for this.

The Queen is by far the strongest piece on the board. It is the heart and soul of a well-managed attack which is based on systematic, *completed* development. To move this powerful piece aimlessly and repeatedly dissipates the attacking power of your position. To move the Queen very early while concentrating on a definite but minor goal, is still bad policy; often much more important features are neglected during these short-sighted maneuvers.

Still another drawback to early Queen moves is that they readily expose the Queen to attack by enemy pieces. So we have here the painful paradox that while one player ignores his development with repeated Queen moves, his opponent develops one piece after another with gain of time by simultaneously attacking the Queen!

Your best course, then, is to follow the advice given in Number 1: concentrate on playing out the minor pieces at the beginning of the game; make sure of castling into safety; and develop the Queen only after the opening development has begun to take shape.

FOUR CONSECUTIVE QUEEN MOVES—AND "RESIGNS"

Caro-Kann Defense

WHITE	BLACK
1 P—K4	P—QB3
2 P—Q4	P—Q4
3 P x P	P x P
4 P—QB4	B—B4

It is poor policy for Black to expose his Queen to immediate attack.

5 P x P	Q x P
6 N—QB3	Q—R4
7 Q—N3	Q—N3

Still another Queen move.

8 N—Q5 !	. . . .

If Black now tries to defend the Queen Knight Pawn with *8 . . . Q—QB3*, then the pinning move *9 B—QN5* wins the Queen.

8	Q x Q
9 P x Q	Resigns !

Black cannot meet the double threat of 10 N—B7ch or 10 N—N6, winning the Exchange. If he tries *9 . . . N—R3* then *10 R x N ! , P x R; 11 N—B7ch* wins for White.

The excessive number of Queen moves has resulted in an undeveloped position lacking adequate defensive resources.

BLACK LOSES PRECIOUS TIME

King's Knight's Opening

WHITE	BLACK
1 P—K4	P—K4
2 N—KB3	Q—B3 ?

A thoughtless move. Why use the Queen—the most powerful piece on the board—for such menial work as guarding a Pawn?

(*2 . . . N—QB3* performs the same task much more economically.)

| 3 B—B4 | Q—N3 ? |

A second move with the unfortunate Queen.

| 4 Castles ! | Q x KP ? ? |

And now a third move with the unfortunate Queen. Far ahead in development, White is now ready to exploit the Queen's exposed position.

| 5 B x Pch ! | . . . . |

For if 5 . . . K x B; 6 N—N5ch forking King and Queen.

| 5 . . . . | K—K2 |

5 . . . K—Q1 is slightly better, but the damage is done: Black's King is stranded in the center and has lost the castling privilege.

| 6 R—K1 ! | Q—KB5 |
| 7 R x Pch ! | . . . . |

With a mating attack in the offing, White does not mind sacrificing his Bishop.

| 7 . . . . | K x B |
| 8 P—Q4 ! | . . . . |

Gaining valuable time by again attacking the unfortunate Queen.

8	Q—B3
9 N—N5ch	K—N3
10 Q—Q3ch	K—R4
11 P—KN4ch !	K x P
12 Q—KR3 mate	

An extraordinary game: out of 11 moves, Black made five with his Queen, five with his King. Small wonder that his King was battered into an early checkmate.

Budapest Defense

WHITE	BLACK
1 P—Q4	N—KB3
2 P—QB4	P—K4
3 P x P	N—N5
4 N—KB3	B—B4
5 P—K3	N—QB3
6 B—Q2	N/N5 x P/K4

Thus Black wins back the Pawn offered on his 2nd move.

7 N x N	N x N
8 B—B3	Q—K2
9 Q—Q5 ?	. . . .

A premature attack with the Queen. This is bound to be waste of time, for Black need only protect his Knight and then drive the Queen away.

9	P—Q3
10 P—QN4	. . . .

Pointless. It would be better to develop with 10 B—K2.

10	P—QB3
11 Q—K4	. . . .

White is looking for trouble. His simplest course is 11 Q—Q2, taking the Queen out of danger.

11	P—B4

Even at this point, after two time-wasting Queen moves, White can still save himself by 12 Q—B2. Instead, he imagines that he is keeping the Queen "in active play" with: ·

12 Q—B4 ? ? ?	. . . .

But this is one "aggressive" Queen move too many. **The** White Queen is now lost by force!

12	P—KN4 ! !
13 Q—N3	. . . .

The Queen has no other move.

13	P—B5 ! !
14 P x P	P x P
15 Q x P	. . . .

Still the only move. But now the King file is open, and White is exposed to a ruinous double check.

15	N—Q6 dbl ch
Resigns	

White must move his King, losing the Queen. An impressive example of how early Queen moves expose that powerful piece to persecution by the enemy's minor pieces.

Falkbeer Counter Gambit

WHITE	BLACK
1 P—K4	P—K4
2 P—KB4	P—Q4
3 KP x P	P—K5
4 P—Q3	N—KB3
5 P x P	N x KP
6 P—KN3 ?	. . . .

White guards against the threat of *6 . . . Q—R5ch; 7 P—KN3, N x P; 8 P x N, Q x R.*

But the *developing* move *6 N—KB3* would be a much more effective way of preventing the Queen check.

6	B—QB4
7 Q—K2 ?	. . . .

Having the King and Queen on the open King file may easily lead to trouble for White.

7	Castles !

Black is piling up a great lead in development. He does not fear *8 Q x N,* for then he wins the White Queen with the pinning move *8 . . . R—K1.*

8 Q—B4 ? ? ?	. . . .

Another Queen move, and another serious loss of time in a position which cannot bear the strain.

8	Q—K2 !

Putting the open file to good use. He threatens a nasty discovered check with *. . . N x P* dis ch or *. . . N—B7* dis ch, winning White's King Rook in either event.

9 Q—K2 . . . .

Still another Queen move; but he must try to keep the open file at least partly closed.

9 . . . . B—KN5 ! !

At first sight incomprehensible, this powerful move forces White's Queen off the open King file.

10 Q x B B—B7ch !

If now 11 K—Q1, N—B6ch ! ; 12 P x N, Q—K8 mate! Or, 12 K—Q2, Q—K6 mate!

11 K—K2 N—KB3 dis ch

This brutal discovered check wins White's Queen—a graphic proof of the dangers lurking on the open King file for a King stranded in the center.

12 K x B N x Qch
Resigns

Black exacted a harsh penalty for White's repeated Queen moves.

WHITE'S COMBINATION IS UNSOUND
Queen's Pawn Opening

WHITE	BLACK
1 P—Q4	N—KB3
2 P—QB4	P—Q4
3 P x P	Q x P
4 N—QB3	Q—Q1

Black has lost time with the Queen moves.

5 P—K4	P—K4

A temporary Pawn offer: *if now 6 P x P, Q x Qch; 7 K x Q, N—N5* and Black regains the Pawn favorably.

White's indicated reply is the developing move *6 N—B3*. Instead, he plays a superfluous Queen move that leads to trouble.

6 Q—R4ch ? ?	B—Q2

A typical example of the way in which early development of the Queen exposes that piece to attack by hostile forces of lesser value.

7 Q—N3	. . . .

Here is White's idea: if he retreats 7 *Q—Q1*, there follows 7 . . . *P x P; 8 Q x P, N—B3* and White must lose still more time with still another Queen move. Naturally White does not relish this loss of time. Therefore he intends to part with his Queen Pawn, winning Black's Queen Knight Pawn in return. Black will win White's Queen Knight, but only by losing his own Queen Rook in return.

Thus White reasons, and it sounds very plausible. What he forgets is that he will be making three consecutive Queen moves, ending up with his Queen hopelessly out of play and his other pieces undeveloped.

| 7 . . . . | P x P |
| 8 Q x NP | P x N |

If 8 . . . B—B3 White saves himself with the pinning 9 B—QN5!

| 9 Q x R | . . . . |

Now White's Queen is far from the scene of action, and Black has a free hand in attacking the helpless White King in the center.

9	P x P
10 B x P	B—QN5ch
11 K—K2	B—N5ch
12 P—B3	. . . .

White fares no better with 12 K—K3 for Black still has 12 . . . Q—Q7 mate or 12 . . . B—Q7 mate.

| 12 . . . . | Q—Q7 mate |

A convincing sermon on the subject of making too many Queen moves in the opening. If we compare the sequence of moves 6-9 with the sequence of moves 10-12, we see that a series of excessive Queen moves may often lead to disaster. The Queen is too powerful a piece to be wasted on trifling excursions.

WHITE WINS TWO ROOKS—
AND LOSES THE GAME

Philidor's Defense

WHITE	BLACK
1 P—K4	P—K4
2 N—KB3	P—Q3
3 P—Q4	N—KB3
4 P x P	N x P
5 B—QB4	B—K3
6 B x B	P x B
7 Q—K2	. . . .

White develops the Queen this early because he is carried away by the double threat of 8 Q x N and 8 Q—N5ch which will win a Pawn.

7	P—Q4
8 Q—N5ch	N—QB3

Now White can win a Pawn, but the price is too steep: *9 Q x NP ? ? , N—N5; 10 Q—N5ch, P—B3; 11 Q—R4, N—B4 ! !* and White's Queen is lost (*12 Q—R3, N x Pch or 12 Q x N, N—Q6ch*).

9 N—Q4	. . . .

Still threatening to win a Pawn, but he is neglecting his development.

9	Q—Q2 !

Defending with a developing move—and at the same time preparing an extraordinarily deep reply to White's coming Pawn grab.

10 Q x NP	. . . .

76

Still another Queen move—but it does not seem to lose any time because of the attack on Black's Queen Rook.

| 10 . . . . | B—N5ch ! ! |
| 11 P—QB3 | . . . . |

Now three Black pieces are attacked. Are White's repeated Queen moves justified after all?

11	N x N ! !
12 Q x Rch	K—B2
13 Q x R	. . . .

White's Queen moves have been very profitable, but . . .

| 13 . . . . | Q—N4 ! ! |
| Resigns | |

There is no way for White to prevent . . . Q—K7 mate. The position has a beautiful logic all its own: White's Queen is far, far away from the scene of action; all the other White pieces are on their original squares. Too many Queen moves!

GRABBING PAWNS THOUGHTLESSLY

ADVANTAGE in material is the deciding factor in most games of chess. Consequently, you must always be on the lookout to capture material without yielding up the same amount of material to your opponent.

But the opportunity to capture material is not always a blessing. The capture may have serious drawbacks attached to it. Sometimes an innocent-looking Pawn may turn out to be protected indirectly, and capturing the Pawn may involve you in heavy losses. So the first caution about capturing is to examine the position for any trace of hidden protection.

Even where no such protection is available, the capture may be unfavorable in other ways. Perhaps your King is in need of defense, and a slyly offered Pawn will lure your Queen far away from the defense. You may find that you are capturing a Pawn which is trifling in comparison to the harm caused by leaving your King defenseless.

Such faraway captures by the Queen remind us of the dangers to which that powerful piece is exposed in making repeated moves early in the game. To play the Queen out early, have her capture a distant Pawn or two, expose her to attack by hostile pieces, and then spend more time in getting her back in active play—this big mistake has lost many a game. In the worst of these cases, you may find that a far-ranging capture of a remote Pawn will actually result in your Queen being trapped—lost for a hostile piece of far less value.

In your own games, then, you will avoid Pawn-grabbing moves that either neglect development in the opening stage or spoil vitally important defensive formations in the middle game.

But thoughtless Pawn-grabbing can take other forms. Sometimes a player will deliberately offer Pawns for the sake of the open lines he obtains when these Pawns are cleared out of the way. To capture such Pawns is a double mistake—not only is valuable time wasted in capturing them, but the very capture opens up attacking lines for the opponent.

This is particularly dangerous when you capture center Pawns at a stage when your own King is still in the center. But the outcome can be just as disastrous if you are castled and snatch a Pawn or two on the files leading to *your* castled position. You *may* be able to make up for the time lost; whether you can defend yourself against the assault on the open lines is much more doubtful.

The moral of this chapter is, *don't grab Pawns thoughtlessly!* But if, after taking due precaution, you feel you can safely capture, then act on your convictions.

THE POISONED QUEEN KNIGHT PAWN

Queen's Gambit Declined

WHITE	BLACK
1 P—Q4	P—Q4
2 B—B4	N—KB3
3 N—KB3	P—K3
4 P—K3	P—B4
5 P—B4	N—B3
6 N—B3	P—QR3
7 Q—R4 ?	. . . .

Up to this point White had developed along sound lines. The early Queen move, however, is sheer waste of time.

| 7 . . . . | B—Q2 |

A typical reply to premature development of the Queen. Black threatens *8 . . . N x P* winning a Pawn because of the attack on White's Queen.

| 8 Q—Q1 | Q—R4 |

This move has point because it threatens a pin with . . . N—K5.

| 9 Q—N3 ? | . . . . |

Another time-wasting Queen move. Note that White has taken three moves to get his Queen to QN3—which normally should take a single move.

| 9 . . . . | QP x P |

This looks like a careless move. Oughtn't Black to be defending his unguarded Queen Knight Pawn?

Not when White is about to commit a flagrantly ill-judged Pawn-grab. Chess literature abounds in games where the Queen has been lost after capturing a harmless-looking Queen Knight Pawn which turned out to be quite securely (though indirectly) guarded after all. That is what happens here.

> 10 Q x NP ? ? ?   . . . .

The fourth Queen move out of ten. But this ill-considered capture leads to immediate disaster.

> 10 . . . .   R—R2 !
>   Resigns

A ludicrous tableau. White's Queen is trapped!

Sicilian Defense

WHITE	BLACK
1 P—K4	P—QB4
2 N—KB3	P—Q3
3 P—Q4	P x P
4 N x P	P—KN3
5 P—QB4	N—KB3
6 N—QB3	N—B3
7 P—B3	. . . .

Black should now continue his development with 7 . . . B—N2 and 8 . . . Castles. Instead, he commits an error of judgment by developing his Queen prematurely.

7	Q—N3

This looks promising, as White's Knight at Q4 is now doubly attacked. True, White can defend the Knight with the developing move B—K3—but in that case his Queen Knight Pawn will be deprived of protection. Black is therefore well content with the Queen move, which seems to create a puzzling problem for White.

8 B—K3 !	. . . .

A surprise! White makes the "impossible" move, and leaves his unprotected Queen Knight Pawn in the lurch.

Now Black is confronted with a difficult choice. He can carry out his original intention and capture the Queen Knight Pawn; or he can beat a shamefaced retreat with . . . *Q—Q1.* But if he refuses the Pawn, he loses valuable time, and also confesses that his whole plan was wrong. If he leaves his Queen at QN3, White continues Q—Q2 (protecting the Pawn at QN2 and the Bishop at K3), with the formidable threat of N—K6 attacking Black's Queen.

So, if only as a matter of pride, Black captures the Pawn.

8 . . . .   Q x P ? ? ?

But this is a ruinous blunder, for now the Queen is trapped!

9 N—R4   Q—R6

After *9 . . . Q—N5ch; 10 B—Q2* Black loses his Queen as in the actual play.

10 B—B1 !   Q—N5ch
11 B—Q2   Q—R6
12 N—N5   Resigns

The Black Queen is left without a single flight square—proper punishment for an impetuous Pawn-grabbing expedition.

BLACK'S PAWN-GRABBING OPENS
THE CENTER FILES

Vienna Game

WHITE	BLACK
1 P—K4	P—K4
2 N—QB3	N—KB3
3 P—B4	P—Q4
4 BP x P	N x P
5 N—B3	B—KN5
6 Q—K2	N—B4 ?

He wastes time with the Knight to put it on a worse square. Instead of this third move with the Knight, a simple *6 . . . N x N* was in order.

7 P—Q4	B x N
8 Q x B	Q—R5ch

Black looks forward to *9 Q—B2 (protecting the Queen Pawn), Q x Qch; 10 K x Q, N—K5ch with an easy game.*

| 9 P—KN3 ! | . . . . |

An unpleasant surprise. Black hadn't expected to grab a Pawn, but he captures the Queen Pawn to "save face."

9	Q x QP
10 B—K3 !	Q x P

More Pawn-grabbing and more loss of time.

| 11 Castles | P—QB3 |

White has a considerable lead in development, both center files are open, and Black's King is still in the center. The position is perfect for further sacrifices by White, relying on the use of the open files and the gains of time made possible by Black's Pawn-grabbing.

12 N x P !	P x N
13 R x P	. . . .

Now Black's Queen must lose more time. The most interesting line is *13 . . . Q—K5; 14 B—QN5ch, N—B3; 15 B/K3 x N ! !, Q x Q; 16 B x Nch, P x B; 17 R—K1ch, B—K2; 18 R x Bch, K—B1; 19 R x RP dis ch, K—N1; 20 R x R mate.* A long variation, but once Black captures the Queen, he has no choice.

13	Q—K3
14 B—QB4	Q—K5
15 B x N ! !	Q x Q
16 R—K1ch	B—K2
17 R x Bch	K—B1
18 R—Q8 mate	

White made splendid use of the two open files resulting from Black's immoderate Pawn-grabbing.

CATASTROPHE ON THE OPEN CENTER FILES

French Defense

WHITE	BLACK
1 P—K4	P—K3
2 P—Q4	P—Q4
3 N—QB3	N—KB3
4 P x P	N x P

Repeated moves with the same piece should be avoided in opening play. Hence *4 . . . P x P* would be correct.

5 N—B3	P—QB4
6 N x N	Q x N

Bringing out the Queen at a very early stage—another faulty move, as she will be exposed to attack.

7 B—K3	P x P
8 N x P	P—QR3
9 B—K2 !	Q x NP

The Black Queen goes far afield to grab an unimportant Pawn. Black loses time, his Queen gets out of play, White gets an important open line on the King Knight file. It all adds up to a very unfavorable deal for Black.

10 B—B3	Q—N3
11 Q—Q2	P—K4

Black is far behind in development, and he sees that after the quiet continuation *11 . . . B—K2; 12 Castles (Q), Castles; 13 KR—N1* White has a winning attack on the open King Knight file.

12 Castles (Q) !	P x N
13 B x QP	N—B3

White's sacrifice of the Knight allows him to carry out a swift and merciless attack on the open center files.

14 B—B6 ! !   Q x B

If 14 . . . P x B; 15 B x Nch forces mate.

15 KR—K1ch   B—K2

After 15 . . . B—K3 the pinned Bishop is useless against 16 Q—Q7 mate!

16 B x Nch   K—B1

Or 16 . . . Q x B and White relies on another pin for 17 Q—Q8 mate!

17 Q—Q8ch ! !   B x Q
18 R—K8 mate

A beautifully engineered attack by White, but Black's disastrous Pawn-grabbing gave White his chance.

PAWN-GRABBING ENDANGERS
BLACK'S CASTLED POSITION
King's Gambit Declined

WHITE	BLACK
1 P—K4	P—K4
2 P—KB4	B—B4
3 N—KB3	P—Q3
4 B—B4	N—KB3
5 N—B3	Castles
6 P—Q3	N—N5 ?

After some excellent opening play featuring sensible developing moves, Black goes wrong by moving the already developed Knight a second time.

7 R—B1	N x P ?

Wrong again. True, if 8 N x N ? , Q—R5ch recovers the piece very advantageously for Black. But White has a powerful alternative—to make use of the murderous open King Rook file thus presented to him.

8 R—R1 !	N—N5

Of Black's eight moves, four have been with this Knight!

9 Q—K2	B—B7ch
10 K—B1	N—QB3
11 P—B5 !	B—B4
12 N—KN5 !	. . . .

Beginning a quickly decisive attack on the open King Rook file—for example 12 . . . N—B3; 13 N x RP ! , N x N; 14 Q—R5 and mate follows.

12	N—R3
13 Q—R5	. . . .

88

Now it is clear that Black's senseless Pawn-grabbing has allowed White to mount a ferocious attack. A delightful possibility here is 13 . . . Q—B3; 14 N x RP ! , K x N; 15 B—KN5 and Black's Queen is trapped.

13 . . . .   Q—K1

14 N x RP !   K x N
15 B x N   P—KN3
16 Q x Pch ! !   P x Q
17 B x R mate !

Thus White triumphs on the file kindly opened for him by Black's Pawn-grabbing expedition.

By playing 1 . . . N x N; 2 P x N, B—B4 Black can obtain a definite advantage because of his pressure on White's King Bishop Pawn. Instead of going into this line, however, Black observes that he can win White's Queen Pawn. He attacks the Pawn twice, and it is defended only once.

This position is important because it is *typical*—its basic idea appears and reappears again and again. While the White Queen Pawn *seems* vulnerable, it is actually guarded sufficiently. But, because this protection is indirect, many a player is unable to resist capturing the tempting Pawn.

1 . . . .   N x P ?

The best that Black can hope for after this thoughtless capture is to lose "only" the Knight.

2 N x N   Q x N ? ? ?

After this Black loses his Queen.

3 B x Pch !   . . . .

This is the finesse that Black overlooked! His King is attacked, consequently he cannot stop to save his unguarded Queen, which is also under attack.

3 . . . . .   K x B
4 Q x Q   Resigns

Having lost his Queen in return for a mere Bishop, Black is left with a crushing material disadvantage.

The questions Black should have asked himself, and failed to ask, are, "What happens after I capture the Pawn? Why has he left it unguarded? *Is* it really unguarded?"

BLACK TO MOVE

Here the same theme appears in a more subtle form. Black's Queen is attacked, and 1 . . . Q x QP seems a thoroughly satisfactory reply, as there is no possibility of B x Pch. And yet it would be a mistake to capture the loose Pawn. How does White prove that the Queen Pawn cannot be captured with impunity?

Black's attacked Queen should retreat to a place of safety, *1 . . . Q—Q1, for example, or 1 . . . Q—R3.* Instead, Black captures the Queen Pawn:

    1 . . . .   Q x QP

To refute the capture, White plays a move which at first sight looks nonsensical:

    2 N—Q6 ! !   . . . .

There seems to be no rhyme or reason to this move, as Black can reply *2 . . . Q x N.* But in that event, the unprotected Queen is lost after *3 B x Pch.*

Nor is this all. In addition, the advanced Knight attacks the Black Rook at K1. Against these two threats Black has only one resource:

    2 . . . .   Q—K4

Black makes the best of it.

    3 N x R   Q x N

White has won the Exchange in return for a Pawn—a material advantage that will win the game for him.

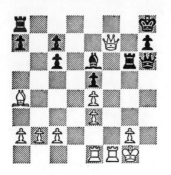

White's choice of a move for his attacked Queen should be influenced by the fact that Black has a powerful attacking position. Black is all set to double Rooks on the open King Knight file, or to proceed even more violently, depending on White's next move.

Even after *1 Q—B3, R/R1—KN1* the concentration of force against White's King-side would eventually be too much for White. Failing to appreciate the power of Black's formation, White completely neglects the defense by playing:

$$1 \text{ Q x BP ? ?} \qquad \ldots \ldots$$

This impetuous Pawn-grab is immediately fatal.

| 1 . . . . | R x Pch ! |
| 2 K x R | R—N1ch |

Battered by the crossfire of three enemy pieces, the lone White King cannot hold out very long. Thus if *3 K—B2, Q—R7ch* and mate next move.

| 3 K—B3 | B—N5ch |
| Resigns | |

For if *4 K—N3, Q—R6ch; 5 K—B2, Q—R7 mate.* (Black can also force mate with *3 . . . Q—R4ch* etc. The absence of the White Queen allows Black to win in a variety of ways.)

WEAKENING YOUR CASTLED POSITION

As you have seen in Number Two, leaving the King in the center often means exposing the King to a dangerous, very possibly fatal, attack. This led us to the conclusion that castling is the best way to safeguard the King.

The castled position, then, is the King's fortress. But, though the King is safer castled than in the center, that does not mean that castling alone assures you complete immunity from attack. If your opponent has an overwhelmingly superior development, he can concentrate more forces for attack than you can supply for defense. Sometimes brilliant sacrifices are available to smash down a defender's barriers.

But in this chapter we are mainly concerned with *Pawn weaknesses* in the castled position. In the case of castling on the King-side, three Pawns are involved: the King Rook Pawn, the King Knight Pawn, and the King Bishop Pawn. As long as all three Pawns are still on their original squares, the castled position remains sturdy and difficult to take by storm.

Yet once a single member of the trio advances, the defender is headed for trouble. For example, suppose the King Knight Pawn advances one square. Then immediately the squares it formerly protected—KR3 and KB3—must receive protection from *pieces*. Worse yet, these squares become targets for enemy occupation. Let a hostile Queen and Knight, or Queen and Bishop, occupy these squares, and you will see the castled position totter and crumble.

The advance of the King Rook Pawn is also dangerously weakening. Very often the attacker is able to sacrifice a piece for the Pawn on KR3, in this way ripping up the castled position and leaving it wide open for large-scale invasion. The advance of the King Bishop Pawn creates similar problems, and very often opens up a vital diagonal for the hostile Bishop.

Another serious consequence of any of these Pawn advances is that they enable the attacker to open lines by advancing his own Pawns and forcing Pawn exchanges. Thus, after Black plays . . . P—KN3, White may reply P—KR4 and P—KR5, exchanging Pawns and thus opening the King Rook file for attack. Or, after White plays P—KR3, Black may react with . . . P—KN4 and . . . P—KN5, likewise obtaining an open file for attack.

Once the attacker succeeds in forcing open a line leading to the castled position, he has enormously improved his prospects of taking the hostile King by storm. As long as the Pawns remain on their original squares, they form a road block for the attacking pieces. After one of the Pawns has advanced, the barrier is much more likely to be breached—by exchanges, by sacrifices, by violent line-opening.

To sum up: you have seen that Pawn advances in front of the castled King can be weakening—even dangerous. You should therefore avoid such advances. Sometimes you are forced to make such advances—but at least you can avoid making them needlessly. *Avoid such Pawn moves if it is at all possible to avoid them!*

Queen-side castling, which we rarely encounter, presents difficulties for the inexperienced player. The castled King has a wider area to guard than on the King-side. Hence the temptation to meet threats with Pawn advances is much stronger in the case of Queen-side castling. This makes it more likely for the defense on this broader front to be upset by violent sacrifices.

BLACK TO MOVE

White's Queen-side castled position is shaky, menaced as it is by Black's Bishops and the open Queen Knight file. Right now the castled Pawn position is intact, but Black's masterly probing soon creates weaknesses that pave the way for brilliant sacrifices.

1	B—Q5 !
2 P—B3	QR—N1 !
3 P—QN3	KR—Q1 !

For *if 4 P x B, then 4 . . . Q x QP wins at once.* White's weakened castled position is now riddled with weaknesses.

4 N—B3   Q x P ! ! !

Beautiful play, made possible by the Pawn weaknesses.

5 P x Q   R x P

Threatens mate.

6 B—K1   B—K6ch ! !
   Resigns

Black mates next move. A convincing demonstration of the disastrous effect of weakening Pawn moves.

HOW PAWN ADVANCES WEAKEN
THE CASTLED POSITION

Ruy Lopez

WHITE	BLACK
1 P—K4	P—K4
2 N—KB3	N—QB3
3 B—N5	P—QR3
4 B—R4	N—B3
5 P—Q3	P—Q3
6 P—B3	B—K2
7 P—KR3	Castles
8 Q—K2	N—K1
9 P—KN4	. . . .

This advance is not weakening as White intends to castle on the Queen-side.

9	P—QN4
10 B—B2	B—N2
11 QN—Q2	Q—Q2
12 N—B1	N—Q1
13 N—K3	N—K3
14 N—B5	P—N3 ?

Impatiently brushing off the powerfully posted Knight. But now his castled position is weakened.

15 N x Bch	Q x N
16 B—K3	N/K1—N2
17 Castles (Q)	P—QB4
18 P—Q4	KP x P
19 P x P	P—B5
20 P—Q5	N—B2
21 Q—Q2	P—QR4
22 B—Q4 !	P—B3
23 Q—R6 !	P—N5
24 P—N5 !	P—B4
25 B—B6 !	Q—B2

Thanks to Black's weakening 14th move, White's pieces have infiltrated powerfully at KR6 and KB6.

| 26 P x P ! | P x P |

| 27 P—N6 ! ! | Q x P |

If 27 . . . Q x B; 28 Q x P mate!

| 28 B x N | Resigns |

Black loses a piece, as *28 . . . Q x B is refuted by 29 R—N1* winning the Queen by a pin. White took advantage of the Pawn weakening in superb style.

HOW PAWN ADVANCES
ALLOW LINE-OPENING

Ruy Lopez

WHITE	BLACK
1 P—K4	P—K4
2 N—KB3	N—QB3
3 B—N5	N—B3
4 P—Q3	P—Q3
5 P—B3	P—KN3

Played in order to develop his King Bishop, but it creates the possibility of a later *P—KR4* and *P—KR5*, opening the King Rook file by P x P.

6 QN—Q2	B—N2
7 N—B1	Castles
8 B—R4	N—Q2
9 N—K3	N—B4
10 B—B2	N—K3
11 P—KR4 !	N—K2
12 P—R5	P—Q4
13 RP x P	BP x P

As predicted. Now White has a formidable attacking weapon in the King Rook file.

14	P x P	N x P
15	N x N	Q x N
16	B—N3	Q—B3
17	Q—K2	B—Q2
18	B—K3	K—R1
19	Castles (Q)	QR—K1
20	Q—B1 !	P—QR4
21	P—Q4 !	P x P
22	N x P	B x N
23	R x B !	N x R

Now White's carefully prepared attack is ready to roll.

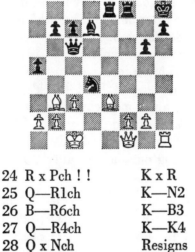

24	R x Pch ! !	K x R
25	Q—R1ch	K—N2
26	B—R6ch	K—B3
27	Q—R4ch	K—K4
28	Q x Nch	Resigns

White mates next move. Note the connection between Black's weakening 5th move, White's line-opening 11th, 12th, and 13th moves, and the brilliant sacrifice on move 24.

Imagine that White's King-side Pawns are still on their original squares. Even if they were, Black's Bishops would still be powerful. But with White's Pawns advanced, his castled position is wide open to attack. The deadly Bishops penetrate into the castled position with irresistible force.

Before we see Black's winning procedure, there is one other aspect of the position that we must study. Note that Black has advanced two of his King-side Pawns without exposing *his* King to danger. Why is the advance of White's King-side Pawns a serious mistake; why is the advance of Black's King-side Pawns of no importance?

What influences our reply is the placement of each player's pieces. White's forces are not posted for attack, so that Black has nothing to fear! Black's Bishops, on the other hand, are trained menacingly on the King-side.

Thus, White's advanced Pawns give Black the *opportunity* for devastating attack. Black's Bishops give him the *means* for carrying out such an attack. Here is how it is done:

1	B—R7ch !
2 K x B	Q—B2ch
3 B—B4	Q x Bch
4 K—N1	Q—N6 mate !

Observe how Black's pieces have infiltrated into the squares weakened by the advance of White's Pawns. Observe, too, that White's pieces can't contribute nothing to the defense.

100

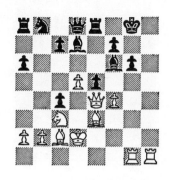

Black has the same kind of weakness as in the previous example—his King Rook Pawn is gone, his advanced King Knight Pawn is a target. As for White, his Rooks have a powerful sweep on open files leading to the Black King. Note also that White's Bishops are aggressively posted.

| 1 R x P ch ! | . . . . |

You can always expect such startling explosions when one player has weaknesses and his opponent has powerfully posted pieces.

| 1 . . . . | P x R |

Declining the Rook doesn't help, for after *1 . . . K—B1; 2 B—B5ch is decisive.*

| 2 Q x NPch | K—B1 |

A pretty alternative finish is *2 . . . B—N2; 3 R—R8ch ! , K x R; 4 Q—R7 mate!*

| 3 B—B5ch | R—K2 |

Or 3 . . . B—K2; 4 R—R8 mate.

| 4 Q x Bch | Resigns |

No matter how Black plays, White ends it all with 5 R—R8 mate. You will find it worth while to study this extremely instructive example. A weakening Pawn move opened the King Rook file, which is bound to serve as White's highway to victory. *The advanced King Knight Pawn serves as a further target which is sure to be demolished by White.* Result: a decisive sacrificial attack.

The absence of even one Pawn from the castled position often exposes the King to a dangerous attack. The reason is that hostile pieces may gain a foothold on squares that are not guarded by the missing Pawn. Here, for example, a spectacular mate is possible.

White's King-side suffers from the disappearance of his King Knight Pawn from KN2. His KB3 and KR3 squares are weakened by the absence of their natural Pawn protector and need to be guarded by pieces. Such defensive needs are wasteful and also have an additional drawback —there is no telling when some startling tactical surprise may crush the defense.

On the surface it seems that White has covered up the gap fairly well. He has swung around his Queen Rook to the defense of the castled position, and his Knight gives added support, though at the cost of dangerously crowding the King's position.

Nevertheless, the organic weakness of the castled position—the absence of the King Knight Pawn—has allowed a threatening rush of Black pieces to the King-side. And here is the result:

1	Q—N7ch ! ! !
2 R x Q	N—R6 mate !

Or 2 Q x Q, N—K7 mate—an equally delightful smothered mate.

BLACK TO MOVE

White has weakened his King-side by playing P—KN3. Worse yet, he has played his King Bishop to Q3 instead of KN2. On the latter square, this Bishop would have guarded the long diagonal against inroads by Black's Bishop. As matters stand, Black can win by means of an effective sacrifice!

Has White developed his pieces effectively? What are the facts? White's Queen is cut off from the King-side and can barely move. The White Rooks stand on closed files; the White Bishops aim along closed diagonals!

So badly jumbled are White's pieces that they can contribute virtually nothing to the defense of the White King.

What of Black's development? His Bishop has an unshakeable grip on the King-side. Black's Queen is aggressively poised for attack. The King Rook can come into action by . . . R—B3.

To sum up: White has weakened his King-side by playing P—KN3. He has failed to neutralize this weakness by striving for a good defensive formation. What happens now?

1	Q x P ch ! ! !
2 K x Q	R—B3 !
Resigns !	

White is helpless against the threat of . . . *R—R3ch* followed by . . . *R—R8 mate*. (See the power of Black's Bishop on the diagonal!)

Black's extra piece is of little value, for his King-side is denuded of protection, and it is on the King-side that the game will be decided. For White can force a fatal weakness in Black's castled Pawn position. Black's King will succumb quickly, deprived of any aid from the other Black pieces.

1 B—B6 !   . . . .

The key to the situation. Black's only answer to the threatened mate is to advance still another Pawn in front of his King.

1 . . . .   P—N3
2 Q—R4   . . . .

Whereas White has three powerful pieces cooperating in the attack, Black's King is on his own—no help from his forces. So Black must rely on King moves or on weakening Pawn moves—feeble resources against White's murderous attack.

2 . . . .   K—R2

Or 2 . . . P—KR4; 3 Q—N5, K—R2; 4 R—R4 and Black has no defense against 5 R x Pch etc.

3 Q x Pch ! !   K x Q
4 R—R4 mate

Right to the bitter end Black's King had no support from the other Black pieces. Note how quickly White triumphed after forcing a weakening in the castled position with 1 B—B6!

WHITE TO MOVE

The first thing you notice here is that White's pieces are posted very aggressively. His Bishop at QN2 hits right at the heart of Black's castled position; his Queen and Knight support the attack; his Rook commands the open Queen file. How does White proceed to force the game?

What use can White make of his superior development? To answer this question, we must first note that Black's pieces are in extremely passive positions. The Black pieces are either defensive or useless.

In one sense, though, Black is lucky. He has no weaknesses on the King-side. Therefore, no matter how formidable White's attacking formation looks, he has no real target. What White must do, then, is to create weaknesses in Black's castled position.

1 N—R6ch ! !   . . . .

This impudent Knight must be captured. *If 1 . . . K— R1; 2 N x Pch forks King and Queen. Even stronger (after 1 . . . K—R1) is 2 Q x BP ! with the irresistible threat of 3 Q—N8 mate.*

1 . . . .   P x N

Now that Black's castled position is breached, White wins quickly.

2 R x N !   Q x R
3 Q—B6   Resigns

He is helpless against the threat of *4 Q—R8 mate,* which has been made possible by the smashing of Black's Kingside.

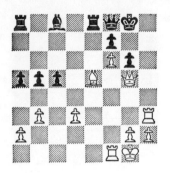

Black's castled position has been sadly weakened. His King Rook Pawn is gone, his King Knight Pawn has had to advance. Meanwhile White has established a menacing Pawn wedge at KB6, and all his pieces are admirably poised for an assault on Black's King. In fact, White forces mate in three moves!

1 Q x P ch ! !   . . . .

A rude shock for Black. But what interests us is this thought: if White can afford to sacrifice his most valuable piece, then Black has indeed damaged his King-side fatally by weakening Pawn moves.

1 . . . .   P x Q
2 P—B7ch !   . . . .

The real point of the sacrifice. The long diagonal becomes completely clear, allowing White to set up a familiar mating pattern. The Rook on KR3, supported by the Bishop, forms this mating pattern.

2 . . . .   Q x P
3 R—R8 mate

One of those combinations that are so distinguished in their artistry that we can play them over again and again and still enjoy them. And again, observe that what makes the artistry possible is *the weakening of Black's castled position.*

Why do players weaken the castled position? Some do not realize the weakening effect of the moves; others cannot help themselves. In this case, it was White's earlier threats that cleverly forced Black to weaken his castled position.

106

BLACK TO MOVE

White has made a serious mistake by castling on the Queenside. Black has concentrated his Rooks for a heavy attack on the open Queen Knight file. White imagines that he has removed all danger by playing P—QN3. But, as so often happens, the moved Pawn is a target rather than a barricade.

That White has a target at his QN3 square is bad enough. What makes matters even worse is that his Queen is paralyzed and his other pieces contribute little to the defense.

This makes Black bold—he looks for a radical solution. Here it is:

> 1 . . . .   R x P ch ! !

Sacrificing a whole Rook to remove the feeble barrier at White's QN3 square.

> 2 RP x R   R x P ch ! !

Encore!

> 3 P x R   Q—Q6ch

Now everything becomes clear. By smashing up White's flimsy Pawn position, Black has been able to strip the White King of all defensive resource.

> 4 K—R2   Q x NP mate

A beautiful combination; but if we ask, what made it possible?—the answer is: *the weakening of White's castled position*. White castled into an open file, and he had a Pawn target that attracted brilliant sacrifices.

107

White is the Exchange ahead—he has a Rook for Knight and Pawn. Hence he seems to have a winning game, with victory not too far away.

Is his immediate task to save his attacked Rook on the QB5 square? Or is there more involved in the position?

What really matters is that Black has fatally weakened his King-side by *the removal of his King Knight Pawn from its original square.* This has created infiltration points at his KR3 and KB3 squares for the White pieces.

So serious are these weaknesses that one's first impression is that White can force checkmate by *1 Q—B6.* Unfortunately, if White moves his Queen from the King Knight file, Black has the reply *1 . . . Q x NP mate.*

Thus the real problem is: how can White execute his mating threat without being exposed to Black's mating threat? White's solution is subtle and effective.

1 R—B8 ! ! !   R x R

The main point is that after *1 . . . B x R* Black no longer threatens mate on the long diagonal but allows *2 Q—B6—followed by 3 Q—N7 mate.*

2 R—Q8ch !	R x R
3 Q x Rch	N—B1
4 Q x N mate	

WHITE TO MOVE

White has sacrificed a Rook to force a fatal breach in Black's castled position. The disappearance of Black's King Knight Pawn has allowed White's menacing Queen to occupy the far-advanced outpost KR6.

White has a sparkling winning method based on the absence of Black's King Knight Pawn from its normal square.

> 1 B—B6 ! !   . . . .

Threat: 2 Q—N7 mate. There is only one reply.

> 1 . . . .   B x B

Now it seems White has shot his bolt. But . . .

> 2 P—K5 ! !   . . . .

Threatens 3 Q x P mate.

> 2 . . . .   N x B
> 3 P x B   Resigns

Now we are back to the first threat of *Q—N7 mate,* and there is nothing that Black can do about it. Note that throughout *his Queen has had no defensive value whatever*.

By parting with his King Knight Pawn, *Black created a fatal breach in his castled position*. White took pitiless advantage of the Black King's exposed state.

GETTING PINNED

THE BEST ADVICE about getting pinned is: Don't!

Pins occur more frequently on the chessboard than any other type of attack. Yet, strangely enough, pins are rarely defined or explained. *A pin is an attack on a piece which screens another piece from attack.* A piece that is pinned is tied down.

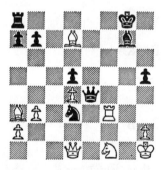

In the above diagram, Black's Queen pins White's Rook. The Queen attacks the Rook, which in turn screens the White King from attack. The Rook is pinned (tied down to its present square) because a move of the Rook would expose the White King to attack by the Black Queen. (As you know, the laws of chess forbid your making any move that exposes your King to attack by a hostile piece.)

To emphasize the helplessness of White's pinned Rook, let us suppose that it is Black's move, and that he plays . . . N—B7ch forking White's King and Queen. One's first thought is to reply R x N, in order to save the menaced Queen. But the pinned Rook is helpless; *it cannot move.* White, in check, must move his King, losing his Queen by . . . N x R.

The pathetic helplessness of White's Rook in the previous diagram is typical of pins where the screened piece is the King.

Where the screened piece is any other piece but the King, the player subject to the pin has greater freedom of action. If the screened piece is a Queen, Rook, Bishop, or Knight, the pinned piece can *legally* move. But though such a move is legal, it is not necessarily advisable. The move of a pinned piece will generally involve a serious loss of material. This is brought out in the following position:

White's Queen, supported by a White Rook, pins Black's Bishop, which is protected only once and cannot be protected additionally. If the Bishop remains on K3, it is lost; if the Bishop moves, the Knight at K2 which it screens is lost. Black can try 1 . . . N—K5, blocking the pin. But after 2 N x N, P x N; 3 Q x P the pin is renewed and White also threatens 4 Q—R7 mate.

The most bearable pins, as far as the defender is concerned, are those where the pinned piece is guarded by a Pawn. In such cases, protection is automatic—and cheap. Where the pinned piece has to be guarded by another piece, you can expect trouble. The pinned piece is tied down, the protecting piece is tied down to the defense of the pinned piece. Thus two units are deprived of much of their mobility and therefore of much of their power.

Another point to remember about the pin is its psychological value. The restraining effect of the pin has a depressing effect on the defender. Pinning and restraining are attacking functions and assure a player the initiative. He has a positive goal—to weaken the pinned piece, to pile up pressure on it, to take advantage of its immobility. The player whose piece is pinned is at a disadvantage. He is at his opponent's mercy, and must often look on helplessly while his pinned piece is being undermined.

It follows, therefore, that you should avoid the pinning of your pieces. Once you are pinned, your freedom of action is restricted, and you are exposed to threats that may cost you the game. Just as it is important not to neglect your development in the opening stage, it is equally vital not to allow your pieces to be pinned later on.

BLACK TO MOVE

When the King Bishop Pawn is advanced after castling, it often happens that a serious weakness is created on the diagonal leading to the King. In this case, it is White who has weakened his position, so that his Knight on this diagonal is in danger. How is Black to exploit this?

Black has a powerful move in:

1 . . . .   Q—N3 !

This pins White's Knight on Q4. The Knight, which screens White's King from attack, is of course unable to move out of the line of attack.

In addition, since the Knight is attacked twice and defended only once, it needs additional protection. But how? If *2 N/B3—K2, P—K4* cruelly exploits the exposed position of the attacked Knight. As it cannot leave its post at Q4, it is lost in return for a mere Pawn.

So White tries a different way:

2 B—K3   . . . .

True, this masks the diagonal, but Black can still win a piece!

2 . . . .   P—K4

It is White's misfortune that he cannot retreat the attacked Knight to a square from which it will defend the Bishop at K3. And if *3 N x N*, Black first plays *3 . . . Q x Bch* and then *4 . . . P x N*.

3 N—R4   Q—R2 !

By keeping his Queen on the diagonal, Black maintains his pin on the Knight at Q4. White resigns, as he can no longer stave off the loss of a piece.

White's course is readily suggested by the uncomfortable position of Black's Bishop and Knight on the King file. Neither piece can protect the other; neither is protected by a Pawn; both are vulnerable to an attack along the King file. This is an ideal set-up for a pinning attack.

With Black's Knight and Bishop established as the vulnerable targets, your only problem is: should White continue with *1 R—K1 or 1 Q—K3*.

As the White Rook is needed at Q1 to guard White's Knight, the Queen move remains the only feasible one:

1 Q—K3   . . . .

Now Black's Knight must not move, for then the Bishop is lost.

Nor will *1 . . . Q—Q3* do, for then *2 N—B6ch* wins the Black Queen.

As for *1 . . . B x N*, this exposes Black to a new pin: *2 R x B, N—Q2 (forced); 3 Q—Q4* and the pinned Knight is lost.

1 . . . .   Q—N1
2 R—K1   . . . .

The Rook (no longer needed at Q1) intensifies the pin. Black's next two moves are forced.

2 . . . .   B x N

Getting out of the pin but running into a worse one.

3 B x Bch   N—B2
4 R—KB1   Resigns

The pinned Knight is lost.

WHITE TO MOVE

White menaces the Black King with his Rook at KN3 and his Bishop at QN3. This creates pins on Black's King Knight Pawn and King Bishop Pawn. However, White's Knight is attacked, and so is his Rook at KN3; his Bishop can be removed by . . . R x B. White's timing must be hair-sharp.

White's first move makes use of both pins and prepares to set up a new pin:

1 Q—N6 !   . . . .

Threatens *2 Q x NP mate*. The Queen is immune from capture, of course, as Black's King Bishop Pawn is pinned.

1 . . . .   **B x R**

The obvious reply.

Blocking the King Knight file with *1 . . . B—N4* does not help: *2 R x B, P x R; 3 P—B6 !* (a new pin!) and Black cannot prevent *4 Q x NP mate*.

2 P—B6 !   **Resigns**

Both Black's King Bishop Pawn and King Knight Pawn are pinned. Black cannot stop *3 Q x NP mate*.

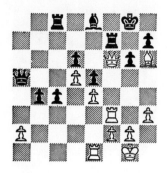

White's Queen, Rook at KB3, and Bishop make up a powerful attacking unit. Balked by the protective Black Rook at its KB2 square, White—almost!—threatens Q—N7 mate or Q—B8 mate. But this Black Rook is under too much pressure, and, worse yet, it gets no help from the Black Queen.

Black has weakened his King-side by advancing the King Knight Pawn. It is this loosening move that has enabled White's Queen and Bishop to take up their invasion posts at the KB6 and KR6 squares.

Momentarily Black's Rook at KB2 valiantly holds the fort. But Black's Queen is far off to one side. This leaves Black helpless against the brilliant *pinning attack* that follows.

1 Q—K7 ! ! . . . .

Beautiful. *If 1 . . . R x Q; 2 R—B8 mate. If 1 . . . R x R; 2 Q—N7 mate.* Thus the crucial Black Rook is pinned two ways, as it screens White's access to two vital squares.

1 . . . . Q—B2

Too late. But Black dare not move his Bishop (to stop the following mate), for then the vital Rook at KB2 falls, with mate the following move.

2 Q—B8ch ! R x Q
3 R x R mate

Black lost because (a) he weakened his castled position; (b) he gave one Rook too heavy a defensive burden; (c) he thus exposed himself to a deadly pin.

BLACK TO MOVE

Material is fairly even—Black has two minor pieces for Rook and two Pawns. But what really counts is the fact that Black's Bishop on the white squares exerts enormous power on the long diagonal. Black unmasks this power with a deadly pin.

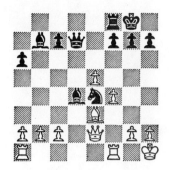

1 . . . .   **N—N6ch !**

A terrible surprise for White. The unexpected check opens up the long diagonal, and brings Black's Queen into action. The effectiveness of Black's attack depends on two pins.

2 P x N   **. . . .**

As the Knight check forks King and Queen, White has no choice: he must capture.

2 . . . .   **Q—R6ch**

White's Pawn at KN2, pinned by Black's Bishop on the long diagonal, cannot capture the Black Queen. It is this pin which assures the success of Black's attack.

3 K—N1   B x Bch
Resigns

If 4 Q x B, Q x P(N7) mate. And if 4 R—B2 or 4 Q—B2, Q x P(N7) mate as well. (The pinned piece has no protective value.)

117

What determines the choice of Black's next move? It is the fact that he controls the open Queen Bishop file. White is on the point of playing B—Q4, which will menace the King-side and also prevent any inroad by a Black Rook at QB6.

1 . . . .   R/B1—B6 !

By playing this move at once Black creates a powerful pin. White's Bishop on Q3, attacked twice, cannot move because that would lose the screened Bishop at K3.

Had Black postponed the Rook invasion by one move, he would have given White time for B—Q4, consolidating White's position against the Rook invasion.

2 Q—K2   . . . .

Forced; but now Black steps up the pinning pressure.

2 . . . .   B—N4 !

Adding to White's troubles—if 3 B x B ? , R x B wins a piece for Black.

3 R/B1—Q1   . . . .

Another forced move.

3 . . . .   Q—B2 !

Based on a plan that is revealed by his next move. White desperately tries to break the pin, but it is too late.

4 B—Q4   R x B !

Creating a different kind of pin.

5 R x R   Q—B5 !
    Resigns

White has no defense against the coming 6 . . . R x R which leaves Black a clear piece ahead.

118

WHITE TO MOVE

Sometimes the utilization of a
pin can be exceptionally subtle.
Here we see at a glance that
White's pin on the King Bishop
Pawn is extremely threatening.
But how is it to be exploited?
The decisive method selected by
White is remarkably imagina-
tive, though dependent on tech-
nical factors.

White's generally more aggressive position justifies his
seeking an immediate decision. We have already concluded
that the pin on Black's King Bishop Pawn will be the winning factor.

       1 B x N !   . . . .

First he removes the valuable defensive Knight.

       1 . . . .   B x B

After *1 . . . P x B* the break-up of Black's castled Pawn
position would lose for him in a number of ways. The
most obvious is *2 Q—N4ch, K—R1; 3 N x Pch* etc.

       2 Q x Pch ! ! !   . . . .

The surprise sacrifice that will take advantage of the pin
on Black's King Bishop Pawn.

       2 . . . .   K x Q
       3 R—R5ch   K—N1
       4 N—N6 !   Resigns

He has no way of parrying the coming R—R8 mate.
(The King Bishop Pawn is pinned, so that . . . P x N is
impossible.)

119

Black's position seems quite secure—until you observe that he has badly weakened his King-side with . . . P—KN3. White's problem is—how is he to take advantage of this weakness? He solves the problem by means of a brilliant combination.

1 R x B ! !   Q x R

Now Black's Knight is pinned—in a particularly dangerous way, too. For this Knight is not protected by a Pawn—thanks to the earlier . . . *P—KN3*. Therefore the pinned Knight must be guarded by pieces—always a dangerous and costly procedure.

2 Q—B3   K—N2

The only other way to protect the pinned Knight is 2 . . . *B—B4*. But then, after *3 N x Bch, P x N; 4 Q—N3 ! ! , K—N2; 5 B x N dbl ch, K x B; 6 Q—R4ch ! , K—K3; 7 R—K1ch,* Black can resign.

3 N/B3—K4 ! !   . . . .

Beautiful play. By sacrificing another piece White crushes Black's resistance to the pin.

3 . . . .   P x N
4 N x P   Q—K3

If 4 . . . Q x N; 5 Q x Nch, K—N1; 6 B—R6 forcing checkmate. Again the weakening of Black's King-side tells against him.

5 B x Nch   K—N1
6 Q—B4   Resigns

There is no defense to the threatened *Q—R6*. White's pin was the weapon that smashed Black's King-side.

120

WHITE TO MOVE

Black seems to have a solid defense against the pin on his King Knight Pawn. But this pin is only the beginning of his difficulties; he has placed all his pieces very awkwardly for defensive purposes. Soon the first pin leads to others even more troublesome.

1 N—N4 ! !	P x N
2 Q x N ! !	. . . .

If now 2 . . . P x Q; 3 R—K8ch, R—B1; 4 R x Pch, K—R1; 5 R x R mate.

2	Q—Q2

The only way to meet the threat of *R—K8ch.*

3 Q—Q5 ! ! !	. . . .

Beautiful play. He pins Black's Rook at KB2 in order to threaten R x Pch.
If 3 . . . Q x Q; 4 R—K8ch forces mate.

3	K—B1

He must get out of the pin. *If 3 . . . P—KN3; 4 R/N3—K3 !* is the winning move.

4 R x P ! !	. . . .

Another superb move. *If now 4 . . . R x R; 5 Q x Q* and the pinned Rook cannot capture White's Queen!

4	Q x Q
5 R—N8 dbl ch ! !	K x R
6 R—K8ch	R—B1
7 R x R mate	

121

WHITE TO MOVE

Black's position seems solid as the Rock of Gibraltar. Especially powerful is his far-advanced Knight at the Q6 square, well guarded by his passed Queen Bishop Pawn. Yet this position is quite deceptive. Relying on pinning technique, White can smash the set-up of Black's forces.

How White can act incisively is not clear, especially since his Queen is attacked. Nor is there a single White piece, with the possible exception of the Knight, which even has the appearance of harboring any aggressive notions.

1 R x N ! !   . . . .

This move looks mysterious; yet it will soon expose Black to a winning attack that is based on a pin.

1 . . . .   P x R
2 N—K6ch ! ! !   . . . .

The point of the previous sacrifice. Black cannot play 2 . . . Q x N because his Queen is pinned.

2 . . . .   P x N

Any move of the Black King would lose the Black Queen.

3 R—B7ch   Resigns

Now everything becomes clear. Black's Queen, being pinned, cannot interpose 3 . . . Q—B2. Consequently he must move his King, allowing 4 Q x Q followed by a quick mate.

122

Here we have one of the rare cases of a pin that does not work. White's Queen is attacked by a pinning Bishop at Black's QR3 square. When the Queen retreats, White will lose the exchange by . . . B x R etc. This seems a good example of the power of the pin, but there is much more to the position!

1 Q x N ! !   . . . .

An amazing move, predicated on the weakness of Black's King-side. If now *1 . . . B x R; 2 R x B* and White has won two pieces for the Rook (a material advantage for him). Of course, Black could still go ahead and win the Queen, getting mated as in the actual play.

1 . . . .   P x Q

Black is skeptical. Mate is now forced.

2 B x Pch	K—R1
3 N—N6ch	K—R2
4 N x R dbl ch	K—R1
5 N—N6ch	K—R2

One forced move after another.

6 N—K5 dis ch !	K—R1
7 N—B7 mate !	

Throughout, *Black's Queen remained a passive onlooker.* Again and again, we find that this is the key to a startling combination. As far as the success of White's combination was concerned, Black's Queen might just as well have been off the board.

FAILING TO GUARD
AGAINST CAPTURES

FEW MISTAKES can be more costly in chess than failing to guard against captures. A capture is often the turning point of a game; it may involve gaining a decisive advantage in material or, in some cases, a vastly superior position.

Sometimes a capture is bound up with a sacrificial combination, in which a piece of great value is given up for one of slight value. Such captures are naturally difficult to foresee. Much more common are those situations in which a capture is quite obvious.

Why are such captures overlooked? Probably because they turn up in positions that seem simple and routine; the player's alertness is lulled; he forgets that almost every position in chess has some element of attack and threat. Positions that are simple on the surface will often turn out, on careful scrutiny, to contain a fantastic wealth of intricate details. If you can acquire the faith that almost every chess position, no matter how simple, has its share of tactical possibilities, you are well on the way to overcoming any tendency to overlook captures.

In the game on page 104, Black overlooks a deadly capture that checkmates him on the 13th move. "Who would have dreamt that it was possible!" is the wondering comment of most chessplayers. Well, the player who saw and

124

executed this combination certainly dreamt it was possible. Whether he found the combination by logical reasoning or by a flash of "inspiration," his example is one that we should all imitate.

WHITE TO MOVE

Without bothering to look very deeply into the position, White snaps at a loose Pawn. It is curious that he fails to see the crushing though obvious reply. This kind of slip often occurs in positions that look too "simple" to require careful appraisal and calculation.

1 Q x RP ? ?   . . . .

This blunder converts a probably drawn position into immediate loss for White.

The chances are that White expected *1 . . . N—K6 ?* in reply.

In that event, *2 R x R ? ? ?* allows *2 . . . Q—N7 mate,* while *2 B x N* is answered by *2 . . . R x Rch* winning the Exchange. However, White has *2 Q—R5ch ! , K—K2; 3 B x N* winning a piece.

But in reply to 1 Q x RP ? ? Black has a devastating alternative:

1 . . . .   N x P ! !

If now 2 R x R ? ? ? , Q—N7 mate.
Or 2 P x N, R x Rch and White loses his Bishop as well.
After 1 . . . N x P ! !, White resigned. The real finesse of this move lies in the fact that it renders Q—R5ch impossible for White, leaving him without a defense.

125

One of the queerest things that can happen in a game of chess is seen when a player actually provokes his opponent to make a capture that wins the game! Even forceful moves may have a drawback—on occasion they stimulate the other player to find an even more forceful reply.

Black's uneasiness about the strong position of White's Bishop is understandable. This Bishop points right at Black's castled position; in combination with White's Queen and Knight, the Bishop may take part in a winning attack.

To ward off danger, Black should play *1 . . . P— KB4 !* as the best means of preventing B x Pch and gaining ground no matter how White replies. Instead, in his anxiety to be rid of the annoying Bishop, Black plays:

1	P—B5 ? ?
2 B x Pch !	K x B

Or 1 . . . K—R1; 2 Q—R5 and Black is in a mating net.

3 Q—R5ch	K—N1
4 N—N5	Resigns

Black is helpless against the threat of *Q—R7 mate.* If he tries *4 . . . R—K1* there follows *5 Q—R7ch, K—B1; 6 Q—R8 mate.* Naturally *4 . . . Q x N; 5 Q x Q* leaves Black with a decisive material disadvantage.

126

BLACK TO MOVE

White's "fianchettoed" Bishop at KN2 exerts strong pressure along the long diagonal. To neutralize this pressure to some extent, Black should play 1 . . . B—N2. Instead, Black overlooks capture possibilities by a faulty move which further opens the long diagonal.

1	P x P ? ?
2 N—K5 !	. . . .

Now White's Bishop at KN2 strikes along the whole diagonal, threatening *B x R*. Poor Black cannot block the diagonal with *2 . . . N—Q4 ?* for then *3 P x P* wins a piece.

2	P—QB3

Forced. Black expects *3 N x QBP, N x N; 4 B x N, R—N1; 5 P x P* and White has won "only" a Pawn. But White has another capturing possibility, totally unforeseen by Black.

3 B x P ! !	. . . .

A paradox—who would expect White to part with the mighty Bishop? The reply is forced.

3	N x B
4 N x N	Q—B2
5 N x Bch	Q x N
6 B—R3 !	

This explains the "mysterious" capture on move 3. Black's Queen must give way, allowing the loss of the Exchange by 7 B x R, after which White has an easy win based on his advantage in material.

WHITE TO MOVE

Some positions have "danger signals" to warn us. Here is such a position. White's Knight at KB3 is *en prise*. Also the loose position of White's Knight at QB3 may lead to trouble, in view of the powerful thrust of Black's Bishop at KN2 along the long diagonal. Can you see why?

White's immediate problem is what to do about his attacked Knight at KB3. Moving the menaced Knight requires careful analysis.

Thus, if 1 N—KN5, N x P ! ; 2 P x N , Q x N. Or 1 N—KN5, N x P ! ; 2 N x N, B x R.

The right move is *1 N—Q4 !* , salvaging one Knight from attack and *closing the long diagonal* so that the other Knight is no longer menaced. If then 1 . . . P x P; 2 P x P, N x P; 3 N x P and Black's weak Queen Pawn must fall.

Unfortunately for White, he misses this resource and decides on counterattack. Such a policy is always risky, for some hidden possibility may spoil your calculations.

    1 P x P ?   P x N
    2 P x N   . . . .

Anticipating capture by *2 . . . B x P; 3 B x P* etc.

    2 . . . .   N x P ! !

The capture that White overlooked! It unmasks the Bishop on the long diagonal, leaving two White pieces attacked. One of them must be lost.

WHITE TO MOVE

White has a double problem here. He has weakened his King-side with the advance of the King Rook Pawn, and he must therefore be on the alert against any threats on that wing. His other difficulty is that his development has been haphazard and ineffectual.

White would do well to remove Black's aggressively posted Knight at KB5. Instead, he decides on what he thinks is a judicious retreat:

1 B—B1 ? . . . .

This "prudent" move, played to give the King-side additional protection, actually leads to disaster; for now White's Queen is no longer protected.

1 . . . . N x RPch !

Taking admirable advantage of the weakness of White's castled Pawn formation.

White must capture the intruder.

2 P x N N—Q5 !

Now the other Knight becomes troublesome. White cannot play *3 P x N ? ?* because his Queen is unguarded. (This is the consequence of 1 B—B1?)

3 Q—Q3 N—B6ch

Black has a field day on the smashed-up King-side. White cannot move his King, for this allows *4 . . . Q—R7 mate*. Therefore White must give up his Queen, suffering a decisive loss of material.

4 Q x N R x Q
Resigns

129

The essential point about this position is that as long as the Queens remain on the board, White has attacking chances; if the Queens are removed, Black reasons, White will have a lost endgame because of the awkward position of his Rooks. Black is therefore unduly eager to bring about the exchange of Queens.

While it is true that White's Rooks would be badly posted in an endgame, they are placed very effectively for attacking purposes in the above position. Black completely misses the point by offering the exchange of Queens with:

1	Q—Q4 ? ?

Theoretically this may seem an excellent move. In actual fact, it loses on the spot.

2 R x NPch !	K x R
3 Q—N3ch	K—B3

If 3 . . . K—R2; 4 Q—N6ch forces mate. (This explains why Black's Queen was needed at Q3.)

4 R x Pch	K—K2
5 Q—N5ch	Resigns

White mates next move.

In the diagramed position, Black should first have consolidated his position with some such move as . . . *R—B3* before offering the exchange of Queens.

Countless games have been lost in just this way—overlooking some small but vital tactical detail.

BLACK TO MOVE

Tactical oversights sometimes come about because a player is so preoccupied with long-range problems that he misses the down-to-earth capturing possibilities that must be watched for from move to move. This kind of absent-mindedness brings about Black's downfall here.

Though a Pawn ahead, Black is definitely on the defensive. White's Queen, Rook, and Bishop all exert powerful pressure, while Black's pieces can barely find a square to move to.

Black's immediate problem is to do something about his doubly-attacked Knight. Unfortunately, *if 1 . . . N—Q2; 2 Q—N5 !* leaves Black without a good move—*2 . . . Q—B2 ? ; 3 B—N7ch !* or *2 . . . R x R; 3 Q x Rch, K—B2; 4 Q x P* and wins.

To solve the problem, Black hits on a finesse:

> 1 . . . .   Q—B2 ?

This move—so Black thinks—guards his Knight indirectly, for *if 2 R x N ? ? , Q x Q etc.* But White has another capture which Black overlooked:

2 Q x N !	R x Q
3 R x Rch	K—Q2
4 R—B7ch	Resigns

For Black loses his Queen and remains a clear piece down.

OVERLOOKING A CAPTURE THAT
LEADS TO CHECKMATE!

Queen's Pawn Opening

WHITE	BLACK
1 P—Q4	P—Q4
2 P—K4 ! ?	P x P
3 P—KB3	P x P
4 N x P	. . . .

White has offered a Pawn in the hope of getting a big lead in development. With careful play, Black has nothing to fear.

4	B—N5
5 B—K3	N—QB3
6 P—B3	P—K4

After this optimistic reply Black's pieces are driven back. He gets an easier game with *6 . . . P—K3*.

7 P—Q5	N/B3—K2
8 Q—R4ch	B—Q2
9 Q—K4	P—KB3
10 B—Q3	N—N3 ? ?

Black's last move is quite plausible, and yet it allows a forced mate!

11 Q x Nch ! ! !   P x Q
12 B x Pch   K—K2
13 B—B5 mate !

How did this catastrophe come about? Naturally, Black did not dream that the Queen sacrifice was possible. What features of the position might have helped him to see danger ahead?

In the first place, Black's King is in the center, where, as we know, he is vulnerable. Secondly, the development of his pieces has become tangled up, so that the King can expect no help from his own forces. Finally, Black has advanced the King Bishop Pawn, which opens up a line of approach for White's pieces.

All these factors create danger for Black—but they need not necessarily be fatal. If Black is aware of the difficulty, he will be careful in selecting a Knight move. For example, 10 . . . N—B4 is quite safe and provides relief for the cramped state of Black's pieces. It is the careless 10 . . . N—N3 ? ? , played without understanding of the position, that leads to a catastrophe.

UNDERESTIMATING YOUR OPPONENT'S THREATS

THREATS are harder to see than captures. Some moves threaten checkmate, some threaten captures, some involve a general improvement in position. Some threats are crude, brutal, obvious. Others are unbelievably subtle in their intentions, refined in their execution. Some threats are sound and directed toward winning the game. Others are based on a foolish idea and will prove disastrous for the player who has devised them. Some threats are irresistible, others can be topped by a stronger threat.

In a game between good players, threats and counter-threats are essentially a matter of interplay of ideas and intentions. If each player does not always see through his opponent's threats, he is at least prepared for them. Thus, as in the case of captures, it is important to realize that threats are always possible, *that they must be looked for.*

That is why threats are most dangerous when they are devised by an opponent who seems to have a lost game. When victory seems within your grasp is just the time when you are most likely to underestimate the other player's resources. "Simple" positions, too, are the downfall of many a player who feels that the game no longer requires

careful scrutiny. Overconfidence is unquestionably the
quality that leads many players to overlook their opponents' threats.

BLACK TO MOVE

All that Black sees in this position is that one of his Bishops
is attacked, and that he can capture the advanced White Knight
if he wishes. Yet White threatens
one of the most startling bril-
liancies ever played on the
chessboard. Can you see White's
threat and how to meet it?

Black's safest course is 1 . . . B—K2 avoiding the
opening of the King Rook file and also guarding his Queen
Bishop Pawn.

But Black is blind to the explosive possibilities in the
position and plays:

1	Q—R4ch ? ?
2 P—QN4 ! !	. . . .

After this Black can avoid mate only by losing his
Queen!

2	P x NP
3 Q x Pch ! ! !	. . . .

This was White's hidden threat.

3	K x Q
4 P x B dis ch	K—N3
5 N—K7 mate	

Black is well aware that the open King Knight file may be dangerous for his King. But he feels he has adequate counter-attacking chances on the open Queen Knight file. He is carried away by the idea of playing ... R—N5. This move, he believes, will win a piece for him. He is wrong!

1	R—N5 ?

Now White has to have his wits about him; merely retreating his attacked Queen loses the Knight.

2 B x N ! !	R x Q
3 R x Pch	K—R1

Black saw this far ahead, and he is well satisfied. He expects *4 R—N5 dis ch, B x B; 5 R x Q, R x RP etc.*

But White has an extraordinary continuation:

4 R—N8 dbl ch ! ! ! . . . .

Who can blame Black for overlooking the threat of White's not even bothering to win the Black Queen—but sacrificing a Rook as well ? !

4	K x R
5 R—N1ch	R—KN5
6 R x Rch	Q—N4
7 R x Q mate	

Black went wrong by ignoring the threat of his open King Knight file. The cautious 1 . . . K—R1 ! would have neutralized the attack and maintained his counter-attack as well.

136

Black has a powerful attacking position. His Bishop has a sweeping diagonal; his Knight is strongly centralized; both Rooks are on open files; there is a devastating threat of . . . *Q—R5*, with the murderous double threat of . . . *Q x RP mate* or . . . *Q x BPch* and . . . *N—N6 mate*. How is White to defend himself?

To meet the threat of . . . *Q—R5*, White chooses the most obvious method—a line that is absolutely ruinous!

1 P—N3 ? ?   . . . .

Thus he prevents . . . *Q—R5*—or so he thinks. But this purely mechanical move fails to provide against the formidable concentration of Black's forces against White's King.

The move that Black chooses in reply seems fantastic, but only on the surface. Actually it is quite logical because it is based on the activity of the other Black pieces.

1 . . . .   **Q—R5 ! ! !**

Now Black threatens 2 . . . Q x RP mate!

How is White to defend himself? If he tries *2 P x Q, then 2 . . . R—N3ch; 3 Q—N4, R x Qch; 4 K—R1, N x P mate.*

So, after 1 . . . Q—R5 ! ! ! White resigns!

Now go back to the diagram. White could have countered the threat with *1 Q—B3.* Then if *1 . . . Q—R5; 2 P—R3* and White is secure—at least for a while.

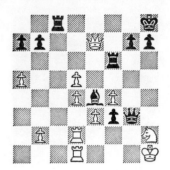

White has just played Q—K7, satisfied that by threatening Q x B he wards off the terrible threat of . . . P—B7 dis ch. Note that White is not afraid of . . . B x P (renewing the threat); for then he can play P—K4, blocking out the Bishop. Nevertheless, White overlooks still another threat at Black's disposal.

| 1 . . . . | Q—K8ch ! ! |

Who can blame White for not seeing this move, which looks utterly nonsensical?

And yet capturing the Queen loses very quickly, as you will see. Therefore White considers what happens if he fails to capture the Queen.

For example: *2 N—B1, R—R3ch; 3 R—R2, Q—B7 ! !* ; and White is comically helpless against the coming *4 . . . Q—N7 mate.* (The Rook at KR2 is pinned!)

Or 2 N—B1, R—R3ch; 3 K—N1, P—B7ch; 4 R x P, R—R8 mate.

2 R x Q	P—B7 dis ch !
3 Q x B	P x R(Q)ch
4 K—N2	Q x Rch
Resigns	

Hopelessly behind in material, White has nothing to play for.

Black's inspired Queen sacrifice is an example of chess imagination at its very finest. White provided against the immediate discovered check, but he failed to realize that Black's sly postponement of the discovered check could actually increase its power enormously.

138

Can you see what White is
threatening? Black misses it
completely, because he ignores
his weakness on the first rank.
How can Black make his position reasonably safe?

Black sees a chance to win White's King Rook Pawn.
Without stopping to look any further than this shallow possibility, he plays:

   1 . . . .   P—N3 ?

With *1 . . . Q—B2* Black could have parried White's
threat.

   2 Q—B7 ! !   . . . .

Threatens 3 Q x R mate or 3 Q—KN7 mate.

   2 . . . .   N—K3

If 2 . . . R x Q; 3 R—Q8ch with mate next move.

   3 R—Q8 ! !   . . . .

This dazzling stroke is much more forcing than *3 Q x N,
P x N*—which leads to nothing for White.

   3 . . . .   Q—B8ch

Desperation. *If 3 . . . N x R; 4 Q x R mate or 4 Q—
KN7 mate. If 3 . . . R x R; 4 Q x BPch, K—N1; 5 N—
K7 mate!*

   4 K—R2   Q—B5ch
   5 K—R3   Resigns

Black cannot capture the White decoy Rook. Meanwhile
he is helpless against a variety of mating threats, the most
brilliant being *6 Q—KN7ch ! !* , N x Q; 7 R x Q mate.
White's Queen was diabolically active; *Black's Queen did
nothing for the defense.*

139

White appears to have a lost game. He cannot move his Knight—for example 1 N—B4 ? ? , Q x Q; 2 R x Q, R—Q8ch forcing mate. Yet White deliberately played for this position, relying on a winning threat that Black has completely overlooked. What is White's resource that Black missed?

One can hardly blame Black for not forseeing the line of play by which White forces victory. Even the crippled Knight plays a part!

    1 R—B6 ! !   . . . .

Threatens *2 R x Pch ! , P x R; 3 Q—B7 mate.*

    1 . . . .   KR—B1

If 1 . . . P x R; 2 Q—B7 mate.

    2 Q—B5ch   K—N1
    3 R x Rch   R x R
    4 Q x Rch ! !   . . . .

The second point of White's magnificent plan.

    4 . . . .   K x Q
    5 R—K8 mate !

Beautiful play indeed; yet, can we completely excuse Black for failing to see White's subtle resource?

Take another look at the diagramed position. What hint is there of things to come? Note that Black's forces are badly split, with his Queen and Bishop practically out of play. When you study the situation carefully, you see that the Black King must really fend for himself, and can get little assistance from his forces. These factors are the key to Black's defeat.

140

WHITE TO MOVE

Black has just played . . . P—KR3, under the impression that this wins White's Bishop. This reasoning seems convincing, as a move of the menaced Bishop will lose the White Queen. How does White's aggressively posted Rook at KN3 spoil this plausible plan?

| 1 B—B6 ! ! | . . . . |

This is the spectacular threat that Black has completely overlooked.

| 1 . . . | Q x Q |

Black must capture, as his Queen is unguarded.

2 R x Pch	K—R1
3 R x P dis ch	K—N1
4 R—N7ch	K—R1
5 R x B dis ch	K—N1

These "windmill" moves are amusing—but not for Black!

| 6 R—N7ch | K—R1 |

The time has come for White to win back the Queen.

| 7 R—N5 dis ch | K—R2 |
| 8 R x Q | K—N3 |

A slight consolation for Black—he regains the lost piece.

| 9 R—R3 | K x B |
| 10 R x Pch | Resigns |

With three Pawns down, Black has nothing to play for.

BLACK IS SHOWN THE THREAT—
AND MISSES IT!

Petroff's Defense

WHITE	BLACK
1 P—K4	P—K4
2 N—KB3	N—KB3
3 N x P	P—Q3
4 N—KB3	N x P
5 Q—K2	Q—K2
6 P—Q3	N—KB3
7 B—N5	B—K3
8 N—B3	QN—Q2

Since neither player can develop his King Bishop both are likely to castle Queen-side.

9 P—Q4	P—Q4
10 Castles	P—B3

Not good. Since he will probably castle on the Queen-side, the Pawn weakness will endanger Black's castled position.

11 K—N1	P—KR3
12 B—B4 !	Castles

142

13 Q—R6 ! !   . . . .

This unwelcome intrusion was made possible by Black's weakening 10th move. *If now 13 . . . P x Q ? ? ; 14 B x QRP mate!*

The fact that Black does not capture the Queen indicates that he sees through this variation. This in turn should give him the key to White's threat—but it doesn't!

13 . . . .   **N—R4 ? ?**

Best was *13 . . . Q—N5*, countering the threat by preventing the sacrifice which follows:

         14 Q x BPch ! ! !   P x Q
         15 B—R6 mate !

Another example of the weakening effect of a Pawn advance on the castled position.

LOSING A WON GAME

OF ALL the different kinds of mistakes in chess, losing a won game is undoubtedly the most exasperating. No other mistake is more likely to rob you of self-confidence.

What do we mean by a "won game"? When you have a demonstrable mate, a sizable material advantage, a decisive attack, you have a won game. Some advantages are clearer than others; for example, a forced "mate in three" brooks no argument, whereas the advantage of a piece ahead may allow the losing side to play on for a long time.

The ways in which players lose won games can be grouped under a fairly small number of types. Some, when they have an advantage in material, seek complications instead of exchanging remorselessly. As the game simplifies, the excess of material becomes more telling; contrariwise, obscure complications give the prospective loser a chance to turn the tables and befuddle his opponent.

Faulty execution of a winning combination has lost many a game on the very brink of victory. In such cases a player sees the winning idea, plays the winning sacrifice and then inverts the order of his follow-up moves or misses the really clinching point of his combination.

A fault shared by many players is the habit of drifting aimlessly once they have achieved a winning position. Like the man who can't bring himself to say goodbye, they dawdle and delay, seemingly unable to bring the game to a successful conclusion. Even great masters have suffered from this affliction.

Closely related to this psychological handicap is the notion that once a player has achieved a decisive advantage —winning a Rook, for example—he can relax, take it easy, and let nature take its course. This often turns out disastrously, especially against an opponent who is determined and resourceful.

Quite different, but equally unsuccessful, is the player who gives way to despair all too soon. He may even go so far as to resign in a position where he has a quick forced mate!

Most of the faults that turn a won game into a lost one are really aspects of character and temperament. Post-mortem analysis shows us what went wrong in the last game, but does not tell us what to do in the next game. To acquire the ability to win won games consistently, you must train yourself to play with determination, to play at all times the best chess of which you are capable, and to give equal care to every type of position.

It will help you to remember that every player has the shattering experience of losing a won game. Every great player owes a good deal of his success to his ability to apply himself to all types of positions; and even the best players have their lapses from time to time.

WHITE TO MOVE

At first sight, we get the impression that White is in a bad way. His vulnerable Queen Pawn, attacked three times, must go lost. Yet White has deliberately aimed for this position! He senses a weakness of Black's first rank—despite the Black King's "loophole" at his KR2 square.

| 1 Q x R ! ! | . . . . |

An amazing resource which should win quickly.

| 1 . . . . | R x Q |

White has a forced win—*if he plays the right move.*

| 2 R—B8ch ? ? | . . . . |

But this is *not* the right move. Black has a winning defense.

| 2 . . . . | R—Q1 |
| Resigns | |

White is left with a Rook for the Queen—a hopeless disadvantage. Now let us retrace our steps and see where White went wrong. Start from the diagramed position:

1 Q x R ! !	R x Q
2 R—K8ch !	K—R2
3 R(B1)—B8	. . . .

To stop the threatened R—R8 mate, Black must submit to ruinous loss of material—for example *3 . . . R—Q1; 4 R (K8) x R, Q x R; 5 R x Q* and White has an overwhelming advantage in material.

146

A Rook up, Black nevertheless finds White's far advanced Queen Pawn a troublesome enemy to contend with. However, by playing the careful 1 . . . R—Q1, Black can consolidate his position and eventually win the game. Note that after 1 . . . R—Q1 the reply 2 Q—B8ch ? ? would be faulty.

If Black plays *1 . . . R—Q1.* the reply *2 Q—B8ch ? ?* will not do; for after *2 . . . R x Q* White would find to his horror that the contemplated *3 R x R* mate is impossible—his Rook is pinned at KB2!

In the actual game, however, Black's move in the diagramed position was:

1 . . . .   R—KN1 ? ? ?

After this disastrous blunder, White can force checkmate by *2 Q x Rch ! , K x Q; 3 P—Q8(Q)ch, Q—K1; 4 Q x Q mate.*

But White did not play this line. Instead, he *resigned!*

Such misjudgments of position are all too frequent. Once White saw that he could not force checkmate after *1 . . . R—Q1,* he completely lost heart and did not even bother to look for the obvious checkmate available after *1 . . . R—KN1.*

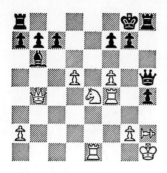

BLACK TO MOVE

After winning a Pawn in the opening Black has been playing a patient defensive game and trying to get his harried King to a place of refuge. He must now meet the threat of 1 N—B6ch !, P x N; 2 R—N4ch, K—R2; 3 R x P winning his Queen. What is Black's best continuation of his skilful defense?

Black can meet the threat of N—B6ch and at the same time get some much-needed development by playing . . . R—R3. In that case he remains a Pawn to the good and has little to fear, as his King is safe from attack.

1 . . . .   P—KB3 ?

A double mistake: he fails to get the King Rook into the game, and he does not parry White's threat.

2 N x Pch !   P x N
3 R—N4ch   Q x R

This loss of the Queen is unavoidable, for *if 3 . . . K—B2 ? ; 4 Q—K7 mate. Or if 3 . . . K—R2; 4 Q—K7ch* and mate follows.

4 Q x Qch   K—B1
5 R—K6   R—R3
6 Q—KB4 !   K—N2
7 R—K7ch   K—B1
8 Q x Rch   K x R
9 Q—N7ch   Resigns

For after *9 . . . K—Q3; 10 Q x KBPch* White's passed Pawns assure him an easy win.

148

BLACK TO MOVE

Black has received the odds of Queen Rook. White is so far behind in material that he sees his only hope of victory in a complicated line of play that will befuddle his weak opponent. This explains White's next move, which, unsound as it is, gives Black several ways to go wrong.

1 N x BP ! ?   . . . .

It is not easy for Black to find the right reply to this surprising move.

Thus, *if 1 . . . B x N ? ? ; 2 N—Q6ch* winning Black's Queen because Black's Bishop on K2 is pinned.

Or if 1 . . . K x N; 2 B x Bch, Q x B; 3 N—N5ch, B x N; 4 R x Q, K x R; 5 Q—N4ch, winning either Black's Bishop on KN4 or his Knight on Q2. The resulting position would be lost for Black because of the exposed position of his King.

The right way is *1 . . . Q x N/B2 ! ; 2 N—Q6ch, B x N; 3 B x B, Q—B3* and Black has nothing to fear from any discovered check by White's Bishop on K6. With his enormous material advantage, Black would win without much trouble.

Bewildered by the complications, Black plays:

1	KN—B3 ? ?
2 N/B7—Q6ch	K—B1
3 N x Q	

And White wins easily.

BLACK TO MOVE

With a piece ahead, Black is quite confident of winning. His confidence is justified, but caution is indicated too. Black's problem is that his Bishop is attacked, and his Bishop in turn guards his Rook at K6. The proper course is 1 . . . Q—Q3 followed by 2 . . . R—K3 and all's well.

With ordinary care, Black's material advantage will yield him an easy win. Certainly there is little point in his embarking on risky tactical complications.

Actually it is White who needs the tactical complications. Why? Being substantially behind in material, he stands to lose if the game continues placidly. Therefore a policy of "mixing it" is psychologically favorable for White.

It is Black's misfortune that he sees a move which he thinks is a "killer." Here it is:

$$1 . . . . \qquad \text{R—K5 ?}$$

Deliberately offering the Bishop. Now *if 2 Q x B ? ?*, *R—K8ch* wins the Queen. Or *if 2 R x B ? ?*, *R x R* and Black is a Rook ahead.

So far, so good; but White has still another move which Black has completely overlooked.

| 2 N x R ! ! | B x Q |
| 3 N—B6 ! | Resigns |

Black has no way of meeting the menace of R x N mate. His foolish search for complications has lost a won game.

WHITE TO MOVE

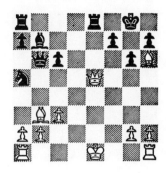

Though White threatens Q—N7 mate, he cannot carry out his threat because of the pin on the King file which wins his Queen. In the actual game, White was so depressed that he *resigned*. Had he been alert, he would have found a way to force victory in this desperate-looking situation. How?

1 B x Pch !   . . . .

This looks like a "spite check"—the last gasp before resigning.

1 . . . .   K x B

Forced—not that Black seems to have anything to worry about, as he still maintains the pin.

2 R—KB1ch   K—N1

Again forced. But now White has run out of checks—or so it would seem.

3 R—B8ch ! !   . . . .

Another spite check? No, much better than that—White forces Black to give up the pin on the Queen. Result: White's mating threat comes to life.

3 . . . .   R x R
4 Q—N7 mate !

Remember, none of this happened! White resigned in the diagramed position, unaware that he had a checkmate within his grasp!

Black can win a piece for several Pawns by 1 . . . P x N, remaining with a won game. Unfortunately, he sees a way to win the Exchange. Without any attempt to check the soundness of the idea, Black plunges into his combination. Only two moves later, he finds that he is checkmated!

Instead of playing the simple winning move *1 . . . P x N,* Black rushes into an "attractive" combination:

1	Q x Rch ?
2 K x Q	N x Pch

The point of Black's sacrifice. His Knight cannot be captured, as White's Bishop is pinned by a Black Rook. Thus Black wins White's Queen by a forking check which attacks White's King and Queen at the same time.

3 K—K3	N x Q

Now Black expects *4 N x B,* leaving him with the material advantage of a Rook for a Bishop. But he is in for a disagreeable shock:

4 P—R7ch !	K—R1

If 4 . . . K—B1; 5 P—R8(Q)ch and wins.

5 N—B7 mate !

The careful *1 . . . P x N* would have won for Black. The careless *1 . . . Q x Rch ?* lost for him.

How
to Play
the White Pieces

Book Three

Chapter One

HOW TO CONTROL THE CENTER

YOU ARE about to start playing a game of chess. The pieces and Pawns are all set up in their proper opening positions. You are playing White. What is the basic thought that will guide you through the opening during the first few moves?

You know that it is important to bring out your pieces quickly and effectively. You have been told that it is a good idea to begin by moving up one of your center Pawns. You have been advised to control the center.

"Control the center"—that is the basic idea of opening play. But just what is the center? how do you control it? and why is it important to control it?

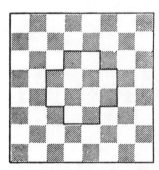

1

The squares inside the heavy lines make up the center.

The center, as you can see from Diagram 1, is made up of the squares King 3, Queen 3, King Bishop 4, King 4, Queen 4,

155

Queen Bishop 4, King Bishop 5, King 5, Queen 5, Queen Bishop 5, King 6, Queen 6.

When you post ("centralize") your pieces in the center, they have their greatest range and power. Once you play them to the center during the opening, they can be moved quickly to other sectors as the course of the game requires.

We often use the term "center" in a restricted sense, referring only to the inner four squares: King 4, Queen 4, King 5, and Queen 5. These are the most effective squares for center Pawns. Why? Because a Pawn at King 4 or Queen 4 prevents hostile pieces from establishing themselves at the center squares controlled by that Pawn.

"Controlling the center," then, means *posting your Pawns and pieces in such a way that you have a decidedly more powerful grip on the center than your opponent has.*

White has the first move. Consequently his chance of controlling the center is a pretty good one. Now let us turn to some examples which show what you do to Black if you get control of the center.

GIUOCO PIANO

WHITE	BLACK	WHITE	BLACK
1 P—K4	P—K4	3 B—B4	B—B4
2 N—KB3	N—QB3	4 P—B3	. . . .

2

White intends to form a broad Pawn center with P—Q4.

156

Black must fight for the center here by playing 4 . . . N—B3, attacking White's King Pawn. Then, after 5 P—Q4, PxP; 6 PxP, B—N5ch; 7 B—Q2, BxBch; 8 QNxB, P—Q4! Black has successfully achieved a foothold in the center.

Instead, Black loses his way in a clumsy line of play:

4	Q—K2	8 P—QR4	P—QR3
5 P—Q4	B—N3	9 N—R3	B—N5
6 Castles	N—B3	10 N—B2	Castles(K)
7 R—K1	P—Q3	11 N—K3!	. . . .

White's powerful Pawn center stifles Black's pieces and deprives them of adequate scope.

(Note how effectively White's Knight has reached the center by a roundabout route.)

If now 11 . . . B—KR4; 12 N—B5! drives back the Black Queen.

And if 11 . . . BxN; 12 PxB, PxP; 13 N—B5! again drives back the Queen.

So Black's Queen Bishop makes a sorry retreat all the way back.

11	B—B1	13 B—KN5	PxP
12 N—Q5!	Q—Q1	14 PxP	B—N5

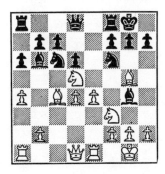

3

Black desperately hopes to consolidate his position with . . . BxP.

White's pin on Black's King Knight threatens to rip up Black's King-side with fatal effect. In order to get the most out of the pin, White advances his King Pawn, thus making use of his overwhelming Pawn center:

15 P—K5!	BxN		18 BxN	PxB
16 QxB!	NxQP		19 Q—R6	Resigns
17 Q—KR3	PxP			

Black surrenders because after the coming 20 NxKBPch he will have to give up his Queen to stop checkmate.

White won this game by exploiting Black's failure to enforce a timely . . . P—Q4, which would have given him a fair share of the center. (See the first note.)

In the next game, Black again neglects to fight for the center with . . . P—Q4. White soon crushes him in an even more brutal manner.

SICILIAN DEFENSE

WHITE	BLACK		WHITE	BLACK
1 P—K4	P—QB4		6 B—K2	B—N2
2 N—KB3	P—Q3		7 B—K3	Castles
3 P—Q4	PxP		8 P—B4	N—B3
4 NxP	N—KB3		9 N—N3	B—K3
5 N—QB3	P—KN3		10 P—N4!	. . . .

4

White will get an overwhelming position unless Black counters energetically with . . . P—Q4!

10 ....   N—Q2??

White can now start a savage Pawn-storming attack which opens up lines of attack against Black's King. After 10 . . . N—Q2?? White is not hampered by any Black counterplay.

11 P—KR4!	P—B4	16 Castles (Q)	NxNch
12 P—R5!	N—B4	17 BPxN	R—B1
13 RPxP	RPxP	18 QR—N1	B—B4
14 NPxP	PxP	19 B—B4ch	P—K3
15 Q—Q2!	PxP	20 Q—R2!	Q—B3

White is ready for the final attack.

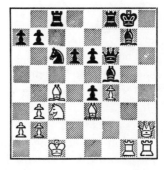

5

White's brilliant sacrifices make the most of his open lines.

21 N—Q5!!	PxN	24 RxBch!	KxR
22 BxQPch	B—K3	25 Q—R7ch	K—B3
23 BxBch	QxB	26 R—R6 mate	

In this game we have seen how White punished Black for neglecting the center.

In the game that follows, White builds up an overwhelming center that is the keystone of a winning attacking formation. Black's opening lapses contribute to the formation of this center.

WHITE	BLACK		WHITE	BLACK
1 P—Q4	N—KB3		4 P—K3	P—Q4
2 P—QB4	P—K3		5 P—QR3	BxNch?
3 N—QB3	B—N5		6 PxB	Castles

6

White has the makings of a mighty center formation.

Thanks to Black's faulty exchange on the fifth move, White has a Pawn on Queen Bishop 3. This Pawn strengthens White's center formation by giving additional protection to White's Queen Pawn.

As a result of White's fourth move, his King Pawn had the function of guarding White's Queen Pawn. But now the King Pawn can disregard its defensive job. White therefore forms the plan of advancing P—K4 (move 16!).

In order to play P—K4 White needs several preparatory moves. In the following play, he supports the intended P—K4 with moves 8, 9, 11, 12, and 14.

Once the White Pawn arrives at King 4, White will have a strong Pawn center that will batter down Black's weakened resistance.

WHITE	BLACK		WHITE	BLACK
7 PxP	PxP		12 P—B3	Q—B2
8 B—Q3	P—QN3		13 BxB	NxB
9 N—K2	B—R3		14 Q—Q3	N—N1
10 Castles	P—B4		15 B—Q2	N—B3
11 N—N3	R—K1		16 P—K4!	. . . .

160

A very difficult situation for Black. If he captures White's King Pawn with his Queen Pawn, then White recaptures with his King Bishop Pawn. This maintains White's overwhelming center and opens up the King Bishop file for White's attack.

Black therefore stands pat in the center. White continues powerfully with P—K5, *chasing away Black's last protective piece on the King-side.*

| 16 .... | QR—Q1 | 18 P—KB4! | N—R4 |
| 17 P—K5! | N—Q2 | 19 N—R5 | P—N3 |

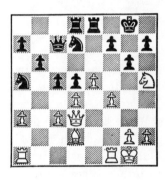

7

The stage is set for a dynamic concluding attack by White.

20 P—B5!!	PxN	23 B—N7ch	RxB
21 B—R6!	K—R1	24 PxRch	K—N1
22 P—B6	R—KN1		

After 24 . . . KxP White has the same winning reply.

| 25 RxP!! | Q—B3 * | 27 Q—B5 | N—QB3 |
| 26 QR—KB1 | Q—R3 | 28 RxN | Resigns |

For if 28 . . . RxR; 29 Q—B8 mate.

A wonderfully instructive game. A comparison of Diagram 6 with Diagram 7 shows clearly how the formation of White's

---

* After 25 . . . KxR; 26 QxP White threatens to obtain a new Queen with discovered—and double!—check. On 26 . . . R—KN1; 27 R—KB1ch wins easily.

overwhelming center left Black with a steadily deteriorating game.

In the next game White wins convincingly when Black runs into trouble by mistakenly giving up a snug defensive position in the center.

QUEEN'S INDIAN DEFENSE

WHITE	BLACK	WHITE	BLACK
1 P—Q4	N—KB3	5 Castles	QN—Q2
2 N—KB3	P—QN3	6 QN—Q2	P—K4
3 P—K3	B—N2	7 P—K4	PxP?
4 B—Q3	P—Q3	8 NxP	P—N3?

White has the makings of a powerful attacking position, thanks to two serious blunders by Black.

Black's seventh move has opened up the game and brought a White Knight to a good post in the center.

Black's eighth move is another lapse. White's Knight at Queen 4, cooperating with his Bishop at Queen 3, is now able to invade Black's territory with menacing effect.*

9 B—N5!   P—QR3   10 B—B6   Q—B1

8

White now follows up with an astonishing advance in the center, made possible by Black's faulty seventh move.

---

* Black should have played 8 . . . P—QR3 in order to prevent the following invasion by White's Bishop.

162

| 11 P—K5!! | PxP | 13 NxB | B—Q3 |
| 12 Q—B3! | BxB | 14 N—B4! | .... |

9

White has prevented 14 . . . Castles,
which loses the Black Queen after 15
NxB, PxN; 16 N—K7ch etc.

| 14 .... | P—K5 | 16 Q—B3! | Q—N2 |
| 15 R—K1 | P—R3 | 17 NxBch | PxN |

As a result of the surrender of the center on move 7, White
has completely disorganized Black's game. White now wins
back his Pawn.

| 18 RxPch! | K—B1 | 20 B—B4 | QR—QB1 |
| 19 R—K7! | K—N2 | 21 Q—QN3 | .... |

White threatens mate on the move.

| 21 .... | P—Q4 | 23 RxPch | K—N1 |
| 22 N—K5 | QR—K1 | 24 Q—N3! | .... |

(see Diagram 10 on page 14)

White sees that Black cannot guard against the mate by 24
. . . NxN. That would lose Black his Queen, so he tries a last
desperate resource, but White winds up brilliantly.

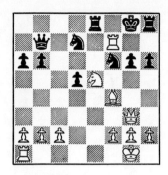

10

Again White menaces mate on the move.

24	....	P—KN4
25	BxP!	RxN
26	BxN dis ch	KxR

27	Q—N7ch	K—K3
28	BxR	Resigns

White threatens QxR as well as R—K1 with devastating effect. Black has paid a heavy price for giving up the center at move 7.

In each of the games in this chapter we have seen how White has punished Black for giving up control of the center. Throughout the rest of this book you will see repeatedly how important it is to maintain a foothold in the center.

Chapter Two

HOW TO EXPLOIT
YOUR SUPERIOR DEVELOPMENT

ONE OF our most important tasks in the opening stage is bringing out our pieces so they will play an active and aggressive role. This process is called "development."

Because White enjoys the theoretical advantage of moving first, there is always a likelihood that his development will proceed more rapidly than Black's. For White, neglected development may mean nothing worse than *losing the initiative.* For Black, the same sin may mean *losing the game.*

How do players go wrong in the opening? There are certain failings that we observe in game after game. One player moves the same piece again and again, neglecting to develop his other forces and neglecting to get his King into a safe haven.

Another player injudiciously spends time capturing a relatively unimportant Pawn, losing priceless time in the chase.

Other players develop hesitantly and with lack of foresight, moving pieces to squares from which they will be driven away. Soon, to their great astonishment, they find themselves in a straitjacket position which developed inexorably from their poor opening play.

In the first illustrative game White proves that Black's faulty development is definitely a case of too little and too late:

FOUR KNIGHTS' GAME

WHITE	BLACK		WHITE	BLACK
1 P—K4	P—K4		4 B—N5	N—Q5
2 N—KB3	N—QB3		5 NxP	Q—K2
3 N—B3	N—B3		6 N—B3	. . . .

11

White has given his opponent the choice between 6 . . . NxP and 6 . . . NxB. Which is right and which is wrong?

At first glance we feel rather suspicious about Black's procedure. He has moved his Queen Knight twice, and he has played out his Queen very early.

These moves are not quite so bad as they seem. The repeated moves of White's King Knight have canceled out the Black Knight's loss of time.

The position of the Black Queen is definitely bad. Black should therefore play 6 . . . NxB; 7 NxN, QxPch. This forces the exchange of Queens, so that Black no longer suffers from the disadvantage of having developed his Queen too early.

6	NxKP?		9 QxN	Q—B4
7 Castles!	NxQN		10 R—K1ch	B—K2
8 QPxN	NxNch *		11 B—Q3	. . . .

---

* If 8 . . . NxB White wins the Queen by 9 R—K1.

166

White has powerful pressure. He is ahead in development. and if Black castles, White replies 12 Q—K4! winning a piece because Black has no time to guard his menaced Bishop on account of the mating threat.

| 11 .... | P—Q4 | 13 B—KB4 | Q—KB3 |
| 12 B—K3 | Q—Q3 | 14 QxP!! | .... |

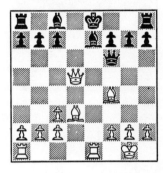

12

Can White afford to offer the Bishop?

The capture 14 . . . QxB? would lead to disaster because of 15 B—N5ch! Thus if 15 . . . K—B1; 16 Q—Q8ch!! and mate next move.

Or 14 . . . QxB?; 15 B—N5ch!, P—QB3; 16 BxPch, PxB; 17 QxQBPch winning the Queen Rook with easy victory in sight.

White has a powerful attack because Black's botched development has exposed the Black King to frightful dangers.

| 14 .... | P—B3 | 15 Q—K4 | B—K3 |
| | 16 QR—Q1! | Castles(Q)? | |

White has disguised his attacking plan so subtly that Black is lulled into a false sense of security.

(see Diagram 13 on page 18)

| 17 QxBPch!! | PxQ | 18 B—QR6 mate |

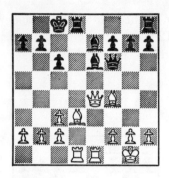

13

White has set an incredibly sly trap!

In this game White brought about Black's downfall by exploiting his thoughtless development or no development. In the following game, Black goes Pawn-hunting, while White goes King-hunting. In this unequal struggle White naturally holds all the trumps.

EVANS GAMBIT DECLINED

WHITE	BLACK		WHITE	BLACK
1 P—K4	P—K4		4 P—QN4!?	B—N3
2 N—KB3	N—QB3		5 P—QR4	. . . .
3 B—B4	B—B4			

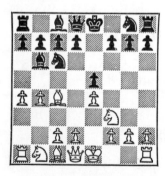

14

White threatens to win a piece with P—R5 etc.

The opening moves are extremely interesting. On move 4

168

White offered a Pawn in order to divert Black's pieces and gain time. (The further course of the game will show what White had in mind.)

But Black was not obliging. He simply retreated his attacked Bishop, wisely avoiding complications that might prove exceedingly troublesome.

However, in playing 5 P—QR4 White poses a new problem. If Black keeps his wits about him, he can react calmly with 5 . . . P—QR3! so that if 6 P—R5, B—R2. In that case his Bishop is perfectly safe and White has made no headway.

Instead, Black becomes rattled and goes in for an orgy of Pawn captures. This is just what White was waiting for.

5	NxP?	9 Castles	PxP
6 P—R5	B—B4	10 Q—N3	Q—K2
7 P—B3	N—QB3	11 NxP	P—Q3
8 P—Q4	PxP	12 B—KN5	Q—Q2

White is considerably ahead in development as a result of Black's time-wasting Pawn captures. Black's position is already seriously compromised.

Thus, if he tries 12 . . . P—B3 White wins by 13 BxN, PxB; 14 N—Q5, Q—Q1; 15 N—N6!!

Another unpleasant possibility is 12 . . . N—B3; 13 N—Q5, Q—Q1; 14 NxNch, PxN; 15 BxPch etc.

13 P—K5!	PxP	15 NxN	BxN
14 QR—Q1!	N—Q5	16 KR—K1	Q—B4 *

With all his pieces in action against only two Black pieces, White must win. White's King is quite safe, Black's King is in mortal danger.

---

* Black intends to answer 17 RxB with 17 . . . QxB.

15

White's Rooks are all-powerful on the center files.

| 17 BxPch! | QxB | 18 RxPch! | Resigns |

For if 18 . . . BxR; 19 R—Q8 mate.

And if 18 . . . K—B1; 19 Q—N4ch, P—B4; 20 RxB!, PxQ; 21 R—Q8ch, Q—K1; 22 R/K5xQch, K—B2; 23 N—K4. White comes out at least a piece ahead.

White's vigorous reaction to Black's ill-judged Pawn-grabbing was very instructive.

In the next game White demonstrates that thoughtless moves ruin Black's prospects of achieving a satisfactory development.

KING'S INDIAN DEFENSE

WHITE	BLACK	WHITE	BLACK
1 P—Q4	N—KB3	8 P—KR3	B—K3?
2 P—QB4	P—KN3	9 P—Q5	PxP
3 N—QB3	B—N2	10 BPxP	B—Q2
4 P—K4	P—Q3	11 Castles	N—K1
5 P—KN3	Castles	12 B—K3	P—N3?
6 B—N2	P—B3	13 P—B4	P—B3?
7 KN—K2	P—K4		

What are the factors that have provided White with such a splendid position?

170

16

White has brilliant encirclement plans —Black's pieces face a dreary prospect.

Black has played thoughtlessly. His eighth move was a futile provocation which lost time. The retreat 11 . . . N—K1 makes sense if followed up by . . . P—B4 fighting for a foothold in the center.

But Black completely overlooks the possibility of playing . . . P—B4. First he wastes more time with 12 . . . P—N3? and then he plays the timid, self-blocking 13 . . . P—B3? His pieces have no future and no scope.

White's indicated strategy is to tie up Black's position still more, and that is exactly what he does.

14 P—B5!	P—KN4	16 N—N3	B—KB1
15 P—KN4	R—B2	17 R—B2	N—N2

17

White can go ahead with his plan, for though Black has rearranged his pieces, they have become even more ineffectual than before.

When you have an advantage in space and mobility—as

White has here—the indicated course is to increase that advantage. White therefore plays to open up the King Rook file, *which will become his exclusive property.*

18 B—KB1!	B—K1	21 PxP	RPxP
19 R—R2	P—QR4	22 Q—B3!	R—N2
20 P—KR4!	P—R3	23 Q—R1!	....

Now that White monopolizes the open King Rook file, he is able to penetrate into Black's position with fatal effect.

18

White's attack must succeed: Black's pieces are posted too awkwardly to have any defensive value.

23	N—Q2	25 Q—R7	K—K2
24 R—R8ch	K—B2	26 N—R5	Resigns

For if 26 . . . BxN; 27 PxB and there is no defense against White's coming P—R6 which will win a piece. White's logical and consistent play in this game is a perfect example of how to demolish a cramped position.

In this game White's prime task was to refute a development that was planless. White's hard-hitting play left Black with a middle game position which offered no hope of unscrambling his pieces.

In the next game Black embarks on a devilishly plausible counterattack. But White has a surprising refutation.

172

QUEEN'S GAMBIT DECLINED

WHITE	BLACK		WHITE	BLACK
1 P—Q4	P—Q4		5 N—B3	PxP
2 P—QB4	P—K3		6 P—K4	P—B4
3 N—KB3	N—KB3		7 BxP	PxP
4 B—N5	B—N5ch		8 NxP	Q—R4

19

Does White have a lost game as a result of Black's powerful-looking Queen move?

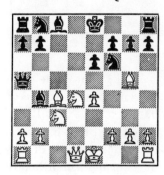

Black threatens to win a piece by . . . QxB or by . . . BxNch. But White has an extremely subtle defense!

9 BxN!	BxNch		11 K—B1	QxBch
10 PxB	QxBPch		12 K—N1	. . . .

Now we can appreciate the depth of White's plan:

Black is just on the point of playing 12 . . . PxB with a piece to the good. But he realizes that White would continue 13 R—B1 attacking the Queen with decisive effect.

So Black concludes that he must refrain from "winning a piece" as he finally perceives the far-reaching effect of White's resourceful ninth move.

Black thought he was seizing the initiative. Actually it is White who is doing the attacking, and he presses his advantage vigorously.

12	N—Q2		14 BxP	KR—N1
13 R—B1!	Q—R3		15 B—R6	. . . .

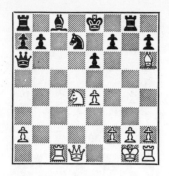

20

White has shattered Black's position.

Thanks to White's ingenious play, the result of Black's Queen moves is that his Queen is shunted off to the side. White has seen to it that Black's King cannot possibly find a safe haven, and that his pieces cannot co-operate effectively.

White's King is quite safe and his King Rook will soon be developed in unorthodox fashion. Meanwhile White has his eye on the most serious weakness in Black's game: his isolated and indefensible King Rook Pawn.

15	N—B3		18 Q—B2!	R—N3
16 P—K5	N—Q4		19 P—R5!	R—N5
17 P—KR4!	B—Q2			

White has left Black no choice, for if 19 . . . RxB; 20 Q—Q2! wins the Rook!

Thus White succeeds in capturing the weak King Rook Pawn, which in turn gives him a menacing passed Pawn. *Black cannot put up proper resistance because his faulty development has split his forces.*

20 QxP	K—K2		22 B—N7!	Q—R6
21 R—R4!	KR—N1		23 B—B6ch!	K—B1

White's coming attack, which relies on the power of the

174

mighty passed Pawn, cannot be stemmed by Black's disorganized forces.

21

White can now play 24 R—B7!! for if 24 . . . NxR; 25 P—R6!! and Black is helpless against 26 QxRch!! and 27 P—R7ch etc.

24 R—B7!!	NxB	25 PxN	Q—Q3
	26 P—R6!!	Resigns	

There is no defense to the coming 27 Q—N7ch!!

With this sparkling example we conclude the study of faulty development on Black's part and how White exploits it. The faulty development has taken different forms, but in each case White's resulting initiative has led to a quick decision. Study White's procedure in each of these games and you will find opportunities to use similar methods in your own games.

Chapter Three

HOW TO EXPLOIT
YOUR SUPERIOR MOBILITY

YOU WILL FIND, almost without exception, that when you have
the better development, your pieces have more mobility than
your opponent's forces. Remember that the first move gives
you a springboard for getting ahead in development—and for
having more mobility than Black has.

Mobility, as you saw in the first chapter, is connected with
having a powerful position in the center. The stronger your
position in the center, the more mobility your pieces will
have. In the following game White emphasizes this point very
strongly.

ALEKHINE'S DEFENSE

WHITE	BLACK		WHITE	BLACK
1 P—K4	N—KB3		3 P—Q4	P—Q3
2 P—K5	N—Q4		4 P—QB4	N—N3

Black has developed one piece, White hasn't developed any
at all. Yet White has considerable mobility, as his center
Pawns dominate the center and many avenues of development are open to his pieces.*

---

* Black's lead in development is academic, as his Knight can accomplish very
little from Queen Knight 3.

22

Though Black is ahead in development, White has more mobility!

White's immediate aim is to support his powerful Pawn center by advancing his King Bishop Pawn.

5 P—B4	PxP	7 B—K3	B—N2
6 BPxP	P—KN3	8 N—QB3	P—QB4

The advance of Black's Queen Bishop Pawn is logical, as it breaks up the center. (On 9 P—Q5, BxP; 10 BxP Black has a playable though clearly inferior game, as his Knight at Queen Knight 3 is sadly lacking in mobility.)

Instead, Black tries to win a Pawn outright. The attempt is disastrous, because White leaves Black with an unbearably cramped position. White now makes admirably effective use of his superior mobility.

9 P—Q5	Q—B2?	12 NxQPch	K—B1
10 P—Q6!	PxP	13 NxB!	NxN
11 N—N5!	Q—K2	14 BxP!!	Resigns

An extraordinary finish. If 14 . . . QxB; 15 Q—Q8 mate. Thus White wins the Queen by force.

White succeeded admirably in this game because **Black** started an attack on White's center and failed to follow it **up.** This gave White time to exploit his superior mobility to **the** utmost.

23

White is still behind in development and ahead in mobility.

The remaining games in this chapter are more orthodox, for White has superior development, superior mobility, and control of the center in each case.

FRENCH DEFENSE

WHITE	BLACK		WHITE	BLACK
1 P—K4	P—K3		3 N—QB3	PxP
2 P—Q4	P—Q4		4 NxP	. . . .

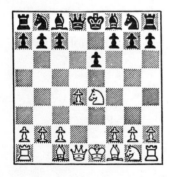

24

White's dominating position in the center makes it likely that he will have vastly superior mobility in the middle game.

White has a free hand in the center, thanks to Black's colorless third move.

White's Knight is strongly centralized at King 4; his Queen Pawn controls the important center square King 5.

4	....	N—Q2		7	Castles	NxN
5	N—KB3	KN—B3		8	BxN	N—B3
6	B—Q3	B—K2		9	B—Q3	....

White's game is noticeably freer.

| 9 | .... | P—QN3? * | | 11 | N—B6 | Q—Q3 |
| 10 | N—K5! | Castles | | 12 | Q—B3! | .... |

Very clever. White threatens to win a whole Rook by 13
NxBch.

If 12 . . . B—N2?; 13 NxBch and White wins a piece.

Black must therefore develop his Queen Bishop to Queen 2,
where it has no mobility. Thus White's lead in mobility becomes even more pronounced.

12	....	B—Q2		15	KR—K1	KR—K1
13	NxBch	QxN		16	Q—R3!	....
14	B—KN5	QR—B1				

Now White threatens 17 BxN followed by 18 QxRPch.

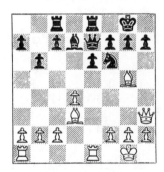

25

*White's pressure against Black's King-
side is irresistible.*

White's superior mobility has provided him with a devastat-

---

* Black's position is cramped, but he can at least make a fight of it by playing
9 . . . P—B4.

ing King-side attack. If now 16 . . . P—KR3; 17 BxP!, PxB; 18 QxRP and Black is helpless against the coming 19 R—K5 and 20 R—KN5ch.

Or if 16 . . . P—N3; 17 Q—R4, K—N2; 18 R—K4! and White's pin leads to Black's downfall after 19 R—KB4.

With his next move Black admits his despair.

16	Q—Q3	19 R—K3	QxP
17 BxN	PxB	20 P—QB3!	Resigns
18 Q—R6!	P—KB4		

If Black retreats 20 . . . Q—N2 or 20 . . . Q—Q3, he must give up his Queen after 21 R—N3. Otherwise, White forces checkmate with 21 R—N3ch etc.

White had an overwhelming advantage in mobility from the third move on as a result of Black's passive play.

In the following game Black fights hard to maintain his grip on the center. But his development is slow and cramped, and White plays with masterly consistency for domination of the open lines.

PHILIDOR'S DEFENSE

WHITE	BLACK	WHITE	BLACK
1 P—K4	P—K4	5 B—QB4	B—K2
2 N—KB3	P—Q3	6 Castles	P—B3
3 P—Q4	N—KB3	7 P—QR4	....
4 N—B3	QN—Q2		

White has already put his finger on the weakness of Black's position:

The development selected by Black is slow, clumsy, and cramped. White notes especially the lack of mobility of Black's Bishops. His King Bishop is blocked by his Queen's Pawn; his Queen Bishop is blocked by his Queen Knight.

180

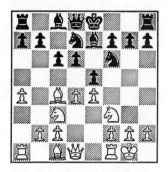

26

White has an advantage in the fact that Black's Bishops have very little scope.

White's policy from now on will be to create more open lines for his own forces and at the same time to restrain Black from freeing himself.

7	Q—B2	12 N—R4!	N—R4
8 Q—K2	P—KR3	13 N—B5	B—B1
9 B—R2	N—B1	14 B—K3	P—KN3
10 Q—B4!	N—K3	15 QR—Q1!!	....
11 PxP	PxP		

White's last move looks like an oversight, but it isn't. He loses no time occupying the open Queen file, even though his Knight is attacked.

This is how White reasons:

As Black has not yet castled, he is unable to bring a Rook to the Queen file to dispute White's occupation of that open line.

Furthermore, because Black's King is still in the center, he cannot hope to win a piece with impunity. Thus if 15 . . . PxN; 16 PxP, N—Q1; 17 N—Q5!, Q—R4; 18 N—N6!!, PxN; 19 RxNch!, KxR; 20 QxKBP and Black's King perishes in the crossfire of the enemy pieces.

This fascinating variation, which deserves the most careful study, is a magnificent example of White's power of superior mobility.

15	B—Q2	18 P—B4!	PxP
16 N—N3	N—B3	19 BxBP	Q—N3ch
17 P—R3	B—N2	20 K—R1	N—R2

White has increased his mobility still more by opening the King Bishop file. Thus he is ready for action on two open files.

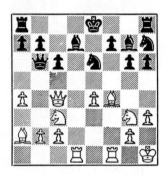

27

White can now win by a very brilliant combination.

| 21 RxB! | KxR | 22 B—K3!! QR—KB1 |

He might just as well resign. If 22 . . . QxB; 23 RxPch, K—Q1; 24 QxN forces mate.

23 RxPch!!   Resigns

For if 23 . . . RxR; 24 QxNch, K—Q1; 25 BxQch, PxB; 26 QxR and Black is hopelessly behind in material.

White's play was a masterpiece of consistently utilizing superior mobility. From the very start White took merciless advantage of Black's lack of mobility. He never gave Black a chance because he never allowed Black's pieces to cooperate properly.

In the next game White neatly combines superior mobility with control of the center and lasting King-side attack.

182

WHITE	BLACK		WHITE	BLACK
1 P—Q4	P—Q4		3 N—KB3	N—KB3
2 P—QB4	PxP		4 N—B3	P—K3

White now seizes on the fact that with his second move Black has given up his hold on the center. Black should therefore play . . . P—B4 as soon as possible in order to fight for a foothold in the center. Because he holds back timidly, White gains an overwhelming position in the center by energetic play.

5 B—N5!	B—K2		8 BxP	N—Q2
6 P—K4!	P—KR3?		9 Castles	Castles
7 BxN	BxB		10 P—K5!	B—K2

28

White's formation is aggressive, while the outlook for Black's pieces is very poor.

White has driven a wedge into Black's position by advancing his King Pawn to King 5. One important consequence is that he has prevented Black from bringing his Knight to King Bishop 3. This is the best square for a Knight defending the King-side. It follows that the combination of White's aggressive position in the center, plus the aggressive position of his pieces, foreshadows a powerful attack by White.

Note in the following play how White uses the square King 4 as a steppingstone for transporting his pieces to the King·

183

side. We know from the start that his onslaught will be successful because Black has so little maneuvering space for defensive purposes.

11 Q—K2	R—K1	14 KR—K1	N—B1
12 QR—Q1!	P—QB3	15 Q—N4	P—QN3
13 Q—K4!	Q—B2	16 Q—R5	B—N2

The position begins to look very threatening for Black. White now proceeds to bring more pieces to the King-side. Because of the cramped position of his forces, Black cannot defend with equal vigor.

29

White again gets more pieces into the attack by using the square King 4.

17 R—K4!	B—N5	20 N—N5!	R—K2
18 R—N4	BxN	21 N—K4!	R—Q1
19 PxB	K—R1	22 R—Q3!	P—QB4

At last Black plays the move that he should have played early in the opening. But White is now ready for the final attack, having maneuvered his Knight into position for a deadly stroke. He has also moved his Queen Rook into position for the final attack.

23 N—B6!   . . . .

With the brutal threat 24 QxRPch!!, PxQ; 25 R—N8 mate. White's superior mobility has become overwhelming.

184

Of course, if Black tries 23 . . . PxN then 24 QxRPch and 25 Q—N7 mate.

| 23 .... | N—N3 | 24 R—R3 | Resigns |

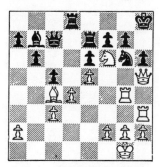

30

White has left Black no move to hold the position.

White's overwhelming plus in mobility has left Black without any satisfactory defense.

Thus if 24 . . . PxN; 25 QxPch, K—N1; 26 Q—R8 mate. Or 24 . . . PxP; 25 Q—N5!!, QxB; 26 RxPch!, PxR; 27 QxP mate.

White never gave Black a chance after Black's all too passive handling of the opening.

In the following game White again triumphs after dominating the center and preventing Black from getting his pieces into action. White's Pawn-storming attack follows with crushing—and logical—effect.

SICILIAN DEFENSE

WHITE	BLACK	WHITE	BLACK
1 P—K4	P—QB4	3 P—Q4	PxP
2 N—KB3	P—Q3	4 NxP	....

White has a well centralized Knight established at Queen 4. Black cannot imitate this maneuver. Note also that White

185

controls the important center square Queen 5 with his King Pawn.

On these two grounds it seems likely that White will dominate the center and will therefore enjoy superior mobility.

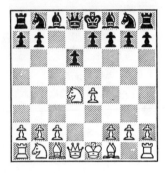

31

There are already strong indications that White may achieve an overwhelming plus in mobility.

4	N—KB3	7 B—K3	B—K2
5 N—QB3	N—B3	8 Castles	Castles
6 B—K2	P—K3		

How has the situation developed as regards mobility? Both White Bishops have free diagonals; both Black Bishops are hemmed in by Pawns. The outlook for Black's game is very unpromising.

In such positions White always has a practical problem: *how can his superior mobility be increased still further?* White solves this problem by a general advance of his King-side Pawns, which will achieve the following:

1. He will congest Black's position more than ever.

2. He will drive away Black's King Knight—his best defensive piece—from King Bishop 3.

3. He will subject Black's position, already cramped unbearably, to a devastating Pawn-storming attack.

9 P—B4	Q—B2	12 P—B5	Q—Q1
10 P—KN4!	P—QR3	13 P—KR4	NxN
11 P—N5	N—K1	14 QxN	....

186

White's plan has made considerable progress. As a result of Black's unpromising opening line of play, White has deprived Black of any constructive plan.*

32

The formidable centralization of White's Queen provokes Black to lose his foothold in the center.

14 . . . .   P—K4?

Very shortsighted. He drives away the Queen, but at the cost of permanently losing Pawn control of his Queen 4 square.

This vital center square now becomes a "hole," completely at the mercy of the White pieces.

| 15 Q—Q2 | N—B2 | 17 R—B2 | B—Q1 |
| 16 B—N6! | Q—Q2 | 18 QR—KB1 | . . . . |

White menaces a decisive breach with 19 P—B6, P—N3; 20 P—R5. Black stops this, but White penetrates in a different way.

| 18 . . . . | P—B3 | 20 P—N6! | P—R3 |
| 19 B—B4ch | K—R1 | 21 B—B7 | Q—B3 |

White can now win by 22 B—K3 and 23 BxP! He plans a much more striking finish.

---

* The continuation . . . B—Q2 and . . . B—QB3 is about the best Black has.

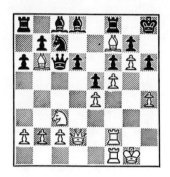

33

There is no defense against White's coming attack.

22 BxN	BxB	23 R—N2!	P—Q4

Desperation.

24 QxRPch!!   Resigns

For if 24 . ˙. . PxQ; 25 P—N7ch, K—R2 and now White captures the Rook, promoting to a Knight (!) and giving checkmate after 25 . . . K—R1; 26 R—N8ch!

The games in this chapter teach a lesson of the greatest practical importance—that when White gets the initiative through superior mobility, he has a lasting advantage that he can increase systematically until he achieves victory.

The first step is to pinpoint Black's faulty strategy. Once you see how he has committed himself to a cramped position, you can find ways to increase your command of the board. You must not swerve from your determination to keep him in a vise; one thoughtless move will often allow the enemy to escape. All five games in this chapter show how you maintain and increase the pressure until Black's position collapses.

Chapter Four

HOW TO EXPLOIT
BLACK'S PREMATURE OPENING UP
OF THE POSITION

THE BANE of many chess books is that they ignore the human factor. You may have read the last paragraphs of the previous chapter with some skepticism. Suppose Black is not satisfied to be trussed up; suppose he fights back? How does White proceed in such cases?

We can approach the problem of cramped positions systematically by dividing such positions into three parts. Those positions in which Black defends passively without any attempt to fight back, have been treated in the previous chapter. Positions in which Black tries to open up the position are the subject of the present chapter. Positions in which Black resorts to counterattack will be the subject matter of Chapter Five.

We start with a game in which Black is so anxious to avoid a cramped position that he opens up the game before castling. This transfers the struggle from a predominantly *strategical* one to a predominantly *tactical* one. The switch, as we shall see, favors White.

SICILIAN DEFENSE

WHITE	BLACK	WHITE	BLACK
1 P—K4	P—QB4	4 NxP	N—B3
2 N—KB3	N—QB3	5 N—QB3	P—Q3
3 P—Q4	PxP	6 B—K2	P—K4

This reminds us of Black's fourteenth move in the previous game (after Diagram 32). Black surrenders control of the important square Queen 4. This gives White a powerful hold on the center and foreshadows a serious lack of mobility on Black's part.

34

White intends to train his guns on the weakness created by Black's last move.

| 7 N—B3 | P—KR3 | 9 Castles | B—K2 |
| 8 B—K3 | B—K3 | 10 Q—Q2 | P—Q4? |

In his anxiety to get a free hand in the center, Black advances forthrightly to get rid of White's control of the Queen 5 square.

Strategically the advance is irreproachable. It has, however, the drawback of provoking a lasting attack by White.

| 11 PxP | NxP | 12 B—QN5! | .... |

By pinning Black's Queen Knight White threatens NxP. This forces one concession after another by Black.

12	P—B3	15 Q—Q3	R—Q1
13 QR—Q1	NxB	16 Q—N6ch	K—B1
14 QxN	Q—N3	17 RxRch	BxR

If 17 . . . NxR??; 18 Q—K8 mate.
If 17 . . . QxR; 18 BxN, PxB; 19 NxP wins a Pawn.

190

35

White is operating with brilliant tactical threats.

18 NxP!	B—QB2

White's threats cannot be met satisfactorily: if 18 . . . NxN??; 19 Q—K8 mate. If 18 . . . PxN; 19 QxB and White has a winning game.

19 N—Q5!	Resigns

A magnificent winning move. If 19 . . . QxB; 20 NxB attacking Black's Queen and also threatening 21 Q—K8 mate. If 19 . . . B/K3xN; 20 N—Q7ch winning Black's Queen.

Thus White faultlessly exploited Black's premature opening up of the position. In the following game Black is strangely inconsistent. First he drifts listlessly into a critically cramped position; then, with equally poor judgment, he strikes out recklessly to achieve freedom. White hits back hard.

KING'S INDIAN DEFENSE

WHITE	BLACK	WHITE	BLACK
1 P—Q4	N—KB3	4 P—K4	P—Q3
2 P—QB4	P—KN3	5 P—KN3	Castles
3 N—QB3	B—N2	6 B—N2	QN—Q2

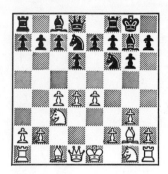

36

White's pieces are likely to have more mobility than Black's forces.

7 N—B3	P—K4	10 B—K3	N—KN1
8 Castles	P—KR3	11 Q—B2	N—N3
9 P—KR3	K—R2	12 P—N3	P—KB4?

Dissatisfied with the slight scope of his forces, Black opens up the position violently. *But White, having much greater mobility,* reacts with brutal effectiveness.

What makes White's reaction all the more powerful is that Black has loosened up the Pawn position in the vicinity of his King. The result is that it is relatively easy for White to penetrate the Black King's defenses.

| 13 QPxP | BPxP | 14 NxP | N—Q2? |

Black takes advantage of the fact that White's King Pawn is pinned on the long diagonal. But this is trifling compared to White's smashing attack against Black's weakened Kingside.

| 15 N/K4—N5ch! PxN | | 16 NxPch | Resigns |

If 16 . . . K—R3 White wins the Black Queen with 17 N—B7 dbl ch or 17 N—K6 dis ch.

If instead 16 . . . K—R1; 17 QxP, QN—B3; 18 PxN, NxP; 19 N—B7ch, RxN; 20 QxR and White is two Pawns and the Exchange ahead. In the face of this crushing material advantage, Black resigns.

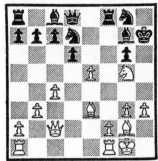

37

White scores a decisive win of material no matter how Black replies.

In this game White profited by Black's cramped game in the opening. Later on, when Black tried to struggle out of his straitjacket, White opened effective lines for his action-greedy pieces.

In the next game Black has a satisfactory opening position, but by thoughtlessly opening up the game he exposes himself to a decisive attack. Again White is alive to the possibilities, and quickly works up a withering attack.

NIMZOINDIAN DEFENSE

WHITE	BLACK		WHITE	BLACK
1 P—Q4	N—KB3		3 N—QB3	B—N5
2 P—QB4	P—K3		4 P—K3	. . . .

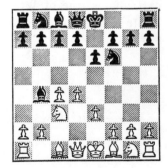

38

In this seemingly conservative variation White's Bishops have enormous potential power.

193

4	Castles	7 N—K2	P—K4
5 P—QR3	BxNch	8 N—N3	P—Q3
6 PxB	R—K1	9 B—K2	QN—Q2

There is a clash of plans here. As in Diagram 6, White wants to open up the position so that his Bishops will have powerful play. Black, on the other hand, should strive to keep the position closed.

10 Castles	P—B4	12 BPxP!	N—N3
11 P—B3	BPxP? *	13 B—N2	PxP?

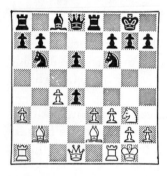

39

White's Queen Bishop has come to life!

White has been on the alert to increase the scope of his Bishops. He is well aware that Black has gone completely astray with his eleventh and thirteenth moves.

The position is opened up for White's pieces, and this is particularly true of White's Queen Bishop. As you will see, White knows just how to derive the maximum benefit from this.

14 P—K4!	B—K3	16 QxP	Q—B2
15 R—B1	R—K2	17 P—B5!	....

As a result of White's masterly fourteenth move he has

---

* This sadly inconsistent move opens up a future for White's Queen Bishop.

194

created a magnificent diagonal for his Queen Bishop and powerfully centralized his Queen at Queen 4.

Thus White is supreme in the center and in the general mobility of his forces. All this may be traced back to Black's mistake in prematurely opening up the position on move 11.

With his last move White increases his mobility and prepares to switch a Rook to the King-side. This will lead to a surprisingly quick decision.

| 17 .... | PxP | 19 B—B1! | Q—N1 |
| 18 RxP | Q—B5 | 20 R—KN5! | QN—Q2 |

White was threatening QxN/B6.

40

White is ready for a bombshell finish.

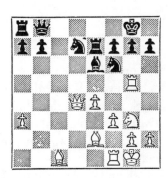

| 21 RxPch!! | KxR | 22 N—R5ch | K—N3 |

Or 22 . . . K—R1; 23 NxN, Q—K4; 24 B—N2!, QxQch; 25 BxQ, NxN; 26 BxNch winning a Rook.

23 Q—K3!   Resigns

White has foreseen that Black will be helpless against the double threat of 24 Q—R6 mate or 24 Q—N5 mate. He has made Black pay a high price for prematurely opening up the position.

The next game shows a still further refinement of this type of mistake. Black prematurely opens up the position *for his opponent* without even seeking any real or imaginary compensation. White's resulting attack, as we might expect, is devastating.

FRENCH DEFENSE

WHITE	BLACK	WHITE	BLACK
1 P—K4	P—K3	5 QN—K2	P—QB4
2 P—Q4	P—Q4	6 P—QB3	N—QB3
3 N—QB3	N—KB3	7 P—KB4	P—B3
4 P—K5	KN—Q2	8 N—B3	. . . .

The very nature of this opening gives White a much freer position. His pieces have more scope, and Black's Queen Bishop is hemmed in for good.

However, White does not have a completely free hand; Black is keeping the White center under pressure by attacking it with his King Bishop Pawn and Queen Bishop Pawn.

Since this is all the pressure that Black has, he ought to increase it by playing 8 . . . Q—N3. By keeping White's center under observation, Black would distract White's attention from his attacking intentions.

41

White is now greatly relieved as Black deprives himself of his only counterplay.

196

8	QBPxP?	12 B—K3	N—N3
9 BPxP	B—N5ch	13 B—Q3	N—B5
10 N—B3	PxP?	14 BxN	PxB
11 BPxP	Castles	15 Castles	N—K2

White has the better development and superior mobility.
Black is limited to a passive role.

| 16 Q—K2 | BxN | 18 N—N5! | B—Q2 |
| 17 PxB | Q—B2 | 19 Q—R5 | P—KR3 |

White has suddenly built up a powerful attack. Black's last
move seems to give him a respite, but White has a surprising
reply.

20 R—B7!!   ....

Apparently a losing move in view of the possible reply
20 . . . B—K1.

But White has a remarkable resource in answer to 20 . . .
B—K1, namely 21 RxP'ch!!, KxR; 22 NxPch, K—N1; 23
Q—N4ch followed by 24 NxQ with a crushing material ad-
vantage for White.

| 20 .... | Q—Q1 | 21 QR—KB1 | N—B4 |

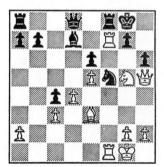

42

*White has a brilliant concluding com-
bination.*

Black has managed to block the open King Bishop file, but White is not impressed. He has concentrated his forces so powerfully on the King-side that he can afford spectacular sacrifices.

22	R(B1)xN!	PxR	27	Q—R6ch	K—B2
23	RxPch!	KxR	28	BxQ	QRxB
24	N—K6ch!	BxN	29	Q—B6ch	K—N1
25	BxPch	K—R2	30	QxBch	K—N2
26	B—N5 dis ch	K—N2	31	Q—K7ch	Resigns

White will advance his passed Pawns in the center to achieve a quick victory by queening a Pawn.

Thus White has made magnificent use of the open King Bishop file presented him by Black's premature opening up of the position.

In each of the games in this chapter Black has opened up the position prematurely. Through this opening up he has made it possible for White to develop an overwhelming attack.

This type of mistake is frequently made in over-the-board play. Consequently the methods adopted in these games by White are of the greatest practical value. By refuting these premature actions, White successfully defends his initiative.

Chapter Five

HOW TO EXPLOIT
BLACK'S PREMATURE COUNTERATTACK

IN THE PREVIOUS CHAPTER we saw how White won consistently by taking advantage of Black's prematurely opening up the position. White, generally being the player with the better development, is generally in position to benefit by the opening of lines.

Premature counterattack presents a much sharper problem. Here Black not only opens up lines—he actually *attacks*. If White reacts carelessly to a premature opening up of the position, he loses his initiative. If he reacts carelessly to a premature counterattack, *he may well lose the game*.

The following games show in an impressive way how White *can react effectively* to such premature counterattacks.

EVANS GAMBIT DECLINED

WHITE	BLACK		WHITE	BLACK
1 P—K4	P—K4		5 P—QR4	P—QR3
2 N—KB3	N—QB3		6 P—R5	B—R2
3 B—B4	B—B4		7 P—N5	PxP
4 P—QN4	B—N3		8 BxNP	N—B3

Black has an excellent development and he is now ready to castle into safety. "This won't do!" says White, and he plays to confuse Black with complicated possibilities.

This crafty move provokes Black to embark on a counter-attack which looks very attractive because it involves a powerful threat.

By playing . . . NxKP, Black threatens a decisive gain of material with . . . NxBP. Yet White is untroubled. He has looked further ahead and has prepared suitable counter-measures.

(Black should play 9 . . . P—Q3, shunning the complications.)

9	NxKP?	11 NxP!	N—Q5
10 Q—K2!	NxBP	12 NxQP dis ch!!	

White's last move seems incomprehensible at first sight. We might even take it for despair, in view of Black's fourfold threat of . . . NxQ or . . . NxR or . . . NxB or . . . NxPch. (Note that 12 QxN??—instead of the move actually played—would not do at all because of 12 . . . NxPch winning White's Queen.)

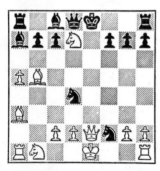

43

White gives up his Queen . . . and wins outright!

12	NxQ	13 N—B6 mate!

White had to be exceptionally resourceful to refute Black's plausible and promising counterattack.

Such premature counterattacks are favorites with daring and aggressive players who are aware that bluff is a potent weapon in chess. When the player of the White pieces is equally daring and has superior development in his favor, the counterattack is likely to grind to an abrupt halt. Here is another case in point:

QUEEN'S GAMBIT

WHITE	BLACK		WHITE	BLACK
1 P—Q4	P—Q4		4 P—K3	PxP
2 P—QB4	PxP		5 PxP	B—N5?
3 N—KB3	P—QB4		6 BxP	....

Threatening 7 BxPch, KxB; 8 N—K5ch coming out a Pawn ahead with a winning position.

From this variation you can see that White realizes the early development of Black's Bishop is ill-judged. But Black is determined to counterattack; White must hit hard to keep his initiative.

6	P—K3		8 N—K5	QxP!?
7 Q—R4ch!	N—QB3		9 NxN	Q—K5ch

The only move, as he obviously cannot play 9 . . . PxN?

10 B—K3	PxN	

Forced, for if 10 . . . QxN??; White pins and wins the Queen with 11 B—QN5.

11 N—B3!	QxP		12 B—Q5!!	....

A complete sermon in one move. White forcefully separates Black's Queen from Black's King. The effect of White's brilliant Bishop move is that Black's premature counterattack disappears in graceful fireworks.

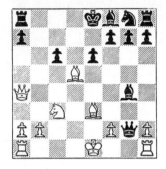

44

White's brilliant 12 B—Q5!! seizes the initiative.

12	....	KPxB
13	QxBPch	K—Q1
14	QxRch	K—Q2

15	Q—N7ch	K—K3
16	Q—B6ch	B—Q3
17	B—B4!!	Resigns

A spectacular finish. After 17 . . . QxRch; 18 K—Q2, QxR; 19 QxBch White mates in two more moves.

White has pitilessly punished Black's premature counterattack which took his Queen hopelessly far afield.

In the following game when Black commits the same mistake, White's punishment is even more forceful.

VIENNA GAME

WHITE	BLACK	WHITE	BLACK
1 P—K4	P—K4	3 B—B4	B—B4
2 N—QB3	N—QB3	4 Q—N4?!	....

This early development of the Queen is wrong on principle. Black's best reply is doubtless 4 . . . K—B1, protecting his King Knight Pawn and threatening to win a piece with . . . P—Q4. Black would thereby lose the castling privilege but would gain time by his attacking threat.

$$4 \dots \qquad Q—B3?$$

Defending and attacking at the same time. Black is so taken with the false economy of this move that he fails to provide for White's ingenious reply.

| 5 N—Q5!! | QxPch | 6 K—Q1 | K—B1 |

White's powerful Knight move has left Black nothing better against the double threat of 7 NxPch or 7 QxNP. So Black has had to move his King after all. White has even more formidable threats in store for him.

| 7 N—R3 | Q—Q5 | 8 P—Q3 | B—N3 |

White was threatening to trap Black's Queen by 9 P—B3!! He has used Black's premature counterattack to box in Black's Queen, which now offers no help to the Black King.

But this is not all: White can now operate on the open King Bishop file, thanks to Black's premature attack with the Queen. This enables White to win quickly by a spectacular, incisive attack.

| 9 R—B1! | N—B3 |

White's threat was 10 NxB, RPxN; 11 RxPch and Black can resign.

45

White is ready to embark on a brilliant sacrificial attack.

10 RxN!   P—Q3

White's sacrifice of the Exchange is based on the idea that if 10 . . . PxR; 11 B—KR6ch, K—K1; 12 Q—N7 the King Rook cannot be saved. Black tries a different way, but White's refutation is sensational:

11 QxPch!!!	KxQ	13 R—N6ch!!	RPxR
12 B—KR6ch	K—N1	14 N—B6 mate!	

Rarely do we see such a convincing refutation of a premature counterattack as White has provided here. The next example is much more difficult for White because the counterattack seems to be based on a fairly reasonable idea. Nevertheless, White sees that Black's counterplay is basically unsound. White follows up that observation with forceful, daring play.

QUEEN'S GAMBIT

WHITE	BLACK	WHITE	BLACK
1 P—Q4	P—Q4	4 P—K3	P—B4
2 P—QB4	PxP	5 BxP	PxP
3 N—KB3	N—KB3	6 PxP	Q—B2?

This premature development of the Queen is definitely out of place, as White has many ways to defend his attacked Bishop.

White deliberately selects a method that will provoke an unsound counterattack by Black.

7 Q—N3!   B—K3??

The very move that White wanted to provoke! Black is under the impression that White cannot capture this Bishop because of the reply . . . QxBch, winning at least a piece.

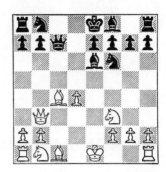

46

White is about to give Black an unpleasant surprise!

8 BxB!!	QxBch	11 QxP	Q—B8
9 K—K2	QxR	12 QxR!	QxPch
10 BxPch	**K—Q1**	13 QN—Q2	N—K5

Now the full depth of White's plan is revealed.

Black's last move is a shamefaced admission that his counterattack has misfired. In reply to 13 . . . QxR there follows 14 QxNch, K—Q2; 15 N—K5 mate.

The move actually chosen is not much of a help, either.

14 QxN/K4	QxR	16 Q—B5ch	K—Q1
15 Q—Q5ch	K—B2	17 B—K6	Resigns

For if 17 . . . N—Q2; 18 Q—B6, N—N3; 19 N—K5 followed by N—B7 mate.

From these games we can see that premature counterattack by Black generally takes the form of an early Queen development. Once this happens, White can generally entice the Black Queen far afield. If this requires substantial offers of material, don't shrink from making them—*provided you can see genuine compensation to reward your sacrifices.*

Chapter Six

HOW TO EXPLOIT
BLACK'S WEAKENING PAWN MOVES

THIS IS a very profitable subject. Familiarity with it will yield you many victories. This is why:

When your opponent weakens his position with ill-judged Pawn moves, he obviously does not know such moves are weakening. If he had that knowledge, he would of course avoid the Pawn moves.

Hence it follows that once Black has weakened his position, he has left himself wide open to powerful moves by which you can take advantage of his weakness. The following games tell you what you need to know in order to take advantage of weakening Pawn moves.

FRENCH DEFENSE

WHITE	BLACK	WHITE	BLACK
1 P—K4	P—K3	5 N—K4	P—KB4?
2 P—Q4	P—Q4	6 N—N5!	B—K2
3 N—QB3	N—KB3	7 N/N5—B3	P—B3
4 PxP	NxP	8 N—K5	. . . .

Black's weakening Pawn advance at move 5 has ruined his position. This move has left a backward Pawn on the King file: the Black King Pawn cannot be defended by Pawns.

White exploits this by posting his Queen or a Rook—or both—on the King file.

Equally disastrous for Black is the fact that Black's fifth move has left his King 4 square a "hole"—a square that Black can no longer protect by Pawn moves.

This makes it possible for White to occupy the "hole" with a Knight. *Posting a Knight on a vital center square* in this fashion is one of the strongest possible moves on the chessboard.

In this first part of the game, White has succeeded in bringing a Knight to the important square. The second part of the game will show you what happens as the result of White's aggressive placement of the Knight.

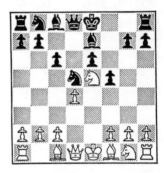

47

White controls the center as a result of Black's faulty fifth move.

8	Castles	11 Castles	R—K1
9 N/N1—B3	P—QN3	12 P—B4	N—B3
10 B—Q3	**B—N2**	13 B—B4	QN—Q2

White's ninth and thirteenth moves have both strengthened his powerful hold on the center. He continues that policy with his next move—a very important one, as we shall see.

14 Q—K2   P—B4

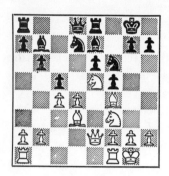

48

White now plays one of the most surprising moves ever made on the chessboard.

15 N—B7!!!　　....

White has not left Black much choice in replying to this amazing move. If he removes his Queen from attack by playing 15 . . . Q—B1, White replies 16 QxP, confiscating the King Pawn. (This is the Pawn weakened by Black's feeble fifth move.)

After this capture, White is threatening a murderous double check. If Black tries 16 . . . K—B1; 17 N/B7—N5 is decisive.

15 ....　　　KxN　　　　　16 QxPch!!!　　....

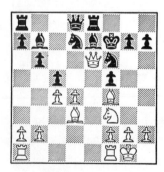

49

White has captured the weak King Pawn in spectacular fashion.

Black's weakening move now leads to his downfall. If 16

. . . KxQ; 17 N—N5 mate! This possibility vividly illustrates White's powerful control of the center.

Refusing the Queen by 16 . . . K—B1 is futile, for then White plays 17 N—N5 with crushing effect.

Black tries another way, but White forces mate in two moves.

| 16 . . . . | K—N3 | 17 P—KN4! | B—K5 |
| | 18 N—R4 mate | | |

The way in which White exploited the weakening of Black's Pawn position was very instructive. In the next game White does an equally good job in taking advantage of a Pawn weakness created by Black.

FRENCH DEFENSE

WHITE	BLACK	WHITE	BLACK
1 P—K4	P—K3	5 N—B3	B—Q3
2 P—Q4	P—Q4	6 B—Q3	Castles
3 N—QB3	N—KB3	7 Castles	N—B3
4 PxP	PxP	8 B—KN5	. . . .

By pinning Black's King Knight, White threatens NxP.

50

White has given Black a troublesome problem: how is he to defend his Queen Pawn?

209

| 8 .... | N—K2?? * | 10 N—KR4! | K—N2 |
| 9 BxN | PxB | 11 Q—R5! | .... |

Black's faulty eighth move has breached his King-side Pawn position. White naturally trains his guns on the gap in Black's castled position.

It is clear that White is taking admirable advantage of the opportunities offered. He has brought a Knight and the Queen into aggressive play. From now on, White keeps bringing more and more pieces to the King-side. In this way White builds up an imposing concentration of force against the Black King.

11	R—R1	14 QR—KB1	Q—B2
12 P—B4	P—B3	15 N—K2!	B—Q2
13 R—B3	N—N3	16 N—N3	QR—KN1

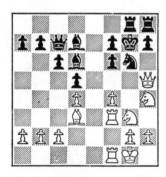

51

White's concentration of force on the King-side is so overwhelming that he can afford to sacrifice his Queen.

To appreciate White's brilliant combination, bear in mind that it is based on Black's *weakening of his Pawn position.*

17 Q—R6ch!!!	KxQ	20 P—N4ch!	KxP
18 N/R4—B5ch	BxN	21 R—N3ch	K—R4
19 NxBch	K—R4	22 B—K2 mate	

---

* Black's best way to meet the threat is 8 . . . B—KN5, counterattacking against White's Queen Pawn.

Striking as this combination is, what really interests us is that White did a masterly job in taking advantage of the gap in Black's King-side.

In the next game, White shows equal skill in exploiting the same kind of weakness in Black's King-side.

QUEEN'S GAMBIT DECLINED

WHITE	BLACK	WHITE	BLACK
1 P—Q4	P—Q4	7 R—B1	P—B3
2 P—QB4	P—K3	8 B—Q3	PxP
3 N—QB3	N—KB3	9 BxBP	N—Q4
4 B—N5	B—K2	10 BxB	QxB
5 P—K3	QN—Q2	11 Castles	NxN
6 N—B3	Castles	12 RxN	P—K4

Starting out with a cramped position—the kind we have studied in Chapter Three—Black has worked hard to free himself.

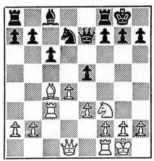

52

White must fight hard to maintain the initiative.

White must be extremely alert now to maintain some initiative.

13 NxP	NxN	15 P—B4	Q—K2? *
14 PxN	QxP	16 P—B5	P—QN4

---

* Black should have played 15 . . . Q—B3.

White's further advance of his King Bishop Pawn will break up Black's King-side Pawn position. Thus White will stamp Black's sixteenth move as a serious mistake.

17 B—N3   P—N5   18 P—B6!   . . . .

53

White breaks up Black's King-side.

White has put his finger on the weakness created by Black's faulty fifteenth move. White's advance of the King Bishop Pawn opens up a dangerous gap on the King-side. From now on, White concentrates his forces more and more powerfully against Black's King.

Note that this process of gathering concentration is typical. First, you pinpoint the weakness. Second, you switch your forces to bear on the weakened point. Third, you deploy your superior forces to crush Black's weakened resistance.

18	PxP	22 Q—Q2	K—R1
19 QRxP	QxPch	23 BxP	QR—B1
20 K—R1	B—N2	24 R/B6—B2	QR—Q1
21 QRxP	Q—K5	25 Q—N5!	R—Q3

White has skilfully brought his pieces to bear on the exposed Black King. His last move threatened 26 Q—B6 mate.

212

54

White's magnificently posted pieces are poised for the final attack.

26 B—Q5!!   Resigns

A brilliant final move. White offers his Bishop three ways and attacks three pieces. Black cannot guard his attacked Rook and attacked Queen at the same time and he must therefore resign.

An interesting possibility is 26 . . . RxR so that if 27 RxR???, Q—K8ch leading to mate. However, on 26 . . . RxR White plays 27 Q—N8 mate.

In the next game Black weakens his white squares. White's exploitation of this weakness is a masterpiece of positional maneuvering.

RUY LOPEZ

WHITE	BLACK	WHITE	BLACK
1 P—K4	P—K4	7 B—N3	P—Q3
2 N—KB3	N—QB3	8 P—B3	Castles
3 B—N5	P—QR3	9 P—Q3	B—K3
4 B—R4	N—B3	10 QN—Q2	N—KR4
5 Castles	B—K2	11 P—Q4!	BxB
6 R—K1	P—QN4	12 PxB	. . . .

Black's game is somewhat cramped but it is free from weaknesses. As in the previous game, White must be alert for opportunities to preserve some initiative.

12	N—B5	15 P—Q5!	N—Q1
13 N—B1	Q—B1?	16 BxN!	PxB
14 N—N3	P—N3	17 N—K2	P—N4

One glance at Diagram 55 shows that White's sixteenth move was a masterpiece.

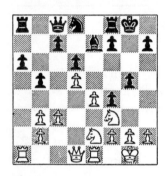

55

White has his strategic goal clearly laid out for him: Black is now very weak on the white squares.

Black made a mistake in allowing his Knight to be exchanged. White showed masterly judgment in making this exchange, which compels 17 . . . P—N4 on the following move.

What White has achieved is that a number of white squares in Black's position are no longer protected by Black Pawns. White's success is particularly notable because of his control and coming occupation of the King Bishop 5 square.

White's interpolation of 15 P—Q5!! was another admirable stroke. He drove back Black's Knight at a time when the Knight had to retreat to the Queen 1 square. At this post the Knight is badly out of play, which will handicap Black in the coming phase.

As we know from previous games, White's next step is *to concentrate his forces for attack*. He devotes his next three moves to posting his Knights aggressively and unassailably.

18 N/B3—Q4	R—K1	19 N—B5	B—B1
	20 N/K2—Q4	. . . .	

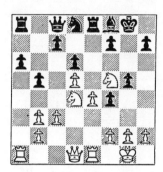

56

Neither of White's powerfully posted Knights can be driven away.

Now that White has established his Knights firmly, his next step is to open the King Rook file. This will enormously increase the attacking potential of his position.

20	. . . .	P—KB3	22 RPxP	P—B4
21	P—N3!	PxP	23 N—B3	N—B2

White has purposely retreated his Knight because he intends to use it for his King-side attack. The next stage in White's build-up of pressure is to attack on the newly opened King Rook file.

24 N—R2!	R—R2	28 NxQP!	R—Q1
25 Q—R5	B—N2	29 NxN	PxN
26 N—N4	Q—Q2	30 N—B5	B—B3
27 K—N2	N—K4	31 R—R1	R—KB1

(see Diagram 57 on page 66)

32 Q—N4!   . . . .

215

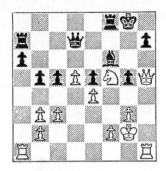

57

White is now ready for the final attack.

White proceeds with the final regrouping of his forces. The immediate threat is 33 RxQRP!, RxR; 34 N—R6ch winning Black's Queen!

32	K—R1	35 QR—R1	R/B1—B2
33 R—R6	P—R4	36 Q—B5	Q—KB1
34 N—K3!	Q—K1	37 N—N4	B—Q1

White now announced mate in three moves: 38 RxPch, K—N1 and now 39 Q—N6ch and 40 R—R8 mate.

The way that White broke through on the open King Rook file from the position of Diagram 57 is most instructive. Looking back over the earlier part of the game, you can appreciate the importance of his opening of the King Rook file by 21 P—N3! You can also see how useful it was for White to force the weakening of the white squares by 16 BxN!

This game is particularly valuable because White has done such a convincing job in exploiting the weaknesses in Black's position. Unlike most of the games in this book, the game had very little in the way of brilliancy. Yet White was in full command of the situation; he pushed his advantage to the utmost.

So far in this chapter we have been studying White's procedure against weaknesses on Black's King-side or in the neighborhood of his King. But weaknesses on the Queen-side, far away from the King, can also be disastrous. Here is an impressive example:

QUEEN'S GAMBIT DECLINED

WHITE	BLACK		WHITE	BLACK
1 P—Q4	P—Q4		5 B—N5	QN—Q2
2 P—QB4	P—K3		6 P—K3	Castles
3 N—QB3	N—KB3		7 R—B1	P—QN3
4 N—B3	B—K2			

58

White has a marked positional advantage because Black has created a "hole" at his Queen Bishop 3 square, which can no longer be protected by a Pawn.

White now sets himself to take advantage of the weakness at Black's Queen Bishop 3 square. Here is White's plan of campaign:

First he plays PxP in order to clear the Queen Bishop file for pressure by his Queen Rook against the weakened point. (Later on you will be able to appreciate the power of this pressure.)

White's next step will be to exchange the white-squared Bishops. In this way he will eliminate the Black Queen Bishop which would have been able to protect the weakened point.

	WHITE	BLACK		WHITE	BLACK
8	PxP!	PxP	11	QxB	P—B3
9	Q—R4!	B—N2	12	Castles	N—K5
10	B—QR6!	BxB	13	BxB	QxB

217

White's plans have proceeded according to schedule. Black's weakened Queen Bishop 3 has been replaced by a weak Queen Bishop Pawn, and White now turns his attention to this Pawn.

59

White is now ready to pounce on the weak Pawn.

14 Q—N7!　　KR—B1　　　　　　　15 NxP!　　Q—Q3

After 15 . . . PxN; 16 RxRch White is the Exchange and a Pawn ahead, with an easy win.

16 RxP!!　　Resigns

White's last move is a brilliant stroke which wins more material than Black can afford to part with. For if 16 . . . QxN?; 17 RxRch wins the Queen.

And if 16 . . . RxR; 17 QxQRch, N—B1; 18 QxR!!, QxQ; 19 N—K7ch followed by 20 NxQ leaves White a Rook ahead.

Finally, if 16 . . . QxR?; 17 N—K7ch wins the Queen.

In this game White carried out his strategical ideas with attacking moves. In the final game of the chapter he operates with strictly strategic methods. While less spectacular, this policy is equally effective.

218

QUEEN'S GAMBIT DECLINED

WHITE	BLACK	WHITE	BLACK
1 P—Q4	P—Q4	4 N—B3	B—K2
2 P—QB4	P—K3	5 B—N5	Castles
3 N—QB3	N—KB3	6 Q—B2	QN—Q2

Even at this early stage White has an inkling of what course the game may take. Black's Queen Bishop is badly hemmed in. White must keep a sharp eye on that Bishop in the hope of keeping the Bishop tied up permanently.

7 R—Q1	P—B3	12 BxP	P—QN4
8 P—K3	P—KR3	13 B—R2	Q—N3
9 B—R4	P—R3	14 Castles	B—N2
10 P—QR3	R—K1	15 N—K5!	QR—Q1?
11 B—N3	PxP	16 P—N4!!	....

White takes advantage of Black's faulty fifteenth move.*

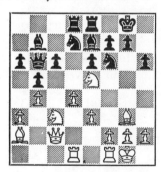

60

White now has a winning positional advantage.

With his last move White has established a lasting bind on the position. By preventing . . . P—B4 for good, he has stamped Black's Queen Bishop Pawn as *a backward Pawn on an open file.* In all the intricate maneuvering that follows,

---

* Black should have freed his Queen Bishop with . . . P—B4.

White keeps his eye on this Pawn and finally piles up enough force to capture it.

But White enjoys still another advantage after 16 P—QN4!! He keeps Black's Queen Bishop hemmed in for good. This means that to all intents and purposes White is playing with a piece ahead.

16	P—QR4	19 N—B5	N—B1
17 N—Q3!	PxP	20 B—N1	B—B1
18 PxP	R—R1	21 P—R3	N—Q4

Now that White has pinpointed the weakness, he goes on to the next phase: piling up on the weakness. First comes a very fine Knight maneuver aimed at transferring his Knight from Queen Bishop 3 to Queen Rook 5. At this latter post the White's Knight will bear down on the weak Queen Bishop Pawn.

22 N—R2!	R—R2	25 N/B1—N3	N—B3
23 P—K4	N—B3	26 N—R5	N—R4
24 N—B1	N/B3—Q2	27 B—KR2	P—N3

White has posted his Knights to the best advantage. His next four moves lead to the capture of the weak Pawn.

| 28 Q—B3! | B—B3 | 30 B—K4! | R—B2 |
| 29 P—K5! | B—K2 | 31 Q—B3! | .... |

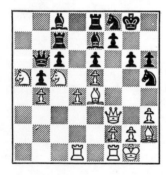

61

White must now win the weak Queen Bishop Pawn.

220

31	....	B—Q2		34	P—Q5!	N—N1
32	NxB	NxN		35	PxP!	NxN
33	NxP	B—B1		36	BxN	RxP *

White has achieved his aim. He now goes on to make use of his superior mobility.

37	B—Q5!	N—N2		43	R—R1	Q—B1
38	BxR	NxB		44	R—R8	Q—B8ch
39	R—Q6!	BxR		45	K—R2	P—B3
40	PxB	R—Q2		46	QxP	N—N2
41	R—Q1	K—R2		47	Q—B8	P—N4
42	B—K5	Q—R3		48	BxN!	Resigns

After 48 . . . RxB White mates by 49 Q—B5ch, R—N3; 50 R—R7ch, K—R1; 51 Q—B8ch! etc.

The games in this chapter give us a very clear and thorough method for White's procedure against weaknesses. The earlier White recognizes these weaknesses, the better for him. Even at a very early stage of the game, they give him a target to aim at; they provide a complete plan of the game. Once the target is created, White need not drift or guess; by concentrating on the target, he is playing the strongest and most logical moves.

---

* If Black captures the Bishop, the reply 37 PxPch is deadly.

Chapter Seven

HOW TO EXPLOIT
BLACK'S ERRORS OF JUDGMENT

ERRORS OF JUDGMENT, like weakening moves, enable you to train your forces on a target. Errors of judgment on Black's part provide you with a ready-made plan of attack.

However, you have to be alert to note these errors of judgment. If the lapse is ignored, Black may very possibly escape without serious damage. In each of the following games White is well aware of the lapse as soon as it happens, and vigorously turns it to his advantage.

In the first game, Black makes a plausible move that ruins his chances of achieving a normal development. White's method of exploiting this error of judgment is simple but highly effective.

The simplifying variation White adopts in this game is rather deceptive. Black is set for an easy game, but White knows how to create unexpected difficulties.

FOUR KNIGHTS' GAME

WHITE	BLACK	WHITE	BLACK
1 P—K4	P—K4	4 B—N5	B—N5
2 N—KB3	N—QB3	5 Castles	Castles
3 N—B3	N—B3	6 BxN	. . . .

222

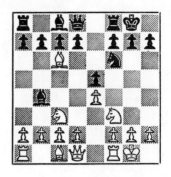

62

White will get his big opportunity as Black proceeds to make an error of judgment.

6	NPxB?

By capturing with the Queen Pawn, Black opens up a line of development for his Queen Bishop.

The text, on the contrary, blocks the Bishop's development.

Here White sees his chance—*to make use of the superiority in development that he is bound to obtain because Black's Queen Bishop is immobilized.*

7 NxP	R—K1	9 PxB	NxP
8 P—Q4	BxN	10 R—K1!	....

Very powerful. White's Rook move creates serious difficulties for Black. If 10 . . . N—B3; 11 B—N5 gives White a lasting and annoying pin. If 10 . . . NxQBP; 11 Q—B3 and White attacks the Knight and also threatens QxKBPch.

10	N—Q3

Now Black's Queen Pawn·cannot move, and it is not clear how his Bishop is to be developed. Credit this to White's pressing Rook move. White has made important progress by ruining Black's prospects of development.

In the following stage White builds up strong pressure on the King-side, which lacks proper protection.

223

If 11 . . . P—B3; 12 B—R6, P—N3; 13 NxNP! and White wins.

12 B—R3   R—Q1   13 R—K3!   . . . .

While Black works hard to unscramble his pieces, White increases his pressure on the King-side. Note the helplessness of Black's Bishop.

| 13 . . . . | N—B4 | 15 Q—R5 | P—N3 |
| 14 R—B3 | P—Q4 | 16 N—N4! | Q—R1 |

A queer-looking move, but White has the whip-hand in any event because of his powerful accumulation of forces on the King-side.

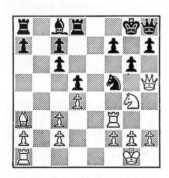

63

White's lead in development is now decisive.

17 Q—N5   B—K3   18 RxN!   Resigns

For if 18 . . . BxR; 19 N—R6ch, K—N2; 20 NxBch, K—N1; 21 B—K7 threatening to win the Queen with 22 B—B6 or to win a Rook with 22 BxR.

White timed his play perfectly to take advantage of Black's error of judgment on move 6. By continuing to pile on pressure relentlessly on the King-side, White emphasized the back-wardness of Black's development.

In the next game White deals with a somewhat different kind of error on Black's part. Starting out with a reasonably satisfactory development, Black undermines the position of his most effective piece.

White must ask himself such questions as: Where is Black's error of judgment? How can I take advantage of that error?

VIENNA GAME

WHITE	BLACK		WHITE	BLACK
1 P—K4	P—K4		3 P—B4	P—Q4
2 N—QB3	N—KB3		4 BPxP	NxP

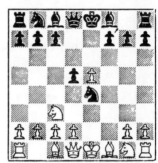

64

White must contend with a powerfully centralized Black Knight.

At a very early stage in the game, White has a serious problem: what is he to do about the effectively posted Black Knight in the center? Exchanging Knights is not aggressive enough, so White spars for time.

5 N—B3	B—QN5		8 Q—K3	N—QB3
6 Q—K2	BxN		9 B—Q3	P—B4
7 NPxB	Castles		10 Castles	P—B5

A critical move which unhinges the support of Black's well posted Knight.

225

This is the mistake White has been waiting for.* The centralized Knight leaves his powerful post. At the same time Black's far advanced King Bishop Pawn becomes an exposed weakness.

12 B—R3!   NxNch   13 QxN!   R—B2

White is playing with superb tactical skill. In reply to 13 . . . NxP he plays 14 Q—R5, attacking the Knight, threatening BxPch with a mating menace, and keeping Black's Rook under attack.

14 QR—K1   . . . .

White's alert play has brought all his pieces into powerful play. His Bishops are magnificently trained for attack. Thus, if now 14 . . . B—K3 (to hold back the threatening King Pawn) White continues 15 Q—R5, P—KN3; 16 BxP!, PxB; 17 QxPch winning the Bishop with two Pawns to the good.

14 . . . .   P—KN4

To guard the advanced Bishop Pawn and to defend the King Rook Pawn against Q—R5.

But White has all the play and now forces the game in a few moves.

15 P—K6   R—N2   16 Q—R5!   . . . .

Now White has the brutal threat 17 P—K7!, NxP; 18 BxN, RxB; 19 QxNPch, K—B1; 20 RxPch, K—K1; 21 Q—N8ch, K—Q2; 22 QxQPch, K—K1; 23 R—B8ch!

---

* 11 . . . B—B4 supports the well posted Knight.

| 16 .... | N—K2 | 17 B—QB5! | N—B3 |

He cannot allow White to play B—Q4.

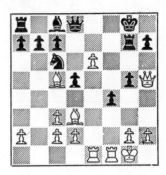

65

White crowns his masterly attack by breaking up Black's position.

| 18 P—K7! | NxP | 19 BxN | Resigns |

If 19 . . . RxB; 20 QxNPch and White wins as in the note to White's sixteenth move.

This game is extremely impressive because of the way that White worked up a devastating attack after Black's error of judgment. White's removal of Black's Knight from the center opened up the lines that White needed for the effective cooperation of his forces.

In the next game, a wrong opening choice by Black leaves him exposed to White's tactical threats. White maneuvers very cleverly to take advantage of the opportunities offered.

FRENCH DEFENSE

WHITE	BLACK	WHITE	BLACK
1 P—K4	P—K3	5 PxP	QxP
2 P—Q4	P—Q4	6 BxN	BxNch
3 N—QB3	N—KB3	7 PxB	PxB
4 B—KN5	B—N5	8 N—B3	. . . .

227

66

White wants to drive off Black's centralized Queen.

In order to drive away Black's Queen from an effective centralized post, White plans to play P—N3 followed by B—N2 with threats against the Black Queen.

8	P—N3	9 P—N3	B—N2
	10 B—N2	Q—KR4? *	

White threatened 11 N—R4 with decisive effect. Black has avoided this threat, but he has put his Queen out of play. White will make good use of the Queen's inactive role.

11 Castles	N—Q2	14 N—R4!	BxB
12 Q—K2	QR—B1	15 NxB	PxP
13 Q—K3!	P—QB4	16 PxP	....

White's Pawn sacrifice is neatly calculated. After 16 . . . RxP; 17 Q—R3!!, P—R4; 18 QR—B1, RxR; 19 RxR White has reduced his opponent to helplessness. (White would then threaten R—B8 mate, and Black would be unable to castle out of danger.)

In offering this variation, White relies on the inactive role of Black's Queen.

---

* Black gets an equal game with . . . Q—K5ch, which practically forces White to agree to the exchange of Queens by 11 Q—K2 etc.

16	Castles	19 P—KB3!	Q—N4
17 Q—K4	R—B2	20 R—B2	R—Q1
18 N—B4	Q—N5	21 P—KR4!	Q—R3

If 18 . . . QxNPch?; 19 R—N2 pins and wins the Queen.

White now begins a very ingenious maneuver to harry the Black Queen and at the same time to exploit the lack of harmony among Black's forces.

22 P—N4!	QxP	23 R—R2	Q—N4

After 23 . . . Q—N6ch; 24 K—R1 White can confidently look forward to trapping the Black Queen.

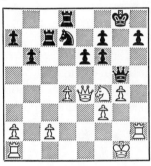

67

White can capture the King Rook Pawn, but he has an even stronger move.

24 NxP!!	PxN	25 QxKPch	....

Now you can see how White's unexpected combination takes advantage of the lack of communication among Black's forces. If 25 ... K—B1; 26 Q—Q6ch wins a Rook. The same is true of 25 . . . K—N2; 26 Q—K7ch.

Black tries a different defense, but White's superior mobility still tells in his favor.

25	K—R1	28 QxRch	N—B1
26 Q—K7	Q—N1	29 QxNch	Q—N1
27 RxPch!	QxR	30 QxPch	Resigns

White has succeeded admirably in carrying out his original aim of exploiting the lack of cooperation between Black's Queen and his other pieces. Black's loss of material makes further resistance hopeless.

In the following game it is up to White to punish his opponent for a slight transposition of moves toward the beginning of the middle game. It is very instructive to see how White carries out this idea.

NIMZOINDIAN DEFENSE

WHITE	BLACK	WHITE	BLACK
1 P—Q4	N—KB3	4 P—K3	Castles
2 P—QB4	P—K3	5 P—QR3	BxNch
3 N—QB3	B—N5	6 PxB	P—Q3

Here White faces the same kind of problem as in the play following Diagram 38. He wants open lines for his pieces— particularly the Bishops—while Black's interests are best served by a closed position.

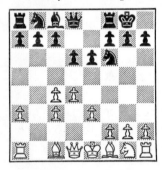

68

White needs open lines for his coming attack.

7 B—Q3	P—B4	10 Castles	P—QN3
8 N—K2	N—B3	11 P—B4	B—R3? *
9 P—K4	N—K1!	12 P—B5!	P—K4

* By playing 11 . . . P—B4! Black would have avoided the terrific attack that follows.

230

White has just the kind of position he was aiming for, thanks to Black's carelessness at move 11. White can now force a breach in Black's King-side position and just keep on piling up pressure against Black's game. In this way he takes advantage of the fact that Black's pieces are poorly placed for defensive purposes.

69

White can force a weakness in Black's King-side by a very surprising move.

13 P—B6!!   . . . .

This amazing move breaks up Black's King-side no matter how he plays.

After 13 . . . NPxP; 14 B—R6 White has achieved his objective. Black's King-side formation is then similar to the one in Diagram 51. The Black King is exposed to attack, and White simply continues to bring additional pressure to bear. (The actual continuation of the game proceeds along similar lines.)

If Black tries 13 . . . NxBP White can still inflict the unwieldy doubled Pawn on him by playing 14 B—N5. White would then have lasting pressure by means of the pin supported by his Rook on the open King Bishop file.

13 . . . .   K—R1   14 P—Q5   N—R4
         15 N—N3!   . . . .

White's Knight now comes into play very strongly. He is indifferent to the loss of a Pawn by 15 . . . BxP; 16 BxB, NxB for after 17 PxPch, NxP; 18 B—R6 his attack rolls on undiminished.

15	PxP	17 Q—R5	BxN
16 N—B5	B—B1	18 PxB	R—KN1

To force a clearly winning position White only needs to bring his King Rook into the attack.

This he now proceeds to do, applying the formula which has been used so often by White in these games. First he determines where the weakness lies; then he concentrates his forces on the weak spot; finally, he attacks in overwhelmingly superior strength.

In this case the weakness is Black's exposed King-side, *created by White's brilliant thirteenth move.*

19 R—B3!   ....

Threatening mate in four moves beginning with 20 QxRPch!!

19	R—N2	21 R—R3	N—KN2
20 B—R6	R—KN1	22 Q—R4!	Resigns

Black is helpless against the coming 23 B—N5, P—R4; 24 QxPch!!, NxQ; 25 RxNch, K—N2; 26 B—R6ch and mate next move.

The power of White's concluding attack has amply proved the correctness of White's judgment in making the surprising Pawn advance on move 13.

In this last game, as in all the games in this chapter, we have seen how White takes advantage of Black's error of judgment. The important requirement, as far as White is concerned, is alertness. If White is watchful enough to see how Black's plans are spoiled by a hasty move, then that observation is half the battle.

Nor can White afford to be dogmatic. He applies whatever attacking methods are needed to refute Black's play, and he does not mind changing his plans as the occasion requires.

Thus, in this game, White wanted originally to get good attacking diagonals for both Bishops. Yet after his twelfth move White had to reconcile himself to the fact that his white-squared Bishop was destined to play a minor role. There were two reasons why White accepted this philosophically.

In the first place, the Pawn moves that shut in *this* Bishop (9 P—K4 and 13 P—B6!!), opened the diagonal for White's black-squared Bishop. Secondly, Black had so many inactive pieces that the blocking of the King Bishop was of minor importance.

This kind of elasticity is an important quality in a chess-player. We're often told that a plan is important; unfortunately, we hear less often that a plan needs modifying as the original conditions are modified. In all the games in this chapter, White is very sensitive to *the changes in Black's policy that are the results of errors of judgment*. The result, as you have seen, is effective attack and quick victory.

Chapter Eight

OPENING MISTAKES
WHITE SHOULD AVOID

So FAR you have seen the methods by which White exploits Black's mistakes in the opening and the early middle game. *These methods are valid and useful as long as White does not violate the rules of good opening play.*

It is therefore vital for you to be forewarned against the danger of losing the initiative when you play White.

This danger comes from neglect of your development. You may damage your development by losing time or by developing pieces inefficiently.

There are some openings in which the defects are so obvious that these openings have been partly or completely discredited. Many years ago, when opening theory was not so well understood as it is today, some of these openings were popular. In the course of time their serious defects became all too clear. Such openings are described in Chapter Nine, but here we want to emphasize several of them, pointing out their defects in some detail:

The Center Game offers a good example. Here are the opening moves:

WHITE	BLACK
1 P—K4	P—K4
2 P—Q4	PxP
3 QxP	N—QB3

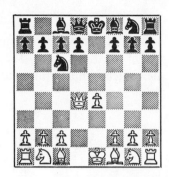

70

White's Queen must retreat with loss of time.

Black's last move gains time by attacking the Queen. White must now move the Queen out of attack, giving Black another tempo for development. What usually happens is that White plays 4 Q—K3 and Black replies 4 . . . N—B3, developing another piece.

To understand what has happened, you must realize that in effect *Black has taken over the role usually held by White.* It is no longer White who is a move ahead; Black has the initiative.

The same mistake on White's part appears in milder form in the Scotch Game:

WHITE	BLACK
1 P—K4	P—K4
2 N—KB3	N—QB3
3 P—Q4	. . . .

To advance in the center and to open up a line for the Queen Bishop seems very good on general principles. But the advance of the Queen Pawn is not well timed.

3	PxP
4 NxP	. . . .

By recapturing, White moves his Knight a second time and thus wastes a move.

Black, by way of reply, develops with gain of time. He can

play 4 . . . B—B4, developing a new piece and gaining time by threatening to win White's Knight.

Or Black can play 4 . . . N—B3, likewise developing a new piece and gaining time by threatening to win White's King Pawn.

4 . . . .   N—B3

71

White is on the defensive: he must defend his King Pawn.

In this case White's shortcomings are not fatal. However, any possibility of keeping Black's position under pressure is gone.

Another kind of mistake to avoid with the White pieces is to develop inefficiently. Note this in Alapin's Opening:

WHITE	BLACK
1 P—K4	P—K4
2 N—K2	. . . .

As you know, White almost invariably plays 2 N—KB3. You may have wondered why White should not play 2 N—K2. There are two reasons for this.

On King 2 the Knight blocks the development of White's King Bishop and thus holds up White's whole development. Furthermore, N—K2 is passive whereas N—KB3 is aggressive, attacking Black's King Pawn.

In view of these defects, N—K2 is ruled out as a worthwhile move.

236

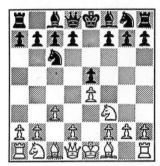

72

White's last move was much too passive.

A similar example appears in Ponziani's Opening:

WHITE	BLACK
1 P—K4	P—K4
2 N—KB3	N—QB3
3 P—B3	. . . .

73

White's last move blocks his development.

White's last move deprives his Queen Knight of its best square. Black replies 3 . . . P—Q4! opening up the position favorably. After 4 PxP, QxP White is unable to attack the Black Queen by 5 N—B3, because 3 P—B3 has made the Knight move impossible.

As in the previous examples, Black has an easy time of it. Black has the initiative and has nothing to fear. From the positions discussed in this chapter, you can see that White must avoid *loss of time as well as ineffectual development*. If White violates these simple rules, *he loses his chance to exploit Black's mistakes in the opening.*

How
to Play
the
Black Pieces

Book Four

Chapter One

HOW TO EXPLOIT WHITE'S WEAKNESSES

BECAUSE Black does not have the first move, we are prone to think of him as being forced onto the defensive from the very start. You often hear extreme views expressed about "White's initiative," and "White's birthright of the first move."

You can be reassured about Black's chances from the very start. All the statistical analyses we have about the results of games show that Black breaks even or else is *very* slightly in the red.

In fact, some modern theorists went to the other extreme and announced ominously that "White's game is in the last throes!"

However, this is definitely going too far. All that we want to establish in this book is that *with best play on Black's part,* White's theoretical advantage will disappear with astonishing rapidity.

And remember this: all talk about White's theoretical advantage presupposes that White will play flawlessly—the first-class chess shown in *Third Book of Chess*, the previous book to this. In actual practice, White often goes wrong in one way or another, giving Black his chance to seize the initiative.

In this volume it is our purpose to study the ways in which Black seizes the initiative. We begin with his methods of exploiting weaknesses created by White.

Weaknesses in the King's position

It often happens that White, in his eagerness to press a real or imagined advantage, allows a weakness to be formed in his position. Black must be alert in observing such weaknesses and pouncing on them. The following two games show how it is done.

QUEEN'S GAMBIT DECLINED

WHITE	BLACK		WHITE	BLACK
1 P—Q4	P—Q4		5 P—K3	Castles
2 P—QB4	P—K3		6 N—B3	P—KR3
3 N—QB3	N—KB3		7 B—R4	N—K5
4 B—N5	B—K2		8 BxB	QxB

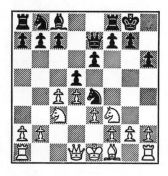

1

Black plays to simplify the position.

Black's handling of the opening deserves close study. His position is cramped, and his Bishop on the white squares has no scope. He therefore exchanges some pieces in order to create elbow room for his remaining forces.

In the position of Diagram 1 he has already achieved a promising set-up. Thus, if 9 NxN, PxN; 10 N—Q2, P—K4! and Black actually wins a piece after 11 NxP?, PxP; 12 QxP??, R—Q1 etc. (In any event, after 10 . . . P—K4! Black has an open diagonal for his Bishop.)

242

Again, after 9 B—Q3, NxN; 10 PxN, PxP Black has freed himself and can play . . . P—QN3 and . . . B—N2 with a splendid diagonal for his Bishop.

9 PxP	NxN	12 P—B4	PxP
10 PxN	PxP	13 BxP	N—B3
11 Q—N3	R—Q1	14 Q—B3	B—N5

2

Black is already operating with threats.

Black has achieved a splendid development, and White finds himself in difficulties. (Black's threat is 15 . . BxN; 16 PxB, NxP—or 16 . . . RxP.)

White can meet the threat with 15 N—Q2, but then he loses more time and allows Black to get further ahead in development. So White retreats his Bishop, but Black has a brilliant resource in reserve.

15 B—K2   BxN!   16 PxB   . . . .

The point of Black's exchange is that the seemingly safe 16 BxB is answered by 16 . . . NxP; 17 BxP, QR—N1; 18 B—R6, Q—B3! (threatens . . . N—B6ch or . . . N—B7ch); 19 PxN, QxB.

In that case, Black's command of the open lines would decide the game quickly in his favor.

| 16 .... | R—Q3 | 17 KR—N1 | .... |

White wants to attack. His threat is 18 P—Q5 (menacing mate), N—K4; 19 P—B4, N—N3 (forced); 20 P—B5, N—K4; 21 P—B4 winning the Knight.

But Black has a masterly reply.

| 17 .... | NxP!! |

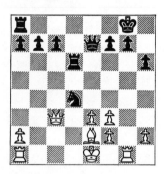

3

Black is counterattacking.

The point of Black's sacrifice is that if 18 PxN, R—K1; 19 Q—K3, R—K3 regaining the piece with a winning game.

| 18 R—Q1 | N—K3 | 19 P—B4 | .... |

Now Black must watch out for 20 P—B5, N—N4; 21 P—KR4 winning the Knight because of the mating threat.

| 19 .... | RxRch | 20 BxR | R—Q1! |

This looks like a blunder. It isn't!

| 21 P—B5 | .... |

(See diagram on top of next page)

4

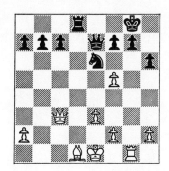

Has Black blundered?

21 ....   Q—Q3!

A powerful thrust which sends White reeling. If 22 PxN???, QxB mate.

22 B—R5   QxP

Now Black attacks two pieces, which reduces White to desperation.

5

Black is well prepared for White's active counterplay.

23 BxPch   K—R1!

Of course Black does not play 23 . . . KxB? allowing White to capture the Knight with CHECK.

24 R—B1   N—N4!   25 Q—B4   ....

Or 25 B—B4, N—B6ch; 26 K—K2, Q—R4! and Black's threat of . . . N—N8 dbl ch is crushing.

6

How does Black exploit the disorganized state of White's pieces?

25 ....   Q—Q3!

White resigns. The threat is 26 . . . Q—Q8 mate or 26 . . . Q—Q7 mate. To parry this threat he must move his Queen, allowing Black to win the Bishop.

Black played very ably to neutralize his initial inferiority in development. White moved his Queen too much in the opening. Black cleverly exploited this mistaken policy by organizing a rapid-fire attack against the White King stranded in the center.

Weaknesses in the castled position

NIMZOINDIAN DEFENSE

WHITE	BLACK	WHITE	BLACK
1 P—Q4	N—KB3	3 N—QB3	B—N5
2 P—QB4	P—K3	4 P—K3	....

(*See diagram on top of next page*)

246

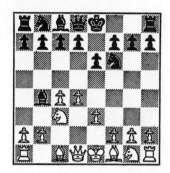

7

Black intends to play an aggressive game.

Black's third move tells us that he means to develop his pieces actively. White's last move, on the other hand, points to a slow or noncommittal development on his part.

4	P—QN3	6 Q—B2	N—K5
5 N—B3	B—N2	7 B—Q3	....

Somewhat belatedly White realizes that Black has a good development and as a result he tries to fight for control of the vital King 4 square. But Black has entrenched himself too well.

7	P—KB4!	10 Castles	R—B3!
8 P—QR3	BxNch	11 N—Q2	R—R3!
9 PxB	Castles	12 P—N3??	....

Black has set a little trap which White has avoided. The trap was: 12 BxN, PxB; 13 NxP, Q—R5 attacking the Knight a second time and threatening mate.

By playing 12 P—N3?? White has avoided the trap; but he has opened up the long diagonal for Black's Queen Knight. Black recognizes possibilities and takes advantage of White's weakened King-side with a final smashing attack.

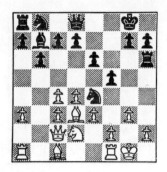

8

Black can now demolish White's King-side.

12 ....   Q—R5!!

First point: if 13 PxQ, R—N3ch; 14 K—R1, NxKBP dbl ch and mate! Throughout the proceedings Black's sinister Bishop at Queen Knight 2 plays an effective role at long distance.

13 N—B3   N—N4!!!   14 PxQ   ....

A delightful possibility prepared by Black is 14 NxQ, N—R6 mate.

14 ....   NxNch

Black is fully prepared for 15 K—R1, to which his answer will be 15 . . . RxP; 16 K—N2 (else . . . RxP mate), N—K8 dbl ch!; 17 K—N3, R—N5ch; 18 K—R3, B—N7 mate.

15 K—N2   N—K8 dbl ch   17 K—B4   R—N5ch
16 K—N3   R—N3ch   18 K—K5   N—B6 mate

(Another way was 18 . . . N—B3 mate.)

Black took superb advantage of White's weakening of the castled position. Despite the general opinion that Black's play

248

must necessarily be defensive, there are frequent opportunities for aggressive play on his part.

In the following game, for example, Black realizes that White goes badly astray when he castles on the Queen-side in the face of a half-open Queen Bishop file. When White aggravates his foolhardiness by presenting a target, in the form of an advanced Queen Rook Pawn, Black is alert to his opportunities. He soon unleashes an attack that rakes White's castled position.

NIMZOINDIAN DEFENSE

WHITE	BLACK		WHITE	BLACK
1 P—Q4	N—KB3		3 N—QB3	B—N5
2 P—QB4	P—K3		4 Q—B2	....

9

Black must fight back in the center.

Black has a serious problem here. White threatens P—K4 with an overwhelming position in the center.

4 ....   P—B4

With this wing thrust at the center, Black restrains his opponent from monopolizing the center.

| 5 N—B3 | N—B3 | 7 B—N5 | B—K2 |
| 6 PxP | BxP | 8 Castles? | .... |

Gaining time for placing a Rook on the Queen file to press down on Black's backward Queen Pawn.

Yet Black realizes that he gains more than White does by this move; any strategical advantage that White may have is canceled out by Black's attacking chances against the exposed White King.

| 8 .... | Q—R4! | 9 P—QR3? | .... |

Now Black has a new target to aim at.

| 9 .... | P—QR3 | 11 B—K2 | B—N2 |
| 10 P—K3 | P—QN3 | 12 N—QN1 | P—N4! |

Black is well aware that open lines against White's King are all-important in this game.

| 13 PxP | PxP | 15 N—B3 | BxP!! |
| 14 Q—Q3 | QR—B1! | 16 BxN | PxB |

Now that Black has scored a bull's-eye on the target, he does not fear White's counterattack.

10

Black's pieces are admirably posted for attack.

Black sees that after 17 QxPch, K—B1; 18 QxB??? he has a mate in two: 18 QxNch etc.

As we'll see in a moment, Black has more sparkling attacking ideas in mind. If 17 PxB, QxPch; 18 K—N1, N—N5 wins.

17 K—N1   BxP!!

Proving that the White King's flight from the "hot" Queen Bishop file did him no good.

Black has worked out this pretty variation after 18 KxB: 18 . . . Q—N5ch; 19 K—B2, N—K4!; 20 NxN, B—K5!! winning the Queen by a double pin.

18 N—R2   N—K4!   19 NxN   B—Q4!

White resigns, as he has no good parry to the threat of . . . QxN mate.

With this dashing game we take our leave of attacks against the castled King and turn to attacks on strategical weaknesses—a very important subject.

Strategical weaknesses

In the following game Black plays steadily, waiting for a "break." Then, realizing that White has made a serious error, Black repulses the attack with cool judgment and calm, accurate appraisal of the situation.

FRENCH DEFENSE (in effect)

WHITE	BLACK	WHITE	BLACK
1 P—K4	N—KB3	4 P—Q4	P—K3
2 N—QB3*	P—Q4	5 QN—K2	P—QB4
3 P—K5	KN—Q2	6 P—QB3	. . . .

After White's timid second move the game has turned into

---

* As indicated in *Third Book of Chess* (pages 26, 88) White's best chance of obtaining an advantage lies in the forthright 2 P—K5 etc.

a French Defense in which Black stands rather well. Note
that Black has some initiative in the center, for his last move
has put White's Pawn under pressure.

6 ....   N—QB3   7 P—KB4   ....

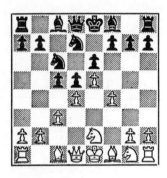

11

*Black is developing more rapidly than
White!*

Black can now put more pressure on White's center with
. . . Q—N3. But he prefers to continue his development in
straightforward fashion. *In fact, Black never moves his
Queen throughout this game!*

7	B—K2	10 PxP	N—N3!
8 N—B3	Castles	11 B—R3?	B—Q2!
9 P—KN3	PxP	12 Castles	R—B1!

The harmonious development of Black's forces is a thing
of beauty. His 10th move made room for his 11th; his 11th
made room for his 12th.

And the object of these moves? Black wants to post his
pieces powerfully on the Queen-side, with such moves as
. . . N—B5. He sees that White's 11th move has sadly weakened his control of the Queen Bishop 4 square.

The play will unfold along these lines: Black brings the
bulk of his forces to the Queen-side to increase his pressure
there. White seeks a counterattack by pressing forward on
the King-side.

Who will succeed? Black's plans have a sound basis, while White's "attack" is a delusion.

13 P—KN4	P—B3!	16 K—R1	N—B5
14 PxP	BxP	17 N—B3	B—N5!
15 P—N5	B—K2	18 Q—K2	R—K1

Since the last note Black has made further progress. He has improved the position of his pieces, and White has forfeited command of another important white square by playing 15 P—N5.

19 Q—Q3   N—Q3!

Directed against White's next move, and also played with a view to . . . N—R4 followed by . . . BxN and . . . B—N4.

20 P—B5   NxBP   21 NxP   B—Q3!

Now Black has distinctly the upper hand, for example: 22 N—B4, N—N5!; 23 Q—Q1, N—B7; 24 QR—N1, N—K6 winning the Exchange—or 23 Q—K2, RxB!; 24 RxR, BxN with the winning advantage of two pieces for a Rook.

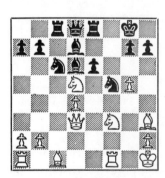

12

*Black is building up a powerful coun-
terattack.*

To avoid the variations just pointed out, White chooses a different way. But it is all one to Black, who continues with remorseless vigor.

22 BxN	PxB		25 N—R4	NxP
23 N—B4	R—K5!		26 Q—KR3	R—B7!
24 Q—N3ch	K—R1		27 P—N6	B—B3!

Presumably White is doing the attacking—but see with what power Black's pieces press down on the King-side! White makes a pathetic gesture toward a mating attack, but Black repulses the attempt with brutal counterstrokes.

28 N—B3	P—KR3		30 BxP	R—KR5!
29 N—K6	NxN		Resigns	

White is of course unable to capture the impudent Rook, and his position is about to topple. Black has shown his contempt for the ill-judged "attack" by not even bothering to move his Queen. It would be difficult to find a more convincing example of the proposition that the attack does not always pay.

In the next game, too, White saddles himself with a positional weakness. Apparently he has compensation in the form of a more aggressive position; and yet Black single-mindedly concentrates on taking advantage of White's real weakness.

QUEEN'S GAMBIT ACCEPTED

WHITE	BLACK		WHITE	BLACK
1 P—Q4	P—Q4		3 N—KB3	N—KB3
2 P—QB4	PxP		4 P—K3	. . . .

Black's acceptance of the gambit on the second move has temporarily cost him control of the center. It is therefore important for him to strike at the center with . . . P—B4.

13

Black's last move fights for control of the center.

Black looks forward to having a comfortable position. He will play . . . P—QR3 and . . . P—QN4, developing his Queen Bishop very favorably at the Queen Knight 2 square.

| 6 N—B3 | P—QR3 | 8 B—Q3 | PxP! |
| 7 Castles | P—QN4 | 9 PxP | . . . . |

This exchange of Pawns has opened a good diagonal for White's Queen Bishop. Yet Black very well knows what he is about, for he has created an isolated Queen Pawn in White's camp. (An "isolated" Pawn is one which lacks protection from Pawns of the same color on adjacent files. In this particular case, White's Queen Bishop Pawn and King Pawn have disappeared.)

An isolated Pawn is always a potential weakness, for it may require defending by valuable pieces. This, then, is why Black isolated the Pawn.

But Black had another reason for this Pawn exchange. When a Pawn is isolated, there are no Pawns left to control the square immediately in front of the Pawn. This square becomes a "strong point" for the enemy pieces, for they

255

can never be dislodged by Pawns. In this case, Black's Queen 4 square is a strong point.

| 9 .... | B—N2 | 11 Q—K2 | Castles |
| 10 B—N5 | B—K2 | 12 QR—Q1 | .... |

Black will now bring his Queen Knight into play, and will then be ready to occupy the strong point at Queen 4.

| 12 .... | QN—Q2 | 13 N—K5 | N—Q4! |

Foreseeing that White will seek the opening of more attacking lines with P—B4 and P—B5, Black plays for simplifying exchanges.

There are two reasons for such exchanges. One is that the fewer pieces there are on the board, the harder it will be for White to complicate the play. The other point is that the fewer pieces on the board, the easier it will be for Black to menace the White Pawn weakness.

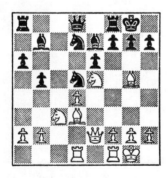

14

Black has occupied the strong point on the Queen 4 square.

14 B—B1   ....

A strange-looking move that enables Black to maintain a clear positional advantage. But this would also be true after 14 BxB, QxB; 15 N/B3xN, BxN. (Remember that simplifying is detrimental to the player with the isolated Pawn.)

| 14 .... | N/Q4xN! | 15 PxN | N—B3 |

Black's exchange of Knights is hard to understand. For now White has acquired a new Queen Bishop Pawn all over again and his Queen Pawn is no longer isolated.

The explanation is that White's Queen Bishop Pawn is *backward on an open file*. It is subject to attack by Black pieces and can be defended only by pieces, not by Pawns.

16 P—QR4?!   Q—Q4!

Threatening mate on the move.

If White parries the mate threat by 17 P—KB4 or P—B3, Black has a powerful reply in 17 . . . P—N5!, again isolating the Queen Pawn and in some cases winning a Pawn.

17 N—B3   KR—B1!

Hitting at the weak Pawn—so that if 18 PxP, PxP; 19 BxNP, RxP. In that case Black again remains with pressure against the isolated Pawn, and the position of his forces is more aggressive.

White tries for something better, and ends up with something worse.

18 B—N2   ....

Black has reason to be gratified at this wretched posting of the enemy Bishop for purely protective reasons.

18 ....   N—K5!

White defends, Black attacks.

If now 19 BxN, QxB; 20 QxQ, BxQ and Black's Bishops have enormous scope while White's positional weakness persists.

Furthermore, Black is well satisfied with the possibilities in 19 PxP, PxP; 20 BxP, NxQBP; 21 BxN, RxB; for then he again has the two-Bishop advantage plus pressure on White's isolated Pawn.

Even more desirable for Black is 19 PxP, PxP; 20 BxN, QxB; 21 QxP, B—R3 winning the Exchange.

19 R—B1   ....

As we have seen from the previous note, Black has forced his opponent to make another unattractive defensive move.

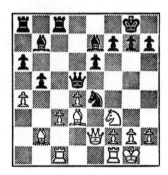

15

Black now establishes a winning advantage.

19 ....   N—N4!

This Knight cannot be captured because of Black's mate threat along the diagonal. And 20 N—K1, N—R6ch; 21 K—R1, N—B5 leaves Black with a positionally won game.

20 PxP	PxP	22 PxN	Q—N4ch!
21 BxNP	NxNch	Resigns	

258

For after 23 K—R1, Black has 23 . . . Q—N5! when White will have to give up his Queen to stop mate.

Black did a very effective job in stamping White's Pawns as weaknesses and in refuting White's attempts to obtain an attacking position.

In the first three games of this chapter we saw how Black lashed out at weaknesses in the White King's position; in the last two games Black succeeded by hammering away at White's positional weaknesses.

But suppose White has no weakness? How do you proceed? The next chapter deals with this problem.

Chapter Two

HOW TO SEIZE THE INITIATIVE

IF YOU ACCEPT the view that White has some initiative by reason of his first move, you will doubtless agree that in actual practice White often loses that initiative with great rapidity.

And, furthermore, if you realize just what is happening, you will be in a position to snatch up White's lost initiative and become the aggressor.

Now, assuming that White does not lose material and does not create weaknesses, just what should Black look for in order to seize the initiative?

There are several ways White can go wrong. He may, for example, play an opening so poor that his theoretical advantage disappears at once. This gives Black his chance.

Or White may play an excellent opening and then ruin his development by a series of foolish, time-wasting Queen moves. Here again Black must be alert to the possibilities.

If Black discovers that White is wasting valuable time chasing a relatively unimportant Pawn, he can use the opportunity to get far ahead in development.

Sometimes White may avoid the sin of greed only to succumb to another fault—bad judgment. Sheer thoughtlessness, inattention, negligence, or happy-go-lucky innocence of a positional trap may ruin White's development. In every case Black should be alert to seize the initiative.

So you see there are many ways for White to go wrong,

260

and it pays Black to keep a sharp lookout for such cases of poor judgment. Now let's see some examples of the kinds of mistakes White may make.

Lost initiative from a poor opening

In this game Black gives us a classic example of slashing attacking play. His play is magnificent, and yet—it all stems from White's faulty opening. Black immediately pounces on the opportunities offered by White's faulty play.

IRREGULAR OPENING

WHITE	BLACK	WHITE	BLACK
1 P—QN4	P—K3	2 B—N2	N—KB3

Even at this early stage we can see the faulty character of White's first move. Black is attacking, White is defending! Black's development will proceed rapidly, while White's will be laborious.

3 P—QR3	P—B4	4 P—N5	P—Q4

Black's Pawns already have a substantial foothold on the center, while White has no Pawns in the center at all. His attempt to improve the situation leads to disaster.

		5 P—Q4?	....

Plausible but weak, as Black promptly proves.

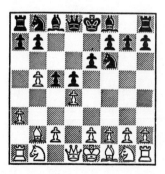

16

Black now seizes the initiative.

5 ....   Q—R4ch!

This forceful move starts a chain reaction. It forces White to play N—QB3 in order to protect his unfortunate Queen Knight Pawn. Then, to protect this Knight, White is forced to develop his Queen in a risky manner. These factors give Black his chance for a brilliant attack.

6 N—QB3	N—K5		8 QxP	B—B4!
7 Q—Q3	PxP		9 QxNP	BxPch

Black's brisk attacking play has shunted White's Queen far from the scene of action and has deprived White's King of the castling privilege. Even at this early stage White's position is shattered.

10 K—Q1   ....

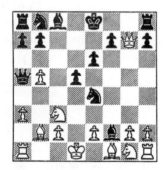

17

How does Black guard his menaced Rook?

10 ....   P—Q5!!

Black ignores the attack on his Rook because he has decided on an all-out attack on the White King. Note, by the way, that 11 NxN? allows 11 . . . Q—K8 mate!

11 QxRch	K—K2!		12 QxB	PxN

In the event of 13 BxP Black intends 13 . . . NxBch; 14 K—Q2, N—K5 dbl ch; 15 K—Q3, Q—Q7ch; 16 KxN, Q—K6 mate.

13 B—B1   N—Q2!!

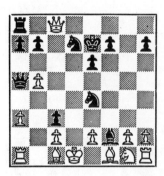

18

Black offers another Rook!

Black has calculated the play very closely. Thus if now 14 Q—B4, R—Q1; 15 Q—N4ch, QN—B4 dis ch!; 16 B—Q2, RxBch; 17 K—B1, R—Q8ch!!; 18 KxR, Q—Q1ch followed by mate.

What now follows is a foregone conclusion, despite White's enormous material advantage. With four powerful attacking pieces at his disposal, Black engineers a sparkling mating attack.

14 QxR   QxNP   16 K—B1   B—K6ch!!
15 B—B4   Q—Q4ch   17 BxB   N—B7!!

White resigns, for after 18 BxN Black replies 18 . . . Q—Q7ch forcing mate in two more moves.

Black has forcefully punished White for losing the initiative by choosing an inferior opening line.

Lost initiative from too many Queen moves

In the next game White starts out with an excellent opening; but then, animated by some perverse suicidal impulse, he lets his Queen drift out of play. Black develops rapidly and forcefully, sacrifices both Rooks, and wins handsomely.

NIMZOINDIAN DEFENSE

WHITE	BLACK		WHITE	BLACK
1 P—Q4	N—KB3		5 PxP	N—R3
2 P—QB4	P—K3		6 P—QR3	BxNch
3 N—QB3	B—N5		7 QxB	NxP
4 Q—B2	P—B4		8 B—N5	P—QR4

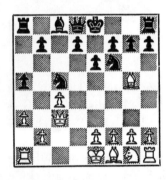

19

A typical situation in the Nimzoindian Defense.

This position is typical of the opening because Black has developed rapidly but has had to give up one of his Bishops in the process.

White should now play 9 P—B3, P—R5; 10 P—K4, P—Q3 leading to a position with chances for both sides. Instead, his weak play enables Black to seize the initiative.

9 Q—K5?	P—Q3		11 Q—B4?	P—K4
10 BxN	PxB		12 Q—R6	Q—N3!

Black has gained two moves for developing his Bishop and

264

has also brought his Queen into active play. White belatedly returns to rational moves, but as Black demonstrates, it is already too late for that.

13 R—N1	B—B4!!	15 QxRch	Q—K2
14 QxBP	BxR	16 QxR	....

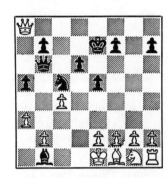

20

Black has a mating attack.

This is the position Black has played for: White's Queen is far afield, and his other pieces are still on their home squares.

16 ....   N—K5!

Threatens mate in two.

17 P—K3   QxNP

Threatening mate on the move.

18 QxRP   QxBPch

White resigns, for if 19 K—Q1, QxBch; 20 Q—K1, Q—Q6ch and mate next move. Black has played with superb energy to exploit White's nerveless loss of the initiative.

Lost initiative from greedy play

In the next game, also, White plays the opening not too badly but Black maneuvers ingeniously to obtain the advantage when White becomes greedy.

FRENCH DEFENSE

WHITE	BLACK	WHITE	BLACK
1 P—K4	P—K3	5 B—Q3	B—Q3
2 P—Q4	P—Q4	6 Castles	Castles
3 PxP	PxP	7 N—B3	N—B3
4 N—KB3	N—KB3	8 B—KN5	. . . .

White has already forfeited part of his initiative by playing 3 PxP and thereby opening the diagonal of Black's imprisoned Queen Bishop. Nevertheless, Black is still under some pressure, mainly because his King Knight is pinned and his Queen Pawn is under attack.

21

How is Black to defend his Queen Pawn?

Black's daring conclusion is that he need not defend his Queen Pawn altogether!* Therefore he plays:

---

* In *Third Book of Chess* (page 59) Black played the timid 8 . . . N—K2?; 9 BxN, PxB; 10 N—KR4! and was roundly trounced a few moves later.

266

8 .... B—KN5!

The first point of Black's play is that if 9 NxP, BxPch;
10 KxB, QxN and he has recovered the Pawn with a good
game.

9 BxN   QxB!   10 NxP   Q—R3!

Now Black threatens 11 . . . BxN and 12 . . . QxP mate.
Nor can White defend with 11 P—KN3?, for then 11 . . .
Q—R4! wins.

True, White can play 11 Q—B1, but after 11 . . . QxQ;
12 QRxQ, BxN; 13 PxB, NxP Black has regained his Pawn
and has a very promising endgame. White therefore selects
what *seems* to be the least evil:

11 P—KR3   ....

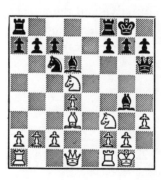

22

Black has seized the initiative.

11 ....   NxP!

Black offers a piece that cannot be accepted, for if 12
PxB???, NxNch; 13 QxN, Q—R7 mate.

12 B—K2   NxNch   13 BxN   BxP!

267

Black, who gave up a Pawn a few moves ago, is now actually a Pawn ahead. White cannot play 14 PxB because of 14 . . . QxP; 15 R—K1, B—R7ch; 16 K—R1, B—N6 dis ch; 17 K—N1, Q—R7ch and mate next move.

14 R—K1	B—K3	16 Q—K2	BxN
15 P—KN3	QR—Q1	17 BxB	BxP!

A neat thrust. If 18 PxB, RxB with a second Pawn to the good.

18 B—K4	R—Q7	19 QxR	B—R7ch!

White resigns, for if 20 K—N2, QxQ; 21 KxB, QxKBPch with a tremendous advantage in material for Black.

Lost initiative from blocked development

It was fascinating to see how cleverly Black snatched the initiative and the attack in this bright little game. In the next game all is tranquil throughout, but the game is if anything even more instructive.

FOUR KNIGHTS' GAME

WHITE	BLACK	WHITE	BLACK
1 P—K4	P—K4	4 B—N5	B—N5
2 N—KB3	N—QB3	5 Castles	Castles
3 N—B3	N—B3	6 BxN	. . . .

In a game in *Third Book of Chess* (page 72) Black played 6 . . . NPxB? This led to lasting difficulties for him because of the Queen Bishop's inability to develop. Here Black recaptures with his Queen Pawn, making it possible for the Bishop to develop effectively.

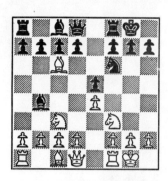

23

How should Black retake?

6	QPxB!	8 B—N5	P—KR3
7 P—Q3	B—Q3	9 B—R4	P—B4!

24

Black has set a subtle trap.

Black's last move not only prevents P—Q4; it also sets a trap into which White falls headlong.

10 N—Q5?	P—KN4!	11 NxNch	....

Likewise after 11 B—N3, NxN; 12 PxN, B—N5 Black has all the play.

11	QxN	14 QxB	QxQ
12 B—N3	B—N5!	15 PxQ	P—KB3
13 P—KR3	BxN	16 K—N2	....

269

The result of Black's positional trap is that he is in effect a piece to the good. White's Bishop is a dead piece, and can play no effective role in the game.

| 16 .... | P—QR4 | 18 R—R1 | K—K3 |
| 17 P—QR4 | K—B2 | 19 P—R4 | KR—QN1 |

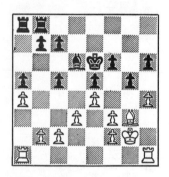

25

Black is a piece ahead!

Black's strategy is delightfully simple. He plays to open a file on the Queen-side, by advancing . . . P—N4 and . . . P—B5. Then his "extra" piece is bound to win for him.

| 20 PxP | RPxP | 22 R—QR2 | P—N4 |
| 21 P—N3 | P—B3 | 23 KR—R1 | P—B5 |

If now 24 NPxP Black wins easily after 24 . . . PxBP; 25 PxP, R—N5 etc.

24 RPxP	PxP/N6	27 P—Q4	R—N4
25 BPxP	RxP	28 R—B4	R—N5
26 R—R4	RxP	29 RxBP	RxP

White resigns, as he is powerless against Black's "extra" piece. There is a great deal to be learned from the way Black seized the initiative by taking advantage of White's careless 10th move.

Lost initiative by an error of judgment

In the following game Black sees his opportunity to seize the initiative when White condemns his King Bishop to lasting inactivity. Then Black continues to exercise cumulative pressure on White's weakened position.

SICILIAN DEFENSE

WHITE	BLACK		WHITE	BLACK
1 P—K4	P—QB4		6 B—K2	P—K4
2 N—KB3	P—Q3		7 N—N3	B—K3
3 P—Q4	PxP		8 Castles	QN—Q2
4 NxP	N—KB3		9 P—B4	Q—B2
5 N—QB3	P—QR3		10 P—B5?	....

26

Black can now take the initiative.

With Pawns on the white squares King 4 and King Bishop 5, White has reduced the mobility of his King Bishop to an alarming extent. If this piece is not "dead," it is certainly "half-dead." Another drawback to White's last move is that it releases pressure on the center, thereby enabling Black to react eventually with ... P—Q4!

10	B—B5		13 Q—K2	QR—B1
11 B—Q3	P—QN4!		14 QR—B1	Castles
12 B—K3	B—K2		15 N—Q2	P—Q4!

271

Declaration of independence. As in the previous game, White's colorless opening has been the first step in Black's seizure of the initiative.

True, Black permits White to get rid of the useless Bishop and cancel Black's pressure on the half-open Queen Bishop file. But Black exacts a heavy price: the opening of the Queen file for Black's forces.

16 BxB	QPxB	18 PxP	BxP
17 P—QR3	P—N5!	19 P—N4	....

A gesture toward attack on the King-side. But Black is well prepared for it. The permanent result is a weakness that Black will exploit later on.

19	BxN	23 K—R1	KR—Q1
20 PxB	Q—B3!	24 Q—K2	P—R3
21 Q—N2	N—B4!	25 R—R1	Q—Q3
22 BxN	QxBch	26 KR—Q1	....

27

Black is ready for the final blow.

26 ....   Q—B3!

Black threatens 27 . . . RxN!; 28 RxR, NxKP and wins because of the menace of a murderous discovered check.

272

If now 27 R—KN1, RxN!; 28 QxR, NxKP; 29 Q—N2, N—B7 mate. Or if 27 R—K1, NxNP! winning a Pawn.

| 27 K—N2 | R—Q3! | | 29 K—B3 | Q—Q2! |
| 28 P—R3 | QR—Q1! | | 30 K—K3 | .... |

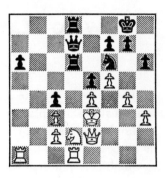

28

How does Black add the last bit of pressure that topples White's position?

White has rushed in his King to the center to bolster his position. But Black's mighty pin on the Queen file leaves White helpless while the Black Knight makes a lengthy trip to Queen Knight 4.

| 30 .... | N—K1! | | 32 RxKP | N—N4! |
| 31 R—R5 | N—B2! | | 33 R—Q5 | .... |

Losing the Exchange by 33 RxN is even worse.

| 33 .... | RxR | | 35 Q—B3 | NxRch |
| 34 PxR | NxP | | Resigns | |

White has no compensation for the loss of the Exchange. Having seized the initiative at an early stage, Black made admirable use of it thereafter.

Thus, in all the games in this chapter, we have seen the various ways that Black can seize the initiative in consequence of faulty play by White.

Chapter Three

HOW TO PLAY AGAINST GAMBITS

TO KNOW how to refute a gambit is one of the most important qualifications for playing the Black pieces skillfully.

Gambits are among the most critical tests that confront you as a chessplayer.

Gambits are those openings in which Black quickly receives some material "on spec" because White hopes to bewilder or terrify him.

Some players, when they meet a gambit, put up only token resistance. Others fight back sturdily. What produces defeat in one case, and victory in another?

To succeed against a gambit, you must keep two valuable principles in mind:

(1) In a gambit, the *initiative* is much more important than material advantage. Aim cold-bloodedly and consistently for the initiative.

(2) Remember this: You can use the material advantage you have received as an excellent means of seizing the initiative. Very often the best use you can make of this material advantage is *to give back the extra material* to your opponent!

Why? Because your opponent needs a move or two to pick up the sacrificed material. If you are alert, you can make use of that time to further your development, your plans, your attack. In short, watch for a chance to seize the initiative!

274

Psychological warfare

You can learn a great deal from the way Black handles this game. He produces a finish which is among the most artistic ever seen in a game of chess. That alone is a broad hint that he seized the initiative at a fairly early stage.

But what is even more important is the mood in which he plays a gambit. "I'm not afraid of your gambit," he seems to tell White, "and at the same time I don't intend to put myself to a lot of trouble holding on to the Pawn. In fact, you can have it back any time you please—it's a matter of indifference to me.

"To force my pieces into a twisted, cramped position for the sake of holding onto a Pawn—that's not for me! I want to draw the sting out of your gambit and play the game *my* way.

"If you want to exchange. pieces, O.K. If you want to exchange Queens, that's O.K. And if you want to get a bad game by sticking stubbornly to your so-called 'gambit attack,' that's surely O.K."

BISHOP'S OPENING

WHITE	BLACK	WHITE	BLACK
1 P—K4	P—K4	4 P—QB3	B—B4
2 B—B4	B—B4	5 P—Q4	PxP
3 P—QN4	BxNP	6 PxP	B—N5ch!

29

Black plays to exchange pieces and ease his defensive problems.

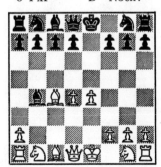

275

Black has little to fear from White's gambit, which aims at a powerful center and rapid development. By offering to exchange pieces Black hopes to save time.

Of course, White can avoid an exchange by 7 K—B1. But in that case he loses the castling privilege—surely a plus for Black.

7 K—B1?!	B—R4*	9 BxP	Q—K2
8 Q—R5	P—Q4!	10 B—R3	N—KB3!

A long-foreseen resource, without which things might be critical for Black.

Black well knows that 11 BxQ, NxQ; 12 B—R3 is now White's best course. But Black also knows that a gambit player never contents himself with such picayune lines. The aggressor dreams of the Grand Attack!

11 BxPch?	QxB	14 N—KB3	B—Q2
12 QxB	N—B3	15 QN—Q2	NxNch
13 Q—R4	NxKP	16 NxN	Castles(Q)

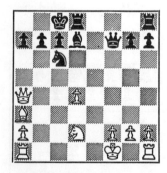

30

Black has a vastly superior position; he has smashed White's flimsy gambit attack.

---

* Black does not mind 8 BxPch, KxB; 9 Q—R5ch, P—KN3; 9 QxB, N—QB3 whereby Black gains plenty of time in exchange for the returned Pawn.

Black has a splendid development. His King is perfectly safe. White's forces are disorganized and he cannot castle his King into safety.

Black's play has been first class, psychologically as well as technically. With moves 6, 8 and 10 he has turned White's jaunty gambit into a miserable failure. From now on, Black has it all his own way.

| 17 QR—N1 | Q—Q4! | 19 R—Q1 | KR—K1! |
| 18 N—B3 | B—B4 | 20 B—B5 | .... |

Black's initiative is now so powerful that he can allow himself a beautiful Queen's sacrifice.

31

Black's Queen sacrifice will leave White defenseless.

| 20 .... | QxN!! | 22 K—N1 | R—K3 |
| 21 PxQ | B—R6ch | 23 Q—B2 | RxP! |

Another winning way is 23 . . . N—K4!

24 BxR   NxB

White resigns because after 25 Q—Q3 Black mates by 25 . . . R—N3ch etc. or by 25 . . . N—K7ch etc.

277

Aggressive counterattack

In the next game, too, the defender proclaims very quickly that he is not interested in defending. He captures the gambit Pawn on move 2, returns a Pawn on move 4.

Black's paradoxical theory is that White's gambit move 2 P—KB4 is precisely the move that is to give BLACK a powerful attack. And that is the way that Black executes his attack, helped by White's greediness.

To appreciate this game to the full, you must bear in mind that Black is a very powerful player, while White is comparatively weak. Consequently, Black is not impressed by his adversary's choice of an aggressive opening.

From the start, Black reveals his disrespect for his opponent. The cocky 4 . . . P—QN4! tells the story. It proclaims that Black is not interested in any measly gambit Pawns.

The mere moves of this game do not tell the whole story. Black plays energetically, joyously, aggressively: he is out to win. He has no trouble crashing through White's mediocre defense.

BISHOP'S GAMBIT

WHITE	BLACK	WHITE	BLACK
1 P—K4	P—K4	4 K—B1	P—QN4!?
2 P—KB4	PxP	5 BxNP	N—KB3
3 B—B4	Q—R5ch	6 N—QB3	. . . .

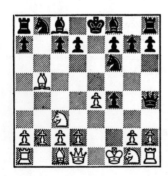

32

Black plays for a brisk attack against White's King, which has lost the castling privilege.

Black has already given notice that nothing less than monopolizing the attack will suit him. This has the psychological effect of scaring White out of the resourceful attitude he needs for coping with the attack.

6	N—N5	8 N—Q5	N—Q5!
7 N—R3	N—QB3	9 NxPch?*	....

Black's policy has succeeded. White is so confused that he misses his last chance of a proper defense.

| 9 .... | K—Q1 | 10 NxR | .... |

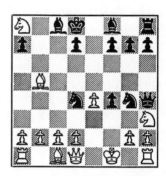

33

Black can win material or continue the attack. Which should he choose?

The simplest course for Black is 10 . . . NxB and in due course he will pick up the White Knight in the corner. This would give Black a winning material advantage, and most players would choose this safe and sane course. But Black reasons differently: he wants to win quickly and elegantly; and so he does.

| 10 .... | P—B6! | 11 P—Q3 | P—B3 |

---

* Here White misses his last chance to hold the game by 9 B—K2. Earlier, he had better moves in 6 N—KB3, driving off Black's Queen by attack, and in 7 or 8 Q—K1, disconcerting Black by offering the exchange of Queens.

Black's play here is an object-lesson for the student. His tenth move was a real battering ram, breaking up White's King-side formation no matter how White plays. Black realizes full well that White's inability to castle is an important asset for the Black attack.

Now, most are apt to get overconfident in such a situation. Not so Black. Though he is concentrating on a brilliant attack, he does not fail to provide against the threatened 12 B—N5ch winning his Queen.

12 B—QB4   P—Q4!   13 BxP   B—Q3!

Black is weaving a diabolical plot. With his sly twelfth move he opened the diagonal for his Queen Bishop. With his thirteenth move he got his other Bishop into the attack. Can you see why Black played these moves? If not, you will find them explained in the note to Black's sixteenth move.

14 Q—K1   PxPch   15 KxP   . . . .

34

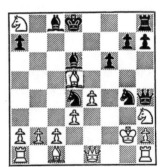

Black has set the stage for a very beautiful Queen sacrifice.

15 . . . .   QxNch!!

The move that Black has been angling for.

16 KxQ   N—K6 dis ch

Now we see that Black's twelfth move made this discovered check possible.

Note also that White's K—N3 is ruled out because of Black's thirteenth move.

17 K—R4   N—B6ch   18 K—R5 B—N5 mate

Black played with true artistry and wound up with a brilliant finish.

Here is how the game would have ended after 14 P—B3: 14 . . . PxPch; 15 KxP, QxNch!!; 16 KxQ, N—K6 dis ch; 17 K—R4. Now Black has to choose a different course from the one used in the actual game:

17 . . . N—N7ch; 18 K—R5, P—N3ch; 19 K—R6, B—B1 mate!

Parrying a surprise gambit

The following game is one that needs to be studied in terms of personalities. Black is a twelve-year-old youngster who grew up to become World Champion. His opponent is an experienced, mature player who hopes to outwit the boy by adopting a complicated gambit attack.

HAMPPE-ALLGAIER GAMBIT

WHITE	BLACK	WHITE	BLACK
1 P—K4	P—K4	5 P—KR4	P—N5
2 N—QB3	N—QB3	6 N—KN5?!	P—KR3
3 P—B4	PxP	7 NxP!?	KxN
4 N—B3	P—KN4		

Black's situation is one that might well trouble a sophisticated master. His King is exposed to attack and can never castle. True, he is a piece ahead, but White can pick up some Pawns in the following play, leaving him almost equal in material.

The real difficulty for Black is that he is likely to fall badly behind in development. Apparently White has done well in chooosing this tricky, complicated opening.

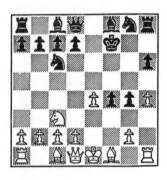

35

Black must evolve a resourceful plan.

8 P—Q4	P—Q4!	10 K—B2	P—N6ch
9 PxP	Q—K2ch!	11 K—N1	....

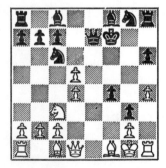

36

Black is about to spring a clever surprise.

A glance at Diagram 36 gives the impression that Black has virtually committed suicide. He has already lost two Pawns for the sacrificed piece, and after his attacked Knight moves he will lose a third and fourth Pawn. Worse yet, Black will be hopelessly behind in development.

282

11 . . . .   NxP!!

With this magnificent resource Black reveals that he understands very well how to free himself from an uncomfortable bind. The move is hard to see, if only because it leaves Black behind in material—though not for long.

12 QxN   Q—B4!!

Now we see the point of Black's sly countersacrifice: if 13 QxQ??, BxQch and mate next move!

13 N—K2	Q—N3!	14 QxQ	RPxQ

Black still threatens mate!

15 N—Q4	B—QB4	16 P—B3	R—R5

Black plays with remarkable ingenuity. He now threatens 17 . . . RxN!; 18 PxR, BxPch and mate follows.

If White tries 17 P—N4, then 17 . . . RxNP! smashes his defense.

Aside from these tactical details, Black has buried White's King Rook for the rest of the game.

17 B—K2	BxNch	19 P—N3	N—B3
18 PxB	RxQP	20 B—N2	R—Q7!

Of course not 20 . . . RxP?; 21 B—B4 and Black loses the Rook because of the pin.

In this situation White can avoid loss of a piece with 21 BxN, KxB; 22 B—B3. But then, with a Pawn down, he has no counterchances in the cut-and-dried endgame that would follow. So he tries a different way, but Black is ready for him.

| 21 B—R5ch | NxB! | 22 BxR | P—B6! |
| | 23 PxP | N—B5! | |

37

The concentrated attack of Black's pieces must be decisive.

If now 24 R—K1, Black has a lovely finish with 24 . . . B—R6!; 25 B—K5, R—KN7ch; 26 K—B1, R—KB7 dbl ch; 27 K—N1, R—B8 ch!; 28 RxR, N—K7 mate!

| 24 B—K5 | R—KN7ch | 26 K—K1 | N—Q6ch |
| 25 K—B1 | R—KB7ch | Resigns | |

Black wins the Bishop, leaving White in a hopeless situation.

A fascinating game because of the way that Black spiked the unfamiliar gambit attack and seized the initiative. (The Black pieces were played by José Raoul Capablanca.)

Diverting the gambit attack

Though artless greed proves White's undoing in this game, Black deserves lots of credit for leading him astray. On move 3 Black is offered material, which he respectfully declines. Then, only two moves later, *he* is offering material!

Soon Black has a surprisingly powerful initiative which results in a convincing win. Above all, note how he refuses to be appeased by material gain, and always searches for the most incisive move.

284

VIENNA GAME

WHITE	BLACK
1 P—K4	P—K4
2 N—QB3	N—KB3
3 P—B4	P—Q4

WHITE	BLACK
4 BPxP	NxP
5 Q—B3	N—QB3!

38

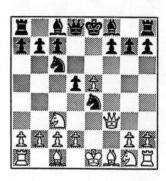

Black's last move reveals his intentions to counterattack.

Black plays boldly for counterattack, instead of being concerned about his doubly attacked Knight at the K5 square.

Black knows, to be sure, that 6 B—N5 is White's best reply—but he hopes that White will play 6 NxN? expecting 6 . . . NxP?? when 7 Q—KN3! wins a piece!

6 NxN?	N—Q5!	7 Q—B4	PxN

If now 8 QxKP??, B—KB4 when Black wins.

8 B—B4	B—KB4	9 P—B3!?	P—KN4!

Black is too crafty to snap at 9 . . . N—B7ch; 10 K—Q1, NxR; 11 QxB. For in that case White threatens mate, with plenty of time to pick up the wandering Black Knight afterwards.

In the event of 10 Q—B1 (in reply to Black's last move),

Black has the delightful line 10 . . . N—B7ch; 11 K—Q1???, N—K6ch winning White's Queen.

10 BxPch   KxB   11 Q—B2   . . . .

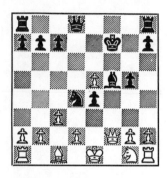

39

Should Black play to win more material?

Again Black has the tempting . . . N—B7ch within his reach. But after 12 K—Q1, NxR; 13 QxBch, K—N2 he is bound to lose his wandering Knight and his King is somewhat exposed.

So, Black correctly reasons, he is not going to part with his initiative for such a doubtful gain. Instead, he hits hard with:

11 . . . .   P—K6!!

The first point of Black's sly idea is this: 12 QxP???, N—B7ch winning White's Queen!

Another fine point of Black's plan is that though he must apparently lose a piece when his Knight moves, he manages to hold on to his material advantage.

12 Q—B1   PxPch!

Black continues to find the strongest moves. If now 13

286

BxP, Black replies now 13 . . . N—B7ch with a decisive gain of material—even a mate in some cases.

| 13 K—Q1 | PxB/Qch | 14 KxQ | P—N5! |

Black would not mind 15 PxN, for then he could force mate by 15 . . . B—R3ch; 16 K—Q1, QxPch etc.

| 15 P—N4 | Q—N4ch | 16 K—Q1 | R—Q1! |

White resigns in this hopeless situation, 17 PxN, RxPch being obviously disastrous for him.

Black's brisk counterattack made mincemeat out of White's slovenly set-up.

Neutralizing White's initiative

In this game, as in the previous one, Black's initiative is the deciding factor. But the mechanics of victory are different. In the previous game Black tempted White to succumb to fatal greed; while in this game White fails because he loses time in the opening.

Note, too, that Black's play here is just as consistent, just as grimly efficient, as in the previous game. But instead of spectacular play we have here Black's smooth, logical, irresistible piling up of pressure that leaves White helpless.

FALKBEER COUNTER GAMBIT

WHITE	BLACK	WHITE	BLACK
1 P—K4	P—K4	5 N—Q2	PxP
2 P—KB4	P—Q4	6 BxP	NxP
3 KPxP	P—K5	7 N—K4	N—N5!
4 P—Q3	N—KB3	8 B—N5ch	P—QB3!

Black's shrewd thrust at move 7 has given him the initiative, which cannot be taken away from him even by the simplifying exchange of Queens.

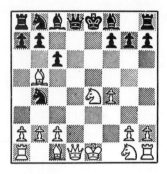

40

Despite the coming exchange of Queens, Black already has his opponent on the defensive.

White's game is already in need of vitamins. Certainly there is no chance for the dashing kind of play White seeks when he plays a gambit.

9 QxQch	KxQ	12 K—Q1	P—B3
10 B—R4	B—KB4	13 N/N5—B3	N/N1—R3!
11 N—N5	K—K1		

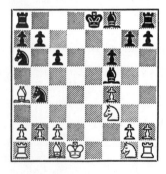

41

Black's position gathers power from move to move.

Thanks to Black's forceful play, White's original lead in development has evaporated and his pieces are awkwardly placed.

With skillful change of pace Black has alternated between

288

attacking and developing moves. He is now ready for . . .
N—B4 and also . . . R—Q1ch. These moves will increase his
positional advantage.

14 P—QR3	R—Q1ch	17 B—N3	NxB
15 B—Q2	N—Q4	18 PxN	B—Q3
16 K—K2	N—B4		

Black keeps hammering away at White's game. Now that
Black has two Bishops against Bishop and Knight, he pro-
ceeds to use the Bishops to press down all the harder on
White's position.

| 19 P—N3 | K—B2 | 21 K—B2 | B—N3ch |
| 20 R—QB1 | B—B2 | 22 K—N2 | KR—K1 |

42

*Note how Black's Bishops have be-
come stronger.*

Black has all his pieces in magnificent play and continues
to pile on the pressure relentlessly. White, on the other
hand, is still unable to develop his King Knight and King
Rook at this late date.

Now Black continues in the same forceful style to wind
up with a crushing finish.

23 P—R3	N—K6ch		26 B—B3	N—Q8
24 K—R2	R—Q6		27 P—N4	B—K5
25 P—QN4	R/K1—Q1		28 N—K1	....

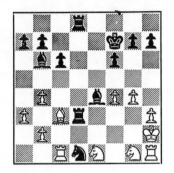

43

Black must come out at least a piece ahead.

28 ....   R—Q7ch!
Resigns

After 29 BxR, RxBch Black wins pretty much as he pleases.

The moral we derive from all these games is that in gambits, the initiative matters most of all. What we have seen in this chapter is that Black is most likely to succeed when he spots the factors that will give him the initiative; when he fights consistently for these advantages; and when he hits hard, once he has achieved those advantages.

These are the ways in which Black successfully hammers away at gambits.

290

Chapter Four

HOW TO DEFEND AGAINST A
POWERFUL ATTACK

A FAMOUS English philosopher once wrote, "He is happy whose circumstances suit his temper; but he is more excellent who can suit his temper to any circumstance."

So it is with chessplayers. They love the attack above all; they want to attack at all times, and at all costs. But this kind of chess is akin to an exclusive diet of nesselrode pie.

Chess positions are of all kinds, and we cannot always choose what kind of game we are going to have. If we dislike certain types of positions, our gleeful opponents will be sure to inflict them on us.

Defensive ability is an important quality in chessplayers, and one that will give satisfaction and win many points. Besides, though some of us may flinch from defensive tasks, we really have the determination and perseverance to fight through to victory in a defensive position.

Of course, at some point or other a well-conducted defense must take the form of dynamic counterattack, or even outright attack. This is the reward and even the duty of good defensive play. The following examples show you how it's done.

Maneuvering in a crowded position

Crowded positions are undesirable because your pieces cannot operate to the best advantage. A great master was fond of saying that "crowded positions carry within themselves the germ of defeat." By this he meant that a player afflicted with a cramped position would gradually be pushed to the wall.

The best way to handle a crowded position is to avoid it. But all the best principles and maxims in the world cannot save us from sometimes getting into unfavorable or difficult situations.

If your pieces are in a crowded position, you must always be on the lookout for opportunities to free yourself. This is easier said than done, for you may look and look for many moves, while the opportunity for freedom may come at only one point and may be rather hidden at that.

Nevertheless the advice is valuable: *watch for a chance to free yourself*. To be aware of the difficulty and to be determined to solve it, is often half the battle. If you can figure out the freeing method in advance, that is a great help.

Here is a useful hint, illustrated in the following game: *the thrust for freedom will generally come in the center*.

OLD-INDIAN DEFENSE

WHITE	BLACK	WHITE	BLACK
1 P—Q4	N—KB3	5 P—K4	B—K2
2 P—QB4	P—Q3	6 B—Q3	Castles
3 N—KB3	QN—Q2	7 Castles	PxP!?
4 N—B3	P—K4	8 NxP	R—K1

Black "surrendered the center" on move 7. He now has no Pawn on his fourth rank, while White has two Pawns on *his* fourth rank.

The result is White's Pawns control more center squares

than Black's Pawns do. Black's pieces have less maneuvering space in the center than White's pieces do.

9	P—QN3	N—K4
10	B—B2	P—QR3
11	B—N2	B—Q2

12	P—KR3	B—KB1
13	P—B4	N—N3

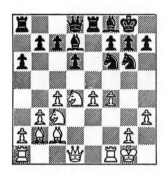

44

Black must now maneuver ingeniously in the center.

Black's position looks uncomfortably cramped, but he has his compensations. By attacking White's King Pawn, he limits White's freedom of action. Also, Black is well posted to prevent the aggressive advance P—K5.

But Black has other ideas. His main idea is to free himself some time later by . . . P—Q4. First he must play . . . P—B3 to make that move possible. Second, he must play . . . P—Q4 at a time when the powerful reply P—K5 is not feasible.

The later course of the game will show how Black carries out his idea.

14	Q—B3	P—B3!
15	QR—K1	P—N4!

16	Q—Q3	Q—B2
17	K—R1	....

Black's judgment has been vindicated. White's development looks very impressive, but with P—K5 or P—KB5 ruled out, Black has little to fear.

(Why is P—KB5 ruled out? Because the move allows . . .
N—K4, giving one of the Black Knights a magnificent and
unassailable center post..)

17 . . . .   QR—Q1   18 B—N1   P—N5!

45

*Black is gradually freeing his posi-
tion.*

Black has made considerable progress. By driving off
White's Queen Knight, he brings himself an important step
nearer to playing . . . P—Q4. (White will now have one
piece less bearing down on the important Queen 5 square.)

Black has scored another point as well. By making White's
P—QN4 impossible, he is able to establish a Black Knight
at his Queen Bishop 4 square. From that point the Knight
will bear down strongly on the center.

19 N—Q1   B—B1!   21 N—B5   N—B4!
20 Q—KB3   N—Q2!   22 P—N4?   N—K3!

Alertly taking advantage of White's weakening 22nd move,
Black attacks the King Bishop Pawn and prepares for the
final freeing maneuver.

23 Q—N3   B—N2!   24 P—KR4   P—Q4!!

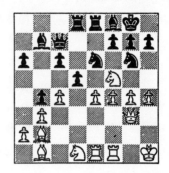

46

Black has freed his game!

At just the ideal moment, and with the maximum amount of impact, Black has freed his game.

Note that . . . P—Q4!! is very strong because it opens up the diagonal leading to White's King. Consequently this brings Black's cooped-up Bishop at the Queen Knight 2 square into powerful play.

Note, also, that Black gains time by playing . . . P—Q4!! since he is attacking White's King Bishop Pawn.

Note, finally, that White's reaction of P—K5 loses all impact because of Black's grip on the long diagonal.

25 P—K5	P—B4!	26 PxP	RxP

Now that the diagonal of his Bishop at Queen Knight 2 is fully open, Black threatens all sorts of brutal discovered checks, such as . . . RxN dis ch or . . . R—Q6 dis ch.

Black has arranged matters so cunningly that he can answer 27 B—K4 with 27 . . . RxN! and wins.

27 K—N1	R—Q7!	28 N/B5—K3	. . . .

Something had to be done about the threat of . . . R—N7ch. (In the event of 28 R—B2, Black has a winning reply in 28 . . . R/K1—Q1.)

But Black's next move (menacing . . . Q—R8 mate!) forces White's surrender.

| 28 .... | Q—B3 ! | 29 R—B3 | QxR |

White resigns. Black's skillful maneuvering in his crowded position was extremely impressive. He knew he had to free his game and he knew how to go about it.

Defense by counterattack

When you play the Black pieces, you are frequently called upon to make a sharp, accurate appraisal of what your opponent is aiming for.

We more or less take it for granted that White has the birthright of the attack, and that he is entitled to the initiative. However, there is no guarantee that White's judgment is always sound, and that his execution of the attack is always impeccable.

As player of the Black pieces, it is your job to assess the position; decide how much stress it can stand; coolly weigh the likely success or failure of White's efforts. If you conclude that the attack will be insufficient, you can look for counterattack.

Should you decide that White's efforts on the King-side are unlikely to succeed, you can counterattack on the other side of the board. Such Queen-side counterattacks are quite common. In the following game Black carries out this plan with commendable skill.

QUEEN'S GAMBIT DECLINED

WHITE	BLACK	WHITE	BLACK
1 P—Q4	P—Q4	5 P—K3	QN—Q2
2 P—QB4	P—K3	6 B—Q3	PxP
3 N—KB3	N—KB3	7 BxBP	P—QN4
4 N—B3	P—B3	8 B—Q3	P—QR3

Black's Queen Bishop is blocked by his Pawn at King 3. His last three moves have been directed toward opening a new, clear diagonal for the Bishop. Black needs one more move (. . . P—B4!) to achieve this objective.

9 N—K4*	P—B4!	11 NxQN	BxN
10 PxP?	NxP	12 Castles	B—N2

47

Black is ahead in development!

How did Black obtain his lead in development? He took advantage of White's faulty maneuver in moving his Queen Knight three times—only to exchange it off. White's 10th move was another time-waster, aiding Black's development.

White ought to take a very modest view of this situation. Instead, he strives for attack.

Is Black impressed? Not at all. With his lead in development and perfectly solid King-side position, he need not fear any coming attack.

13 P—QN3	Castles	15 R—B1	QR—B1
14 B—N2	Q—K2	16 Q—K2	B—R6!

---

* White's most forceful line is 9 P—K4, P—B4; 10 P—K5, PxP; 11 NxNP with a complicated game.

Black intends to concentrate on the Queen-side. By removing White's protective Queen Bishop he will be able to play . . . N—Q4 and . . . N—B6, planting the Knight with great effect in White's position.

| 17 KR—Q1 | N—Q4! | | 19 QxB | P—N5! |
| 18 B—N1 | BxB | | 20 Q—K5 | N—B6! |

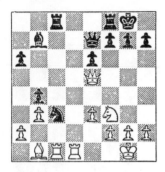

48

Black has achieved his objective on the Queen-side.

Black has a won game, for if now 21 R—Q2 or 21 R—K1, he plays 21 . . . N—K7ch! with decisive effect. White must therefore carry out the attack he has been plotting for some time.

| 21 RxN | PxR! | | 23 Q—R5ch | K—N1 |
| 22 BxPch | KxB | | 24 N—N5 | .... |

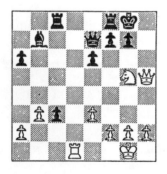

49

Black is threatened with mate on the move.

Black must do something about the threat of 25 Q—R7 mate.

24 ....   B—K5!!

This nonsensical-looking move is actually a brilliant resource that gains a priceless tempo. (After White's reply he will no longer threaten mate!)

25 NxB   P—B7   26 R—QB1 KR—Q1!

Black avoids a sly trap here: if 26 . . . Q—R6?; 27 N—B6ch!, PxN; 28 Q—N4ch and White forces a perpetual check!

27 P—KR3   ....

On 27 P—KR4 Black planned 27 . . . Q—R6; 28 N—N5, QxRch; 29 K—R2, R—B2 and White has nothing: 30 Q—R7ch, K—B1; 31 Q—R8ch, K—K2. Black is then safe, with an overwhelming material advantage.

(Black could win by the same line after the move actually played by White; but he prefers a different, prettier line.)

27 ....   P—B4   29 QxQ   R—Q8ch
28 N—N5   QxN!   30 K—R2   ....

Here we have the point of Black's Queen sacrifice. If 30 RxR, PxR/Qch and Black is a Rook ahead.

30 ....   RxR

White resigns. A masterly effort by Black. He appraised the situation correctly; this led him to start a Queen-side demonstration which soon showed up the futility of White's efforts.

Note that Black's Queen-side demonstration resulted in the passed Pawn which eventually won the game for Black!

Defending against a violent attack

Very often a chessplayer is called upon to defend himself against a violent attack. In the nature of things, Black is generally the player who has to do the defending.

For most of us, defense is an irksome chore. It requires lasting attention; it puts you under great strain; it gives you the double task of not only foreseeing your future defensive resources, but foreseeing your opponent's future attacking resources!

However, good defensive play is highly rewarding. So few players have mastered it that possessing this skill puts you ahead of your opponents. Good defensive play salvages many a game that is really lost or one that only looks lost.

Too many players forget that attack is only a part of chess, and that we cannot always have the kind of positions we like. If you have patience and faith in the resisting power of defensive positions, you will win many more games.

The following example shows what can be done to hold the fort against an attack which is persistent, forceful, and inventive.

BISHOP'S GAMBIT

WHITE	BLACK	WHITE	BLACK
1 P—K4	P—K4	5 N—QB3	Q—K2
2 P—KB4	PxP	6 P—Q4	N—B3
3 B—B4	N—K2	7 N—B3	Q—N5
4 Q—R5	N—N3	8 Q—Q5	N—Q1

As you can see, Black is very tenacious. He has captured the gambit Pawn on move 2, and he means to hold on to it no matter what difficulties may arise to plague him.

This type of defense against a gambit is not recommended in Chapter 3; but it is precisely this kind of stubbornness that will lead to a very cramped game for Black—the kind of position we want to study at this point.

| 9 P—QR3 | Q—K2 | 11 Q—KR5 | P—QB3 |
| 10 Castles | P—Q3 | 12 B—Q2 | .... |

50

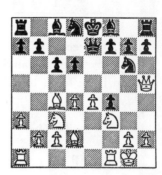

Black plans to castle on the Queen-side.

Black is far behind in development, and he must plan to get his King into safety before White finds some violent method to open up the center lines.

Black therefore gets the idea of preparing for Queen-side castling. However, White spoils this plan.

| 12 .... | N—K3 | 13 QR—K1! | Q—B2! |

Black realizes that his plan won't work: if 13 . . . B—Q2; 14 P—Q5!, N—B2; 15 PxP, PxP and his Queen-side is too exposed for castling there.

| 14 P—Q5 | N—Q1 | 15 P—K5 | .... |

(See diagram on top of next page)

51

Black's position looks lost!

It would seem that Black cannot defend his King against White's vigorous onslaught in the center. Most players would give up hope here, but Black has just begun to fight.

15	QPxP!	17 K—R1	Castles
16 NxP	B—B4ch!	18 PxP	....

The way Black saved himself from disaster by finding a way to castle, verges on the miraculous!

But he is by no means out of danger. For example, if now 18 . . . PxP?; 19 NxN, RPxN; 20 QxB and White has won a piece.

However, Black finds a magnificent counterstroke in this critical situation:

$$18 \ .... \qquad B—K6!!$$

Attacking White's undefended Bishop. If now 19 BxB (the natural reply), QxN! and no matter how White plays, he loses a piece! For example, 20 QxQ, NxQ and both White Bishops are attacked.

The consequence is that White decides to sacrifice a piece to keep the attack boiling at full force. True, Black's position is still full of hazard, but now White has to take chances too.

302

19 N—B3   BxB!

With this move Black gives his opponent an unpleasant choice. If now 20 NxB, PxP and White's attack has petered out ingloriously, with Black triumphantly clutching his extra (gambit) Pawn.

So, White decides to sacrifice a piece—a psychological victory for Black.

20 N—KN5!   P—KR3

The only reply to White's threat of mate on the move.

21 QxN   PxN   22 N—Q5!   ....

Attacking Black's Queen and also threatening 23 N—B6ch, K—R1; 24 Q—R7 mate. But even in this crisis Black finds a way out.

22 ....   QxP!

Black is not afraid of the following forking check!*

23 N—K7ch   K—R1

52

Black is still holding his own!

---

* Black can escape by 22 . . . PxQ; 23 NxQ dis ch, K—R2; 24 NxR, BxR; but he prefers to fight it out in the hardest variation.

Black's resourceful defense holds in every line.

Thus if 24 NxQ, PxQ and he remains a piece ahead.

Or 24 Q—R5ch, Q—KR3 with the same result.

Finally—and this was the crucial variation calculated by Black—if 24 BxP, NxB!; 25 NxQ, BxR; 26 N—K7!, B—Q7; 27 Q—R5ch, N—R3; 28 N—N6ch, K—N1; 29 NxR, KxN and Black's material advantage of three minor pieces against the Queen should win the game for him.

24 QxP/N5	Q—KR3!		25 Q—QB5	N—K3

Directed against the threat of 26 N—N6ch. White is still making attacking gestures, but Black has the game well in hand.

26 BxN	BxB		27 R—K5	B—K6!

White was threatening to win Black's Queen with R—R5. But now Black is ready to seize the attack.

53

Black has survived the storm of attacking threats.

28 Q—N5	P—KN3!		29 QxP	K—N2

Now the initiative is in Black's hands. He threatens 30 . . .
QxPch!!; 31 KxQ, R—R1ch and mate next move.

30 Q—B3	QR—Q1	33 QxQB	QxQ
31 P—R3	Q—R5	34 PxQ	R—R1ch
32 N—B6	B—N5!	35 R—KR5	PxR

White resigns.

This game, a masterpiece of superb defensive play, shows
what can be accomplished by tenacious and ingenious defense. Few games will ever call for such difficult maneuvering in the face of so powerful an attack.

The King as a fighting piece

The most important of all our defensive jobs is protecting
the King from harm. Though most players err on the side of
neglecting this task, they sometimes go to the other extreme
and become too cautious.

There are times when firmness and daring are called for
—times when routine caution is not good enough. In the
following extraordinary game, Black is well aware of the
need for bold handling of his King.

CARO-KANN DEFENSE

WHITE	BLACK	WHITE	BLACK
1 P—K4	P—QB3	5 B—KB4	N—B3
2 P—Q4	P—Q4	6 N—Q2	P—KN3
3 PxP	PxP	7 KN—B3	B—N2
4 P—QB3	N—QB3	8 P—KR3	N—K5

An adventurous move which leads to a very difficult game
for Black.

| 9 NxN | PxN | 10 N—Q2 | P—B4 |

The only practicable way to guard the King Pawn; but after White's reply Black will be unable to castle.

11 B—B4! ....

54

Black is unable to castle.

As the position now stands, Black cannot get his King into a safe position and he cannot post his Rooks for rapid action.

True, Black has a makeshift solution in 11 . . . P—K3, which makes castling possible. But then the Pawn at King 3 is a lasting weakness—always under attack by White's King Bishop. Worse yet, Black's Queen Bishop is then a permanent prisoner.

Black therefore comes to a courageous and highly unconventional decision:

11 .... P—K4!!   12 PxP NxP

This Knight has to be captured, as Black threatens . . . NxB or . . . N—Q6ch; with a fine game in either case.

13 BxN BxB   14 Q—N3 Q—N3!

Naturally Black offers the exchange of Queens, for then all danger to his King will vanish.

306

55

Black's King is ready to embark on a long tour.

15 B—N5ch	K—K2!	18 Castles(Q)	B—K3
16 N—B4	Q—B4	19 B—B4	BxB
17 NxB	QxN	20 QxB	KR—Q1!

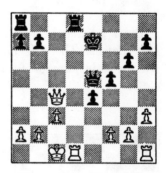

56

Black's King is about to advance fearlessly.

Black's last move is a daring one; his King is about to end up well in the opponent's camp. The brilliant originality of Black's plan is that he foresees that his King, paradoxically enough, will be quite safe.

21 Q—N4ch   K—B3!!

The only correct move. Black realizes that if his King goes to King Bishop 2, his Queen Knight Pawn is lost with check. If his King goes to King 1, White plays QxNP threatening QxKRP followed by QxNPch.

22 QxNP	Q—B5ch		23 K—N1	QxP

As a result of this capture, Black has a passed King Pawn which is ready to march down to the queening square as soon as the storm has passed. This means, in technical language, that White has a lost endgame in prospect unless he can win by attack. Consequently, the safety of Black's King is the key factor in the following play.

Black does not fear 24 QxKRP, for his King Knight Pawn is guarded, thanks to his 21st move. Furthermore, if 24 QxKRP, Black replies 24 . . . QxKNP, with *two connected passed Pawns*—an overwhelming positional advantage. So White tries a different way.

24 Q—B6ch	K—N4!		25 P—R4ch	K—N5!!

Black's King, as a fighting piece, heads for White's King-side Pawns. There is now a possibility that Black's King will be able later on to attack White's Pawns (. . . K—N6 etc.).

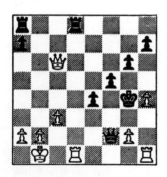

57

Black's King is attacking!

26 QR—KB1   Q—N3!

Offering the exchange of Queens; this is about the same

308

as inviting White to commit suicide. White's reply threatens 28 Q—K2ch and 29 R—R3 mate!

27 Q—B4   R—Q7!

Black parries the mating threat and menaces mate on his own. Black now wins easily by stepping up the pressure.

28 P—N4	Q—K6		31 R—B4ch	K—N6!
29 R—R3	Q—N3		32 Q—Q5	R—QB1
30 R/R3—B3	RxNP		33 Q—Q7	Q—R3

White resigns. (If 34 P—R4, Q—B5.) One of the most original games ever played, and one of the finest examples of cool, resourceful chess under very trying circumstances.

Recovery from a lost position

So far we have seen some very fine play by Black. In actual practice, of course, his play is not always very fine. Often, indeed, he plays badly and finds himself with a lost game. Yet he must not give up in despair after such poor play, for there is often a possibility of redeeming the most disastrous situations. And, as far as the score table is concerned, a botched game that is resourcefully salvaged is worth just as much as a masterpiece.

KING'S INDIAN DEFENSE

WHITE	BLACK		WHITE	BLACK
1 P—Q4	N—KB3		5 N—B3	Castles
2 P—QB4	P—KN3		6 B—K2	P—K4
3 N—QB3	B—N2		7 Castles	PxP
4 P—K4	P—Q3		8 NxP	R—K1

Black has exchanged Pawns early in order to provide a long, free diagonal for his fianchettoed Bishop. This exchange is questionable, however, as White's pieces obtain great freedom of action.

With his 10th move (. . . P—B3) Black weakens his Queen Pawn. His intentions, to be sure, are of the best: he wants to make room for the Queen so that he can assure communication between his Rooks.

9 P—B3	QN—Q2	12 B—K3	Q—B2
10 B—N5	P—B3	13 QR—B1	N—N3
11 Q—Q2	Q—N3	14 KR—Q1	KN—Q2

As we anticipated, Black finds his position cramped. He is not clear about what he wants or what he can achieve, and his maneuvering and regrouping is not getting him very far. His last move gives White the opportunity for a very promising attack.

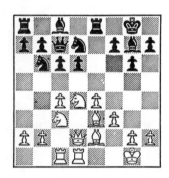

58

Black has overlooked White's combination.

15 N/Q4—N5! . . . .

This is the move that Black failed to foresee.

15 . . . . PxN 16 NxP Q—Q1

Black is on the run now.

17 NxQP N—K4

310

To retreat 17 . . . R—B1 allows White to recover his piece (with a Pawn plus) by 18 NxB, RxN; 19 P—B5 etc.

18 P—B5! N/N3—Q2   19 P—B6?   . . . .

The correct course—the one that Black feared—was 19 P—B4, N—QB3; 20 B—QB4. In that case Black has a Knight for two Pawns but he can hardly move a piece. This course would have been fatal for him.

In playing as he does, White seeks to regain the sacrificed piece. He succeeds—but only on Black's terms.

19 . . . .   NxQBP!

Black finds the best move.

Note that 19 . . . PxP?? would be ruinous after 20 NxR, QxN; 21 P—B4 etc.

20 NxB   RxN   21 QxN   . . . .

White has regained his piece, but now comes Black's stunning refutation.

59

How does Black save the game?

21 . . . .   B—Q5!!

A masterstroke. If 22 QxQ, BxB CHECK wins a piece for Black.

And if 22 BxB? White loses his Queen.

22 RxB	NxR

Now White's best is 23 QxQ, NxBch; 24 K—B2, KRxQ when Black will win nevertheless with the Exchange for a Pawn. However, White goes to pieces:

23 B—QN5?	RxRch	25 BxQ	R—Q1!
24 BxR	QxQ		Resigns

For after the Bishop leaves the Queen 7 square, Black wins the other Bishop by . . . N—K7ch.

Black's resilience in a very difficult situation is in striking contrast to White's tragic collapse.

The games in this chapter have highlighted the cold-blooded resourcefulness that Black must bring to difficult defensive situations. Such positions are very trying; but, by virtue of their very difficulty, they present a challenge that is worth meeting and worth surmounting.

Chapter Five

HOW TO SEIZE THE ATTACK

SO FAR WE have seen how Black defends, how he reacts
to gambits, how he seizes the initiative, how he counterattacks. Now we want to see situations in which a serious
flaw in White's game gives Black a chance for a slashing
all-out attack.

One word of warning: when playing the Black pieces, do
not embark lightly on an attacking policy. Note in each of
the following games that White compromises his game in
some fashion, while Black maintains an impeccable position.

Exploiting White's faulty development

VIENNA GAME

WHITE	BLACK		WHITE	BLACK
1 P—K4	P—K4		3 P—B4	P—Q4
2 N—QB3	N—KB3		4 BPxP	NxP

60

Black's Knight is splendidly cen-
tralized.

5 N—B3   N—QB3   6 B—Q3?   P—KB4

White cannot very well play BxN now, as he would lose further time—and his King Pawn as well. He therefore captures Black's King Bishop Pawn in passing. This returns Black's King Knight to the King Bishop 3 square. But meanwhile White's Queen Pawn cannot advance. The result: at the end of the game, White's Queen Bishop and Queen Rook are still on their original squares.

7 PxP e.p.   NxBP   8 Castles   B—B4ch

Development with gain of time. Note that White is unable to reply P—Q4.

9 K—R1   Castles   10 B—N5   N—KN5!

Threatening to win the Exchange by . . . N—B7ch.

If White tries 11 P—Q4, then 11 . . . NxQP; 12 NxN, RxRch; 13 QxR, BxN and Black is a Pawn ahead.

Thus Black wrests another concession from White: giving up his developed Bishop, White increases Black's lead in development and his attacking prospects.

11 BxN   PxB   12 P—Q4   B—Q3

Black's attack has become very powerful; he threatens to win the Exchange by . . . B—R3.

13 P—KR3   B—R3!!

61

Can Black afford to ignore the attack on his Knight?

314

14 PxN	BxR	15 QxB	RxN!!

With this sacrifice, Black establishes the soundness of his previous sacrifice. First point: if 16 PxR, Black has a quick mate with 16 . . . Q—R5ch etc.

Second point: if 16 QxR, Q—R5ch—and now if 17 Q—R3, Q—K8 mate. Or 17 K—N1, Q—K8ch; 18 Q—B1, B—R7ch winning White's Queen.

But the best is yet to come.

16 Q—K1	Q—R5ch!!	17 QxQ	R—B8 mate

Thus we see that Black's brilliant attack succeeded because White's Queen Bishop remained at home.

Exploiting White's neglected development

This game is a joy to play over because Black never misses a chance to find an energetic move. His play is forceful but not brash. White, on the other hand, dawdles. First he hits out aimlessly—and then strikes at the wrong target.

SCOTCH GAMBIT

WHITE	BLACK	WHITE	BLACK
1 P—K4	P—K4	3 P—Q4	PxP
2 N—KB3	N—QB3	4 B—QB4	N—B3

Ignoring the defense of his Queen Pawn, Black strikes at White's King Pawn.

5 P—K5	. . . .

White, too, intends to attack.

62

How does Black save his Knight?

$$5 \ldots \quad P—Q4!$$

Instead of defending, Black attacks!—and opens up the diagonal of his Queen Bishop at the same time.

6 B—QN5	N—K5	8 NxN	PxN
7 NxP	B—Q2	9 B—Q3	B—QB4

Black's obvious eagerness to attack is perfectly well grounded in the fact that he has two extra pieces in play.

$$10 \ BxN \qquad \ldots$$

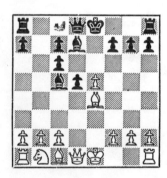

63

Should Black recapture?

$$10 \ldots \quad Q—R5!$$

The alternative 10 . . . PxB is quite satisfactory, but Black's Queen move brings still another piece into play—threatening mate, by the way.

11 Q—K2	PxB	12 B—K3	B—KN5!

Forcing a crisis, for if 13 Q—Q2 Black leaves his opponent without an adequate reply by playing 13 . . . R—Q1.

13 Q—B4	. . . .

Apparently crushing: if Black moves his attacked Bishop, the Queen fork 14 QxQBPch seems deadly.

13	BxB!

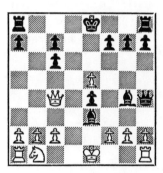

64

Black has started a crisp winning combination.

On 14 QxQBPch Black intends 14 . . . B—Q2!!; 15 QxRch, K—K2!!; 16 QxR and Black forces mate beginning with 16 . . . QxBPch.

Suppose, however, White interpolates 16 P—KN3 in this variation? Then Black wins with 16 . . . BxPch!; 17 KxB, P—K6ch! If now 18 KxP, Q—N4ch wins White's Queen, and if 18 K—N1, P—K7! decides.

Finally, if 18 K—K1, Q—QN5ch; 19 P—B3, QxNP; 20 QxR, B—N5! and Black forces mate.

| 14 P—KN3 | Q—Q1!! | 16 K—B2 | Q—B6ch |
| 15 PxB | Q—Q8ch | 17 K—N1 | .... |

On 17 K—K1 Black had 17 . . . QxKPch; 18 K—B1, B—R6 mate.

| 17 .... | B—R6! | 19 QxRch | K—K2 |
| 18 QxQBPch | K—B1 | Resigns | |

White's Queen is *en prise* and he cannot stop mate. Beautiful play by Black.

Exploiting White's faulty plan

Sometimes White gets a good development and then embarks on a faulty plan. It takes a sharp eye to see the flaw in White's procedure. In the following delightful game Black takes admirable advantage of White's shortcomings.

GIUOCO PIANO

WHITE	BLACK	WHITE	BLACK
1 P—K4	P—K4	3 B—B4	B—B4
2 N—KB3	N—QB3	4 P—B3	....

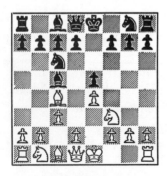

65

Black must decide on his policy in the center.

318

White intends to play P—Q4. Then, if Black exchanges Pawns, White gets a powerful Pawn center and an ideal development. Black therefore determines to avoid the exchange of Pawns.

4	P—Q3	9 R—K1	Castles
5 Castles	B—N3!	10 P—QN4	K—R1!
6 P—Q4	Q—K2	11 B—R3	N—KN1!
7 P—QR4	P—QR3	12 P—N5	N—R4!
8 P—R3	N—B3	13 NxP	....

Since . . . PxN??? would lose the Queen, Black seems to have blundered. How does he regain his Pawn?

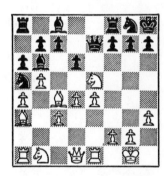

66

Black seizes the attack.

13 ....   P—KB3!

With this powerful reply Black completely turns the tables. If the attacked Knight moves, Black wins a piece. Thus he forces White's reply.

| 14 BxN | BPxN! | 15 B—R2 | KPxP |

If now 16 BPxP, Q—B3 is much in Black's favor.

16 N—Q2   BxP!

319

67

Black's surprise sacrifice is only the beginning.

On 17 PxB Black intends 17 . . . Q—N4ch; 18 K—B1, RxPch!!; 19 KxR, P—Q6 dis ch with a crushing attack.

| 17 N—B3 | B—N5 | 18 BPxP | PxP! |

For on 19 PxP Black continues 19 . . . BxN; 20 PxB, Q—N4ch; 21 K—B1, QxPch and is ahead in material.

19 Q—Q3	BxN	21 K—B1	N—B5!
20 PxB	Q—N4ch	22 B—B1	Q—R4
		23 PxP	RxP!!

68

Black has given his opponent another unpleasant surprise.

The point of Black's last sacrifice is that if 24 QxN, Black wins with 24 . . . R—KR6!

| 24 BxN | RxR! | 25 Q—Q1 | RxB! |

White resigns, for if QxR B1, R—KR6! wins.

320

OPENING MISTAKES BLACK
SHOULD AVOID

AS WE'VE pointed out earlier, an opening mistake on White's part may cost him the initiative; an opening mistake on Black's part may cost him the game. If Black plays well, White's advantage of the first move will be neutralized from the start; if Black plays badly, White's advantage will result in a quickly winning game.

The dangers of thoughtless development

In the following game Black begins with inexact moves and soon finds himself in a hopeless position:

WHITE	BLACK	WHITE	BLACK
1 P—Q4	P—Q4	2 N—KB3	N—QB3

A doubtful move, because Black needs to advance the Queen Bishop Pawn to free himself.

	3 P—B4	P—K3?	

Again he cramps his game voluntarily. 3 . . . B—N5 is more promising.

	4 N—B3	PxP?	

Now he surrenders the center. Eventually White will react powerfully with P—K4.

5 P—K3	N—B3	9 Q—B2	N—K2
6 BxP	B—N5	10 B—R3	P—B3
7 Castles	BxN?	11 P—K4	P—KR3?
8 PxB	Castles	12 QR—Q1	B—Q2

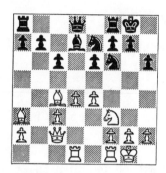

69

Black has played the opening very badly.

Black's thoughtless development has left him in a hopeless position. Blocking his Queen Bishop Pawn on move 2, he is now unable to play the freeing move . . . P—QB4.

Having hemmed in his Queen Bishop on move 3, he has condemned this piece to lasting uselessness.

By surrendering the center on move 4, Black gave his opponent a chance to build up a mighty center.

The exchange on move 7 created a magnificent diagonal for White's Queen Bishop.

On move 11 Black weakened his King-side, making it easier for White to conduct an attack against the Black King.

The dangers of ignoring the center

Having an adequate command of the center is a life-and-death matter for Black. What happens if he ignores the center is well illustrated in the following opening:

322

WHITE	BLACK		WHITE	BLACK
1 P—Q4	P—KN3?		2 P—K4	B—N2

Black's fianchetto of his King Bishop is premature. His poor timing has allowed White an overwhelming Pawn center.

3 N—QB3	P—Q3		5 B—QB4	P—K3?
4 N—B3	N—Q2?		6 Castles	N—K2?

70

The Black pieces have no striking power.

Any expert player would dismiss Black's position as lost.

White has complete control of the center, while Black has neither center Pawn on the fourth rank.

White's Knights are developed aggressively on the third rank; Black's Knights go timidly to the second rank.

Black's fianchettoed King Bishop accomplishes nothing, while his other Bishop is already destined to be a "problem child." White's Bishops, on the other hand, will have bold, free diagonals.

The dangers of a planless opening

Sometimes Black's positional blunders are not so gross, and therefore perhaps not so easily recognizable; yet the results are equally disastrous. In the following example, Black's hit-or-miss development ruins his prospects.

WHITE	BLACK		WHITE	BLACK
1 P—K4	P—QN3?		2 P—Q4	B—N2

Black has made the same kind of mistake as in the previous example.

3 B—Q3	P—K3		4 N—KR3	....

Usually it is not good play to develop a Knight *away* from the center. Here the move is good because it prepares for the line-opening advance of White's King Bishop Pawn.

4	P—Q4		5 P—K5!	....

Black has belatedly advanced in the center, but White's reply creates difficulties for Black: he can no longer play ... N—KB3.

5	N—K2		7 P—KB4!	B—K2
6 Castles	N—N3		8 P—B5!	....

Black has had to develop his King-side pieces ineffectually, and his Queen Bishop has no scope. His position offers no promise whatever, and he will soon be exposed to a violent attack by White's well-placed forces. Since Black's pieces are not very active, his chances of successful resistance are microscopic.

These three samples of poor play can therefore serve as horrible examples of what Black must avoid in the opening. He need not find the *ideal development* or the *very best moves*. But he does need moves that give him a fighting chance, a basis for planning, a hope that he will have something to say about how the game unfolds. If he can achieve these substantial goals, he can truly say that he knows how to play the Black pieces.

How
to Win
When
You're Ahead

Book Five

Chapter One

SUPERIOR FORCE SHOULD WIN!

THE BASIC PROPOSITION of this book is that you can win when you're ahead because, in chess, *superior force should win!* There may have been times in your own games when you have been ahead in material without being able to win. If that is the case, this book should help you greatly. Once you have *adequate* force, you must be able to win with it.

It is easy to see that when you're a Queen ahead, or a Rook, or even a Bishop or Knight ahead, the win is easy. In master games, when a player loses a piece the end is a foregone conclusion and he generally resigns.

But suppose you're "only" a Pawn ahead? To win a Pawn is much more common than to win a piece. And, as you will see, most master games are decided by an extra Pawn.

Most games of amateurs could likewise be decided by the advantage of a Pawn if—and this is a very big if— the ordinary chessplayer knew how to make use of his extra Pawn.

That is what most of this book is about—how to make use of a Pawn ahead. Here you will see how the Pawn becomes increasingly important as we come to the endgame stage. In the opening, when there are a great many pieces on the board, an extra Pawn may seem a trifling matter. But in the endgame, with perhaps only a King and Pawn left against a King, the extra Pawn looms very large indeed as it proceeds inexorably on its way to the queening square.

There, in a single sentence, you have the secret of the extra Pawn's power—its power to become a Queen on reaching the eighth rank. In this book you will have many examples of the Pawn's power. By studying these examples you will learn tò win many more games. You will learn to win when you're ahead.

The elements of Checkmate

The most basic examples of the use of superior force are the elementary checkmates:

> King and Queen vs. King
> King and Rook vs. King
> King and two Bishops vs. King
> King and Bishop and Knight vs. King

These checkmates are achieved on the open board. That is, no forces are present other than the units named.

Why are these checkmates important?

They represent the minimum force necessary for checkmate; but with such force it is possible to achieve checkmate no matter how the opponent plays. The player who is familiar with these checkmates can see that there is a purpose in chess. The player who is not familiar with these checkmates is necessarily at a loss in understanding how to bring a game to a satisfactory end.

Knowing these checkmates, then, is the first step toward playing decisive chess with a clear goal before you.

Checkmate with the Queen

(See diagram on top of next page)

1 K—B2	K—Q4	5 K—B4	K—N3
2 K—Q3	K—B4	6 Q—Q7	K—R3
3 Q—B6	K—Q4	7 K—B5	K—R4
4 Q—K7	K—B3	8 Q—R7 mate	

328

1

WHITE TO MOVE

White brings his King towards the center, cuts down the mobility of Black's King, and then drives him to the side of the board where the checkmate will take place.

Another standard checkmate position would have arisen if White had played 8 Q—N5 mate.

2

BLACK IS CHECKMATED

Starting from Diagram 1, the Black King had a great many alternative possibilities. However, the standard procedure, as outlined in the caption to Diagram 1, would have been exactly the same.

Checkmate with the Rook

Checkmate with the Rook is not quite so easy. This stands to reason, as the Queen has the combined powers of the Rook and Bishop.

3

WHITE TO MOVE

Again White brings his King to the center and then cuts down the Black King's mobility, forcing him to a side row.

329

1 K—N2	K—Q5	4 K—B4	K—K5
2 K—B2	K—K5	5 R—K1ch!	K—B4
3 K—B3	K—K4	6 K—Q4	K—B5

Note what happened at move 4: when the Kings face each other horizontally or vertically, a Rook check greatly limits the Black King's mobility. (White's next move will repeat the maneuver.) As a result, the Black King is now limited to three files.

7 R—B1ch!	K—N4	9 K—K5	K—N4
8 K—K4	K—N3	10 R—N1ch!	K—R4

Now Black's King is marooned at the side of the board. The end is nigh.

11 K—B4	K—R3	13 K—B6	K—R1
12 K—B5	K—R2	14 K—B7	K—R2

15 R—R1 mate

4

BLACK IS CHECKMATED

This Rook checkmate ended with the same type of position as the Queen checkmate in Diagram 2. There is one important difference, however: The extra power of the Queen gives it an alternative checkmate position. This is not true in the case of the Rook.

Checkmate with the two Bishops

Just as the Rook is weaker than the Queen, the Bishop or Knight is weaker than the Rook.

A single Bishop or a single Knight cannot enforce checkmate. In fact, even two Knights cannot enforce checkmate.

Two Bishops, however, can force checkmate. The process, though a bit lengthy, is fascinating because it gives us a glimpse of the power of the two Bishops on the open board.

330

5

WHITE TO MOVE

Unlike the Queen or the Rook, the two Bishops can give checkmate only on one of the four corner squares. The Black King is well situated here for a prolonged resistance.

1 B—K1	K—Q6	4 K—B3	K—B6
2 K—N2	K—K7	5 K—K4	K—B5
3 B—KB2	K—Q6	6 B—Q4	K—N5

6

WHITE TO MOVE

White has brought his King into action, and his next job is to drive the Black King to a side row. The process is slow but sure.

7 B—Q1	K—B5	10 B—QB5	K—R3
8 B—QB2	K—N5	11 K—B6	K—R4
9 K—Q5	K—N4	12 B—Q6	K—R3

7

WHITE TO MOVE

White has driven the Black King to the side. Note how powerfully the Bishops cooperate. The final phase is to drive the Black King to his King Rook 1 square, where he will be checkmated.

331

13 B—N4	K—R2	15 B—Q3ch	K—R2
14 K—B7	K—R3	16 B—B5ch	K—R1

17 B—K4 mate

8

BLACK IS CHECKMATED

White brought his King to the center, drove Black's King to the side, and was then ready for the kill. His smoothly cooperating Bishops finally checkmated the Black King on a corner square.

Checkmate with the Bishop and Knight

This mate is really difficult, and even experienced players have been embarrassed by the requirement of forcing the checkmate in 50 moves.

9

WHITE TO MOVE

To bring about this checkmate requires the highest degree of cooperation of the checkmating forces. The mate can only take place on a corner square of the same color as those on which the Bishop travels.

1 N—N3ch	K—B3	6 K—Q5	K—B2
2 K—N4	K—Q4	7 N—B5	K—B3
3 B—B3ch	K—Q3	8 N—Q6	K—N3
4 N—Q4	K—K4	9 K—K5	K—N2
5 K—B4	K—B3	10 B—K4	K—N1

10

WHITE TO MOVE

The hard-working White pieces have at last driven the Black King to the side. Next comes the task of forcing him to a white corner square—his Queen Rook 1. This requires patience!

11 K—B6	K—R1
12 N—B7ch	K—N1
13 B—B5	K—B1
14 B—R7	K—K1
15 N—K5	K—B1

16 N—Q7ch	K—K1
17 K—K6	K—Q1
18 K—Q6	K—K1
19 B—N6ch!	K—Q1
20 B—R5	K—B1

11

WHITE TO MOVE

White has accomplished the hardest part of his task. Yet, though the Black King is momentarily only two squares away from the corner, it will still take nine moves to finish the job.

21 N—B5	K—Q1
22 N—N7ch	K—B1
23 K—B6	K—N1
24 K—N6	K—B1

25 B—N4ch	K—N1
26 B—B5	K—R1
27 N—B5	K—N1
28 N—R6ch	K—R1

29 B—K4 mate

12

BLACK IS CHECKMATED

One of the best ways to get an insight into the powers of the pieces is to practice these checkmates alone or with a friend.

Why superior force should win

From these basic checkmates we learn, then, that there are certain material advantages which enable us to force checkmate.

However, an advantage in material has many other uses. Nor do we have to wait to remove almost all the pieces from the board in order to win the game.

For example: you have seen how to checkmate a lone King with your King and Queen. Now, suppose you have White in a game which starts like this:

1 P—K4	P—K4	4 Q—K2!	N—KB3??
2 N—KB3	N—KB3	5 N—B6 dis ch!	B—K2
3 NxP	NxP?	6 NxQ	KxN

You have won Black's Queen, and given up a mere Knight in return.

How will the game proceed from this point? The superior power of the Queen is bound to tell in your favor. Think of all the long-range swoops the Queen is famous for; all the double attacks; all the divergent checks.

Clearly you will be able to make all sorts of attacks that Black, *with his disadvantage in material,* won't be able to meet adequately. After all, there will be more power in your attacks than he can muster for defense.

334

In short: your initial material advantage will lead to greater material advantage.

You can also make use of your material advantage in another way. The more you swap down, the nearer you bring Black to that dread endgame stage where he cannot hope to escape checkmate. So, sometimes when you threaten to exchange, he will evade the transaction even if it costs him some material.

Of course, he may not be content to let you whittle down his forces more and more. Realizing the hopelessness and dreariness of his situation, he may resign—conceding that "superior force should win."

Now let's suppose you win a Rook early in the game. Here again, by threat of exchange or by overwhelming force, your material advantage will help you to win.

Suppose you win a Bishop or a Knight?

The picture is still the same, despite the fact that neither of these pieces can force checkmate. In the earlier part of the game they can exert their superior force for many purposes, such as winning Pawns.

Winning Pawns? Surely that means very little. Most players lose Pawns without a qualm. And of course it's absurd to think of a Pawn forcing checkmate.

Yet this attitude of contempt, widespread though it is, is based on a serious fallacy. Because the Pawn has the potential power of becoming a Queen through promotion at the eighth rank, the Pawn is actually of great value.

Among masters, the advantage of a Pawn habitually decides the fate of a game—*of championship tournaments and title matches*. To take one example, the great 34-game struggle between Alekhine and Capablanca in 1927 made Alekhine World Champion when he scored the decisive win through the advantage of a "mere" Pawn!

This same advantage would also be decisive in the games of lesser players, if only they knew how to make use of it.

It is the purpose of this volume to deal with this vitally practical problem. By learning how to win when you're ahead, you will greatly increase the number of your victories.

Before we turn to some of the important features of utilizing a material advantage, we need to be very clear about the value of each piece in relation to the others.

The relative values of the pieces

QUEEN .... 9 points
ROOK .... 5 points
BISHOP .... 3 points
KNIGHT .... 3 points
PAWN .... 1 point

For most readers this table of values will be in the nature of review, but let's dwell briefly on what it tells us.

The Queen is by far the strongest of the forces, not to be parted with unless you obtain heavy compensation.

Two Rooks, worth ten points, are somewhat stronger than the lone Queen.

Bishop and Knight, known as "minor pieces," are each valued at 3 points. You may therefore readily exchange a Bishop for a Knight, or a Knight for a Bishop.

A Rook is definitely worth more than a minor piece (5 points vs. 3 points).

A Rook is worth more than a minor piece plus a Pawn (4 points).

Two minor pieces (6 points) are worth more than a Rook (5 points).

To play chess well, it is absolutely essential to have a thorough grasp of the relative values of the forces.

Without this knowledge, you cannot even know whether you are ahead or behind in material. You are also at a loss, without this knowledge, when it comes to exchanging pieces. A player who does not know the values of the pieces has no way of knowing whether an exchange is desirable or not.

Again, a player who lacks this knowledge is greatly limited in his use of threats. To be able to threaten your opponent's forces, you need an exact notion of what you propose to capture and what you may be called upon to give up.

We have said that superior force should win, by and large. It should win most of the time, or generally. There are important reasons for using these limiting phrases so repetitiously.

The painful fact is that superior force does not *always* win. Why?

In the first place, there are certain rare theoretical positions—stalemate situations, for example—in which superior force does not win. As a rule, however, the player who has his wits about him can avoid such disappointments.

A second exception to the rule that superior force should win, lies in the possibility of sacrifices. These are brilliant moves that give up material purposely, with a view to obtaining adequate, or more than adequate, compensation.

Take the following position as an example:

13

WHITE TO MOVE

White plays 1 QxKPch!!, a beautiful move that forces 1 . . . PxQ. White has either sacrificed or blundered— which is it? The answer: 2 R—K6 mate! It was a sacrifice!

Diagram 13 is a fine example of a sacrifice. Ordinarily, when a player *loses* his Queen for a Pawn, we say the move is idiotic. When a player *gives up* his Queen for a Pawn—and knows what he is doing—we say he is inspired.

If you think about it carefully, you will see that sacrifices are not really an exception to the rule that superior force should win. Sacrifices aim at achieving (a) checkmate or (b) superiority in material. So, although they often shock us, there is indeed method in their seeming madness.

The third exception to the rule that superior force should win is a very sad one. A player with a material advantage *ought* to win. But if he blunders away his advantage, or doesn't know how to make use of it, or lets his opponent slip out of his difficulties, he may very well end up by not winning.

Later on we will pay some attention to the exceptions, just by way of precaution.

But first, let's study the techniques for *winning with superior force*.

Chapter Two

THE POWER OF PAWN PROMOTION

HAVE YOU ever stopped to think that the strongest move on the chessboard—aside from actual checkmate—is the successful queening of a Pawn?

To obtain a new Queen so cheaply is the equivalent of winning your opponent's Queen!

If we think of Pawn promotion in this way, we can understand why the advantage of a Pawn plays such a big role in the games of the masters, and why it should play just as important a part in our own games.

In the two following diagrams we see how Pawn promotion "makes all the difference":

14

WHITE TO MOVE

At this moment White is "hopelessly" behind in material. Without the possibility of queening, he could safely resign. However, he plays 1 P—K8/Qch.

15

BLACK TO MOVE

Black is in check from the new Queen. He must move his King out of check. When he does so,, White remorselessly continues 2 QxR, followed by checkmate.

339

Sometimes, it is true, the newly established Queen is immediately captured. But if there is a recapturing force at hand, the Pawn promotion still turns out to be highly profitable.

An example of material gain by Pawn promotion:

16

WHITE TO MOVE

White plays 1 P—B8/Q. As Black cannot afford to remain a Queen down, he plays 1 . . . RxQ. White of course replies 2 RxRch.

17

BLACK TO MOVE

Black has been able to get rid of the new Queen, but he has had to part with his Rook in the process. White has won a Rook!

The promotion of a Pawn is generally of decisive effect. Note, for example, how the newly created Queen took an active role in the position of Diagram 15. Diagrams 18 and 19 illustrate the same point.

18
WHITE TO MOVE

White plays 1 R—Q8. This is a very common maneuver with a Pawn that is already on the seventh rank, and you will find it very effective. The advanced White Rook blocks off Black's forces from the White Pawn.

19
BLACK TO MOVE

Black can resign. If he takes the White Rook, the passed Pawn recaptures, becoming a Queen. If Black refrains from capturing, the Pawn advances anyway, becomes a Queen, and is safe from recapture.

The all-important Pawn

We saw earlier that a Bishop or a Knight cannot force checkmate. If you are left with King and Knight (or King and Bishop) against a lone King, you cannot win.

But if the Bishop or Knight is assisted by only a single Pawn, then that Pawn, supported by the other forces, advances to the queening square.

20

WHITE TO MOVE

Without the lone White Pawn this position would be a draw. As matters stand, there follows 1 K—N4, K—K3; 2 KxP and then 3 KxP. The White Pawn will then advance to the eighth rank and become a Queen.

The examples in this chapter have shown the tremendous power of Pawn promotion.

However, we must not jump to the conclusion that Pawn promotion is easy to carry out or that it is appropriate in all parts of the game.

Pawn promotion is very rare in the opening, as it takes quite a few moves for a Pawn to reach the eighth rank. And, since there are a great many pieces on the board during the opening stage, the chances of the Pawn's reaching the last rank are slim indeed.

In the middle game the Pawn's promotion chances are somewhat brighter, but here too the game is complicated by various factors, such as attacking play against the King.

It is in the endgame stage, when the Queens have generally disappeared and when relatively few pieces are left on the board, that Pawn promotion begins to take the center of the stage.

It is in these rather simplified endgame positions, too, that the Kings can at last venture out to the center of the board, no longer terrified by the brutal attacking possibilities of the major pieces.

The new mobility of the Kings at this simplified stage reminds us that endings with only the Kings and Pawns on the board are the simplest kind of endings and therefore the logical ones to study first. So we now turn to them.

Chapter Three

KING AND PAWN ENDINGS

IN ONE SENSE, King and Pawn endings are very simple.

The material on the board has been greatly simplified. Only Kings and Pawns remain. Everything else has been swapped off.

However, King and Pawn endings abound in interesting finesses. In that sense, they are far from simple.

We need to be familiar with King and Pawn endings because some of them, as you will soon see, are of a standard form that is always a win.

This means that whenever you can manage to win a Pawn free and clear, you are in effect threatening to swap off all the pieces, reducing the game to a standard King and Pawn ending that is an almost automatic win for you! The threat of this simplification is a potent weapon in your handling of the game.

Passed Pawns

Most King and Pawn play revolves about passed Pawns—their creation and their advance to the queening square. (A passed Pawn is one that is not impeded by hostile Pawns on either of the neighboring files. In Diagrams 21 and 22, White has two passed Pawns.)

Some passed Pawns are especially powerful. We can see this in Diagrams 21 and 22.

21

CONNECTED PASSED PAWNS

White's passed Pawns are connected: they are placed on neighboring files. They are capable of protecting each other without their King's help.

Here is a typical line of play which wins for White in Diagram 21:

$$1 \text{ P—N6} \qquad \text{K—B3}$$

If 1 . . . KxP; 2 P—N7 and the Pawn cannot be prevented from queening.

2 K—B4	K—K2	5 P—B7ch	K—B1
3 K—K5	K—B1	6 K—K6	K—N2
4 P—B6	K—N1	7 K—K7	. . . .

White's King guards the queening square, so that he can now continue with 8 P—B8/Qch with a quick mate in the offing.

22

REMOTE PASSED PAWNS

Here White's Pawns are said to be "remote passed Pawns" or "distant passed Pawns." We use this term because they are too far away from the Black King to be caught by him as they advance to queen.

344

In Diagram 22 White's remote passed Pawns are so power-ful that White can queen a Pawn without the help of his King. This is how he does it:

1 P—N6   ....

(White can also start the same process with 1 P—B6.)

1 ....   K—B3

For the moment the Black King can still catch either Pawn in time.

2 P—B6   K—K3

Else the Bishop Pawn marches through to promotion.

3 P—B7   K—Q2   4 P—N7   ....

Now it is too late for the Black King to catch the Knight Pawn, which will become a Queen on the next move.

23

WHITE TO MOVE

White's remote passed Pawn wins for him without the aid of his King.

In Diagram 23 the play is:

1 P—R4!   K—N2   3 P—R6   K—K2
2 P—R5   K—B2   4 P—R7   K—Q2

And now White plays 5 P—R8/Q and will soon force checkmate. Thus we see from these examples the enormous power of the remote passed Pawn.

Now we come to a basic concept in chess known as the "Opposition." See Diagram 24.

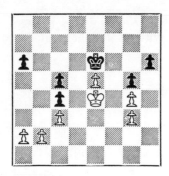

24

WHITE TO MOVE

The Kings are in "Opposition." We use this term when they face each other with an odd number of squares between them. The King that does NOT have to move is said to "have the Opposition."

Before we see what happens in Diagram 24, please study the caption carefully. In the basic King and Pawn endings, which we are now about to study, the winning process often depends on "having the Opposition."

To make our study of Diagram 24 easier, let's assume for the moment that it's Black's turn to move: he plays 1 . . . P—QR4 and White replies 2 P—R4!

Now Black's Pawn moves are exhausted, and he has to move his King. That means that White has the Opposition—Black's King has to give way.

Why is this important to us?

Well, White is a Pawn ahead to begin with. He has a passed King Pawn which is momentarily blocked. If a free path is created for this passed Pawn, White can advance it, supported by its King, to the queening square.

Not only that; if Black's King gives way, White can advance his own King to Queen 5, capturing both weak Bishop Pawns. Here is what happens:

2	K—K2	4 KxP/B5	K—K3
3 K—Q5!	K—Q2	5 K—Q4!	....

Now Black must move his King away from the King Pawn, allowing White to play 6 KxP. Then White is three Pawns up, and he has a new passed Pawn—the Bishop Pawn. By advancing both of his passed Pawns, supported by his King, White must promote to a Queen, leading up to a quick checkmate.

So far all this is clear and convincing, but remember we said in the caption to Diagram 24 that *White moves first.* Given that condition, White must be on the alert. For example, suppose he starts from Diagram 24 like this:

$$1 \text{ P—R4??} \qquad \text{P—R4!}$$

Now White has botched it. He has no Pawn moves, and must move his King. In other words, BLACK HAS THE OPPOSITION!

The consequence? After White moves his King, he loses his King Pawn, and the position is a draw!

Now back to Diagram 24. White *can* win, and this is how:

$$1 \text{ P—R3!!} \qquad \text{P—R4} \qquad 2 \text{ P—R4!!} \qquad ....$$

Note the finesse in making two moves with the Rook Pawn instead of one. Now it is White who after all has the Opposition; Black's King must give way; White plays 3 K—Q5, as shown above, and continues on his way to victory.

This was what we meant when we said that the simple King and Pawn endings are not always "simple." However, their tricky qualities add to their fascination.

25

WHO MOVES?

If Black moves, White wins. If White moves, the position is a draw. In other words: if White has the Opposition, he wins. If Black has the Opposition, he draws.

Diagram 25 is one of the most important situations in basic King and Pawn endings.

If Black moves, here is what happens:

| 1 .... | K—Q1 | 2 P—Q7 | K—K2 |
| | 3 K—B7 | .... | |

And on the next move White plays 4 P—Q8/Q, checkmating quickly.

If White moves first, he cannot win:

1 P—Q7ch   K—Q1

Now the only move to hold the Pawn is 2 K—Q6, but that causes stalemate!

Suppose White tries a different way:

| 1 K—N6 | K—Q2 | 2 K—B5 | K—Q1! |
| | 3 K—B6 | K—B1 | |

Black has maneuvered his King to keep the Opposition. He thus maintains the draw.

The important moral is, then, that in the basic ending of King and Pawn vs. King, *you must make sure that you keep the Opposition.* The method will be explained in later endings.

26

WHITE TO MOVE

Here too White has stalemate troubles. Thus, if 1 K—B5, K—R1; 2 K—B6 and Black is stalemated. How is White to win?

In Diagram 26 White has more material than he needs for winning purposes. Here is how he solves his difficulty, getting rid of the stalemate:

1 P—R8/Qch!   KxQ   2 K—R6!   ....

The point. White has the Opposition. Black's King must give way.

2 ....   K—N1   3 P—N7   ....

Here is a valuable hint about positions where the stronger side's King does not control the queening square: whenever your Pawn advances to the seventh rank *without giving check*, you win the ending.

Black must now play 3 . . . K—B2, whereupon White continues 4 K—R7, making 5 P—N8/Q possible, followed by a quick mate.

27

WHO MOVES FIRST?
It doesn't matter! Because White's Pawn is still on the fifth rank, he can always advance the Pawn at any point where he has lost the Opposition. This will cause Black to give way with his King.

Suppose, in Diagram 27, that Black moves first. Then he has lost the Opposition, and his King must give way:

1 ....   K—Q1   2 K—B7   ....

(Or 1 . . . K—B1; 2 K—Q7 with the same result.)

2 ....   K—Q2   3 P—K6ch   K—Q1

Now White continues 4 P—K7ch followed by 5 P—K8/Q, followed by a quick checkmate.

Now back to Diagram 27. Suppose White moves first? What follows is extremely important, and you must study it until you fully understand it.

White must move his King, and therefore loses the Opposition:

                1 K—Q6   ....

(Note that 1 K—B6 serves the same purpose.)

                1 ....   K—Q1

Black maintains the Opposition. So far so good for Black. But now White has a move in reserve:

                2 P—K6!   ....

(In Diagram 25 White's Pawn was already on the sixth rank, so he no longer had this "tempo" move in reserve!)

                2 ....   K—K1

Black's King must give way. He has lost the Opposition.

                3 P—K7   ....

The Pawn has advanced to the seventh rank *without check*.

As we know from earlier examples, this means that White's Pawn will soon become a Queen and enforce checkmate.

An important moral we deduce from Diagram 27 is this: if your single Pawn has not reached the sixth rank, don't advance it too hastily. Reserve the moves of the Pawn to a time when you will be badly in need of them.

Now let's apply what we've learned.

350

28

WHO MOVES FIRST?

It doesn't matter. If Black moves first, he loses the Opposition immediately, and White wins with ease. If White moves first, he keeps the Opposition with the tempo move 1 P—Q4!

Diagram 28 should offer no difficulties.

If Black moves first, White quickly lays down a path for his Pawn to advance and queen. For example:

1	K—K2	3 K—Q6	K—B1
2 K—B6!	K—Q1	4 P—Q4	K—Q1
	5 P—Q5	....	

Again Black loses the Opposition: 5 ... K—K1; 6 K—B7 etc. or 5 ... K—B1; 6 K—K7 etc. and White's King guards the queening square.

If White moves first in Diagram 28, the procedure is pretty much the same:

1 P—Q4!	K—K2	4 K—B7	K—K2
2 K—B6	K—Q1	5 P—Q5	K—K1
3 K—Q6	K—K1	6 P—Q6	K—B1
	7 P—Q7	....	

Again the Pawn becomes a Queen and forces checkmate.

There is still one more vital point we need to know about King and Pawn endings.

In Diagram 28 White's King was ideally posted—*in front of the Pawn.* However, if the stronger side's King is at the side of the Pawn, or in back of it, and if the weaker side's King is well advanced, the lone King can draw.

29

BLACK DRAWS!

Black is able to draw because, due to the unfavorable position of the White King, Black can always assume the Opposition at the critical moment.

Diagram 29 is a draw no matter who moves first.

Let's see the play with Black moving first. He loses the Opposition at once, but he regains it when he needs it. This will lead in due course to the drawing method of Diagram 25.

| 1 .... | K—Q4 | 2 P—Q4 | K—Q3! |

After 2 . . . K—B5??; 3 K—K4! White wins because Black can never get back the Opposition. (If 3 . . . K—N4; 4 K—Q5!)

| 3 K—K4 | K—K3! | 5 K—Q4 | K—Q2 |
| 4 P—Q5ch | K—Q3 | 6 K—K5 | K—K2! |

If 6 . . . K—B2??; 7 K—K6 and White gets the Opposition after 7 . . . K—Q1; 8 K—Q6. Then if 8 . . . K—K1; 9 K—B7 wins; or 8 . . . K—B1; 9 K—K7 wins in familiar fashion.

| 7 P—Q6ch | K—Q2 | 8 K—Q5 | .... |

A crucial situation for Black. If 8 . . . K—B1??; 9 K—B6 White gains the Opposition and wins. The same thing happens after 8 . . . K—K1??; 9 K—K6.

But Black does have a saving move:

8 ....   K—Q1!!   9 K—B6   ....

Or 9 K—K6, K—K1 with a similar windup.

                9 ....   K—B1!

Now we have the exact position of Diagram 25 with Black having the Opposition and White having to move. As we know from Diagram 25, this is a drawn position.

From our study of the positions in this chapter, you now know which positions to aim for when a King and Pawn ending is in prospect, and which positions to avoid.

You have learned of the importance of the Opposition, and you have seen how you can use it to your advantage by keeping Pawn moves in reserve.

These positions are well worth playing over, preferably with a friend, so that you can iron out any misunderstandings. You will find that familiarity with these endings is very profitable in terms of additional wins you will score.

Chapter Four

ENDGAMES WITH A PIECE AHEAD

ENDINGS in which you are a piece to the good are generally won for you *if you have one or more Pawns*.

If you have a Rook and Bishop (or Rook and Knight) against a Rook, the position usually winds up as a draw. Once in a great while a position turns up where the player with superior forces wins because of some chance finesse. But the general rule is that such positions are drawn.

With Pawns on the board the situation changes radically. When you have at least one Pawn left, *you have a chance of queening it*. At that point your extra piece goes to work for you, and makes your victory possible.

The following endgames will show you how to win the game.

A masterpiece of technique

30

WHITE TO MOVE

Black has three Pawns for a piece. In some situations this would be good enough to draw. Not here, however, as White demonstrates, with power-ful and economical handling of his forces.

354

Positions like this one occur fairly often in over-the-board play. Here are the outstanding features of White's winning method:

(1) White must make the weight of his extra piece tell.

He must place his pieces to the best advantage, menace the hostile Pawns; provoke their advance (which will make them more susceptible to attack); force them into a position where any change will be for the worse.

(2) White must play his King to a centralized position (say the square King 5—or Queen 5 or Queen Bishop 4— where it can put added pressure on Black's game.

(3) White must avoid exchanging Pawns. These Pawns may seem insignificant at the present time but *they are potential queening candidates.* Without these Pawns White cannot win.

(4) Another reason why White must avoid Pawn exchanges is that he means to *win* the Black Pawns; *exchanging* Pawn for Pawn would ruin this plan.

                    1 R—Q3!   ....

Taking an open file, where the Rook will have maximum mobility.

1 ....   P—QR4   2 K—N2!   ....

Another good move. The King heads for the center.

2 ....   K—N2   3 K—B3   K—B3

Black follows suit with his King. He tries to hold as much ground as possible.

                    4 P—KR4!   ....

In order to penetrate further by K—B4 without being driven back by . . . P—N4ch.

Once White gets that far, he can contemplate further penetration—in due time—with R—Q6ch and K—K5.

To learn the most from this ending, you must study White's gradual encroachment of more and more terrain.

$$4 \ldots \qquad \text{R—N3}$$

To guard the third rank from eventual invasion.

4 . . . P—N4 may look good here, but it would weaken Black's King Bishop Pawn. The why and wherefore of this will soon become clear to you.

$$5 \text{ B—B2} \qquad \ldots$$

White dallies with the idea of a frontal attack on the Queen Bishop Pawn by R—B3. But Black is alert and immediately scotches this plan.

$$5 \ldots \qquad \text{K—K4}$$

Now Black threatens 6 . . . P—QB5; 7 R—B3, K—Q5. So White tries a different way.

6 B—N3   K—B3   7 B—B4   ....

Now the Bishop is self-supporting and White's Rook can become active.

7 ....   P—R3   8 K—K3!   ....

Not 8 K—B4?, P—N4ch! exchange Pawns. White's King Rook Pawn is to play an active role.

$$8 \ldots \qquad \text{P—N4}$$

Inevitable. Thus, if 8 . . . R—B3; 9 R—Q7 with unpleasant threats, such as R—QR7.

31

WHITE TO MOVE

White's next move is the key to the ending. It "fixes" Black's King Rook Pawn as a decisive weakness. White also establishes all the remaining Black Pawns as targets.

9 P—R5!!	R—B3	11 R—KR7	K—K4
10 R—Q7	R—N3	12 R—K7ch	K—Q3

Or 12 . . . K—B3; 13 R—QB7 and White wins.

13 R—K6ch	K—B2	14 R—K5!	. . . .

Note that 14 R—N6 also wins. But the text is more in accord with White's plan: he creates an entering wedge for his King.

14	P—B5ch	15 K—K4	R—QB3

If 15 . . . K—B3; 16 R—K6ch, K—B2; 17 R—N6! followed by 18 K—Q5 and White wins.

16 R—K7ch   K—Q1

The alternative 16 . . . K—N3 allows 17 R—N7 followed by R—N6 and K—Q5.

17 R—KN7	R—Q3	19 B—Q5	P—B6
18 K—K5	R—Q5	20 K—Q6	K—B1
	21 R—N8 mate		

White's penetration plan worked out beautifully.

A difficult ending

BLACK TO MOVE

Though Black's play in this ending is highly systematic, the process is extremely interesting. The ending takes a great deal of patience, but Black's logical procedure makes it seem easy!

Black begins with the basic idea that White can never allow the exchange of Rooks.

Once such an exchange takes place, White will be helpless against the advance of Black's King and Bishop to a point where the White Pawns will be defenseless. Then, eventually, Black will queen his remaining Pawn.

(If you are not certain of this, remove the Rooks and play about ten moves for either side.)

The fact that White cannot exchange Rooks, gives Black's forces great power. *It means that Black can consistently strengthen his position by offering the exchange of Rooks.*

White will always have to withdraw from the exchange, giving ground each time. This gives Black the basis for a policy of gradual penetration. (But remember this: Black must never allow the exchange of his lone Pawn.)

Now what is to be the object of Black's pressure? Clearly, White's Bishop Pawn.

The best way for Black to menace it will be to place his Rook on the seventh rank and his Bishop at King 5 or King Bishop 4.

This will reduce White's Rook to complete passivity on the Queen Bishop file. Black can then advance his King with decisive effect.

358

1	R—K5	4 R—B7	K—Q3
2 R—R8	K—B4	5 R—KR7	B—N4
3 R—QB8	R—K1!	6 K—B3	B—R5

Black threatens . . . R—B1ch winning the Bishop Pawn. This forces White's Rook to the second rank.

| 7 R—R2 | R—K5 | 9 R—R2 | R—K6ch |
| 8 R—N2 | K—B4 | 10 K—N2 | B—N4! |

In order to take the seventh rank with . . . R—K7. Black's constriction plan is making progress.

| 11 R—R8 | R—K7 | 13 K—N3 | B—B5ch |
| 12 R—B8ch | K—Q5 | 14 K—N2 | B—Q6! |

Now Black is attacking the vulnerable Pawn twice; and by bringing his Bishop to King Bishop 4 he can hound White's Rook as well.

| 15 K—N3 | B—B4 | 16 R—B7 | R—K1!! |

33

WHITE TO MOVE

Black's masterly retreat with his Rook threatens to force the exchange of Rooks by . . . R—QB1. This explains the purpose behind Black's last two moves.

White is embarrassed for a good move.

If he plays 17 R—QN7 then 17 . . . R—QB1 wins the wretched Bishop Pawn. On other moves of White's Rook along the seventh rank, 17 . . . R—QN1ch wins that Pawn.

| 17 P—B3ch | K—Q6 | | 18 R—B5 | R—QN1ch |

Driving off White's King. His Bishop Pawn is definitely lost now.

19 K—R4	B—K5		22 R—B5	B—B5
20 R—B7	K—B7		23 K—R5	KxP
21 R—B6	B—Q6		24 P—R4	R—QR1ch

White resigns. Black's accurate play was a triumph of logic.

Victory for the passed Pawns

Three Pawns, as we know, are about equal in value to a minor piece. Toward the beginning of the game we generally rate the piece higher, as its chances of being useful are much greater. Toward the end of the game, the Pawns (especially if they have queening possibilities and the position is simplified) may weigh more heavily in the scale.

In the following ending the Pawns are definitely preferable.

34

WHITE TO MOVE

Black's winning plan is based on the fact that White's King has to lose time removing Black's remote passed Queen Rook Pawn. The upshot is that Black's Kingside Pawns prove too much for the unaided Bishop.

| 1 K—N5 | P—B5! |

Black loses no time. Passed Pawns must be pushed!

360

	2 KxP	P—B6

A menacing-looking Pawn.

3 K—N4	K—B5	4 K—B4	K—K6!

Very good. He keeps White's King away from the queening square.

5 K—Q5	P—R4	6 B—Q7	....

On other moves Black simply advances his Pawns and ultimately queens one of them.

6	P—B7	8 K—K5	K—N7
7 B—N5	K—B6	9 K—B4	KxP!

Preparing the advance of the Knight Pawn.

	10 K—K3	P—N6

White resigns, as Black is about to continue victoriously with ... P—N7 and ... P—N8/Q. An instructive ending.

Chapter Five

ENDGAMES WITH THE EXCHANGE
AHEAD

To BE the Exchange ahead—to have a Rook for a Bishop or Knight—generally assures you an easy win. Nevertheless, it is well for you to be prepared for a little trouble, or at least some hard work. The advantage of the Exchange does not win by itself!

The Rook's superior mobility

The following endgame shows what the Rook can accomplish on open lines.

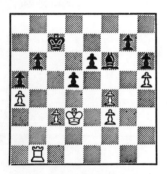

35

WHITE TO MOVE

White has the Exchange for a Pawn. Naturally this makes the win harder than if Black were not a Pawn up.

White's Pawns are all isolated, which gives us a discouraged feeling that they cannot be put to good use. So White must give some thought to the problem of employing these Pawns profitably.

He has one consolation: Black's Pawns are not in very good shape either. Black's King Pawn and his Knight Pawns *require protection by pieces*.

These Pawns are *"backward"* Pawns; they can no longer be protected by neighboring Pawns. They are therefore vulnerable to attack by the Rook. Luckily, the Rook has a lot of scope. It has a choice of three open files.

So, here is White's diagnosis:

To win on the superior mobility of his Rook, he needs to create additional open lines by P—B4! and P—KB5! This will also create points of invasion for his King.

It will not be long before Black will find himself in trouble because his Bishop and King are tied to the defense of weak Pawns.

1 P—B4!	K—B3

Or 1 . . . PxPch; 2 KxP and White has a standing threat of K—N5 (or K—Q5 after P—B5 and the resulting exchange of Pawns).

2 R—N5!	B—K2	3 P—KB5!	. . . .

Splendid timing. Watch how the mobility of White's pieces is increased.

3	QPxPch	4 KxP	PxP
	5 RxBP	B—B3	

Though Black's position *looks* as solid as it did at the beginning, White has actually made great progress.

His next goal: A check on the sixth rank with his Rook, forcing Black's King to retreat.

6 P—B4	K—Q3	7 R—QN5	K—B3
	8 P—B5	. . . .	

Black feels the noose tightening, for if 8 . . . B—R8; 9 R—N1, B—B3; 10 R—K1 and White is ready for the decisive 11 R—K6ch.

| 8 . . . . | B—N4 | 10 R—K6ch! | K—B2 |
| 9 R—K5! | B—B3 | 11 K—N5 | B—Q5 |

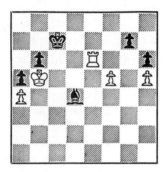

36

WHITE TO MOVE

White is ready to exploit the fact that Black has achieved his best defensive position. The Bishop protects two weak Pawns, and White forces Black to choose between these weak Pawns.

12 R—QB6ch!! . . . .

Magnificent endgame play!

Black's laborious defense topples as a result of this masterstroke, for if 12 . . . K—N2; 13 R—B4, B—N7; 14 R—K4, B—B3; 15 R—K6, B—Q5; 16 R—Q6! and White wins a Pawn, depending on where the menaced Bishop moves.

| 12 . . . . | K—Q2 | 13 R—B4! | B—B4 |
| | 14 R—KN4! | K—K2 | |

He cannot save the King Knight Pawn because he cannot play . . . B—Q5. Thus White's Rook triumphs.

| 15 RxPch | K—B3 | 16 R—N6ch | KxP |
| | 17 RxRP | Resigns | |

For White is about to force an easily won King and Pawn ending with 18 RxP.

364

Delicate Rook maneuvers

From this ending, too, you can learn how to take splendid advantage of the Rook's superior mobility.

37

WHITE TO MOVE

This ending looks easy at first sight. Apparently White need only attack the Black Pawn with his Rook and King, and play RxP, giving up the Exchange to get a won King and Pawn ending. This is easier said than done!

1 R—B7ch!   K—K1

Best. If 1 . . . K—N1; 2 K—B6, B—Q5ch; 3 K—N6, B—K6; 4 R—B5 and the unfortunate mating position of Black's King loses quickly for him.

Thus, if 4 . . . B—Q7; 5 R—Q5! (threatens mate), B—N5; 6 R—Q8ch, B—B1; 7 R—K8 (or any other Rook move on the rank) followed by checkmate next move!

If 4 . . . B—B8; 5 R—B5 wins the same way.

2 R—B5!   . . . .

Now Black's choice of moves is limited.

If 2 . . . B—B8?; 3 R—B5 (threatening mate) wins on the spot.

And if 2 . . . K—Q1; 3 R—B8ch! drives Black's King away, so that after 3 . . . K—B2; 4 K—K5, K—Q2; 5 RxP!, BxRch; 6 KxB, K—K3; 7 K—N5 and White assures the queening of his Pawn (see Diagram 28).

2 . . . .   B—Q7

365

White can now win the Pawn with 3 K—K5, K—K2; 4 RxP?, BxR; 5 KxB. But after 5 . . . K—B3! Black has the Opposition and the position is drawn. (See Diagram 29.)

3 K—B6! ....

Taking advantage of the fact that Black dare not play 3 . . . K—Q1?? or 3 . . . K—Q2?? because of 4 R—Q5ch.

3 .... K—B1

38

WHITE TO MOVE
Now White succeeds in driving off the Black King.

4 R—B5! ....

White threatens mate.

If Black parries with 4 . . . K—K1, then 5 K—N7!! followed by R—K5ch and R—K4. Black's King is then cut off from the King file, so that White can comfortably play K—N6 and K—B5 and then capture the Black Pawn with an easily won King and Pawn ending.

4 .... K—N1   5 R—B8ch! ....

Driving the Black King away.

5 .... K—R2   6 K—B7! Resigns

For now, no matter how Black replies, White plays 7 R—KN8 and 8 R—N4.

Then, with Black's King hopelessly cut off, White continues 9 K—B6 and 10 K—B5, picking off the Black Pawn at his leisure. The resulting King and Pawn ending is an easy win.

White's Rook maneuvers give us a vivid notion of the power of this piece.

Passed Pawns fight for supremacy

39

WHITE TO MOVE

White has the Exchange in return for a Pawn. His King is tied down by a dangerous passed Pawn. In addition, he must watch out for . . . K—Q6—Q7 or else . . . KxP followed by the advance of the Queen Pawn.

White's Rook is bound to do great damage on the seventh rank, but first he must get a shipshape position against Black's threats, so:

1 K—K1!   KxP   2 K—Q2   . . . .

Now White is safe and therefore ready to invade the seventh rank.

2 . . . .   P—QR3   3 R—N7 B—Q6
        4 R—QB7!   . . . .

Forcing the advance of Black's King Rook Pawn, as Black's Bishop is overloaded with defensive tasks. White makes telling use of the Rook's superior mobility.

367

4	P—R4	7 R—K6!	B—B5
5 P—R4	K—K5	8 R—R6	K—K5
6 R—K7ch	K—Q5	9 RxKRP	K—B5

40

WHITE TO MOVE

White's clever Rook maneuvers have won material. He is now ready to advance his own passed Pawn, but he must keep an eye on the possibility of . . . K—B6 and . . . K—B7, whereby Black renews his threats to queen the King Pawn.

10 R—N5! ....

White cuts off Black's King from any attempt to stop the passed Pawn. Black must seize his last desperate chance for counterplay.

| 10 .... | P—Q5 | 12 P—R5 | K—B6 |
| 11 R—N7 | P—Q6 | 13 R—K7 | .... |

White is too wily for 13 P—R6, K—B7; 14 P—R7???, P—K8/Q mate!

| 13 .... | K—B7 | 14 P—R6 | B—N1 |
| | 15 P—R7! | .... | |

Very sly. On 15 . . . BxP White interpolates 16 R—KB7ch! (not 16 RxB??) and *then* picks up the Bishop.

| 15 .... | P—K8/Qch | 16 RxQ | BxP |
| | 17 R—K6 | Resigns | |

White has reduced Black to helplessness in view of the coming RxP followed by the queening of the Rook Pawn.

A very pleasing ending by reason of the Rook's agile maneuvers.

Victory for the minor piece

When a player is the Exchange down and has two extra Pawns by way of compensation, the material may be said to be fairly even. Where the Pawns are passed and well advanced, the Rook is definitely at a disadvantage.

41

WHITE TO MOVE

White is in trouble because his forces are split. His King has to stop one of the passed Pawns; his Rook has to stop the other one. Black's winning plan is to give up his Knight Pawn at the right moment, forcing the queening of his other Pawn.

1 R—N8ch	K—B7	3 R—K8ch	K—B8!
2 K—B2	K—K7	4 R—KB8	P—B7

Now that this Pawn is poised to queen, Black's only problem is to find shelter for his King against the Rook checks.

5 R—B7	K—K7	6 R—K7ch	K—B6
	7 R—KB7ch	B—B5!	

White resigns, as the Bishop Pawn must queen.

Thus we see that when passed Pawns are dangerously far advanced, even a Rook is helpless against them.

ROOK AND PAWN ENDINGS

THIS TYPE of ending occurs more frequently than any other kind of endgame. For this reason it is valuable to know something more about the qualities of the Rook.

One of the most powerful ways to post a Rook is on an open seventh rank. Here your Rook can create havoc among the opposing Pawns.

The Rook can accomplish a great deal when it is on open lines—open files and open ranks.

When you have a passed Pawn, aim to place your Rook *behind* it. Then the Rook aids the Pawn's push toward the queening square.

If your opponent has the passed Pawn, you likewise do best to place your Rook behind the Pawn, not in front of it. In the latter position, your Rook loses much of its mobility, because if it gives up the blockade, the passed Pawn can march toward the queening square.

In this type of ending the Kings, too, play a very active role, guarding their own Pawns and attacking the enemy's.

Remember that when you are a Pawn to the good in a Rook and Pawn ending, you can often reduce your opponent to helplessness by threatening the exchange of Rooks, bringing the game to a simple King and Pawn ending which is easily won.

Two basic endings

The position in Diagram 42 is of fundamental importance, as it shows a basic setup that can often be reached when a player is a Pawn ahead.

42

WHITE TO MOVE

In order to be able to win, White must make room for his King, and he must then shield his King from checks by the Black Rook. White does this by "building a bridge."

1 R—QB1ch   K—N2

White needs a subtle preparatory move before moving his King out and threatening to queen.

Thus, if 2 K—Q7, R—Q7ch; 3 K—K6, R—K7ch; 4 K—Q6, R—Q7ch; 5 K—K5, R—K7ch and it is clear that White is not getting anywhere.

2 R—B4!!	R—B8	5 K—B6	R—KB8ch
3 K—Q7	R—Q8ch	6 K—K5	R—K8ch
4 K—K6	R—K8ch	7 R—K4!	....

Now you can see the point of White's first and second moves. He drove away the Black King, and now he has shielded the White King from checks. The passed Pawn must queen.

The next ending (Diagram 43) shows a stratagem that often proves useful.

43

WHITE TO MOVE

Black threatens to bring his King to Queen Knight 2, winning White's extra Pawn and thereby achieving a draw. But White wins by an "X-ray attack."

| 1 R—R8!! | RxP | 2 R—R7ch | .... |

This X-ray attack forces Black's King to move, after which White plays 3 RxR, followed by a quick checkmate.

Passed Pawns win

In Diagram 44 it takes some neat play to win with the extra Pawn.

44

WHITE TO MOVE

White's Pawn is on the point of queening, but White's King is in check, and 1 K—B8 is futile in view of 1 . . . R—R1ch. To get a hint of the position that White needs, look at Diagram 19.

Believe it or not, the play from Diagram 44 requires White to play his King all the way back to King Knight 2. Thus:

| 1 K—B6 | .... |

If now 1 . . . R—R1; 2 R—B8 forces the queening of the passed Pawn. So Black must keep on checking.

1 ....   R—R3ch

Black hopes for 2 K—K5? when 2 . . . R—KN3, followed by . . . K—R3, will win the dangerous Pawn. But White has a finesse:

2 K—B5!   ....

So that if 2 . . . R—KN3; 3 P—N8/Q!!, RxQ; 4 R—KR7 mate! (See Diagram 4.)

2 ....   R—R4ch   3 K—B4!   ....

And now if 3 . . . R—KN4 White has a pin with 4 R—B5! knocking out the Black Rook and thus forcing the queening of the Pawn.

3 ....   R—R5ch   4 K—B3!   ....

White is endlessly resourceful. This time he figures on 4 . . . R—KN5; 5 R—B5ch, K—R5 (forced); 6 R—B4! again winning by pinning.

4 ....   R—R6ch   5 K—N2   R—R7ch
                6 R—B2!   ....

At last Black is out of checks. His reply is forced:

6 ....   R—R1   7 R—B8!   ....

Of course Black cannot exchange Rooks. Here is his last try:

7	R—R7ch	10 K—Q5	R—R4ch
8 K—B3	R—R6ch	11 K—B6	R—R3ch
9 K—K4	R—R5ch	12 K—N7	Resigns

At last the Pawn is able to queen.

This delightful ending shows how wrong some players are in thinking that endgames do not allow scope for combinative play.

In Diagram 45, however, White proceeds in a highly systematic manner.

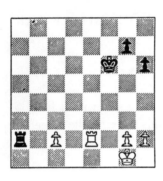

45

WHITE TO MOVE

Note that White's Rook very efficiently cuts off the Black King from contact with White's passed Pawn. On the other hand, White's King can actively support the passed Pawn.

Here is how White proceeds in Diagram 45:

1 K—B2	P—R4	4 K—Q3	R—R1
2 K—K1!	P—N4	5 P—B4	R—Q1ch
3 K—Q2	K—B4	6 K—B3	R—QB1

To prevent P—B5; but White makes progress all the same.

| 7 K—N4 | R—QN1ch | 9 K—N5 | R—QN1ch |
| 8 K—R5 | R—QB1 | 10 K—R6 | R—QB1 |

Now White gets his Rook *behind* the passed Pawn.

| 11 R—QB2! | K—K4 | 12 K—N7! | R—B4 |
| | | 13 K—N6! | Resigns |

46

BLACK TO MOVE

Black resigns because 13 . . . K—Q3??; 14 R—Q2ch loses on the spot; and if 13 . . . R—B1; 14 P—B5 and Black can do nothing against P—B6 and P—B7 and K—N7.

Diagram 47 gives the winner greater difficulties.

47

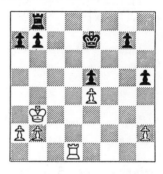

BLACK TO MOVE

Black is a Pawn ahead, but he has no passed Pawn. To get one, he advances his King-side Pawns. His two-to-one majority should give him a passed Pawn.

1	P—KN4!	2 R—KN1	P—N5

If now 3 P—KR3, R—N1; 4 PxP, RxP and Black has his passed Pawn.

3 R—QB1	R—Q1	4 R—B1	R—Q6ch!

Very strong, for if 5 K—B2, R—K6; 6 R—B5, R—K7ch!; 7 K—B3, RxRP; 8 RxPch, K—B3; 9 R—B5ch, K—N3 and Black's *two connected passed Pawns* win quickly for Black by their advance.

5 K—B4	R—Q5ch	8 R—R5	P—N6
6 K—B5	RxP	9 PxP	PxP
7 R—B5	P—R5	10 K—Q5	R—K7!

48

WHITE TO MOVE

As in Diagram 45, the weaker side's King is cut off from the remote passed Pawn. And if 11 RxPch, RxR- ch; 12 KxR, P—N7 and the passed Pawn queens.

11 R—N5	P—N7		13 R—N8	K—B4
12 P—N4	K—B3		14 R—N7	R—Q7ch!

Chasing White's King away from Black's other passed Pawn.

15 K—B4   K—B5

White resigns, as Black's King will support the advance of the King Knight Pawn to the queening square.

Winning simplification

We have previously discussed swapping down to a won King and Pawn ending. Diagram 49 is an example of how to carry out the simplification.

49

WHITE TO MOVE

White has a passed Queen Pawn. Note also that Black's remaining Pawn is weak and White may be able to win it.

1 R—N7ch   K—B1

If 1 . . . K—K1 (to approach the passed Pawn), White has 2 R—N7, winning Black's remaining Pawn.

2 P—Q6   . . . .

Threatening 3 R—N8ch and 4 P—Q7, forcing the queening of the passed Pawn.

2 . . . .   K—K1

Black fights hard. If 3 R—N8ch?, K—Q2. Or if 3 R—N7?, R—K3; 4 P—Q7ch, K—Q1 and Black can draw.

50

WHITE TO MOVE

White wins by giving up his extra Pawn in order to get a won King and Pawn ending.

3 R—K7ch!   RxR   4 PxR   . . . .

If now 4 . . . KxP; 5 K—K5, K—B2; 6 K—Q6, K—B1; 7 K—K6, K—N2; 8 K—K7, K—R2; 9 K—B7 winning Black's Pawn. White then has a standard win as in Diagram 27.

4 . . . .   K—Q2

Black prays for 5 K—K5?, KxP when he has the Opposition and the White King cannot penetrate.

5 K—K4!   K—K1

If 5 . . . KxP; 6 K—K5! and White's King penetrates as in the note to White's fourth move.

6 K—Q5   K—Q2

And, if 6 . . . KxP; 7 K—K5! wins.

7 P—K8/Qch!   KxQ   8 K—K6   Resigns

If 8 . . . K—B1; 9 K—B6 and wins as previously shown.
And in Diagram 51, too, White wins instructively by relying on simplification into a King and Pawn ending.

51

WHITE TO MOVE

White's Pawn position is very unwieldy and his King has no way to play an active role. His logical course is to exchange his advanced Bishop Pawn for Black's Rook Pawn.

1 P—B5ch!   KxP   2 RxPch   . . . .

Now White has created invasion possibilities for his King, and he has obtained a passed Pawn.

2	K—N3	6 P—R5	R—R2
3 R—R8	K—B4	7 R—N3	R—R2
4 R—KN8!	R—B8	8 R—R3	K—N4
5 K—N2	R—QR8	9 K—B3	R—R3

After 9 . . . RxP; 10 RxRch, KxR Black is lost. This will be explained later on.

10 R—R1	K—B4		12 R—R4	K—B4
11 K—N3	K—N4		13 R—B4ch	K—N4
	14 R—N4ch		....	

52

BLACK TO MOVE

*And here, too, if 14 . . . KxP; 15
R—R4ch, K—N4; 16 RxR, KxR
Black is lost, as we shall see later on.*

14	K—B4		17 P—R6	R—R8
15 K—R4	R—R1		18 R—N3	R—R8ch
16 R—N7	R—R1		19 R—R3	R—KN8

And now, if White carelessly plays 20 P—R7???, apparently succeeding in queening the Pawn, Black has a perpetual check with 20 . . . R—N5ch etc.!

20 R—B3ch!	K—N3		22 KxR	KxP
21 R—N3ch!	RxR		23 K—N4	K—N3
	24 K—B4		....	

Now we see why White was so eager to get into the King and Pawn ending at the cost of his extra Pawn. If Black tries 24 . . . P—KB4; 25 K—K5, K—N4; 26 P—B3!, K—N3; 27 P—B4! wins for White, as Black must give up the King Bishop Pawn.

24	K—N2		25 K—B5	K—B2
	26 P—B3!		Resigns	

For if 26 . . . K—K2; 27 K—N6, K—K3; 28 P—B4, K—K2; 29 P—B5 winning the King Bishop Pawn. And if 26 . . . K—N2; 27 K—K6 achieves the same result. A splendid example of efficient endgame planning.

Two Rooks apiece

Endings with two Rooks on a side do not occur very often. However, they are worth noticing for the aggressive power of two smoothly cooperating Rooks. Take Diagram 53 as an example.

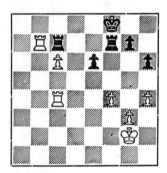

53

WHITE TO MOVE

For White to play 1 RxR?, RxR would be a big mistake, as Black could play . . . K—K2 and . . . K—B3 to win back his Pawn. White must therefore rely on the offensive power of his Rooks.

Therefore, in the position of Diagram 53, White plays:

1 R—R4! . . . .

This clever move threatens to win a Rook by 2 R—R8ch, K—K2; 3 RxRch etc.

Black is in trouble, for if he tries 1 . . . RxQBP?? then 2 R—R8ch, R—B1; 3 RxR mate!

Not much better is 1 . . . RxR; 2 R—R8ch, K—K2; 3 PxR and the Pawn queens.

Even escape by 1 . . . P—N3; 2 R—R8ch, K—N2 will not do for then 3 R/R8—R7! forces the exchange of all the Rooks, whereupon the passed Pawn queens.

1 . . . . R—B1 2 R/R4—R7 . . . .

And now if 2 . . . R—B3 White wins with 3 R—Q7! as his Queen Bishop Pawn is still immune. There might follow 3 . . . P—N3; 4 R/R7—N7, P—R4; 5 P—B7!, K—K1; 6 R—

380

KR7! and Black has no defense whatever to the coming 7 R—N8!

| 2 .... | R—B4 | 3 RxP | RxQBP |
| | 4 R—R7 | .... | |

Threatening mate. The Rooks have tremendous power on the seventh rank, with the result that White wins a second Pawn.

4	K—N1	6 P—R5	R—N6
5 RxP	R—QN4	7 R—N6ch	K—R1
	8 R—B6	....	

Threatening 9 R—B8 mate.

| 8 .... | R—N1 | 9 P—R6 | R—N1 |
| | 10 R/B6—B7 | .... | |

Again threatening mate.

| 10 .... | R—KN3 | 12 RxRch | KxR |
| 11 R—B8ch | R—N1 | 13 R—K7 | Resigns |

For White can win in a variety of ways, such as advancing his Knight Pawn.

This impressive example repeats the lesson taught repeatedly in this chapter—that the Rook unfolds enormous power on open lines.

Chapter Seven

ENDINGS WITH MINOR PIECES

IN ENDINGS with minor pieces we often see a struggle of Bishop against Knight.

There has been much argument pro and con as to which of these pieces is to be preferred. In modern master play the Bishop is the more popular piece, mainly because of its long-range effectiveness. The following endgames illustrate the versatile powers of the Bishop as against a Knight.

The agile Bishop

Although Black is a Pawn ahead, he seems at first to have a puzzling task ahead of him, as his King cannot advance and there seems to be no immediate progress in sight.

54

BLACK TO MOVE

The right way is 1 . . . B—B5! stale-mating White's Knight. This forces the White King to move, so that Black can win another Pawn shortly.

As indicated in the caption to Diagram 54, Black wins quickly with 1 . . . B—B5! paralyzing the Knight. There might follow 2 K—N4, K—Q4 and now Black threatens the devastating march . . . K—Q5—Q6—K7 winning the Knight.

White has nothing better than 3 K—B3, allowing 3 . . . K—B4 which wins White's Queen Knight Pawn. With two Pawns ahead, one of them a passed Pawn, Black wins easily. (Another winning method is 3 . . . P—K5! assuring a successful raid by Black's King.)

In Diagram 55 White is not only a Pawn ahead; he already has a remote passed Pawn. The win may take a little time, but it should be absolutely certain!

55

WHITE TO MOVE

White's passed Pawn splits up Black's forces. The King or Knight—or both—must prevent the Pawn from queening. Meanwhile White invades the undefended Kingside. The first part, as usual, is for him to centralize his King.

| 1 K—B3 | K—K2 | 2 K—K3 | P—B3 |

Necessary before he can play . . . K—Q3. But now his Knight Pawn will be a weakness.

3 K—Q4	K—Q3	5 B—B3	N—B1
4 B—Q1	N—N3	6 P—R4!	N—K2
	7 B—K4!	. . . .	

56

BLACK TO MOVE

Now the Knight is tied to the defense of the weak Pawn. Black's King dare not move, as that would allow penetration by 8 K—B5. The passed Pawn paralyzes the Black King. Hence a weakening Pawn move is forced.

If the Black Pawns get on white squares the Bishop will become fearfully effective, for example: 7 . . . P—B4; 8 B—B3, N—B1; 9 B—Q5, N—K2; 10 B—B7, K—Q2; 11 K—K5 followed by K—B6 winning all the Pawns.

If instead 7 . . . P—R4; 8 P—N3!, P—B4; 9 B—B3, N—B1; 10 B—Q5, N—K2; 11 B—B7, K—Q2; 12 K—K5 as above.

7	P—N4	13 K—B4	N—N1
8 BPxP	BPxP	14 KxP	N—B3
9 PxP	PxP	15 B—B3	N—Q2
10 P—N6!	P—N5	16 K—B4	K—Q3
11 P—N7	K—B2	17 K—B5	K—K2
12 K—K5	P—N6	18 B—B6!	N—N1
	19 B—N5!	Resigns	

Black realizes that although his King can cross to King Knight 2 and prevent White's King Knight Pawn from queening, White can bring his King to Queen Bishop 7, winning the Knight and then obtaining a new Queen. Play this out for yourself!

Diagram 57 shows some exciting possibilities.

57

BLACK TO MOVE

Black is a Pawn ahead and he has a Pawn that is ready to queen. Overconfidence can cause his downfall, thus: 1 . . . B—R3 (or 1 . . . B—R6); 2 P—N6!, P—B8/Q?; 3 NxQ, BxN??; 4 P—N7 and White's Pawn cannot be stopped!

In Diagram 57 Black prudently plays:

1 ....   P—K5!!

This opens up a diagonal to enable the Bishop to stop the Pawn in time.

| 2 PxP | B—R3 | 4 NxQ | BxN |
| 3 P—N6 | P—B8/Q | 5 K—B3 | .... |

On 5 P—N7 Black has 5 ... B—B5 and wins.

| 5 .... | B—R6 | 6 P—K5 | .... |

Threatening 7 P—N7 followed by queening.

| 6 .... | B—B4 | 7 P—N7 | B—R2 |

Just in the nick of time. The rest is a typical ending with a piece to the good. Black either picks up more Pawns or gives up his Bishop for a different kind of advantage.

For example: 8 K—K4, K—B2; 9 K—Q5, B—N1; 10 P—K6ch, K—K2; 11 P—R3, P—R3 and White loses the King Pawn.

8 K—N4	P—R3	14 K—R1	K—B6
9 K—B4	K—B2	15 K—N1	P—R4
10 K—K4	K—K3	16 K—R1	B—R2!
11 K—B4	B—N1	17 P—R4	K—N6
12 K—B3	KxP	18 P—N8/Qch	BxQ
13 K—N2	K—B5	Resigns	

White's last move was nothing but despair—the familiar spite check.

The agile Knight

But it is wrong to despise the Knight, as so many modern players do. This piece can sometimes unleash enormous power, especially where the opponent has most of his Pawns on the same colored square as those his Bishop travels on.

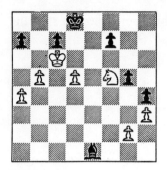

58

WHITE TO MOVE

At the moment White does not have an advantage in material, but he will soon remedy this. The Bishop has the impossible job of defending four Pawns on the black squares. These Pawns in turn deprive the Bishop of mobility.

In Diagram 58 White proceeds with:

1 P—Q6!   ....

This leaves Black no choice, for if 1 . . . B—R4; 2 P—Q7!, B—N3; 3 N—R6!, K—K2; 4 NxP! winning.

1 ....   PxP   2 NxP   ....

And now 2 . . . K—K2 is answered by 3 N—B8ch (forking check) followed by 4 NxP with an easy win for White because of his two connected passed Pawns.

2 ....   P—B3   3 N—K4!   ....

The classic elegance of the Knight moves is delightful. The first point of this move is that 3 . . . P—B4 allows 4 NxP. The second point is that Black cannot play 3 . . . B—B6.

3 ....   K—K2   4 K—N7!   ....

Now comes the third point of the Knight move: Black cannot defend his Queen Rook Pawn with 4 . . . B—B7.

And so White wins the Queen Rook Pawn, which gives him two connected passed Pawns and a technically easy win.

386

Exception to an exception

Diagram 59 illustrates an ending with Bishops on opposite colors.

This is a term we use when one player has a Bishop that travels on white squares, while his opponent has a Bishop that travels on black squares.

It sometimes happens in such endings that the advantage of a Pawn—or even two Pawns—is not enough to win. This is due to the fact that the player with the extra Pawns does not command the squares to which his Bishop does not have access. (See Diagram 77 for an explanation of this point.)

59

WHITE TO MOVE

Relying on the reputed drawing qualities of the Bishops on opposite colors, White exchanges Queens. He overlooks, however, that his Bishop will be tied down by the queening threat of Black's Pawn at Queen Knight 7.

From Diagram 59 play proceeds:

| 1 QxQ | PxQ! | 2 B—Q3 | .... |

White's Bishop must prevent Black's advanced Pawn from queening. Black will therefore advance his two Pawns to one on the King-side with a view to creating *a second passed Pawn.*

2	K—K4	6 B—B2	P—KN4!
3 K—B3	B—B4	7 B—N1	B—Q3!
4 B—N1	K—B3	8 B—B2	P—N5!
5 K—K4	P—R4!	9 PxP	PxP

387

Now Black has his second passed Pawn.

| 10 B—N1 | P—N6 | 11 K—B3 | B—B5 |

If now 12 KxB, P—N7 and the Pawn must queen.

| 12 K—N2 | K—K4 | 13 K—B3 | K—Q5 |

The rest is easy.

14 K—N2	K—B6	16 K—N2	K—B8
15 K—B3	K—Q7	17 B—K4	P—N8/Q
	18 BxQ	KxB	

Thus the queening of the Pawn has won a piece in typical fashion, leaving Black with an easy win.

Squeeze play

In Diagram 60 we see a memorable Knight and Pawn ending in which the winner avoids several crafty traps.

60

BLACK TO MOVE

Black is a Pawn ahead. However, it looks as if his passed Pawn may easily go lost. And, as soon becomes clear, there are other drawing dangers in the position. Nevertheless, Black can win by sacrificing his Knight.

| 1 .... | N—Q6!! |

For if 2 NxN, P—R7; 3 K—N2, KxN and Black wins all of White's Pawns.

388

And if 2 N—R2, K—K7!; 3 K—N3, K—Q7; 4 KxP, K—B7 when White is starved for moves.

| 2 N—N3 | N—K8ch | 4 KxN | KxP |
| 3 K—Q1 | K—Q6! | 5 N—R1 | .... |

Now Black can win back the piece with 5 . . . K—N7?; 6 K—Q2, KxN—but after 7 K—B1, K—R7; 8 K—B2 the game is a draw!

| 5 .... | KxQP! | 6 N—B2ch | K—B6 |

All this is beautifully played. If now 7 NxP, K—N7 trapping the Knight, which can be safely captured this time.

| 7 K—Q1 | P—R7 | 9 N—R1 | P—Q6 |
| 8 K—B1 | P—Q5 | 10 N—B2 | .... |

He tries to trick Black, since 10 K—Q1, K—N7 is hopeless for White.

| 10 .... | P—B4! |

Of course not 10 . . . PxN?? stalemating White.

After 10 . . . P—B4! White resigns, for after 11 PxP, PxN!; 12 P—B6 there follows 12 . . . P—R8/Q mate—the perfect promotion.

Chapter Eight

SUNDRY ENDINGS

IN THIS CHAPTER we study several types of endings that are somewhat more difficult than the ones we have examined so far. In each case, except the last example, one of the players is a Pawn ahead. And in each case, the winning method is highly instructive and of great practical value.

Rooks and minor pieces

Diagram 61 reveals a wealth of tactical detail which is remarkable, considering how many pieces have been exchanged.

61

BLACK TO MOVE

Despite Black's extra Pawn White would have good fighting chances here if Black did not have some clever tactical resources at his disposal.

In Diagram 61 Black plays:

1 ....   P—B6!

First tactical point: if now 2 R—KB2, RxN!; 3 KxR, N—

K5ch followed by 4 . . . NxR and Black has won a piece.

2 R—R1   P—B7!

Second tactical point: if now 3 K—Q3, R—KR4; 4 R—R1, RxP!; 5 RxR, P—B8/Qch.

3 R—KB1	N—B4ch!	4 K—Q3	RxNch!

The third tactical point: Black will come out a piece ahead.

5 KxR	N—K6	6 RxP	N—Q8ch

White had no choice.

7 K—Q4	NxR	9 K—K4	P—R3
8 P—R4	N—N5	Resigns	

For if 10 K—B4, N—B3!; 11 K—K5, P—N4!; 12 PxP, PxP; 13 K—B5, P—N5! Now White can never capture the Knight, for the Black Pawn will queen. Black first confiscates the remaining White Pawn with his King; then he marches the King over to the King-side; finally he escorts his Pawn to the queening square.

In Diagram 62 we are back in the realm of the highly systematic procedure.

62

BLACK TO MOVE

White is a Pawn ahead and he has all the remaining Black Pawns under attack. He also has all the Black pieces in uncomfortable defensive positions. In such situations the attacker's problem is: how can I step up the pressure?

White is well prepared for 1 . . . K—B2 dis ch, which he will answer with 2 K—K5, K—N3; 3 P—N4! (a beautiful pin!), B—Q6; 4 BxPch and 5 K—Q4.

So Black tries a different way, but White has an effective plan at hand.

1 ....   B—Q6   2 B—R2ch   K—Q2 dis ch
                3 K—K5   ....

White threatens 4 B—N1 winning the Bishop Pawn.

                3 ....   K—B2

And now if 4 B—N1, K—N3; 5 P—N4, BxP (thanks to 1 . . . B—Q6).

4 K—Q5 dis ch   K—N3   5 RxRPch!   ....

The point of the subtle King maneuvers.

5 ....   KxR   7 KxP   BxP
6 KxR   B—N8   8 P—N4   K—N2

With two Pawns ahead, the win is no longer difficult. Note how carefully White avoids the difficulties that later turn up in Diagram 77.

9 P—N5!   B—N8   13 K—B5   B—N7
10 K—N4   B—K5   14 P—N6   BxP
11 P—B5   B—B6   15 KxB   P—N4
12 P—B6ch! K—R1   16 P—N7ch! Resigns

For the Pawn queens and immediately forces checkmate. (But note that 16 PxP?? produces stalemate.)

Queen and Pawn endings

These endgames are proverbially difficult, and exasperating too. The player who is behind in material often has a wealth of checks at his disposal. It takes the greatest patience to survive such a series of checks.

Since we are only interested in the principles underlying the winning process, we shall study two comparatively easy Queen and Pawn endings.

63

WHITE TO MOVE

White is a Pawn ahead, but what is more important is that he has two connected passed Pawns on the Queen-side. He means to advance them even if he has to give up several King-side Pawns in the process.

1 Q—Q3	P—B3	4 P—QN4!	Q—R7
2 K—K2	Q—K3ch	5 Q—K2	Q—B2
3 K—Q2	Q—K4	6 Q—Q3	Q—R7

This is where White decides on the all-out push of the Queen-side Pawns.

7 P—N5!	QxNPch	8 Q—K2!	QxRP

Black naturally avoids 8 . . . QxQch; 9 KxQ with a King and Pawn ending which is lost for him because of White's remote passed Pawns.

9 P—N6!   . . . .

64

BLACK TO MOVE

White's material plus has actually turned into a minus, but his Knight Pawn has become very menacing. If now 9 . . . Q—B1; 10 Q—K7ch followed by 11 Q—QB7! forces the immediate queening of the Pawn.

| 9 .... | Q—Q2 | 10 Q—B4! | .... |

With the winning threat of 11 Q—QB7: the pin would force the exchange of Queens, whereupon the remote passed Pawn would decide the outcome at once.

| 10 .... | K—N3 | 12 Q—B2ch! | P—B4 |
| 11 Q—QB7 | Q—K3 | 13 Q—N3! | .... |

Again the sinister motif of the King and Pawn ending which is hopeless for Black.

13	Q—K4	16 Q—N6ch	K—K2
14 P—N7	Q—N1	17 QxRP!	Q—K4
15 K—Q3	K—B3	18 Q—R7ch!	K—K3

An exquisite variation here is 18 . . . K—B1; 19 P—N8/Qch!, QxQ; 20 Q—R8ch. Or 18 . . . K—Q1; 19 Q—R8ch!, QxQ; 20 P—N8/Qch. In either case White wins the Queen by an X-ray attack.

| 19 Q—N8ch | K—K2 | 21 K—B4 | Q—B6ch |
| 20 P—N8/Q | Q—K6ch | 22 K—N5 | Resigns |

With a Queen down, Black has no chance.

In Diagram 65 the winning process is equally interesting.

65

BLACK TO MOVE

Black is a Pawn ahead and it is clear that his hopes of a win rest on the well advanced King Rook Pawn. The proper exploitation of this passed Pawn again depends on an X-ray attack.

In Diagram 65 Black's winning move is:

1 ....   Q—Q4ch!

If now 2 K—B4, P—R7!; 3 Q—B2ch, K—N2 and White is lost, for if 4 QxP, Q—Q3ch winning the White Queen by an X-ray attack.

If 2 K—K3, P—B3 threatens to win at once with . . . Q—K4ch. After White meets this threat, Black advances . . . K—N4, with a lengthy but assured win in sight.

2 K—N3	Q—N7ch	4 Q—Q3ch	K—N2
3 K—R4	P—R7	5 Q—Q4ch	P—B3!

And now White can resign, for after 6 Q—R7ch, K—N3! or 7 Q—Q7ch, K—R3! his Queen has no more checks.

Queen vs. Pawn

This sounds like child's play, but in this special case it is hard work despite the enormous disparity in material.

(See diagram on top of next page)

White wants to bring his own King to the vicinity of the Black King and Pawn in order to construct a mating position.

66

WHITE TO MOVE

If Black's Pawn were less advanced, White would win easily. As it is, the Pawn threatens to queen. Luckily White has an artistic winning method at his disposal.

There is only one way to accomplish this: to give a series of checks designed *to force the Black King in front of his Pawn!* Here's how to do it:

1 Q—N8	K—R7		5 Q—N4ch	K—B7
2 Q—R7ch	K—N6		6 Q—B4ch	K—Q7
3 Q—N6ch	K—B7		7 Q—N3	K—B8
4 Q—B5ch	K—Q7		8 Q—B3ch	K—N8

67

WHITE TO MOVE

At last White has forced the Black King in front of the Pawn, so the Pawn isn't threatening to queen. This gives White a breathing spell, enabling him to rush his King to the scene of action.

9 K—K3!	K—R7		11 Q—R4ch	K—N8
10 Q—B2	K—R8		12 K—K2!	....

Another way is 12 K—Q3!, K—B8; 13 Q—B2 mate— but not 12 K—Q2?? with an inglorious stalemate.

12	K—B8		13 Q—Q1 mate

Chapter Nine

HOW TO SIMPLIFY INTO A WON ENDING

SIMPLIFYING has two aspects.

The player who is ahead in material wants a placid game without complications, so that he can proceed to make use of his extra material without being disturbed by side-issues.

The player who has a material disadvantage naturally avoids simplifying as much as he can, and, just as naturally, seeks complications. The simpler the position, the more assured is his ultimate defeat. Complications, tricks, confusion offer him his best practical chance.

But this is not the only conflict on simplification.

The player who has a material advantage wants to simplify by exchanging *pieces*, particularly the Queen. (The Queen is the great troublemaker in such situations; its long-range potentialities can often stir up an unwelcome surprise.)

However, this same player is opposed to exchanging *Pawns*. We noticed this in a number of earlier endings. His opposition is based on two points.

First, he needs Pawns as queening candidates. (Just think of Diagram 20 in this respect.) The more Pawns he retains, the better his queening chances.

Don't interpret this point too literally. It does not call for a slavish avoidance of all Pawn exchanges; it merely emphasizes the need for caution.

397

As for the player who is behind in material, he avoids the exchange of pieces if he can, but seeks the exchange of Pawns where he can do so.

Removing the Queens

Now let's see some illustrations of how the exchange of Queens is brought about in actual play.

68

WHITE TO MOVE

White is a Pawn ahead and is naturally eager to exchange Queens. This is accomplished directly by a Queen check: 1 Q—K4ch. Whether Black exchanges or allows White to exchange, the Queens disappear.

In Diagram 69 a check again has the desired effect.

69

BLACK TO MOVE

White is two Pawns ahead but he must look forward to a long series of checks. Luckily, when Black tries 1 . . . Q—N4ch White has 2 Q—K2ch! forcing a King and Pawn ending which is effortlessly won for White.

In Diagram 70 Black's immediate resignation comes as something of a surprise.

398

70

BLACK TO MOVE

Though White is a Pawn ahead, it does not seem possible for him to maintain this advantage or turn it to use. Also, the position is so open that Black's chances of perpetual check are very promising.

Yet Black's resignation is quite in order, as we can see from the following play:

1 ....   K—B2

(Or any other King move to the second rank.)

2 Q—Q7ch!   ....

If Black's King goes to the third rank, then 3 Q—Q6ch! forces the exchange of Queens. In that event White's King wins the remaining Black Pawn and advances his own Knight Pawn to queen. Meanwhile Black's King is held in a vise by the White Rook Pawn.

2 ....   K—N1

On 2 ... K—B1 White has 3 Q—Q6ch! and on 2 ... K—R1 White wins as in the text.

3 Q—B8ch!   K—B2

It doesn't matter where the Black King goes.

4 Q—N7ch!   ....

Forcing the easily won King and Pawn ending described in the note to White's second move.

This is a fine example of simplifying technique.

Of course, it isn't always necessary to have a check available to force a simplified position. Any other kind of strong threat can do the trick.

71

WHITE TO MOVE

White is a Pawn ahead and would therefore like to exchange Queens. He doesn't have a check at his disposal, but 1 Q—Q6! does equally well. As Black's Rook is threatened, he has nothing better than 1 ... QxQ; 2 RxQ. Thus White has achieved his objective.

In Diagram 72, too, White does not have a check but he has an equally effective threat.

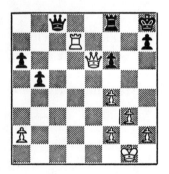

72

BLACK TO MOVE

White is a Pawn ahead. In addition, he has an overwhelming position, in view of the mating threat Q—K7. Thus he forces Black to seek the exchange of Queens even though Black is already behind in material.

1 ....   Q—B8ch

Or 1 ... Q—K1; 2 QxQ, RxQ; 3 R—Q6 winning a second Pawn for White.

2 K—N2   Q—B5   3 QxQ   PxQ
         4 R—QB7   ....

Winning a second Pawn anyway.

| 4 .... | R—QN1 | 5 RxBP | R—N3 |
| | 6 R—B7 | R—N7 | |

If Black's Rook stays on the third rank, White wins by advancing his King-side Pawns, escorted by their King.

7 R—B6	RxRP	12 P—B3	P—QR4
8 RxBP	K—N2	13 P—R4	P—R3
9 R—QN6	R—R4	14 P—N5	P—R4
10 P—N4	R—R5	15 P—B5	R—R8
11 K—N3	R—R6ch	16 R—N7ch	Resigns

White's Pawns advance irresistibly.

Other simplifying methods

In Diagram 73 we see a whole arsenal of threats used by White to force a favorable ending and then win it.

73

BLACK TO MOVE

Momentarily material is even. However, White has the nasty threat of R—Q8ch winning Black's Queen. If Black tries 1 . . . Q—K5ch; 2 P—B3, Q—K6; 3 B—B6!! wins. And if 1 . . . Q—K3; 2 Q—Q3! is decisive.

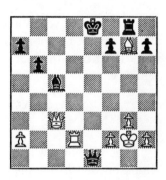

Because of the variations shown in the caption to Diagram 73, Black decides to give up the Queen.

| 1 .... | RxB | 2 R—Q8ch! | KxR |
| | 3 QxQ | .... | |

The Queen is definitely stronger than the Rook and Bishop. The play that follows is a wonderful example of the power of the Queen.

White's immediate threat is 4 Q—K5! attacking the Rook. If then 4 . . . R—N3; 5 Q—R8ch wins a Pawn, likewise after 4 . . . B—B1; 5 Q—N8ch. Finally, if 4 . . . R—N1?; 5 Q—N8ch wins the Rook.

3	R—N3	4 Q—K4!	....

Threatening to win the Queen Rook Pawn with 5 Q—R8ch or the King Rook Pawn with 5 Q—R4ch.

Black must lose one Pawn or the other. Which one is he to preserve? The King Rook Pawn, for if he loses it, White gets a *passed Pawn* at once. This passed Pawn will at once advance—a candidate for queening.

4	P—KR3	6 QxPch	K—B1
5 Q—R8ch	K—K2	7 P—QR4!	....

A clever move. White threatens 8 P—R5 when Black's Pawn cannot recapture because of the pin. The sequel would be 9 P—R6, with a dangerous passed Pawn that would queen quickly.

7	B—N5	9 Q—K5ch	K—N1
8 Q—N8ch	K—N2	10 P—B4	....

A good move which undermines the position of Black's Rook on the third rank because of the possibility of P—B5.

10	R—K3	11 Q—QN5	B—B1

Note that 11 . . . B—B4? is all wrong because of 11 P—R5! and 12 P—R6 with a winning passed Pawn.

12 P—B5	R—Q3	13 K—B3!	....

White brings his King to the Queen-side. He intends to win the Knight Pawn.

| 13 .... | R—Q5 | 14 K—K3! | .... |

To exchange Pawns by 14 QxP?, RxP would run counter to the great principle of avoiding Pawn exchanges. This capture would make White's victory extremely difficult.

14 ....   R—QN5

If instead 14 . . . B—B4; 15 Q—K8ch, K—N2 (he must guard his Bishop Pawn); 16 Q—K5ch and 17 QxR! with an easy win in the King and Pawn ending.

| 15 Q—K8 | K—N2 | 16 K—Q3 | K—N1 |
| | 17 K—B3 | .... | |

Threatening to force a won King and Pawn ending with 18 QxBch!, KxQ; 19 KxR etc.

17 ....   R—N5

He tries to keep White's King from crossing the fourth rank. Thus, if 17 . . . R—N8; 18 K—B4, R—N5ch; 19 K—Q5, R—N7; 20 K—B6 when White keeps the Knight Pawn under attack and advances his King-side Pawns against Black's weakened forces.

18 Q—N5   B—B4

The game is reaching the decisive point.

19 K—N3!   ....

Now Black is lost.

Thus, if 19 . . . R—N5ch; 20 QxR, BxQ; 21 KxB with a won King and Pawn ending.

And if 19 . . . B—Q5; 20 P—B6! (threatening 21 Q—K8ch and 22 QxPch). After 20 . . . BxP White wins easily because of the passed Queen Rook Pawn he gets by 21 QxP.

So Black has nothing better than 20 . . . K—R2. But then

21 Q—B5ch, R—N3; 22 Q—Q7!, BxP; 23 QxPch, B—N2; 24 Q—B5! is decisive.

| 19 .... | K—N2 | 20 P—R5! | Resigns |

For if 20 . . . R—N5ch; 21 QxR, BxQ and now 22 P—R6! forces the queening of the Queen Rook Pawn!

A very fine ending, played in masterly style by White.

In Diagram 74 an extremely subtle maneuver wins for White.

74

WHITE TO MOVE

The most obvious continuation, since White is a Pawn up, is to exchange the Queens and Rooks. But in that case White cannot win!

If White plays 1 QxQch, KxQ; 2 RxRch, KxR the simplification turns out to be faulty because White's King is tied down by Black's passed Queen Rook Pawn. The White King-side Pawns cannot win by themselves, and thus White is held to a draw.

Yet White can win with a subtle waiting move:

1 Q—N6!!   ....

Now Black cannot play 1 . . . K—B1?? because of 2 R—N8 mate.

Nor can he play 1 . . . Q—Q2?? because of 2 R—N8ch, K—K2; 3 Q—N5ch and mate next move.

Nor can Black play his Queen further afield because of the reply QxPch.

404

Therefore Black can only move a Pawn.

If he plays 1 . . . P—R5 then 2 K—B1! If now 2 . . . P—R6 White exchanges all the pieces then plays K—N1—R2 capturing the Rook Pawn and then winning easily by playing K—N4—B5—Q6 etc.

And if Black plays 2 . . . Q—R6ch, White wins with 3 K—N1!, Q—K2; 4 K—R2, P—R6 (forced!); 5 QxRch etc. again winning the Rook Pawn.

| 1 . . . . | P—N5 | 2 PxP | PxP |

Or 2 . . . QxPch; 3 K—K2!, Q—K2; 4 QxRch, QxQ; 5 RxQ, KxR; 6 K—Q2, K—N3; 7 K—B3, followed by K—N2—R3—R4 and KxP winning easily.

| | 3 K—Q1! | Resigns | |

Black gives up because if 3 . . . P—N6; 4 PxP, PxP and now White exchanges pieces followed by 5 K—B1—N2 and KxP.

Or if 3 . . . P—B6; 4 QxRch, QxQ; 5 RxQ, KxR; 6 K—B1 followed by K—N1—R2—N3 and KxP. As already shown, White can then liquidate the Queen-side Pawns and bring his King to the King-side to aid the queening of his Pawns there.

In Diagram 75 White wins by a series of delightful finesses.

75

WHITE TO MOVE

White is a Pawn up but he cannot make any headway in the Rook and Pawn ending. He therefore decides on the maneuver R—K6 followed by R—K5 forcing a won King and Pawn ending.

405

1 R—K6!	K—Q2	2 R—K5!	RxR
	3 PxR	....	

If now 3 . . . K—K3; 4 K—Q4, K—K2; 5 K—Q5, K—Q2; 6 P—K6ch, K—K2; 7 K—K5 followed by 8 KxP and White wins as he pleases.

	3	K—K2!

Setting a sly trap.

If now 4 K—Q4, K—K3! and White cannot win.

For example 5 P—K4?, P—B5! and Black wins the advanced Pawn.

Or if 5 K—B5, KxP; 6 KxP, K—K5; 7 KxP, KxP; 8 P—N4, P—B5. Both players get new Queens and the ending is drawn.

	4 K—Q3!!	....

Now if 4 . . . K—K3; 5 K—Q4 wins as shown in the note to White's third move.

4	K—Q2	5 P—K4!!	....

So that if 5 . . . PxPch; 6 KxP, K—K3; 7 K—Q4, K—K2; 8 K—B5 and White gives up his King Pawn to win both Black Pawns with an easy victory in sight.

5	P—B5!	6 K—K2!!	K—K3

Black's last hope. After the natural reply 7 K—B3??, KxP White loses!

7 K—B2!!	KxP	7 K—B3	Resigns

For he must move his King, allowing 8 KxP with an easy win for White.

An exciting and beautiful ending.

Diagram 76 shows a skillful transition to a won King and Pawn ending.

76

BLACK TO MOVE

Material is even, but Black can force a won King and Pawn ending.

Black's first move is the key to the win:

1	R—B8ch!!	3 KxR	KxR
2 RxR	RxRch	4 K—Q2	K—N7

Black now continues, no matter how White plays, with . . . K—N6 and . . . KxP. This gives him a won King and Pawn ending, along the lines of the play from Diagram 28.

So far we have been making use of valuable rules that help us to win when we're ahead in material.

But these rules are not infallible laws; they are only rules of thumb, and they have occasional exceptions.

In the next chapter we shall study the most important of these exceptions.

Chapter Ten

EXCEPTIONS: MATERIAL ADVANTAGE DOESN'T ALWAYS WIN

WHEN A PLAYER has worked hard to create an advantage in material and then finds that it cannot win anyhow, he is keenly disappointed. Psychologically it is a great help to him to be familiar with some of the common instances where material advantage is futile.

Such knowledge is also of great practical value, too. If you are prepared for the danger, you may know how to forestall it.

Bishops on opposite colors

We were introduced to this type of ending in Diagram 59.

77

WHITE TO MOVE

Though two Pawns to the good, White is powerless to win. His difficulty is that he has no command of the black squares. His Pawns cannot advance and his material advantage is an illusion.

Note this, however: if White's two Pawns were widely separated—say they were a King Bishop Pawn and a Queen Knight Pawn—he would then win. For the defensive forces would be split, with the Black King blockading one passed Pawn and his Bishop holding back the other.

As ~~~ lready know from the play following Diagram 59 ~~~ fense is bound to fail.

~~~ vords, there is nothing dogmatic about this "ex- ~~~ Bishops on opposite colors may draw, they ~~~ depends on the given position. This explains ~~~ on the surface—that in Diagram 59, Black, ~~~ , wins; and in Diagram 77, White, *with* ~~~ .nnot win.

~~~ er "exception to the exception" appears in the ~~~ and Pawn ending following Diagram 62. There ~~~ nite, with two connected passed Pawns, controls squares of both colors.

When material advantage loses

78

WHITE TO MOVE

White is two Pawns and the Exchange down, yet he has a forced win! Why? Because the pin reduces Black's Rook on King Bishop 3 to sheer helplessness.

| 1 RxR | RxR | 2 P—KR4! | .... |

Played to prevent . . . P—KN4 followed by . . . K—N3, whereby Black would free himself and actually win.

White must maintain the pin—that is the secret of the winning method.

| 2 .... | P—R3 | 3 K—N2 | P—KN4 |

Black hopes for . . . K—N3.

Why? Black can never free himself from the pin. He must therefore confine himself to Pawn moves. Sooner or later he will run out of Pawn moves, and he will then have to move his King, losing his Rook.

White's Pawn was so powerful that his Bishop was worth more than Black's Rook!

In Diagram 79 we have another example of *Zugzwang*, a German word describing situations where a player has to lose because it is his turn to move!

79

WHITE TO MOVE

This "exception" is really shocking. If Black were a Pawn ahead, the position would be a draw. With two Pawns up, Black is lost. The reason? His King is in an extraordinary mating net.

1 Q—K7ch!   ....

To this Black has only one reply, for if 1 ... P—N4; 2 Q—K1ch and mate next move.

1 ....   Q—N4   2 Q—K4ch!   Q—N5

Now comes the move that puts Black in *Zugzwang*:

3 Q—K3!!   Resigns

No matter how Black plays, he is forced into a checkmate position. For example:

3 ... P—N4; 4 Q—K1ch and mate follows.
3 ... Q—N4; 4 Q—KR3 mate.
3 ... Q—B4; 4 Q—KN3 mate.

410

Stalemate, the greatest "exception"

Centuries ago, when the stalemate drawing rule was first devised, it was doubtless intended as a punishment for careless or greedy players. Today it is mostly a refuge for desperately ingenious players who manage to find what is sometimes the only way out of an otherwise hopeless situation.

80

WHITE TO MOVE

In Diagram 66 we saw how hard White had to work to win with a Queen against a mere Pawn. In this example, which is even more humiliating, there is no way to win at all!

In Diagram 80 Black's King is in a stalemate position. If the Queen moves off to allow the Black King some elbow room, then Black plays . . . K—N7 and threatens to queen his advanced Pawn. The only way that White can then prevent the Pawn from queening is to check, whereupon the Black King crawls back into the corner.

Verdict: a draw!

81

A DRAWN POSITION!

Move all the forces one row to the left, and White wins easily (Diagram 28). But on the Rook files this type of ending is a draw, no matter who moves first.

If White moves first in Diagram 81, the ending can proceed like this:

1 P—R5   K—N1

When Black has a Knight Pawn, Bishop Pawn, King Pawn, or Queen Pawn, he merely plays his King one square diagonally forward to the next right-hand file, controlling the queening square and winning with ease.

With a Rook Pawn this is impossible, because the King and Pawn are located at the very edge of the board!

2 K—N6	K—R1	4 P—R7ch	K—R1
3 P—R6	K—N1	5 K—R6	....

Stalemate! If Black moves first, the result is the same.

82

WHITE TO MOVE

With a piece and a Pawn to the good, White wins easily: 1 B—Q5ch, K—N1; 2 P—R7ch, K—B1; 3 P—R8/Qch with speedy checkmate in the offing. Yet ... Diagram 83 is a draw!

83

WHITE TO MOVE

This position is a draw no matter who moves first and what White does.

Can you see any essential difference between Diagram 82 and Diagram 83?

If White plays 1 P—R7 in the position of Diagram 83, Black is immediately stalemated.

Other maneuvers do no good, for example:

1 B—K5. Again Black is stalemated. Or:

| 1 K—R5 | K—R2 | 3 K—N6 | K—N1 |
| 2 K—N5 | K—R1 | 4 B—K5ch | K—R1! |

White is making no headway.

The explanation: in order to win this type of ending with a Rook Pawn, its queening square must be of the same color as those the Bishop travels on.

When the queening square is of the right color (Diagram 82) there is an easy win.

When the queening square is of the wrong color (Diagram 83) the position is a draw.

Caution: this applies only to the Rook Pawn. All other Pawns win easily in the analogous situation.

This concludes our survey of the important exceptions to the rule that superior force should win.

Don't let these exceptions dishearten you. They are, after all, the exceptions and not the rule.

By being familiar with these exceptions you will avoid many a painful surprise. You will also be less likely to succumb to overconfidence; and this brings us to our final chapter.

Chapter Eleven

BEWARE OF OVERCONFIDENCE!

NOTHING is so conducive to overconfidence in chess as winning some material from your opponent.

And, by the same token, nothing is so discouraging as losing back that material—or more—through some ill-considered, overconfident move.

Such mistakes, when committed in the opening, may be neutralized later on. A good recovery is even possible after a middle-game mistake. But in the endgame, when the outcome of the game is already in sight, last-minute blunders stemming from overconfidence can be painfully costly.

The element of surprise

Overconfidence breeds error when we take for granted that the game will continue on its normal course; when we fail to provide for an unusually powerful resource—a check, a sacrifice, a stalemate. Afterwards the victim may wail, "But who could have dreamt of such an idiotic-looking move?"

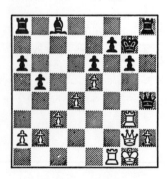

84

BLACK TO MOVE

Black is a piece ahead but he is a bit backward in development. He sees that his Queen Rook cannot be captured because of the reply . . . QxRP mate. This makes him so overconfident that he disdains the careful (and winning) 1 . . . R—QR2.

In Diagram 84 Black blunders with:

1 ....   B—N2??

Black relies on 2 QxB???, QxRP mate. But—

2 RxBPch!!   ....

The brilliant resource that Black completely overlooked.

| 2 .... | KxR | 3 QxBch | Q—K2 |

If the King moves, White captures the Rook with CHECK and still has time to stop Black's mating threat.

4 R—B3ch!   ....

The finesse that really establishes the soundness of the combination.

4	K—K1	8 RxNP	K—B2
5 QxRch	Q—Q1	9 R—N2	K—K1
6 QxQch	KxQ	10 R—N7	R—R6
7 R—B6	K—K2	11 R—QR7	Resigns

Of course White's enormous advantage in material must win easily for him.

Stalemate in master play!

This actually happened to one of the greatest living grandmasters; he overlooked an obvious stalemate possibility.

Sammy Reshevsky had the White pieces in this easily won position in the World Championship Candidate's Tournament of 1953.

85

With two Pawns ahead, White should win in due course. His proper play is 1 R—R8, with a slow but sure win in prospect. Instead, he completely overlooks a stalemate!

White's continuation in Diagram 85 was the thoughtless move:

1 R—KB6??   ....

This gives Black the chance of a lifetime:

1 ....   R—KB6ch!!

Now if 2 K—K2, RxNP; 3 RxPch, KxP and Black has an easy draw, as White's forces are too badly placed to derive any value from the extra Pawn.

2 K—N2   RxNPch!!
Draw

If White captures the impudent Rook, Black is stalemated. If White proudly refuses to capture the Rook, the sequel might be:

3 K—R2	R—KR6ch!!	5 K—B2	R—KB6ch!!
4 K—N2	R—KN6ch!!	6 K—K2	RxP

So White swallows his pride and accepts the draw at once.

416

He who laughs last

With a Pawn ahead, Black was indulging in rather breezy counterplay which eventually led to the position of Diagram 86.

86

WHITE TO MOVE

White attacks the Knight, but his King Bishop is pinned. If White plays 1 BxN, Black replies 1 . . . RxB. However, Black has missed a surprise mating threat.

In Diagram 86 White suddenly unleashes a mating threat.

1 B—B5!!   ....

Attacks Black's Rook and also threatens 2 B—B8ch!, K—N1; 3 B—R6 dis ch and mate next move.

1 ....   B—K2

Black manages to lose "only" the Exchange; but of course this is enough to lose the game.

2 BxR	BxB	5 R—K8	P—B4
3 P—B5!	P—K6	6 B—B4	B—Q3
4 P—B6!	N—K5	7 P—B7!	BxNPch

It doesn't matter what Black does. The passed Bishop Pawn will cost him a piece.

| 8 K—N2 | BxP | 10 RxB | P—B5 |
| 9 R—K7ch | K—B3 | 11 K—B3 | Resigns |

With a Rook ahead, White wins as he pleases.

417

All's well that ends well

But dwelling on the blunders of overconfidence would be a sorry note on which to end this book. So, let's take a last look at a situation in which the prospective winner has become too confident, and yet manages to make a masterly recovery before it's too late.

87

BLACK TO MOVE

With three Pawns to the good, White is understandably lighthearted in this situation. Black's fantastic reply soon shatters this overconfident mood.

	1	R—R8ch?!
	2 KxR	PxP

Neither White's King nor his Rook, so it seems, can stop the Black Pawn from queening.

Nevertheless, White can save the game. To Black's surprise-by-violence he has an even more effective surprise-by-violence.

3 R—KB5!!	KxR	4 P—KN4ch!!	KxP

Now White is ready for the saving move:

5 K—N2	Resigns

For White disposes of the dangerous Pawn and then wins on the Queen-side.

And so White has triumphantly vindicated the thesis of this book: superior force should win!

How
to
Fight
Back

Book Six

Chapter One

COUNTERATTACK—HOW TO MEET
THE CRISIS

NOT SO LONG AGO I read a magazine article about a baseball manager who is famous for his fighting spirit and aggressiveness. I was not surprised to learn that this manager has no equal when it comes to bellowing at an umpire. But, when his team falls behind, this manager "seems to lose interest."

So it is with us chessplayers. *We attack because we like to; we defend because we have to.* We tend to do badly the things we dislike. And, since we dislike to defend, we defend miserably. Thus we lose many games which we might have won—should have won.

Have you ever stopped to think that attacking ability plays a big role in defensive play? Forget about the common assumption that defending means passive maneuvers, patient crawling, endless dread of the decisive blow.

There are many times when you can smash your opponent's attack with one vigorous thrust. If you size up your resources accurately, you can seize the attack for yourself. In other words, play the defense in an aggressive mood. Here's how:

Look for counterplay

Let's look at some actual examples to see the far-reaching difference between active and passive defense. In Diagram 1, for instance, passive play will never do:

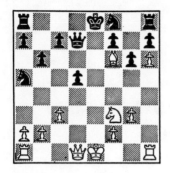

BLACK TO MOVE
At first sight it seems that Black can win a piece by the double attack . . . Q—K3ch.

White's Bishop is attacking Black's King Rook. Black can simply save the Rook with . . . KR—N1. Instead, he tries:

$$1 \ldots \ldots \quad \text{Q—K3ch}$$

Now if White tries to save his menaced Bishop by 2 B—K5? (passive defense), he loses his Bishop after 2 . . . P—KB3.

White must find counterplay—*active* defense! Therefore:

$$2 \text{ Q—K2!} \quad \ldots \ldots$$

By interposing his Queen, White has pinned the Black Queen, and has thus saved his Bishop.

This was a very clean-cut example, in which White was confronted with a stark decision. He *had* to find the right move, otherwise his Bishop would be lost at once.

But sometimes the crisis, though real, is not so obvious to us. In such cases we tend to take it easy, thereby drifting into a lost game. Diagram 2 illustrates this possibility:

422

2

WHITE TO MOVE

White wants to save his attacked King Pawn, and at the same time get a powerful Pawn center, with P—K4. Is the plan good or bad?

White plays the move that looks logical:

1 P—K4   PxP   2 PxP   . . . .

Now Black must look sharp. If he plays the dull 2 . . . N—K2, he has a hopeless position after 3 P—K5, N/B3—Q4; 4 N—K4. In that event, White has a magnificent attacking position, with his open King Bishop file, his powerfully centralized Knight, and his Queen and Bishop poised for action on the King-side. (Even his Queen Rook can be switched quickly to the King-side by means of R—R2 followed by QR—KB2.)

So here is the crisis. Black can play listlessly, falling into a helpless defensive position—or, he can strike out boldly at the one weakness in White's position. Namely:

2 . . . .   NxQP!

This wins a Pawn and destroys White's mighty Pawn center and his beautiful attacking position. For if now 3 PxN, QxPch winning White's Queen Rook! Vigorous counterplay solved Black's problem.

423

In Diagram 3 we come back to a situation where the crisis is drastic and immediate. Black's position is threatened so strongly that he seems quite lost:

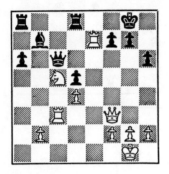

3

BLACK TO MOVE

White threatens QxBPch followed by QxNP mate. He also threatens to win a piece by RxB or NxB. Can Black hold the position?

Most players would see no way for Black to save himself in this predicament. And yet there is a way out—if only Black is determined!

His problem is this: how can he parry the mate threat without losing his Bishop? If there is a way, it must be based on a *counterthreat*—a threat of mate, for example. And Black finds the resource he needs:

1 ....   Q—KN3!

This defends against White's mate threat of QxBPch etc.

At the same time Black indirectly defends his Bishop by threatening . . . Q—N8ch followed by checkmate on the back rank. In other words, White must now stop to prevent this checkmate, giving Black the time to salvage his Bishop.

Thus you see how Black, by his alert counterplay, saved a position which many players would have dismissed as hopeless.

Find the hidden flaw

The first step toward becoming a skilful defensive player, then, is to handle the defense in an aggressive spirit. If you do that, you can find subtle defensive resources that other players would not dream of. By seeking active counterplay, you will often upset clever attacking lines. Better yet, you will upset your opponent.

Diagram 4 offers a good example of such a refutation:

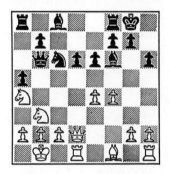

BLACK TO MOVE

Black's Queen is attacked; so is his Queen Pawn. Naturally he will save his Queen. Does that mean his Queen Pawn is lost?

No doubt of it—this is a difficult situation for Black. If he saves his Queen by 1 . . . Q—B2, then White simply continues 2 QxQP with a Pawn to the good.

Or if Black tries 1 . . . Q—N5, White has 2 QxQ, PxQ; 3 N—N6, R—N1; 4 NxB, RxN followed by 5 RxP and again White has won a Pawn, leaving Black without compensation.

Must White win a Pawn—or is there some sly, hidden resource for Black? There is, if Black is alert enough to search for it. Here it is:

1 . . . .   Q—B2   2 QxQP   . . . .

Now comes a stinging surprise:

2 ....   R—Q1!!

Giving away the Queen?

3 QxQ   RxRch   4 N—B1   B—Q1!!

The beautiful point of Black's exceptionally clever play. White's Queen is trapped, and White has nothing better than to give up the Queen for a minor piece. In that case, Black will have a Rook for a minor piece and Pawn. This advantage of "the Exchange" will assure Black victory in the endgame.

Black's play in Diagram 4 was remarkably fine. But the way White fights back in the position of Diagram 5 is even more fascinating, especially from a sporting point of view. Here White evolved his defense in a very difficult position, with all the spectators certain that Black was building up a brilliant winning position.

5

BLACK TO MOVE

Materially the position is about even, as Black has a Rook and two Pawns for two minor pieces. Positionally, however, Black has a very strong game with one of his Rooks on the seventh rank.

426

The powerful position of one of Black's Rooks on the seventh rank gives Black formidable mating threats. The situation is all the more difficult for White because his forces are scattered, and his Queen is unable to get back to the King-side. (Note, for example, that Q—B1 or Q—K2 is impossible.)

Well aware of the strength of his position, Black tries to achieve a decision on the King-side. He starts with:

1 ....   Q—B1

This looks terrifying, as Black threatens 2 . . . RxKNPch! If then 3 PxR, Q—B7ch and mate next move. If, instead, 3 K—R1, RxRPch!; 4 KxR, Q—B7ch forces mate.

How is White to defend? If he tries passive play with 2 R—KB1, Black has 2 . . . RxRch; 3 QxR, Q—QB4ch winning White's Knight. That would leave Black with two Pawns and the Exchange ahead—an easy win for him.

So White does the best he can:

2 BxR   QxB

Apparently Black has calculated beautifully. He threatens 3 . . . Q—N7 mate.

If White tries 3 Q—B1—this seems the only defense—there follows 3 . . . R—N7ch!; 4 QxR, QxRch followed by 5 . . . QxN. With two Pawns ahead, Black would have an easy win in the Queen and Pawn ending.

So there you see White's predicament—either he gets mated (immediate death), or he loses the ending (slow death, with torture). Or . . . is there some way out for White? There is—and what a way!

3 N—B6ch!!   Resigns!!

Black resigns although he's on the point of administering checkmate! Why?

In the first place, if Black plays 3 . . . PxN he allows White to snatch the attack: 4 Q—K8ch, K—N2; 5 R—Q7 mate. Bravo!

And if Black plays 3 . . . QxN, White has 4 Q—N3ch winning Black's Rook and coming out a Rook ahead.

Finally, if Black tries 3 . . . K—B2 (or 3 . . . K—R1; 4 Q—K8 mate), White has a neat checkmate with 4 Q—K8ch!, KxN; 5 R—Q6ch, K—N4; 6 Q—N6 mate!

Admittedly, White's resource was not easy to see. And why? Because few players, threatened with mate on the move, would have the imaginative daring to try to fight their way out—*to hit back*, instead of being resigned to a hopeless endgame.

In Diagram 6 you can see the same point illustrated even more forcefully. White's pieces are beautifully posted—and yet his Queen is lost! What would you do in such a position —would you resign, or would you look for some way out?

6

WHITE TO MOVE

White's Queen is lost. How should he proceed? Is his game hopeless, or does he have some subtle, deeply hidden resource that wins for him?

There is a clue to White's procedure in this fact: Black's

King has a very shaky position, right in the middle of the board and facing White's businesslike Rook on the Queen file.

Well, what then? Suppose White gives a discovered check:

1 N—B3 dis ch   K—B1

As it happens, Black can hold out longer with 1 . . . B—Q2. But why play this chicken-hearted interposition when he can win White's Queen?

So, here we have the critical position. What can White do to make up for the threatened loss of his Queen? Is there any resource which offers the slightest hope in this desperate situation?

2 NxN!!   . . . .

If now 2 . . . PxN; 3 QxBch and White's Queen is safe, with a piece to the good. But Black is relentless:

2 . . . .   BxQ

What now?
Well, White has a check. Let's try it:

3 B—K6ch   K—N1

And now another check:

4 N—Q7ch   K—B1

Wonderful! White has a perpetual check by moving his Knight back and forth. His faith in the strength of his position has been justified.

But wait . . . this is a dangerous moment. What a pity if White, in a moment of relief because he's managed to save

the game, misses the fact *that he has a forced checkmate!*
This is how:

5 N—B8 dis ch! K—N1   6 R—Q8ch   N—B1
                   7 RxN mate

White's uphill struggle was very rewarding. It takes a lot
of courage to fight on in a situation where the Queen is
irretrievably lost.

But note this, which is typical: instead of giving way to
despair, White calmly sized up the position and made the
best possible use of the factors favoring him. In this case it
was the splendid attacking position of his pieces poised to
smite the Black King that gave White the all-important
hint.

One point that's rather puzzling: how was White able to
unleash such a powerful attack without having the services
of his Queen? The answer is partly, as we've seen, that
Black's King was badly exposed to attack. But this isn't the
whole answer. The other vital element was the fact that
Black's Queen was not in a position to aid the defense.

And so it turned out that White's loss of the Queen was
minor—but only because he hit back, immediately, with all
the forces at his command.

In the position of Diagram 7, on the other hand, everything is deceptively serene. Black is a Pawn ahead, and
while his pieces are somewhat awkwardly placed, he seems
to have no reason to worry.

7

WHITE TO MOVE

Black is all set to answer an astonishing sacrifice with an even more astonishing reply.

White has deliberately headed for this position, as he has a very powerful-looking move which seems to give him an overwhelming positional advantage:

1 RxP? ....

Black's first reaction might well be one of terror as he considers the consequences of 1 . . . QxR?; 2 P—Q6.

The fight against White's formidable passed Queen Pawn seems hopeless, for example:

If 2 . . . Q—N2; 3 PxN, BxP; 4 BxB, QxB; 5 Q—Q5ch winning Black's Queen Rook.

Or if 2 . . . Q—Q1; 3 PxN, BxP; 4 BxB winning the same way.

The same motif appears after 2 . . . Q—B3; 3 PxN, B—KN2; 4 Q—Q5ch!, QxQ; 5 P—K8/Qch and wins.

Black, in despair, might try 2 . . . RxP; 3 BxR. But then White wins back his Pawn and remains with a vastly superior position.

This is a very useful position to study; it is in just such situations that a player, confronted with several unattractive possibilities, loses his head completely. The strain proves too much for the player who is on the defensive.

But in this case Black plays with admirable poise, unleashing a counterattack which leaves White with a lost game.

$$1 \ldots \quad \text{N—B4!!}$$

A magnificent move, which to begin with, takes the sting out of White's contemplated P—Q6.

In addition, look at Black's threats: 2 . . . QxR or 2 . . . BxB or 2 . . . N—K6. His keen, alert countermove has snatched the initiative from White.

If White tries 2 RxB, RxR; 3 PxN, then 3 . . . BxB leaves Black the Exchange ahead.

Or if 2 RxB, RxR; 3 BxB, then Black has a crushing reply in 3 . . . N—K6.

White tries a different way, but Black still remains with a winning game.

2 BxB	QxR	3 B—R3	N—K6
4 Q—B1	. . . .		

Now Black has two ways to proceed. He can play 4 . . . Q—Q2 attacking White's Knight and thus winning a second Exchange. Or he can play 4 . . . Q—KN2, with the idea of playing for a King-side attack.

Actually Black made the second choice, but this no longer concerns us here. What interests us is that Black, confronted by a stern challenge, met the crisis with a superb countermove that turned the game in his favor.

So there you have the moral of this chapter. Beware of passive defense that may force you into a straitjacket position. Look for defensive moves that are active and aggressive. Don't be satisfied merely with moves that blunt the hostile attack. Look for moves that enable you to take the attack into your own hands. The examples in this chapter show you how it's done.

Chapter Two

RESOURCEFUL DEFENSE—
HOW TO SIMPLIFY

No SOONER have I convinced you of the value of *active* defense than I must add a word of caution.

Alert, aggressive defense is fine, but it isn't always possible. What do you do when it isn't possible? Do you just allow the attack to overwhelm you? Do you give up hope, resigning yourself to the inevitable? Or do you look for some resource against your opponent's attack?

Simplify!

Few of us realize that one of the best weapons against an attack is to play for exchange of pieces. An attack flourishes on complications, on the efforts of powerfully posted pieces aimed at cramped positions.

Every time you simplify, you remove a hostile piece that might have done a great deal of damage. You're also removing a unit of your own that might have been idle or useless. But above all, you're whittling down the force of your opponent's attack; *you're reducing the danger to which you're exposed.*

And remember this: if you're ahead in material, simplifying is even more useful to you. For you not only smother the attack, you also bring the game to the ending stage where you can make the best use of your extra material.

433

To see how quickly simplifying puts an end to an attack, let's study some particularly effective examples.

8

BLACK TO MOVE

Black is well ahead in material, but his position is uncomfortable. What is his most forcing line?

In Diagram 8 Black breaks the force of the attack once for all by playing:

1 ....   Q—R8ch!

This neat resource leaves White no choice.

2 KxQ   N—B7ch

And Black continues with 3 . . . NxQ. With the Queens gone, Black has nothing to fear. He wins easily, thanks to his extra material.

The situation in Diagram 9 is much more puzzling. Black has a piece for a Pawn, but one of his Rooks is attacked and cannot move. But this attacked Rook is the key to his defensive position, guarding his attacked Bishop! In short, Black has a baffling problem. How is he to solve it?

434

9

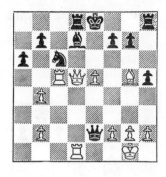

BLACK TO MOVE

In this difficult defensive situation, Black can easily go wrong. For example if 1 . . . B—K3??; 2 QxRch!, NxQ; 3 RxN mate.

Should Black try 1 . . . N—K2, the sequel might be 2 Q—Q6, N—B4; 3 QxBch!, RxQ; 4 R—B8ch and mate next move.

Or 1 . . . N—K2; 2 Q—Q6, N—B1; 3 RxN! and wins.

For such picayune defensive tries we can only comment pityingly, "Black isn't using his head."

No; such uninspired moves will never do. The right way is a drastic simplifying move:

1 . . . .   QxRch!!

This breaks the attack.

2 QxQ   B—N5!!

Splendid play.

If now 3 BxR, BxQ and Black is a piece ahead with an easy game.

Or 3 QxRch, NxQ with the same result.

Or 3 QxB, PxQ; 4 BxR, KxB—again with the same result.

In each case Black has a clear win with his extra material. And he has smashed White's attack.

How to prepare simplification

Though simplifying may be desirable in certain positions, it may sometimes require some preparation. This is the case, for example, in Diagram 10.

10

BLACK TO MOVE

Though two Pawns ahead, Black is in difficulties. How can he steer into a favorable endgame?

Black is subjected to a double pin, and in addition he must guard against the menace of P—B5. The fact that he is two Pawns ahead indicates the course he should adopt.

It's well worth while giving up one of his extra Pawns if he can thereby simplify the position. In that way he will no longer be subjected to attack; and, what is equally desirable, he will be able to win the endgame with his extra remaining Pawn.

Black's course is therefore clear:

$$1 \ldots \ldots \qquad Q\text{—}B2!$$

Black unpins his Bishop. He thereby threatens . . . BxB—not to mention . . . Q—N3ch forcing the exchange of Queens.

$$2 \text{ BxB} \qquad \text{PxB}$$

See how nicely Black's plans have developed. If now 3 RxP, Q—N3ch; 4 QxQ, PxQ; 5 BxN, PxB; 6 RxKBP, RxP and Black wins the endgame with his extra Pawn.

3 R/K1—K3 ....

Momentarily preventing the exchange of Queens as . . .
Q—N3 will not be a check.

3 .... R—KB1!

Well played. He unpins 'the Knight, threatening . . . N—
Q4. This would drive away White's Rook from King 3, thus
preparing the way for . . . Q—N3ch and the exchange of
Queens.

Black has left his opponent at a loss for a good continuation. White feels there is nothing better to do than to regain
one of his Pawns. So:

4 BxN	RxB	6 RxR	Q—N3ch!
5 RxP	RxR	7 QxQ	PxQ

Black has achieved his purpose. By simplifying, he has
relieved the pressure on his game. The attack is over, and
Black will win the endgame with his extra Pawn.

In Diagram 11 Black is faced with a much more difficult
defensive task. He is a Pawn down, his King is insecure,
and there is an immediate threat of RxB.

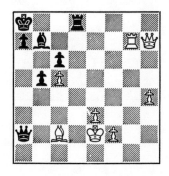

11

BLACK TO MOVE

*What move satisfactorily guards
Black's menaced Bishop in this difficult situation?*

Instead of resorting to passive defense, Black finds a magnificent resource:

$$1 \dots \quad \text{P—N5!!}$$

This threatens . . . P—N6 and thus induces White to simplify. But what is this?—isn't Black's Bishop attacked?

$$2 \text{ RxB} \quad \text{Q—R3ch!}$$

The other point of Black's previous move. By opening up the diagonal for this check, he made it possible to win the Rook.

| 3 B—Q3 | QxR | 5 P—R5 | P—N6! |
| 4 QxQch | KxQ | 6 P—R6 | . . . . |

An exciting ending. Black has calculated well, having foreseen that if 6 K—Q2 (instead of White's last move), then 6 . . . P—N7 wins at once!

| 6 . . . . | P—R4! | 7 P—R7 | P—R5 |

12

WHITE TO MOVE

Black's Rook is more agile than White's Bishop; and Black's connected passed Pawns are more menacing than White's Rook Pawn.

Black has shown splendid judgment in playing for simplification. Though the ending is close, it favors him in all variations.

Consider this possibility: 8 K—Q2, P—R6; 9 K—B3, P—R7; 10 K—N2, RxB!!; 11 P—R8/Q, R—Q8!

If now 12 Q—R7ch, K—R3 and Black wins with the coming . . . P—R8/Qch. Beautiful play!

8 B—B4   ....

Now Black can win by 8 . . . P—N7; 9 B—R2, P—R6; 10 B—N1, R—KR1; 11 K—Q2, RxP! for if 12 BxP, P—R7 and the Pawns queen.

But Black has had enough excitement, and decides on a simpler course which is just as convincing:

8 ....   R—KR1

Black's idea is that if now 9 B—N8, then 9 . . . P—N7 forces the Bishop to return to Rook 2, allowing . . . RxP in reply.

9 B—Q3   P—R6

White resigns, for if 10 B—N1, P—R7 is deadly. Black's incisive timing has made this endgame a pleasure to play over. But even more admirable was his foresight in playing for simplification. In this way he neutralized all attacking possibilities on White's part and prepared for a winning endgame.

Patient defense

Aggressive defense is good—if you can achieve it. Simplifying is good—if you can achieve it. But what do you do where neither of these methods is possible? In that case you must bide your time—not with passive squirming, but by constantly remaining on the lookout for aggressive counterplay and useful simplification.

How the defender can work toward these goals is shown in the following play, which is more difficult than in the previous examples.

13

WHITE TO MOVE

Black is two Pawns ahead with a solid position. But when White hits out boldly, Black cannot depend on his material advantage alone.

Many players in Black's position (Diagram 13) would think, "It's all over but the shouting." They would therefore be unprepared for the vicious attack now unleashed by White.

Of course, White gets nowhere with 1 BxN (hoping for 1 . . . BxB????; 2 QxRP mate). Black replies 1 . . . RxB! with nothing to fear. But White has a different way:

1 BxPch   . . . .

This is not sound. But Black, as you will see, must be wary.

1 . . . .   NxB

Black is not afraid of 2 BxB, QxB; 3 R—KR4 despite its deadly appearance. For then he interpolates 3 . . . Q—B3! (threatening mate in two) and thereby gaining time to protect the Knight with 4 . . . Q—B4.

2 R—KR4	BxB	4 RxB	PxR
3 RxN	B—R3	5 QxRP	. . . .

440

White threatens a murderous attack with 6 R—K3 followed by R—N3ch and mate. Luckily, Black has provided against this seemingly decisive attack.

	5	R—N2!!

But not 5 . . . P—B3??; 6 Q—N6ch, K—R1; 7 R—K3 and Black can resign.

	6 R—K3	P—B3!

Now that he has guarded his second rank with his previous move, Black need not fear 7 Q—N6ch. (He has the convincing reply 7 . . . R—N2.)

	7 R—N3ch	K—B2

Note how artfully Black has combined the details of his defensive plan. He is safe against 8 R—N7ch (or similar moves), because his Rook at Queen Knight 2 is guarded by his Bishop.

Black has defended successfully; White has shot his bolt. The rest is easy.

	8 P—B4	Q—N3ch

If now 9 K—R1, Q—QN8ch!!

9 K—B1	K—K1	10 P—B5	P—K4
11 R—N6	B—N4ch		

White resigns. An impressive example of resourceful defensive play by Black.

In Diagram 14 Black's problem is just as difficult, though somewhat different. He is a piece and a Pawn to the good, but his King is uncastled and condemned to an exposed position in the center.

Worse yet, White's pieces are all developed and aggres-

441

sively placed, whereas Black's development has been greatly delayed.

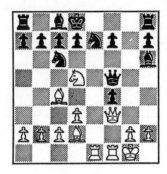

14

WHITE TO MOVE

Black's problem is: can he defend himself successfully despite his arrears in development?

If Black is left in peace for a move or two, he can play . . . P—Q3 and . . . B—K3—or else he can simplify with . . . NxN etc. Consequently, if White is to achieve anything with his attack, he must try to force the pace right now. Thus the next few moves will be critical for both sides.

| 1 B—B3 | KR—N1 | 2 B—B6 | B—N4 |

Black must get rid of the pin at once.

3 RxN!?   . . . .

White hopes for the following tricky variation: 3 . . . NxR; 4 NxN, QxB; 5 NxR, Q—N2; 6 P—KR4!, BxP; 7 QxP, B—N4; 8 QxKBP and White has regained the lost piece.

3 . . . .   BxB!

Alert defensive play, after which White must beat a retreat. Meanwhile, the exchange of pieces has eased Black's game.

442

| 4 R—K4 | B—N4 | 6 P—KR4 | BxP |
| 5 P—KN4 | Q—N3 | 7 QxP | P—Q3 |

Now Black is ready for . . . QxPch. This threat—for it is a threat—forces White to gobble a Pawn or two. But the result is the exchange of Queens, whereby Black eases his position still more.

| 8 QxBP | QxQ | 10 RxRP | NxB |
| 9 RxQ | N—K4! | 11 RxN | P—B3 |

Black's game is still unwieldy—but in no danger. With the Queens off the board, he has nothing to fear.

| 12 N—B7 | R—N1 | 14 R/B4—B7 | KxN |
| 13 R—B4 | B—K2 | 15 RxBch | K—N3 |

We need not follow the play any further. With a piece to the good and his King in perfect safety, Black is sure to win.

We have so far learned a number of valuable defensive techniques. We have seen that the defender must strive to be alert and aggressive. We have noted the value of simplifying in order to break up the strength of the attack.

Nor is this all. We have seen that sometimes the defender must hold out for a number of moves, patiently but resourcefully biding his time until he is safe from danger.

In the next chapter we turn to another important facet of defensive play. This coming chapter stresses the point that the defender can sometimes succeed only by drastically limiting his goals. If you understand this paradox and put it to good use, you will avoid many a lost game.

Chapter Three

HALF A POINT IS BETTER THAN NONE

A GREAT WRITER once observed that you can tell a master by the way he limits his ambitions. There is a lot of truth in this observation.

Have you ever realized how your ambitions become broader or narrower during the course of a game? When your opponent is attacking fiercely and when you're hard pressed, you'd be very glad to escape with a draw. Yet, a moment later, when the pressure has eased off, you've forgotten all about your worries, and you play headlong for a win.

Some players are even more optimistic, or shall we say, more stubborn. Even in the most difficult situations, they insist on "all or nothing"—win or lose. And very often they lose precisely because they refuse to concede the half point. (In competitive play, a win equals one point, a draw equals a half point.)

What I'm getting at is this: there are some positions so difficult to defend that you do well to accept a draw. Very often, to despise the possible draw means a forced loss. Sometimes it means a likely loss, or a grim, uphill fight at best.

Consequently, to force a draw in such a difficult position is a real achievement. Some players still look on a draw as a disgrace or a misfortune; however, when you look at the following examples, you will realize how much skill and artistry go into the job of forcing a draw in a lost position.

444

Drawing by perpetual check

A perpetual check is often a welcome resource in disagreeable situations. Take Diagram 15 as a case in point.

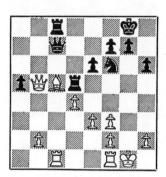

15

BLACK TO MOVE
*With a Pawn down, Black welcomes
the opportunity to force a draw by
perpetual check. How?*

Black finds a wonderfully ingenious resource to draw the
game:

| 1 .... | QxPch! | 2 KxQ | R—R4ch |

And now, believe it or not, Black has a forced draw even
though he is a Queen down!

| 3 K—N3 | R—N4ch | 4 K—B4 | R—B4ch |

White agrees to a draw, for after 5 K—N3, R—N4ch;
6 K—R3, R—R4ch he still cannot make any headway.

In this example you see with beautiful clarity the useful-
ness of forcing a draw in a position that would be lost by
the usual run-of-the-mill moves. And who can deny that
Black displayed the highest artistry in finding this exquisite
resource?

When we turn to Diagram 16, we find that the defender is
in an even more desperate situation. White threatens Q—N7

445

mate. If Black defends with 1 . . . QR—N1 or 1 . . . N—N3, then 2 Q—B6ch forces checkmate.

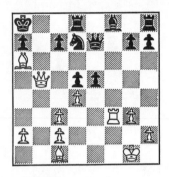

16

BLACK TO MOVE
Can Black save the game? If so, how?

Black's position is desperate; no doubt of it.

But note this: in order to build up his attack, White had previously sacrificed a Rook. With a Rook ahead, Black can well afford to give up material in order to escape from the mate trap.

Is there some counter-sacrifice that offers a way out? Let's try the only possibility:

1 ....   N—B4!!

Splendid play! The point is that if 2 PxN (again threatening mate), Black wins with 2 . . . QxPch forcing the exchange of Queens and a winning endgame, thanks to his material advantage.

Thus Black has prevented Q—N7 mate, and meanwhile he threatens . . . NxB, squelching the attack once for all.

But suppose White plays 2 B—R3, with a view to 3 BxN and wins? Can Black still hold out? Yes!—his position holds by a hair, but it holds. In the event of 2 B—R3, Black parries deftly with 2 . . . Q—Q2!!

In that case, 3 QxQ, NxQ is equivalent to resignation on

White's part. Thus he is forced to play 3 PxN, allowing Black to continue 3 . . . QxQ with a winning endgame.

White sees that this won't do at all. This time he's the one who's happy to take a perpetual check. So:

2 Q—B6ch   K—N1   3 Q—N5ch   K—R1

Drawn. Both sides must be content with the drawn result. White draws despite his material minus; Black draws despite the mating menace.

In Diagram 17 the play is even more exciting. White is the great Professor Anderssen, one of the finest attacking players in the history of the game. The Black pieces are played by Zukertort, his most brilliant pupil. Both of these masters of sparkling combinative play outdo themselves in conjuring up magnificent resources.

17

WHITE TO MOVE

White, who is two Pawns and the Exchange down, must stake everything on his attack. Black is hard put to it to escape disaster.

White begins an extraordinarily brilliant attack with:

1 Q—N5!   . . . .

This threatens 2 Q—R6 followed by mate. What is Black to do?

1 ....   Q—Q7!

A superb defense which parries White's threat and in turn threatens . . . QxP mate. At this point, most players handling the White pieces would resign. But White finds an amazing resource:

2 N—B5!!   ....

A move that sparkles with pretty possibilities.

For example, if 2 . . . QxB; 3 N—K7ch, K—R1; 4 RxPch, KxR; 5 Q—R4 mate.

Or 2 . . . QxPch; 3 QxQ, BxQ; 4 N—K7ch, K—R1; 5 NxPch!, PxN; 6 P—B7 dis ch followed by mate—or 5 . . . K—N1; 6 N—K7ch, K—R1; 7 RxP mate.

Black finds the only defense:

2 ....   QxQ

Has White gone mad? Black has not only won the Queen; he actually threatens mate on the move. But Black will be happy to get a draw!

3 N—K7ch   K—R1

Apparently White has shot his bolt.

4 NxPch!!   ....

As we have seen earlier, Black gets mated if he plays . . . PxN or . . . K—N1. He must give back the Queen.

4 ....   QxN   5 BxQ   ....

And now if 5 . . . PxB; 6 P—B7 dis ch forces mate!

5 ....   R—Q7!

With formidable counterthreats. White is now happy to take the perpetual check:

6 RxPch   K—N1   7 R—N7ch   Drawn

Black cannot avoid the perpetual check. White must take it because he is still a Rook down. One of the finest examples of master chess ever played.

Drawing by stalemate

The examples of perpetual check we've just seen have an almost miraculous quality about them. They remind us that if we have faith, we can often achieve the impossible.

To bring about a stalemate is in the nature of things just as miraculous. An opponent who is good enough to win material from you ought to be good enough not to let you hoodwink him with a stalemate. And yet these miracles do happen.

An extraordinary instance occurred in the position of Diagram 18, in which White, with two Pawns to the good, allowed his alert opponent to escape with a draw.

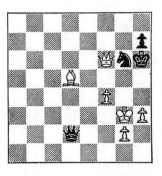

18

WHITE TO MOVE
What is the best way for White to guard his attacked Bishop?

White's Bishop is attacked. There are many ways to meet the threat, but it was White's misfortune to overlook a delightful tactical possibility.

449

One of the simplest ways to continue was 1 Q—N5ch, K—N2; 2 B—B3. Instead there followed:

1 B—B3??   . . . .

What could be more plausible? And yet the move is an unforgivable blunder. For now the Black King is in a stalemate position. Black pounces on his chance to escape from a lost game.

1 . . . .   Q—KB7ch!!

Draw! For after 2 KxQ Black is left without a move. Nor will 2 K—R2 help, for then Black plays 2 . . . Q—N6ch! or 2 . . . Q—N8ch! Similarly, on 2 K—N4 Black has 2 . . . Q—N6ch! etc. Imagine White's chagrin!

In the position of Diagram 19 the play proceeds in an even more spectacular manner. Here it's not a question of either player blundering. White makes an ingenious attempt to win; Black foils him in an even more ingenious manner!

19

WHITE TO MOVE
White's winning plan will tax Black's defensive resources to the utmost.

The powerful position of one of his Rooks on the seventh rank gives White an ingenious winning idea:

1 RxN!   . . . .

Expecting 1 . . . . RxR; 2 NxP and wins because of the double threat of 3 R—R7 mate or 3 NxR.

Black is apparently lost, but he finds a masterly defense based on a piquant stalemate idea.

1 . . . .   R—KR4ch!

A mysterious-looking move which is the basis of Black's plan.

| 2 K—N1 | RxR | 3 NxP | R—R8ch!! |

The first point!

| 4 KxR | R—K8ch | 5 K—R2 | R—KR8ch!! |

The final point. After 6 KxR Black is stalemated. A witty finish.

Our final example of stalemate is equally amusing. In the position of Diagram 20 Black finds himself in an apparently hopeless situation. White has four Pawns for the Exchange, and Black's King is exposed to attack.

20

BLACK TO MOVE

Black's position seems ripe for resignation. Instead, he forces a sensational draw.

What now happens is almost too good to be true. However, it did happen in an international masters' tournament!

1 ....   RxKRPch!

White can hardly decline the Rook, as this would cost his Bishop.

2 KxR   Q—K3ch!!!

And who could expect such a move?

3 QxQ   Drawn

Black is stalemated! Unfortunately, White's comment is not on record.

Drawing by repetition of moves

This drawing method is not too frequent, but it has produced some remarkable finishes. It implies an equilibrium of forces, in which both players are compelled to draw because they have no better line of play. Diagram 21 is a good example.

21

WHITE TO MOVE

Black threatens 1 . . . RxBch!; 2 KxR, R—Q8 mate.

Because of the variation just pointed out, White decides to unpin his Rook:

452

1 K—R1!   ....

White is momentarily safe, but now Black finds an even more vicious pin:

1 ....   Q—K7!

Threatens 2 . . . RxBch or 2 . . . QxBch followed by mate. And of course White must not play 2 RxQ?? because of 2 . . . RxB mate. So White defends with:

2 K—N1!   Q—K6!

Renewing the threat of . . . RxBch followed by . . . R—Q8 mate.

3 K—R1!   Q—K7!   4 K—N1!   Q—K6!

Abandoned as a draw. Neither player can vary from the prescribed sequence without losing. A fine example of ingenious play on both sides.

Diagram 22 illustrates the same delicate technique, but in an even more attractive form.

22

WHITE TO MOVE

Though a Knight and a Pawn to the good, White is apparently lost. If he moves his Queen off the King Knight file, he gets mated.

White cannot move his Queen, true. But he can resort to our tried and true resource: counterattack. Therefore:

1 R—N5!   ....

Masterly play! If 1 . . . QxR; 2 QxRch wins.

Worse yet, Black's Queen is rooted to the spot, for 1 . . . Q—B5? or 1 . . . Q—K3? allows 2 Q—N7 mate.

How then does Black protect his Rook?

He doesn't! Instead, he counterattacks:

1 ....   R—K1!

Threatening . . . R—K8 mate. Now he threatens . . . QxR as well.

White finds the only way to parry both threats:

2 R—N1!   R—KN1!

Naturally. In view of his material minus, Black must renew his attack on the White Queen.

3 R—N5!   ....

Just as naturally, White must renew *his* attack on the Black Queen.

3 ....   R—K1!   4 R—N1!   Drawn

The forced back-and-forth moves of the Rooks lead to a forced draw.

All these examples have been vastly entertaining and equally instructive. They reinforce the moral that a draw is a perfectly welcome and legitimate goal in desperate positions where you can see no better solution. For half a point is better than none; a draw is better than a loss.

454

Chapter Four

THE DEFENSE FUMBLES

So far we have seen the triumphs that alert and accurate defense can achieve. But, as you know from your own experience, defense can be a very spotty affair. A superb move may be followed by one that brings down the whole position with a crash.

It's heartening and instructive to study examples of good defense. It's even more instructive to study examples of faulty defense, so that we know what to avoid. And such instances of faulty defense give us a sobering realization of what we must do in our own games to avoid disaster.

The right way and the wrong way

Most catastrophes of defense come about because a player chooses the wrong move. One move spells salvation, the other means defeat. So, one bad choice and the game is lost.

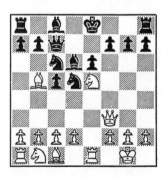

23

WHITE TO MOVE

White's next move is obvious, while Black's reply is far from obvious! Black's best reply to 1 NxN is 1 ... Castles!

Diagram 23 shows us such a position. Black's snap judgment loses for him very quickly.

Relying on a multiplicity of pins, White slyly played:

1 NxN!   . . . .

Black, without much thought, replied:

1 . . . .   PxN?

This loses, as White now convincingly proves.

2 QxN   . . . .

Now Black is shocked into the realization that he is stymied by no less than three pins. Thus 2 . . . KPxQ or 2 . . . BPxQ are altogether impossible. And 2 . . . PxB is possible though not desirable, because of the reply 3 QxR.

Will 2 . . . B—Q2 save the day for Black? No; White simply retreats 3 Q—K4 or 3 Q—B3 and his attacked Bishop is still immune.

And so Black, with a piece down and no way of regaining it, is hopelessly lost.

Let's go back to Diagram 23, and see how Black *should have played*. After 1 NxN the right reply was 1 . . . Castles! In that case, with Black's King removed from the King file, White can no longer play QxN. Another feature is that White's Knight at Queen Bishop 6 has no escape! Black must therefore regain the piece.

It is true that White can play 2 NxP coming out a Pawn ahead. However, Black can still fight on; there is a great deal of play left in the game. Consequently 1 . . . Castles! was the right defensive move.

In Diagram 24 Black goes wrong in very much the same way.

456

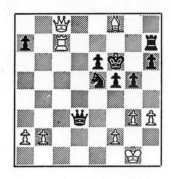

24

WHITE TO MOVE

Black's King is hard pressed; nevertheless he can hold out with best play.

Though Black's King is in hot water, we must admit that Black has set up his defense very cleverly. If for example 1 RxR, Black plays 1 . . . N—B6ch. If then 2 K—R1??, Q—B8 mate. White must therefore play 2 K—N2, whereupon 2 . . . N—K8ch forces a draw by perpetual check (3 K—N1, N—B6ch; 4 K—N2, N—K8ch etc.).

White therefore tries a swindle:

1 B—K7ch!?   K—N3??

And Black succumbs! The rest is agony.

2 QxPch	K—R4	4 B—Q6	PxP
3 QxN	P—B5	5 Q—K8ch	Resigns

For if 5 . . . K—R5; 6 PxPch, KxRP; 7 Q—R5 mate. And if 5 . . . Q—N3; 6 Q—K2ch wins.

Now let's go back to Diagram 24 and see how Black *should have played*.

After 1 B—K7ch!? Black's proper reply is the seemingly dangerous 1 . . . RxB! In that case 2 Q—B8ch? fails after 2 . . . R—B2.

Consequently White must play 2 Q—KR8ch. Then Black has nothing to worry about after 2 . . . K—N3.

For if 3 QxN, RxR; 4 QxR, Q—N8ch and Black's game is perfectly satisfactory.

And if 3 RxR, N—B6ch; 4 K—N2, N—K8ch when Black draws by the perpetual check already shown.

But, as we've seen, Black made the wrong choice and lost the game.

In the position of Diagram 25, the contrast between the right way and the wrong way is even more glaring.

25

WHITE TO MOVE

By playing 1 RxP??!, White sets a trap which Black can refute in the most incisive manner. But Black also has a chance to go wrong!

Here is what happened:

$$1 \text{ RxP??!} \qquad ....$$

A baleful trap.

$$1 .... \qquad Q—N3ch$$

Good enough, though not the most direct course.

$$2 \text{ K—N2} \qquad QxR???$$

Of all the defensive blunders I have ever seen, this one is undoubtedly the worst!

3 N—K7ch   K—R1   4 QxPch!!   KxQ
              5 R—R1 mate

458

A spectacular finish, and perhaps we can forgive Black for missing it. Here is how he *should* have played:

$$1 \text{ RxP??!} \qquad \text{BxN!}$$

Black attacks the Queen and keeps the threat . . . Q—N3ch in reserve. Thus he must win at least a piece and the flashy checkmate is ruled out.

There was still another way for Black to handle this situation correctly:

$$1 \text{ RxP??!} \quad \text{Q—N3ch} \qquad 2 \text{ K—N2} \qquad \text{BxN!}$$

Again Black wins a piece and eliminates the flamboyant checkmate.

Walking into it

One of the worst types of defensive blunders comes about when a player walks into a trap that has been deliberately set for him. Nothing, in fact, is so conducive to blundering as the belief that your opponent has blundered. Our powerful sense of elation blinds us to the possibility that there is more to the position than meets the eye.

Thus, in Diagram 26 Black sees that he can win a piece. Before going any further, he grabs the loose Knight—to his sorrow.

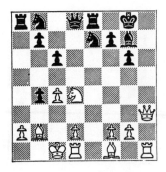

26

BLACK TO MOVE
What is White's threat, and how can Black guard against it? Should Black accept or decline the Knight?

In the position of Diagram 26 White threatens 1 N—K6! If then 1 . . . PxN; 2 Q—R7ch and 3 QxB mate. Or if 1 . . . BxBch; 2 KxB, PxN; 3 Q—R8ch, K—B2; 4 R—R7 mate.

The best way for Black to guard against the threat seems to be 1 . . . N—B1. If then 2 N—K6?, BxBch; 3 KxB, Q—B3ch and Black prevents the mate and wins a piece as well.

Instead of all this, Black plays very naively. He sees that he can capture the Knight; he goes right ahead without asking himself why this opportunity has been made to order for him.

1 . . . .   BxN??   2 Q—R8ch!!   . . . .

This will hurt a bit.

2 . . . .   BxQ   3 RxB mate

Now it is all clear. The White Knight was merely bait.

In Diagram 27 the bait is even more valuable, so that you would expect Black to be correspondingly more careful. This time White has obligingly left his Queen on a square where she can be captured.

27
BLACK TO MOVE
Should Black capture the Queen?

Black's decision to capture the Queen is, as we shall see, a blunder. However, it is to some extent an excusable blunder. He sees White's second move, but overlooks his third. And this third move, you will have to admit, is not an easy move to foresee.

1 ....   NxQ?   2 RxPch   K—R1

This much Black foresaw. He knows there is no good discovered check, because White's Bishop at Knight 2 is under attack.

But what about a *double check?*

3 R—N8 dbl ch!   ....

This is the move that Black overlooked.

3 ....   KxR   4 R—KN1ch   Q—N4
              5 RxQ mate

In Diagram 28, too, the defender's failure to fathom the point of White's attack is pardonable. Few combinations have ever been played to equal this one in subtlety.

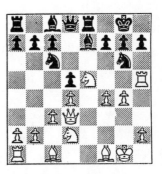

28

WHITE TO MOVE

Black does not dream that White is planning a very brilliant attack.

White's opening move is well calculated to confuse his unsuspecting opponent:

$$1 \text{ N/Q2—B4!!} \quad \ldots$$

This fantastic move is probably best answered by 1 . . . B—B3 creating an escape hatch for the Black King. Why the King needs an escape, will soon become clear.

Instead of weighing the possibilities, Black grabs the offered Knight.

$$1 \ldots \quad\quad\quad \text{PxN}$$

And now what?

$$2 \text{ QxN!!} \quad\quad \ldots$$

Threatening 3 QxRPch, K—B1; 4 Q—R8 mate. (This explains why Black should have made room for his King's escape.)

$$2 \ldots \quad\quad\quad \text{RPxQ}$$

Black sees that after 2 . . . BPxQ White forces mate by 3 BxPch, K—R1; 4 NxP mate or 3 . . . K—B1; 4 NxPch!, PxN; 5 R—R8 mate. (Another indication of the Black King's need for fresh air.)

$$3 \text{ NxNP!} \quad\quad \ldots$$

Threatens 4 R—R8 mate.

| 3 . . . . | PxN | 4 BxPch | K—B1 |

Such moves as . . . Q—Q4 and . . . B—K3 would only delay the mate without stopping it.

$$5 \text{ R—R8 mate}$$

462

If Black's failure to foresee this glorious combination was forgivable, we can hardly say the same for Black's lapse in the position of Diagram 29. There he has a solid defensive position; but he fails to realize that the blockade on King Bishop 2 is necessary to hold his position together.

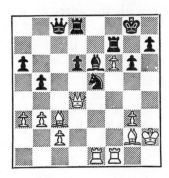

29

BLACK TO MOVE
What would happen if Black moved his Rook from King Bishop 2?

White's position is generally more aggressive, but Black seems safe as long as he keeps up the barricade at King Bishop 2. But Black does not realize the importance of this blockade, for he plays:

1 ....   R/B2—Q2?

This allows White to open the long diagonal leading to Black's King Knight 2 and King Rook 1. It also makes it worthwhile for him to sacrifice the Exchange in order to operate on the long diagonal.

2 RxN!   PxR   3 P—B7ch!   ....

Very fine. He forces the opening of the diagonal. (On the other hand, after 3 QxP?, Black would resume the blockade with 3 ... R—KB2 or 3 ... B—B2.)

3 ....   RxP   4 QxP   ....

White threatens Q—R8 mate. And if 4 . . . RxR; 5 Q—N7 mate. Now we can appreciate the power of White's attack along the diagonal.

| 4 .... | K—B1 | 5 Q—N7ch! | .... |

With this pretty move, White forces the game. If now 5 . . . K—K1; 6 Q—N8ch, K—K2; 7 B—N4ch, K—Q2; 8 RxRch and Black gets mated.

| 5 .... | K—K2 | 6 B—N4ch | Resigns |

Black is helpless. If he tries 6 . . . R—Q3 then 7 RxRch, BxR; 8 Q—K5ch, Q—K3; 9 BxRch is crushing.

Or if 6 . . . K—Q2; 7 RxRch, BxR; 8 QxR mate.

Black's swift collapse came about after he opened the gates to the enemy by giving up the blockade at King Bishop 2.

In this chapter you have seen some of the ways in which the defense can go wrong. It is lack of alertness, lack of aggressive spirit, that leads a player to surrender so readily to his opponent's intentions. So, be warned: the defense does not play itself. Eternal vigilance is the price of successful resistance.

Chapter Five

HOW TO FIGHT BACK: PRACTICAL EXAMPLES

IT'S ONE THING to know how to fight back, it's another thing to be able to do it yourself in your own games!

So, for the balance of this book let's look at complete games. We'll see how mistakes are made early in the play. We'll observe how these mistakes lead to mounting difficulties. We'll watch the critical position arrive, and we'll be able to judge whether or not the player who is under pressure is able to solve his problem successfully.

After studying these models of *complete games,* you'll be able to counterattack a great deal more competently in your own games.

Faulty defense

First, let's see what happens when a player gets himself into a lot of trouble and can't get out of it. If this player hits back, it's with nothing stronger than cream puffs.

IRREGULAR DEFENSE

WHITE	BLACK	WHITE	BLACK
1 P—K4	P—K3	2 P—Q4	P—KN3?

With the game barely started, Black has committed a mistake which should lose the game for him.

465

Why this move is wrong can best be understood if we ask this question: What is Black's best second move?

The right way was 2 . . . P—Q4! In that case Black fights for control of the center squares. By disputing control of the center squares, he struggles to get just as good a foothold in the center for his pieces as White has for *his* pieces.

So, by playing 2 . . . P—KN3?, Black has ignored the fight for control of the center. His pieces will therefore lack mobility; they will have little scope; they will be forced into a crowded, defensive formation.

As the play unfolds, you will see how the violation of these guiding principles causes Black's game to fall apart.

| 3 B—Q3 | B—N2 | 5 N—K2 | P—N3 |
| 4 B—K3 | N—K2 | 6 N—Q2 | B—N2 |

30

WHITE TO MOVE

Black's pieces have a cramped position with no prospects of active play.

The game is proceeding according to our diagnosis. Black's position is very cramped, and he has no positive plan available. Even at this early stage he has nothing to look forward to but pure defense; not a very heartening prospect.

But White, as you will see, has a much freer game and a choice of possible initiatives.

7 Castles   P—Q4

This comes late in the day. White responds with an aggressive advance.

8 P—K5   Castles   9 P—KB4   P—KB4

The right strategy for Black. Since his mobility is limited, he plays to barricade the position. Then, when White tries to attack, he may not be able to get through the barriers Black has set up.

This is a plausible defensive notion. Unfortunately, the weight of experience is against it. In chess, it's generally true that where there's a will, there's a way. White has more mobility; he has the initiative; he has the future. If he proceeds aggressively, he can break through.

Even against a solid defense? Yes, even then. For in a defensive position where the defender's pieces are crowded together—as they are here—his pieces aren't worth very much. Consequently, a sacrifice of material on the attacker's part involves no great risk.

The defender's trouble, you see, is that he cannot rally his cramped and ineffectual pieces very rapidly to the scene of action. Consequently, his King's position is likely to be overrun while his useless pieces straggle idly, far from the scene of battle.

10 P—KR3   N—Q2   12 P—B3   P—B5
11 K—R2   P—B4   13 B—QB2   P—QR3

Black is dallying with a slight attempt at counterplay. He wants to advance his Queen Knight Pawn and Queen Rook Pawn and force open a file on the Queen-side by a Pawn exchange. (For example, . . . P—QN4, . . . P—QR4, . . . P—N5 and . . . PxP.)

He hopes in this way to distract White's attention from the

King-side. But of course this is a futile hope, for White's corresponding advance on the King-side is intended to smoke out Black's King.

So here you have a valuable maxim of defensive play: don't expect to entice your opponent from maximum goals by tempting him with low-grade bait.

14 N—B3   P—R3?

And this move gives aid and comfort to the enemy. By moving another Pawn on the King-side, Black weakens his castled position. With his last move, he has undermined the support of his King Knight Pawn. This will eventually make possible White's winning sacrifice against the weakened point.

Another objection to Black's last move is that it is inconsistent. Since he had announced his intention of counter-attacking on the Queen-side, he should have played . . . P—QN4. Instead, Black vacillates. He doesn't know what he's doing; he doesn't know what he ought to do. In his ignorance, he is pulling down the pillars of his own defensive structure.

15 P—KN4!   K—R2   16 KR—N1!   ....

White, on the other hand, is well aware of what his position calls for. He is prepared to open up a file on the King-side, and he has placed heavy artillery on the file that he intends to open—the King Knight file.

16 ....   KR—N1   17 Q—K1   N—QB3?

Granting that Black's position should be lost in any event, he makes it too easy for his opponent. You've already seen from the note to his fourteenth move that his King Knight Pawn has been weakened. In its present state it is no longer guarded by a Pawn. *Therefore it must be guarded by pieces.*

468

Consequently Black's Knight at King 2 was doing a useful job guarding his King Knight Pawn. But now Black has moved the Knight away, so that this weak Pawn has lost one of its main supports.

18 N—R4! Q—KB1?

Wrong. White's last move menaces the weak King Knight Pawn, which needs more protection. Thus 18 . . . N—B1 was indicated.

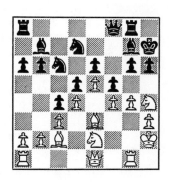

31

WHITE TO MOVE

Black has weakened his position irretrievably and he will now succumb to a crushing attack.

Black has created a weakness (the unprotected King Knight Pawn) in his position.

He has removed a piece that guarded the Pawn, and he has neglected to bring additional support to the Pawn.

Now he pays the penalty for his faulty defense as White breaks through with a sacrifice:

19 NxNP!!   . . . .

Black cannot very well decline the Knight.

If for example 19 . . . Q—B2; 20 PxP, PxP; 21 N—R4, N—K2; 22 NxP!, NxN; 23 N—N3. In that case White wins the pinned Knight, remaining with a material advantage and a crushing attack against the Black King.

| 19 .... | KxN | 20 PxP dbl ch | .... |

Now White smashes through by opening up the King Knight file. (He prepared for this with his eleventh, fifteenth, and sixteenth moves.)

Black has little choice here, for if he tries 20 . . . K—R2 then 21 PxP dis ch shatters his position.

| 20 .... | K—B2 | 22 P—B5ch | K—K2 |
| 21 PxPch | KxP | 23 Q—R4ch | K—K1 |

Black's King is being driven around brutally. Black is still ahead materially with a piece for two Pawns. However, this means little in a situation where White's forces are all-powerful, whereas Black's pieces are cramped, crowded, and ineffectual. (Re-read the note to Black's ninth move, in which the likelihood of such a situation was prophesied.)

| 24 P—B6 | .... |

White's onrushing Pawns have irresistible dynamic power.

Thus, if Black tries 24 . . . B—R1 White simply continues with 25 RxR, QxR; 26 R—KN1, Q—B1; 27 BxP. In that case, White has a third Pawn for the sacrificed piece, and his attack rolls right on.

| 24 .... | BxP |

Black gives back the piece in order to break the force of the advancing Pawn rush. However, this fails to improve Black's position appreciably, as his King remains exposed to attack by White's splendidly posted pieces.

| 25 PxB | RxR | 26 RxR | NxBP |

Black's return of the extra piece hasn't pacified White.

The Black King still finds himself in the crossfire of the White pieces.

27	B—N6ch	K—Q2		29	BxP	Q—R1
28	B—B5ch	K—K1		30	R—N7	N—KN1

32

WHITE TO MOVE

As a result of his faulty development and faulty defense, Black now succumbs to a forced checkmate.

Black has come to the end of the road. White now announces mate in three moves by 31 B—N6ch, K—B1; 32 Q—B4ch, N—B3; 33 QxN mate. Note the concentration of four White pieces—Queen, Rook, and two Bishops—against Black's wretched King.

Black relied on the Pawn barrier to protect his King from harm. This reliance was based on a faulty notion—that once the position was barricaded, it would stay that way. This is the essence of bad defensive thinking. If the attacker is alert and aggressive enough, he will always find a way to break through.

When you're on the defensive, then, it's your chief job to watch for that deadly moment, and prepare for it. How? One way is to try to give your pieces the utmost mobility, so that you will be able to counterattack.

If the position is not suitable for counterattack, then mobility is still something you want to aim for. As long as your pieces have freedom of action, you can bring them quickly to the threatened zone. Above all, avoid the kind of position Black gets in Diagram 31, where his Queen is stuck in the mud and the three Queen-side pieces have nothing whatever to say about the fate of their King.

But this game is not a typical creditable defensive effort. Black made every conceivable defensive mistake, and thoroughly earned his disastrous defeat. In the remaining games we'll see what happens when the defender does a good job.

Gradual counterplay

The next game is one of my favorites in this field. Black starts off with a cramped position by the very nature of the opening. But, as you will see, he is well aware of the danger. He concentrates on developing his pieces effectively, and tries constantly to put them on the best squares.

Having accepted a gambit in the opening, Black is a Pawn ahead to begin with. But he doesn't clutch this Pawn like a miser: as early as the sixth move, he's ready to return it. This is important; for many a defender has ruined his position beyond redemption by greedily clinging to material.

Even when Black loses the castling privilege, he is not dismayed. The danger is minimal because his development is satisfactory. Consequently White cannot exploit the lack of castling.

In due time Black's counterattack sets in. It will come to you as a complete surprise. But, after you've played over the whole game, you'll do well to return to the position of Diagram 34, and arrive at a clear understanding of what Black did and why he succeeded in doing it.

This is a game which will repay your playing over many times. It is a very deceptive-looking game, for Black plays so well that he makes the job of defense and counterattack look easy. It isn't!

EVANS GAMBIT

WHITE	BLACK		WHITE	BLACK
1 P—K4	P—K4		3 B—B4	B—B4
2 N—KB3	N—QB3		4 P—QN4	....

This is one of the most interesting of all the gambits. White offers a Pawn in order to build up a strong Pawn center and to gain time to get a big lead in development. If Black does not look sharp, he may find himself overwhelmed by a powerful White initiative.

4 ....   BxNP

In the light of the previous comment, this is a momentous decision. Black is taking on a big responsibility, but, as we shall see from his following moves, he knows how to hold his own.

5 P—B3   B—R4   6 P—Q4   P—Q3!

33

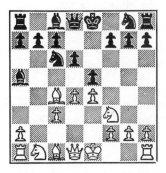

WHITE TO MOVE

With his last move (6 . . . P—Q3!) Black has set his opponent a very difficult problem.

Black's 6 . . . P—Q3! is a good move in the technical sense. Its psychological impact is even greater. By playing this move Black keeps a Pawn in the center and prepares for the development of his Queen Bishop. So far, so good.

But the move has a deeper meaning. It indicates that Black is prepared, even at this early stage, to return the extra Pawn. White can win back his Pawn with 7 PxP, PxP; 8 QxQch, NxQ; 9 NxP. But in that case the Queens are gone and so are White's chances of attack. Black simply continues 9 . . . B—K3 with a prosaic endgame that understandably has no attractions for White.

White naturally avoids this simplifying possibility, but he is undoubtedly shaken by the revelation that Black is less interested in material than he is in breaking the attack.

7 B—KN5	P—B3	8 Q—N3	. . . .

Typical play in a gambit: try to upset your opponent with surprise moves. If Black plays 8 . . . PxB then 9 BxN (threatening mate) with a wide-open position and chances for both sides.

8	KN—K2

Black meets the threat in the most economical way—by developing a piece.

9 B—B7ch	. . . .

White wastes a move in order to force Black's King to move and thereby render castling impossible for Black. Ordinarily this would be a very serious defect in the defender's position. Not so here, as Black continues to defend with great care.

9	K—B1	10 B—R5	. . . .

Threatening Q—B7 mate.

But Black parries the threat easily enough, at the same time making room for the development of his Queen.

10	N—N3	11 B—K3	Q—K2

Notice how Black is carefully concentrating on development of his forces.

12 Castles	B—N3	13 QN—Q2	B—K3!

Well played. Either White's Queen must move off her aggressive diagonal, or White must seal up the center with P—Q5. If he advances the Pawn, then there is no chance for him to get an open file for attack.

14 P—Q5	....

Contrary to appearances, this advance does *not* cost Black a piece. *Counterattack* is the answer!

14	N—R4	15 Q—N4	B—Q2
	16 P—B4	N—B5!	

This represents further progress for Black.

White is now compelled to play the following exchange, which gives Black two Bishops against a Bishop and Knight. As you'll see, the Black Bishops will become magnificently active, while White's minor pieces will scurry around in search of something to do.

17 BxN	PxB	18 N—R4	....

Black was threatening to win a piece by . . . P—N3. Bit by bit we see Black switching from defense to attack.

18	Q—K4!

A further improvement in Black's position: strong centralization of his Queen, attack on White's Bishop, and threats on other lines as well.

Black is really forcing the pace now, for if 19 B—B3, Q—N4!; 20 P—N3, PxP; 21 RPxP, QxNPch and White can resign with a clear conscience.

Hard pressed, White resorts to a "swindle."

19 B—N6!?   ....

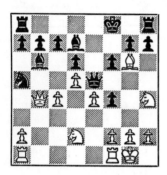

34

BLACK TO MOVE

If 19 . . . PxB??; 20 NxPch wins White's Queen. But Black has a much better move, namely?

Of course Black has no trouble seeing through White's flimsy trap.

But the real danger facing Black is that he will play the attractive 19 . . . Q—N4. In that event there follows 20 N/Q2—B3, Q—R3; 21 B—B5 and—with the decentralization of Black's Queen—White's game has improved considerably.

Instead, Black starts a remarkable combination:

19 ....   BxPch!!

Forcing White to capture, as he cannot allow 20 . . . BxN. Nor can White play 20 RxB? as this would lose his Queen Rook.

20 KxB   Q—Q5ch   21 K—K2   ....

476

Again Black has forced White's reply. For if 22 K—B3, Q—K6 mate; or if 22 K—K1, QxRch.

21 ....   B—N5ch

Remember that Black has to be very sure of what he's doing! For he's sacrificed a piece, and his Knight is under attack.

If White tries 22 N/Q2—B3, Black replies 22 . . . NxP maintaining winning pressure. One remarkable possibility is 23 B—B5, P—KN3! (not 23 . . . BxB??; 24 NxQ); 24 BxB, QxKPch; 25 K—Q1 forced, N—K6ch winning White's Queen.

22 N/R4—B3   PxB   23 QxN   ....

Black is still a piece down for several Pawns, but his Queen is in the thick of the fray, whereas White's Queen is useless.

23 ....   RxP

A remarkable situation in which the pin by the Black Bishop prevents White from playing 24 NxQ or 24 NxR.

24 R—KN1 P—KB4!

Beautiful play. If now 25 PxP, R—K1ch; 26 K—Q1, and Black can capture either Rook with his Queen!

Or 25 PxP, R—K1ch; 26 K—B1, Q—Q6ch!; 27 K—B2, Q—K6ch; 28 K—B1, Q—K7 mate.

25 QxBP   Q—K6ch

Forcing White's reply, as 26 K—Q1 allows . . . QxRch.

26 K—B1   PxP!

477

For if 27 NxR, Q—K7 mate. All this is calculated by Black with a rare combination of verve and accuracy.

| 27 QxQPch | K—N1 | 28 NxP | Q—Q6ch! |

White resigns.

If he plays 29 K—B2, Black winds up with 29 . . . QxN/B6ch; 30 K—K1, Q—K7 mate.

Or 29 K—K1, R—K1! and White's helplessness is pathetic. (Thus, on 30 NxR or 30 N/B3—Q2 Black has 30 . . . Q—K7 mate.)

A masterly example of how the defender brings out his pieces, consolidates his position, and gradually switches to counterattack. Even Black's final attack is a tribute to his earlier maneuvering; for his careful early play is what has made it possible for each Black piece to be on the right square at the right time.

The precious half-point

In this game, too, we see wonderfully alert defense and counterattack by Black. True, he "only" draws, but his defensive task is more difficult. This is a case where drawing a game is a very creditable achievement, one that you can be proud of.

KING'S GAMBIT

WHITE	BLACK	WHITE	BLACK
1 P—K4	P—K4	2 P—KB4	PxP

Black accepts the gambit. He knows he's in for trouble, and he means to fight back as hard as he can.

Right here you can see how important a player's opening

478

attitude is. If he begins in a mood of indifference or ignorance, he may be smashed by the gambit before he ever finds out what's happening to him. On the other hand, if he knows the score, he's prepared from the very start to fight hard. Consequently, the resulting difficult positions don't come as a great shock to him.

As you study the further play, you will see how important a role this attitude plays.

3 N—KB3   P—KN4

And this move too is a calculated risk. Black defends his advanced King Bishop Pawn, which will soon be under attack. However, in providing this protection, Black is weakening his King-side: he has created a breach in his King-side Pawn formation.

Later on White will take advantage of his weakness to start a powerful attack in that sector. But Black is well prepared for it.

4 P—KR4   ....

Now the game is already in a critical stage. White breaks up Black's Pawn-chain so that both advanced Black Pawns will be liable to capture—and meanwhile Black's weakness on the King-side persists. (If Black ever castles King-side, his King will be sadly exposed to attack.)

4 ....   P—N5   5 N—K5   ....

Now Black can defend his King Knight Pawn with 5 . . . P—KR4. But after 6 B—B4, N—KR3; 7 P—Q4 White would have a lead in development, a strong center, and the certainty of winning the gambit Pawn. Black would have a lasting defensive and the inferior position.

So Black realizes that passive, witless defense will not do. What he wants is: systematic development and counterattack. So:

5 ....　　　　N—KB3!

35

WHITE TO MOVE
Black must strive for counterattack.

By developing his King Knight, Black announces that counterattack will be the keystone of his policy from now on. The game gets very involved as both players fight for the attack.

6 B—B4　　　　P—Q4

Thus he parries the attack against his Pawn at King Bishop 2.

7 PxP　　　　B—N2!

More development!

8 P—Q4　　　　....

White is now ready to play BxP.

8 ....　　　　N—R4!

Black guards the threatened Pawn and at the same time he sets a trap.

480

If White plays 9 NxNP? then 9 . . . N—N6! gives Black a winning game. For after 10 R—R2 (necessary to prevent . . . QxRP), Q—K2ch White is at a loss for a good move.

For instance: 11 K—B2, BxN; 12 QxB, BxPch and mate next move. Or 11 B—K2, BxN winning. Or 11 K—Q2, N—K5ch!; 12 K—Q3, BxN; 13 QxB, N—B7ch winning the Queen.

This whole sequence, you observe, is based on counter-attack.

| 9 N—QB3 | Castles |

Black cannot leave his King in the center, so he castles. But, with his King-side Pawns so far advanced, he may easily find himself in a very dangerous position.

| 10 N—K2 | . . . . |

This at last wins back the gambit Pawn, opening files on the King-side at the same time. Move by move the situation becomes more critical for Black.

| 10 . . . . | P—B6 | 11 PxP | PxP |
| 12 NxP/B3 | P—N4! | | |

This is the kind of move we like to see when we're playing over a game. Such a move comes as a complete surprise; there is a great deal of thought behind it; and for good measure, it's a strong move.

In this case, the idea behind 12 . . . P—N4! is to give Black strong play on the diagonal leading from his Queen Rook 1 to his King Rook 8. Thus, if 13 BxP, QxP with a promising position for Black—quite in line with his ambition to counterattack.

White, being a very aggressive player, prefers to aim for attack.

| 13 B—N3 | B—N2! | 15 N—N5! | N—KB3 |
| 14 Q—Q3 | QBxP | 16 R—B1 | .... |

White builds up the attack very skilfully. His immediate threat is 17 RxN followed by 18 QxRP mate. But Black finds ingenious counterplay:

16 ....   R—K1!

This creates a flight square for Black's King and consequently lifts the mating threat. In addition, Black's Rook at King 1 has menacing intentions along the open King file.

17 RxN!?   ....

36

BLACK TO MOVE

Although Black is no longer subjected to a mate threat, he must nevertheless play very resourcefully to hold the game.

Black's reply is forced, as 17 . . . QxR? will not do because of 18 BxB.

| 17 .... | BxR | 18 QxRPch | K—B1 |
| | 19 NxP! | .... | |

A brutal move. If Black replies 19 . . . BxN?? then QxB

482

mate. If he tries 19 . . . Q—K2?? (threatening mate) White has 20 B—R6ch and mate next move.

Even 19 . . . Q—Q2? will not do, for then comes 20 B—R6ch, K—K2; 21 N—K5 dis ch and Black loses his Queen.

Despite the desperate appearance of his position, Black finds a way out: he resorts to a counter-sacrifice of the Exchange!

19 ....　　RxNch!

One must marvel at Black's calmness in the face of so many dangers.

20 KxR　　Q—K2ch

Here is a subtle point of Black's defense: if now 21 K—B1?, QxN; 22 B—R6ch, B—N2 dis ch! and Black remains a piece ahead!

21 K—Q3!?　　....

An ingenious move which leads Black astray. Black now sees that after 21 . . . BxN?; 22 B—R6ch, K—K1; 23 R—K1!, QxR; 24 QxBch followed by 25 QxBch White has a winning attack.

But what Black misses is that after 21 . . . QxN!; 22 B—R6ch, K—K1; 23 R—K1ch, B—K2 he has a satisfactory defense as well as a material advantage.

In his search for active counterplay Black misses this fairly obvious point in favor of a subtle defensive resource.

21 ....　　B—B5ch?!　　　　22 BxB　　PxBch

If now 23 KxP, QxNch forcing the exchange of Queens and leaving Black with a won ending.

23 K—B3!　　....

37

Should Black play 23 . . . QxN winning a piece?

It would be very poor judgment on Black's part now to win a piece by 23 . . . QxN. For after 24 B—R6ch White would regain the piece with a winning game: 24 . . . B—N2; 25 Q—R8ch etc. or 24 . . . K moves; 25 Q—K4ch winning the Black Rook.

| 23 . . . . | BxPch! |

Black figures on 24 KxB?, N—B3ch; 25 KxP, N—K4ch and the concentrated attack of Black's pieces is decisive. For example: 26 K—Q4, R—Q1ch!—or 26 K—B3, Q—B4ch; 27 K—Q2, NxN and White is helpless.

| 24 KxP | . . . . |

Now it would be suicide for Black to play 24 . . . QxNch?; 25 QxQch, KxQ; 26 KxB, leaving White with two Pawns ahead in an easily won ending.

| 24 . . . . | B—N2 |

After this prudent retreat, Black's position looks solid, while White's looks flimsy. However, Black is two Pawns down, so both players are satisfied with a draw.

| 25 N—N5 | N—B3 | 26 Q—B5ch | . . . . |

If now 26 . . . Q—B3??; 27 N—R7ch wins the Queen.

26 ....   K—K1   27 Q—N6ch   ....

Attacking Black's Knight and therefore forcing his reply.

27 ....   K—Q2   28 Q—B5ch   K—K1

At this point the game was abandoned as a draw, for both players realized that discretion is the better part of valor in this position.

Despite the fact that Black missed a win at move 21, this is a very valuable game to study. In fact, Black's lapse gives the game a more realistic flavor, and makes it more true to life.

The main impression we get from such a game is that a hard-fought draw is in many ways more creditable than an easy win achieved over flabby opposition. Black had to be alert from start to finish; time and again it seemed that he could no longer avoid disaster.

From a game such as this one you can learn how much patience and sheer stubbornness are required to hold out in a difficult defensive position.

Passive defense becomes active

This is the hardest of all defensive achievements: to switch from passive defense, when you are subject to every whim and choice of your opponent. Few problems in chess are more trying; few require more ingenuity, more sheer fighting spirit, than the often arduous job of freeing yourself and asserting your own will. A difficult job, but not an impossible one. The main requirement is to know the score, and know what you want to do. Some players are so overwhelmed by the routine of being on the defensive that they never even think of trying to fight their way out.

In the following game the defense is handled by a great master. Though his position is originally very constricted, he works energetically to achieve a position in which he is attacking instead of defending. The switch comes so suddenly that the opponent is caught off balance.

QUEEN'S GAMBIT DECLINED

WHITE	BLACK	WHITE	BLACK
1 P—Q4	P—Q4	2 P—QB4	P—K3

This move is so conventional that we may too easily forget its consequences.

By playing 2 . . . P—K3 Black makes sure of having a Pawn in the center. In this way he prevents White from gaining too much ground in that all-important sector of the board.

On the other hand, 2 . . . P—K3 has a very serious drawback. It blocks the development of Black's Queen Bishop. So, even at this early stage Black must keep his wits about him and realize that the restricted mobility of this Bishop may cause him a lot of trouble in the future.

To recognize your problems this early in the game is a valuable asset. If you know what your problem is, you can be on the lookout for ways to solve it. (Many a player has lost games on the Black side of this opening, precisely because he was unaware of the defect in his position. Being unaware of his handicap, he simply drifted along placidly without making any effort to free the imprisoned Bishop.)

3 N—QB3	N—KB3	4 B—N5	QN—Q2

Now the imprisonment of Black's Queen Bishop seems worse than ever. However, this is only a temporary state of affairs.

486

| 5 P—K3 | P—B3 | 7 Q—B2 | Castles |
| 6 N—B3 | B—K2 | 8 P—QR3 | R—K1 |

38

WHITE TO MOVE
Black's position is extremely constricted.

One look at this diagram shows us the difficulties confronting Black. White's pieces have freedom and scope. Black's forces have developed modestly and are huddled together with very little mobility.

| 9 R—B1 | PxP |

And now, by removing his main center Pawn, Black allows his opponent a free hand in the center. (For example, he makes possible such moves as 12 N—K4! and 17 P—K4, whereby White gains ground in the center and emphasizes the superior aggressiveness of his own formation.)

Does this mean that 9 . . . PxP is a blunder? Not at all. Black has a very good reason for this move: it is the necessary preliminary to an exchange of pieces. The value of such an exchange will soon become clear to you.

| 10 BxP | N—Q4 | 11 BxB | QxB |

What has happened as the result of the foregoing exchange of pieces? Black has exchanged his rather poorly posted King Bishop for White's actively posted Queen Bishop. That certainly represents an improvement in Black's game.

Furthermore, as a result of the exchange, Black's Queen is now developed at King 2. That too is an improvement. This specific example shows why players with constricted positions are advised to seek simplifying exchanges. In this way they get rid of fairly inactive pieces in return for the opponent's active pieces. That's just what has happened here.

                    12 N—K4!   ....

Following the above reasoning, White purposely avoids another exchange.

12 ....   N/Q4—B3   13 N—N3   ....

Black is of course still thinking of how to develop his Bishop. At first sight 13 . . . P—K4 looks like the answer to all of Black's difficulties, as it opens up the diagonal of his imprisoned Bishop. However, after 13 . . . P—K4; 14 N—B5 Black finds that he is still under pressure in a characterless, backward position that holds out no possibilities for him.

Hence Black bides his time about playing . . . P—K4.

                    13 ....   P—B4!

An excellent move which holds out a vague promise of freedom for the Bishop some day—by an eventual . . . B—Q2 and . . . B—B3. But the day of liberation is still distant.

14 Castles   PxP   15 NxP   N—N3
                16 B—R2   R—N1

A strange-looking move, but Black does not want to commit himself with . . . P—K4. We criticize aimless drifting, but purposeful waiting moves of this kind are commendable.

39

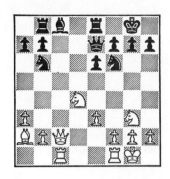

WHITE TO MOVE

Black has not yet managed to free his game, but his position shows no weak points.

17 P—K4	. . . .	

This advance in the center has the effect of limiting Black's mobility, as . . . N—Q4 is impossible. However, Black maneuvers calmly in the small amount of terrain left to him.

| 17 . . . . | R—Q1 | 18 KR—Q1 | B—Q2 |

At last the Bishop is developed! But Black still has far to go before he can free himself.

| 19 P—K5 | . . . . |

Despite its aggressive appearance, this move opens up possibilities which Black is not slow to seize. However, the advance of the Pawn sets a subtle positional trap: if now 19 . . . N/B3—Q4—which looks so natural!—White replies 20 N—K4 followed by N—Q6 with a very powerful game. With the White Knight posted firmly in the heart of Black's position, Black would be in serious trouble.

| 19 . . . . | N—K1! |

This move, which few players would find, guards against the danger of N—K4 followed by N—Q6.

20 B—N1   ....

Threatening checkmate. Black is forced to weaken his King-side castled position.

20 ....   P—N3

One must admire the patience with which Black meets every new difficulty!

21 Q—K4   B—R5!

At last Black's vigilance is rewarded. The Bishop comes into play aggressively.

Of course White could simply reply R—Q2, but psychologically the liberation of the Bishop is distasteful to him. He therefore drives the Bishop back. However, in order to do this, he has to advance Pawns, with the result that he creates points of invasion for Black's forces. This will be explained in the following note.

22 P—QN3   B—Q2   23 P—QR4   ....

White has had his way. But meanwhile, by advancing his Pawns, he has opened up his Queen-side to possible invasion by the Black Knights. Later on, when Black's counterattack is at floodtide, he will be able to post his Knights aggressively on the Queen Knight 5 and Queen Bishop 6 squares. And all this thanks to the Pawn moves that Black has slyly provoked!

23 ....   N—Q4

And note this: as a result of White's aggressive-looking P—K4 and P—K5, Black is able to post his Knight on the "eternal square" Queen 4. Things are beginning to look up for Black.

24 B—Q3   QR—B1

Now he threatens to win the Exchange with . . . N—B6. (See the note to White's 23rd move.)

25 B—B4   B—B3!   26 NxB   PxN

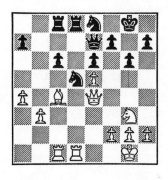

40

WHITE TO MOVE

Black has made headway. He is at last rid of his worrisome Bishop, and his Knight at Queen 4 is a tower of strength.

27 R—Q3   N—N5!   28 R—KB3   R—B2!

Preparing to double Rooks on the open Queen file. The Knight has left the excellent square at Queen 4 for an even more aggressive one at Queen Knight 5. But just as Black is at last asserting himself, a new danger looms up:

29 P—R4   . . . .

White will advance this Pawn in order to weaken Black's castled position. So Black still has a hard fight on his hands.

29 . . . .   R/B2—Q2   30 P—R5   Q—N4!

Counterattack! He threatens . . . QxR.

491

31 R—K1   R—Q5!

Counterplay in the open file.

32 PxP!   . . . .

Offering his Queen. The idea is: 32 . . . RxQ?; 33 PxBPch,
K—B1 (forced); 34 PxN/Q dbl ch, KxQ; 35 NxR, Q—N3;
36 N—Q6ch, K—K2; 37 R—B7ch. Now Black must give
up his Queen, and after 37 . . . QxR; 38 NxQ, KxN he is a
Pawn down with a lost ending.

32 . . . .   RPxP!

Black is not taken in by the Queen sacrifice. In fact, he's
preparing a Queen sacrifice of his own.

33 Q—K2   R—Q7!   34 Q—B1?   . . . .

The most judicious line was 34 Q—K3, with an even ending after the exchange of Queens. But White, who has had
the initiative throughout, cannot reconcile himself to equality.
This is the turning-point of the game.

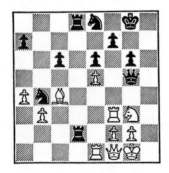

41

BLACK TO MOVE

*White threatens to win the Exchange
by N—K4. How does Black meet the
threat?*

34 . . . .   N—B7!

Black ignores the threat because he intends to sacrifice his Queen.

35 N—K4   QxKP!!

Now at last, Black has shed the role of defender and has seized the initiative. If now 36 NxR, QxR and Black is a Pawn up in the endgame.

36 N—B6ch   QxN   37 RxQ   NxR/B3

What are the consequences of Black's combination? He has ample compensation for his Queen, having won Rook, Knight, and Pawn in return.

But the main point is that Black is now the attacker and no longer the defender.

38 R—B1   N—K5!

Black's Knights dominate the board. The immediate threat is 39 . . . RxP, forcing an endgame in which Black is two Pawns ahead. White avoids this hopeless ending, but the Black Knights continue on their merry way.

39 B—K2   N—Q5!   40 B—B3   NxBP!

Now the threat is 41 . . . NxBch; 42 PxN, R—Q8! forcing an ending in which Black is two Pawns ahead.

White escapes this, but the Black Knights force a decisive penetration into the White King's position:

41 Q—B4   N—Q6!   42 R—B1   N—K4!

Black forces a decisive breach in the White King's position. Black is not only ahead in material; his forces are more active and he has a winning attack.

43 Q—N4   N/K4xBch   44 PxN   N—K7ch

45 K—R2   N—B5 dis ch

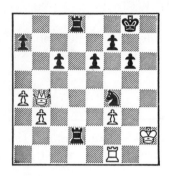

42

WHITE TO MOVE

Black now forces the White King back to the last rank.

Now White doesn't like the idea of having his King trapped on the first rank, and hemmed in by Black's powerful Rook on the seventh rank. However, in the event of 46 K—N3, Black has a pretty win with 46 . . . P—N4! threatening 47 . . . R—N7 mate.

And no matter how White squirms in this variation, Black has a forced win. Thus if 47 R—B2, RxR; 48 KxR, N—Q6ch winning the Queen.

Nor can White escape with 47 R—KN1. For in that case Black plays 47 . . . R/Q1—Q5!; 48 Q—N8ch, K—N2; 49 Q—K5ch, P—B3; 50 Q—B7ch, K—N3. Now White is out of checks, and Black winds up relentlessly with 51 . . . N—R4ch and 52 . . . R—R5 mate.

These variations are enjoyable to play over, but there is a moral to them. Black's pieces are making use of the counterattacking resources he developed earlier in the game when his prospects looked much less attractive. That is to say, Black is benefiting by his policy of finding good squares for his Knights and setting up his Rooks on the Queen file. Thanks to those laborious preparations, Black is now master of the whole board.

494

46 K—R1   R/Q7—Q5!

It comes as a surprise that Black is giving up the Rook's powerful post on the seventh rank. But his control of the Queen file is the compelling factor leading to victory.

47 Q—K7   K—N2!

This innocent-looking move suddenly highlights the fact that Black has still another open file at the disposal of his rambunctious Rooks—the King Rook file. And there's a cruel irony in the fact that it was White himself who opened that file while he was following up what he was sure was a winning attack! (See White's 29th, 30th, and 32nd moves.)

Black's threat in this position is 48 . . . R—R1ch; 49 K—N1, R—Q7; 50 R—B2, N—R6ch with disaster for White.

48 Q—B7   . . . .

By keeping the Knight under attack, White prevents the variation just shown—for Black cannot play . . . R—Q7.

However, since Black's pieces are so magnificently posted, he has no trouble in finding a different way.

48 . . . .   R/Q1—Q4!

Notice how Black's admirable attacking play continues to pivot around the open Queen file. He has in mind a combined operation with his three pieces which will crush White.

49 R—K1   R—KN4!

With the nasty threat of winning the White Queen by . . . N—Q4! This would attack the Queen and also threaten

495

. . . R—R5ch winning the Queen in any event. For example: 50 . . . N—Q4; 51 Q—R2, R—R4 pinning the Queen.

Nor is 50 R—K5 of any use to White, for then comes 50 . . . R—Q8ch; 51 K—R2, R—N7 mate.

50 QxQBP   R—Q1!   Resigns

Black's last, very quiet move left White no defense. The immediate threat was 51 . . . R—KR1 mate. If White tries 51 Q—B3ch, P—K4!; 52 RxP then Black has 52 . . . R—KR1 mate.

What a change there has been from Black's laborious defensive maneuvering in the early part of the game to his crisp, forceful attacking thrusts in the second part! This game is one of the most instructive examples I know of this change from the defensive to the offensive.

I have treated this game in great detail because I think it is important for the student to see what he's up against, and how he ought to go about solving the problems of practical play. You may not be able to play the defense and counterattack this well, but the game sets a worthwhile goal for you to achieve: how to fight back in a position where your opponent has greater mobility and better prospects.

Chapter Six

POINT OF NO RETURN

In almost every game of chess there comes a crisis that must be recognized. In one way or another a player risks something—if he knows what he's doing, we call it a "calculated risk."

If you understand the nature of this crisis; if you perceive how you've committed yourself to a certain line of play; if you can foresee the nature of your coming task and its accompanying difficulties, all's well. But if this awareness is absent, then the game will be lost for you, and fighting back will do no good.

One of the things that makes the masters the great players they are is just this awareness of "the point of no return." They know when they have committed themselves irrevocably. At that point they begin to play with all their determination, all their ingenuity. In the following game, for example, the point of no return comes as early as White's fourth move, and as you study his play there is not the slightest doubt in your mind that he's well aware of the crisis.

KING'S GAMBIT

WHITE	BLACK	WHITE	BLACK
1 P—K4	P—K4	3 P—B4	PxP
2 N—QB3	N—QB3	4 P—Q4!?	....

One of the riskiest forms of the King's Gambit, this brings us to the point of no return as far as this game is concerned.

White hastens to form a broad, powerful Pawn center, but at the cost of exposing his King to attack. It makes quite a difference in this opening whether White is an inexperienced player who cannot foresee the dangerous consequences of Black's reply, or whether he is a great master who well knows that from now on he must be unremittingly on his guard.

4 ....   Q—R5ch

The point. Black drives the White King to King 2. Thus White has lost the castling privilege, and in addition, he blocks the development of White's King Bishop. This sounds like the haphazard play of a tyro. And yet, precisely because White knows he's reached the point of no return, he makes these hardships dissolve as if they had never existed.

5 K—K2	P—Q3	7 BxP	Castles
6 N—B3	B—N5	8 K—K3!	....

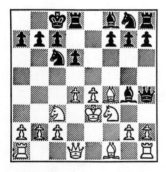

43

BLACK TO MOVE
What does White threaten?

Because White knows that every move must tell in this critical situation, he plays with great resourcefulness. By unpinning his previously pinned Knight, he now threatens NxQ, winning a piece!

But the King move has other important meanings. For example, it protects the Bishop at King Bishop 4, while at the same time making room for the development of the other White Bishop.

8	Q—R4	10 P—QR3!	BxN
9 B—K2	Q—R4	11 KxB!	....

Black expected 11 BxB, P—KN4; 12 B—N3, B—N2; 13 N—K2, P—R4; 14 P—R3, N—B3 and Black has good attacking possibilities.

But after the surprising King move, White can answer 11 . . . P—KN4 with 12 P—QN4!, so that after 12 . . . Q—N3 he has 13 B—K3 with a number of powerful threats, such as P—Q5 or N—Q5 or N—R4, harrying the Black Queen.

11	Q—R4ch	13 P—QN4!	P—KN4
12 K—K3	Q—R5	14 B—N3	Q—R3

Black thinks he has the attack, but he's quite wrong. White has the makings of a very strong attack on the Queen-side. He has a valuable line for his King Rook on the open King Bishop file. He is well ahead in development, and the astonishing fact is that his King is snug and safe behind the rampart of White Pawns.

As for Black, his forces are divided and undeveloped. His Queen is out of play and will be useless in the coming play.

15 P—N5	QN—K2	17 K—B2	N—N3
16 R—KB1!	N—KB3	18 K—N1	Q—N2

By now there's no doubt that White has survived the crisis. His King is artificially castled and quite safe. Meanwhile, Black's King is headed for trouble.

| 19 Q—Q2 | P—KR3 | 21 P—N6!! | RPxP |
| 20 P—QR4 | R—N1 | 22 RxN! | QxR |

White's play is very fine. By means of 21 P—N6!! he forced open an important line to be used in attacking the Black King. And with 22 RxN! he removed the one Black piece which might have hindered the progress of the coming attack.

| 23 B—N4ch | K—N1 | 24 N—Q5 | Q—N2 |
| | 25 P—R5 | .... | |

44

BLACK TO MOVE
Is 25 . . . P—N4 a good defense?

White's policy is naturally to open a file against the Black King. If Black tries to cross his intentions by playing 25 . . . P—N4, White still breaks through, thus: 26 P—R6, P—N3; 27 P—R7ch, K—N2; 28 P—R8/Qch, RxQ; 29 RxR, KxR; 30 NxBPch, K—N2; 31 N—K8, Q—R1 (what a move!); 32 Q—B3 and White must win.

500

| 25 .... | P—KB4 | | 26 RPxP! | .... |

Ignoring the attack on his Bishop, as he threatens mate beginning with 27 R—R8ch!

| 26 .... | QBPxP | | 27 NxP | .... |

Another winning line is 27 Q—B3 (threatening 28 NxP and 29 R—R8 mate). If then 27 . . . R—B1; 28 Q—R3 decides at once.

| 27 .... | N—K2 |

Or 27 . . . K—B2 allowing 28 Q—B3ch with crushing effect.

Again and again we must marvel at the skill with which White has changed the scenery. His King is perfectly safe, while Black's King is nothing but a punching bag.

| 28 PxP | .... |

Still menacing. This time he threatens 29 Q—B3, N—B3; 30 R—R8ch, K—B2; 31 N—Q5ch, K—Q2; 32 P—B6 dis ch winning Black's Queen.

| 28 .... | Q—B2 | | 29 P—B6! | .... |

So that if 29 . . . QxP; 30 Q—B3, N—B3; 31 R—R8ch, K—B2; 32 N—Q5 mate!

Black avoids this, but he soon has to undergo such a grievous loss of material that it might be considered equivalent to resigning.

29	N—B3		33 PxQ	NxP
30 P—B4	N—R2		34 Q—R7ch	K—B2
31 Q—R2	N—N4		35 R—B1ch	N—B3
32 N—Q5	QxN		36 RxN mate	

Thus you see how White's superb timing and awareness of the crisis saved the game for him. His alert capture with the King at move 11 was the turning-point of the struggle. Very few players could have seen this startling possibility. Credit it all to White's recognition of the point of no return.

In the next and final game, we have one of the finest examples of a crisis which develops toward the end of the opening. Once this point of no return is reached, each player knows exactly where he stands, and exactly what he must do to achieve success and avoid failure. The tension increases to an almost unbearable degree as each player follows his indicated course to the foreordained conclusion.

QUEEN'S GAMBIT DECLINED

WHITE	BLACK	WHITE	BLACK
1 P—Q4	P—Q4	3 N—QB3	N—KB3
2 P—QB4	P—K3	4 B—N5	B—K2

This is a totally different kind of opening from the one we saw in the previous game. Here there will be no immediate danger for either King; the goals, at least for the time being, will be vaguer, and the chances of coming to grips will be more remote.

5 N—B3	QN—Q2	6 R—B1	Castles
	7 P—K3	P—QN3	

In order to develop his Bishop on the long diagonal. Now the crisis gradually shapes up.

45

WHITE TO MOVE

Black tries to solve the problem of developing his Queen Bishop.

| | 8 PxP | .... |

Now if Black retakes with his Knight, he will allow White to lord it over the center (by means of P—K4 later on, for example). Black therefore recaptures with his King Pawn, in order to retain a firm grip on the center squares.

8	PxP	9 B—Q3	B—N2
10 Castles	P—B4		

If White exchanges Pawns at this point, he allows Black some additional freedom. Besides, White wants to plant a centralized Knight at the King 5 square. For this purpose he needs to keep his Queen Pawn at Queen 4.

| 11 R—K1 | P—B5 |

White has passed the point of no return. He has allowed Black to establish *a Queen-side majority of Pawns.* That is to say, Black's three Queen-side Pawns (Queen Rook Pawn, Queen Knight Pawn, and Queen Bishop Pawn) are opposed by White's two Queen-side Pawns (Queen Rook Pawn, Queen Knight Pawn). If Black systematically advances his Queen-side Pawns, he will eventually obtain a far advanced passed Pawn.

503

Unless White is able to set up some countervailing advantage, the Black passed Pawn will win the game for Black. Since White deliberately allowed this dangerous state of affairs to arise, we say that he's passed the point of no return.

| 12 B—N1 | P—QR3 | 14 P—B4 | R—K1 |
| 13 N—K5! | P—N4 | 15 Q—B3 | N—B1 |

Black, you will observe, has set his Queen-side Pawns in motion. What is White's counterplay? To attack on the King-side. So, from now on, you will see that White tries to build up an attack on the King-side. Black wants to prepare the advance of his Queen-side Pawns, but he also needs to take time out to try to construct a foolproof defense for his King.

16 N—K2	N—K5	19 Q—N3	P—B3
17 BxB	RxB	20 N—N4	K—R1
18 BxN	PxB	21 P—B5	Q—Q2

Both sides are making progress, though Black underestimates the dangers of his position and is inclined to proceed too slowly.

| 22 R—B1 | R—Q1 | 23 R—B4 | Q—Q3 |
| | 24 Q—R4! | QR—K1 | |

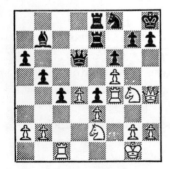

46

WHITE TO MOVE
What is the proper plan for White?

504

If Black is given enough time, he will advance his Queen-side Pawns. White must therefore attack as rapidly as possible on the King-side. The way to do this is to open a file on the King-side by advancing the King Knight Pawn.

White's proper course was therefore 25 N—B2! (making way for the Pawn), B—Q4; 26 P—KN4!, P—R3 (preventing P—N5); 27 Q—N3! (to play up the King Rook Pawn), P—N5; 28 P—KR4! and White is ready to advance P—N5 as a counterpoise to Black's nasty threats on the Queen-side.

Instead, White misses the point:

25 N—B3?   . . . .

This is wrong, as it neglects the possibility of advancing the King Knight Pawn. Aside from that, this Knight move is waste of time, as the Knight will soon be driven away by . . . P—N5.

25	B—Q4	27 R—B1	P—N5
26 N—B2	Q—B3	28 N—K2	Q—R5

Now White is hard pressed. To begin with, the threat of . . . QxP has to be met.

29 N—N4!   . . . .

Very neat. If 29 . . . QxP?; 30 NxP!, PxN; 31 QxBPch and wins. Black must guard against the threat.

29	N—Q2	30 R/B4—B2! . . . .

Another brilliant resource, which combines threats on the King-side with indirect defense of the Queen-side. After 30 . . . QxP; 31 N—B4, B—B2; 32 N—N6ch, BxN; 33 PxB White's attack must succeed.

For example: 33 . . . P—R3; 34 NxRP!!, PxN; 35 QxRPch, K—N1; 36 R—B5! whereupon the coming 37 R—R5 decides in White's favor.

Or 33 . . . N—B1; 34 NxP!, PxN; 35 RxP, K—N1; 36 R—B7 and White wins.

| 30 .... | K—N1 | 31 N—B1 | P—B6! |

Thus Black at last obtains the dangerous passed Pawn whose existence was prophesied by 11 . . . P—B5. White's situation is now truly desperate.

32 P—QN3!	Q—B3	34 N—R2	P—R5
33 P—KR3	P—QR4	35 P—N4	PxP
	36 PxP	....	

The tension mounts from move to move. Black must stop for a moment of consolidation to hold back White's attack by 36 . . . P—R3! Then after 37 Q—N3, N—B1!; 38 P—R4, N—R2! White is still unable to play P—N5. With his King-side attack stymied, he would be truly helpless against Black's Queen-side attack.

| 36 .... | R—R1? |

This is truly the point of no return for Black. Once he allows White's next move, he is doomed to defeat.

| 37 P—N5!! | R—R6 | 38 N—N4! | .... |

47

White's ingenious and courageous counterattack saves the game for him.

Black now wins a Pawn, which gives him two connected passed Pawns on the Queen-side. Since they need only a few moves to advance to the eighth rank and queen, and since the bulk of White's forces is on the King-side, it would seem that White is hopelessly lost.

38 ....   BxP

After the game, 38 . . . RxP, giving up the Exchange, was suggested in order to preserve the Bishop for defending the King-side. However, this ingenious notion would not have sufficed. For example:

38 . . . RxP; 39 NxR, BxN; 40 R—KN2, K—R1; 41 PxP, PxP; 42 N—K5!, NxN; 43 PxN and now White wins after 43 . . . RxP; 44 Q—R6! — or 43 . . . P—B7; 44 P—K6! and wins.

But after his last move (38 . . . BxP) Black expects 39 NxB?, RxN; 40 R—KN2, R—N7! and Black's Queen-side counterplay wins for him.

Instead, White lets the Bishop dangle and gains a valuable tempo:

39 R—KN2!   ....

If now 39 . . . PxP; 40 QxP, K—B1; 41 NxB, RxN; 42 P—B6 and White's attack crashes through to victory.

| 39 .... | K—R1 | 40 PxP | .... |

If Black tries 40 . . . NxP here, then 41 N—K5, Q—K1; 42 N—N6ch wins for White.

| 40 .... | PxP | 41 NxB! | .... |

An important part of his attack. He now eliminates the Bishop, which protects Black's King Knight 1 square.

| 41 .... · | RxN | 42 N—R6! | .... |

Now the absence of the Bishop tells cruelly against Black. White threatens 43 R—N8 mate; and if 42 . . . R—K1; 43 N—B7 mate!

42 ....   R—N2

The only move. But White has some beautiful resources.

| 43 RxR | KxR | 44 Q—N3ch!! | .... |

So that if 44 . . . K—B1; 45 Q—N8ch and 46 QxR— magnificent chess!

44 ....   KxN

And now, in the event of the plausible 45 R—B4? Black plays . . . R—N8ch etc. getting a draw by perpetual check.

But White has a resource which he foresaw a good many moves ago.

45 K—R1!!!   ....

Threaten 46 R—KN1 and 47 Q—R4 mate! Black is lost.

45	Q—Q4	49 RxQ	PxR
46 R—KN1	QxBP	50 Q—Q6ch	K—R4
47 Q—R4ch	Q—R4	51 QxN	P—B7
48 Q—B4ch	Q—N4	52 QxP mate	

In these two thrilling games you have seen telling examples of one of the most important concepts in chess—the crisis which forces a player to continue on a certain course. You have seen the enormous advantage enjoyed by the player who is familiar with the theory of the point of no return. To be unaware of this critical point leaves the attacker, as well as the defender, at the mercy of his opponent. To possess this knowledge gives you the most valuable, and perhaps least understood, of all the weapons you can use to fight back when you're hard pressed by enemy attack.

How
to Play
the King Pawn
Openings

Book Seven

White's game is discredited from the very start by his premature development of the Queen. This enables Black to seize the initiative at move 3 by counterattacking against the White Queen. *Not recommended for White.*

WHITE	BLACK		WHITE	BLACK
1 P—K4	P—K4		2 P—Q4	PxP
3 QxP	N—QB3			

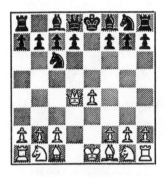

1

(Position after 3 ... N—QB3)

Black's gain of time enables him to take the lead in development.

4 Q—K3	N—B3

An amusing sample of White's difficulties is: 5 B—B4, N—K4; 6 B—N3, B—N5ch; 7 P—QB3?, B—B4!; 8 Q—N3??, BxPch!! and Black wins the Queen by a Knight fork.

5 N—QB3	B—N5

Another way is 5 ... B—K2; 6 B—Q2, P—Q4; 7 PxP, NxP; 8 NxN, QxN and Black's game is decidedly freer.

6 B—Q2	Castles		7 Castles	R—K1

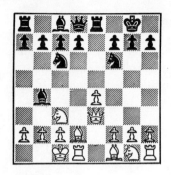

2

(Position after 7 . . . R—K1)

*White's most likely move is 8 Q—N3
or 8 B—B4.*

If White tries 8 B—B4 now, Black can win a Pawn with
8 . . . BxN; 9 BxB, NxP (not 9 . . . RxP??; 10 BxN! winning).

But then White has fairly good attacking prospects after
10 Q—B4, N—B3; 11 N—B3, P—Q3; 12 N—N5, B—K3;
13 B—Q3.

Therefore Black answers 8 B—B4 by 8 . . . N—QR4!;
9 B—Q3, P—Q4! with a fine initiative. This explains White's
Pawn sacrifice on the next move:

| 8 Q—N3!? | NxP | 10 B—KB4 | Q—B3! |
| 9 NxN | RxN | 11 N—R3 | .... |

If 11 BxP?, P—Q3!; 12 BxP, Q—R3ch!; 13 K—N1,
BxB; 14 QxB, QxQ and wins.

| 11 .... | P—Q3 | 12 B—Q3 | R—K1 |

Black is a Pawn ahead with a perfectly safe game. (He
can also try the more complicated 12 . . . N—Q5!; 13 B—K3,
R—N5; 14 BxN, RxB; 15 P—QB3, BxP!; 16 PxB, R—
KN5; 17 Q—K3, QxPch; 18 B—B2, QxQch; 19 PxQ, RxP
with a won ending thanks to his four Pawns for the piece.)

This dashing attempt to seize the attack by sacrificing two Pawns can yield White a very powerful attack if Black does not defend carefully. However, as you will see, Black has several satisfactory defenses. Consequently, the Danish should be ventured only against weak opponents.

WHITE	BLACK	WHITE	BLACK
1 P—K4	P—K4	2 P—Q4	PxP
3 P—QB3		....	

3

(Position after 3 P—QB3)

Black's simplest course is now 3 ... P—Q4!; 4 KPxP, N—KB3!; 5 P—QB4, P—B4 (or even 5 ... P—B3!) with an excellent game.

3	PxP	4 B—QB4	....

If White decides to sacrifice only one Pawn by 4 NxP, Black is safe enough after 4 ... P—Q3; 5 B—QB4, N—QB3.

Black has nothing to fear from 6 Q—N3 because of 6 ... N—K4! Somewhat more troublesome for him is 6 N—B3, B—K3!; 7 BxB, PxB; 8 Q—N3, Q—B1; 9 N—KN5, N—Q1; 10 P—B4, B—K2; 11 Castles, BxN; 12 PxB, N—K2; 13 B—K3, N—B2; 14 R—B2, Castles; 15 QR—KB1, N—N3! Black is still a bit uncomfortable, but the extra Pawn must tell in his favor.

| 4 .... | PxP | 5 BxNP | .... |

The classic position of the Danish Gambit.

Even simplifying and returning the extra material may not give Black a safe game: 5 . . . P—Q4; 6 BxQP, N—KB3; 7 BxPch!, KxB; 8 QxQ, B—N5ch; 9 Q—Q2, BxQch; 10 NxB, P—B4; 11 KN—B3, B—K3; 12 N—N5ch, K—K2; 13 NxB, KxN; 14 P—B4. White will castle Queen-side and advance his formidable mass of King-side Pawns. Black is in trouble.

| 5 .... | P—QB3! | 7 N—B3 | N—Q2 |
| 6 N—QB3 | P—Q3 | 8 Castles | N—B4 |

4

(Position after 8 . . . N—B4)

Black's position, though somewhat cramped, is unassailable. After . . . B—K3 he can catch up in development, and eventually his two extra Pawns must win for him.

This opening is considered inferior because it allows Black to seize the initiative by playing 2 . . . N—KB3 with counter-attack. However, Black must be on the alert for *transpositions* into other openings that may produce an unpleasant surprise.

WHITE	BLACK		WHITE	BLACK
1 P—K4	P—K4		2 B—B4	N—KB3

5

(Position after 2 . . . N—KB3)

White's colorless second move has enabled Black to take the offensive. White can try 3 N—QB3, transposing into the Vienna Game, page 14.

3 P—Q3	P—B3

Continuing his aggressive policy by preparing . . . P—Q4. (If 3 . . . B—B4; 4 P—B4 transposes into the King's Gambit Declined, page 22.)

Should White try to seize the initiative with 4 P—B4, there follows 4 . . . PxP; 5 BxP, P—Q4!; 6 PxP, NxP with a fine game for Black.

And on 4 Q—K2 Black gets a splendid attack at the cost of a Pawn: 4 . . . B—K2; 5 P—B4, P—Q4!; 6 KPxP (6 BPxP, NxP! is also good for Black), KPxP; 7 PxP, NxP; 8 BxP, Castles; 9 N—QB3, N—Q5; 10 Q—Q2 and now Black has 10 . . . B—QN5 with an excellent game—or 10 . . . P—QR3; 11 KN—K2, P—QN4; 12 NxN, QxN; 13 B—QN3, B—QN5; 14 Castles QR, P—QR4! with a winning attack.

4 N—KB3   P—Q4!

Black has an unbearably cramped game after 4 . . . P—Q3?

| 5 PxP | PxP | 6 B—N3 | .... |

6

(Position after 6 B—N3)

The subtle point of Black's play is that after 6 . . . B—N5ch! White cannot interpose 7 N—B3? because of 7 . . . P—Q5!

6	B—N5ch!	9 P—Q4	P—K5
7 P—B3	B—Q3	10 N—K5	N—B3
8 B—N5	B—K3	11 NxN	....

If 11 P—KB4, P—KR3!; 12 B—KR4, P—KN4!; 13 PxP, BxN; 14 PxB, N—KN5! with a powerful game for Black.

| 11 .... | PxN | 12 P—B3 | .... |

After 12 Castles, Black escapes from the pin with 12 . . . Q—B2!

| 12 .... | P—KR3 | 13 B—KR4 | .... |

Not 13 BxN, QxB; 14 PxP?, Q—R5ch etc.

| 13 .... | P—N4 | 14 B—KB2 | PxP |
| | 15 QxP | N—K5 | |

Black's position is more aggressive, and therefore more promising.

VIENNA GAME

As in the Bishop's Opening, White gives Black a chance to counterattack with 2 . . . N—KB3. The struggle for control of the center is a very lively one. This opening always leads to interesting play because of the sharp clash of ideas.

(a) 3 P—B4 Variation

WHITE	BLACK
1 P—K4	P—K4
2 N—QB3	N—KB3

WHITE	BLACK
3 P—B4	P—Q4
4 BPxP	NxP

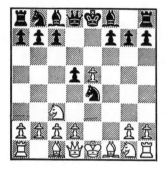

7

(Position after 4 . . . NxP)

If now 5 Q—B3, N—QB3!; 6 B—N5 (not 6 NxN?, N—Q5!; 7 Q—Q3, PxN; 8 QxP, B—KB4!), NxN; 7 NPxN, Q—R5ch; 8 P—N3, Q—K5ch with a favorable endgame for Black.

WHITE	BLACK
5 N—B3	B—K2
6 P—Q4	Castles

WHITE	BLACK
7 B—Q3	P—KB4!
8 PxP e.p.	BxP!

If now 9 Castles, N—B3 and Black maintains material equality. Nor can White capture twice on his King 4 without losing a piece. *The position is even.*

(b) 3 B—B4 Variation

WHITE	BLACK	WHITE	BLACK
1 P—K4	P—K4	2 N—QB3	N—KB3
	3 B—B4	NxP!?	

519

Leads to wild and woolly chess. A quieter and perfectly satisfactory alternative is 3 . . . N—B3; 4 P—Q3, N—QR4; 5 B—N3, NxB; 6 RPxN, B—N5 etc.

        4 Q—R5   . . . .

Threatens mate. The tame 4 NxN is good for Black (4 . . . P—Q4! etc.).

4 . . . .   N—Q3   5 B—N3   N—B3

So far so good, but now White again threatens mate, forcing Black to give up the Exchange.

6 N—N5!?	P—KN3	8 Q—Q5	Q—K2
7 Q—B3	P—B4	9 NxPch	K—Q1
	10 NxR	P—N3	

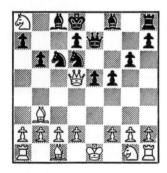

8

(Position after 10 . . . P—N3)

A very unclear situation, despite all the analysis that has been lavished on it.

After 11 P—Q3, B—QN2; 12 P—KR4, P—B5! (stops B—N5) Black has a powerful attack for his minus material. Thus, if 13 Q—B3, N—Q5; 14 Q—R3, B—KR3; 15 B—Q2, P—K5 *with a winning game for Black.*

On the other hand, after 11 N—K2!, B—QN2; 12 Q—B3, N—Q5; 13 NxN!, BxQ; 14 NxB, *White's material advantage should win for him.*

One thing is certain: White's repeated Queen moves leave him with a dangerously retarded development.

520

KING'S GAMBIT

This is the classic attacking line in the King Pawn openings. White offers a Pawn early in the opening in order to obtain a powerful Pawn center and an attack via the King Bishop file. Superior development for White generally gives him a winning attack. Superior development for Black generally gives him a winning defense.

(*a*) King's Knight's Gambit with 3 . . . P—KN4

This is the oldest and most complicated form of the King's Gambit.

WHITE	BLACK		WHITE	BLACK
1 P—K4	P—K4		2 P—KB4	PxP
	3 N—KB4	P—KN4		

Black's idea is to guard the Gambit Pawn at his King Bishop 5.

White can try to break up the Black Pawn formation with 4 P—KR4, but Black has a good reply in 4 . . . P—N5 driving the Knight back. If then 5 N—N5?!, P—KR3 and White is forced to play 6 NxP (Allgaier Gambit), which leaves him with inadequate material for the Knight after 6 . . . KxN.

More reasonable, after 4 P—KR4, P—N5 is 5 N—K5 (Kieseritzky Gambit); but after 5 . . . N—KB3; 6 B—B4, P—Q4!; 7 PxP, B—N2; 8 P—Q4, N—R4! Black has a splendid game.

4 B—B4   . . . .

Black must be wary hereabouts. The over-anxious 4 . . . P—KB3?? leads to disaster after 5 NxP!, PxN; 6 Q—R5ch, K—K2; 7 Q—B7ch, K—Q3; 8 Q—Q5ch, K—K2; 9 Q—K5 mate.

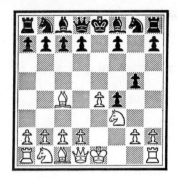

9

(Position after 4 B—B4)

White aims to develop quickly, while Black hopes to maintain his extra Pawn safely.

After 4 . . . P—N5 (too hasty) ; 5 Castles!?, PxN we have the famous Muzio Gambit. Then, after 6 QxP White has a magnificent development in return for his sacrificed piece. Black does well to avoid this hazardous line of play. Therefore:

| 4 . . . . | B—N2 | 6 P—Q4 | P—KR3 |
| 5 Castles | P—Q3 | 7 P—B3 | N—QB3 |

10

(Position after 7 . . . N—QB3)

Black's sober development has given him a solid position which seems shatterproof.

| 8 P—KN3 | . . . . |

Logical: he tries to break up Black's Pawn-chain. Naturally Black does not oblige by replying 8 . . . PxP and thus opening the King Bishop file for White.

| 8 . . . . | B—R6! |

By attacking White's Rook, Black gains time to complete his development. *The game is complicated, with approximately even chances.*

(b) King's Knight's Gambit with 3 . . . B—K2

This line and Variation *(c)* are favored by modern players as being simpler and less risky than Variation *(a)*.

WHITE	BLACK		WHITE	BLACK
1 P—K4	P—K4		2 P—KB4	PxP
3 N—KB3	B—K2			

There is more to this innocent-looking move than meets the eye, for if 4 P—Q4?, B—R5ch and White's King is forced to a bad square.

4 B—B4   . . . .

As usual, a developing move is best. If now 4 . . . B—R5ch; 5 K—B1 and White stands well despite the loss of castling. Black continues the policy of sound development with:

4 . . . .   N—KB3

If now 5 P—Q3, P—Q4! with an excellent game.

5 P—K5   N—N5!

11

(Position after 5 . . . N—N5!)

Black's advanced Knight is well placed. For example 6 N—B3, N—QB3; 7 P—Q4, P—Q3!; 8 P—KR3?, B—R5ch!; 9 K—B1, N—B7! and Black wins.

523

Also good is 6 . . . P—Q3; 7 PxP, QxP and Black has a fine development with nothing to fear.

$$7 \text{ P—Q4} \qquad \text{P—Q4}$$

If now 8 B—Q3, P—KN4! and Black stands well.

8 PxP e.p.　　　BxP　　　　　　9 R—K1ch　　N—K2
10 P—KR3　　　N—KB3

Black has a splendid position, and White still has the vexing problem of recovering the gambit Pawn.

(c) King's Knight's Gambit with 3 . . . P—Q4

WHITE	BLACK	WHITE	BLACK
1 P—K4	P—K4	3 N—KB3	P—Q4
2 P—KB4	PxP	4 PxP	N—KB3

White can now try to complicate matters with 5 B—N5ch, but Black simply replies 5 . . . P—B3, with a splendid game after 6 PxP, PxP; 7 B—B4, N—Q4!

For example 8 Q—K2ch, B—K2; 9 P—Q4, Castles; 10 BxN, PxB; 11 BxP, B—R3! Or 8 Castles, B—Q3; 9 Q—K2ch, B—K3 and Black has a fine game.

5 N—B3	NxP	6 NxN	QxN
7 P—Q4	. . . .		

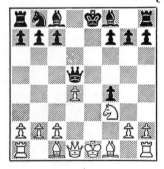

12

(Position after 7 P—Q4)

White hopes to regain his Pawn by 8 BxP, for if then 9 . . . Q—K5ch; 10 Q—K2 pins Black's Queen.

7 ....   B—K2!

This sound developing move indirectly guards the gambit Pawn, for if 8 BxP??, Q—K5ch wins the Bishop.

8 P—B4   Q—K5ch   9 K—B2   B—KB4
            10 P—B5   ....

With the powerful threat of 11 B—N5ch followed by 12 R—K1.

10 ....   N—B3!   11 B—N5   Q—Q4!

Prudently removing his Queen from the open King file.

12 BxP   Castles QR

13

(Position after 12 . . . Castles QR)

Black has a fine game because of his pressure on White's weak Queen Pawn. If now 13 B—K3, B—B3! etc.

Black has escaped unscathed and has a fine game. A remarkable variation here is 13 B—K3, B—B3!; 14 Q—R4, B—K5! with this possibility: 15 BxN, QxB; 16 QxP, BxN; 17 PxB, BxP!; 18 BxB, RxB; 19 Q—R8ch, K—Q2; 20 QxR, QxQBP! and though Black is a Rook down, he has a winning attack!

(d) King's Bishop's Gambit

WHITE	BLACK		WHITE	BLACK
1 P—K4	P—K4		2 P—KB4	PxP
3 B—B4	....			

14

(Position after 3 B—B4)

This opening is out of fashion as Black has easy counterplay with . . . N—KB3 and . . . P—Q4.

| 3 .... | N—KB3! | 4 N—QB3 | P—B3! |

Preparing the counterthrust . . . P—Q4! If now 5 P—K5, P—Q4! with an aggressive game for Black.

| 5 Q—B3 | .... |

Vainly trying to stop Black's next move. If instead 5 P—Q4, B—N5!; 6 Q—B3, P—Q4!; 7 PxP, Castles! and Black is well ahead in development.

| 5 .... | P—Q4! | 7 P—Q3 | B—KN5 |
| 6 PxP | B—Q3 | 8 Q—B2 | Castles |

Black's marked lead in development gives him much the better game. A plausible continuation to emphasize this advantage is the following:

9 BxP	R—K1ch	12 QN—K2	NxP
10 K—B1	P—QN4	13 BxN	PxB
11 B—QN3	P—N5	14 Q—N3	BxNch
	15 NxB	Q—B3!	

Black wins, his chief threat being 16 . . . RxN!
The moral of all these variations is that if Black fosters his development carefully and avoids confusing complications, he remains with much the better game.

KING'S GAMBIT DECLINED

By refusing to accept the gambit, Black hopes to avoid prepared variations and dangerous attacks. In general, therefore, the play in this opening is less critical than in the gambit accepted.

(a) 4 B—B4 Variation

WHITE	BLACK		WHITE	BLACK
1 P—K4	P—K4		2 P—KB4	B—B4

The key move to the whole situation. If now 3 PxP??, Black has the crushing reply 3 . . . Q—R5ch forcing checkmate or winning a Rook.

3 N—KB3	P—Q3		5 N—B3	N—B3
4 B—B4	N—KB3		6 P—Q3	. . . .

15

(Position after 6 P—Q3)

Black can try the aggressive but risky course 6 . . . B—KN5; 7 N—QR4, BxN; 8 QxB, N—Q5; 9 Q—N3!? with highly complicated play. The following recommendation is safer and simpler by far.

6 . . . .   B—K3!

Even game. Black has nothing to fear after 7 BxB, PxB; while if 7 B—N5, P—QR3; 8 BxNch, PxB; 9 P—B5, B—B1

527

he has two serviceable Bishops and the freeing move . . .
P—Q4.

(b)   4 P—B3 Variation

WHITE	BLACK		WHITE	BLACK
1 P—K4	P—K4		3 N—KB3	P—Q3
2 P—KB4	B—B4		4 P—B3	. . . .

16

(Position after 4 P—B3)

White hopes to build a strong Pawn center by continuing with P—Q4. Black must counterattack precisely.

4 . . . .   N—KB3!

Better than 4 . . . B—KN5; 5 PxP!, PxP; 6 Q—R4ch!, B—Q2 (forced); 7 Q—B2 and White's game is freer.

Likewise after 4 . . . P—B4; 5 BPxP, QPxP; 6 P—Q4!, KPxP; 7 B—QB4!, N—KB3; 8 P—K5, N—K5; 9 PxP, B—N5ch; 10 B—Q2, BxBch; 11 QNxB, N—QB3; 12 P—Q5 Black's game is very difficult because White's center Pawn position is so powerful.

5 PxP	PxP		8 P—K5	N—Q4
6 P—Q4	PxP		9 B—QB4	B—K3
7 PxP	B—N3!		10 Q—N3	Castles

Even game, in view of the strong position of Black's Knight at Queen 4. Though White's Pawn center looks formidable, it may become weak later on after a well-timed . . . P—KB3.

FALKBEER COUNTER GAMBIT

Counter gambits must be viewed with skepticism. It is generally doubtful that Black can snatch the initiative at an early stage. In this opening, for example, Black's policy of temporarily—and in some cases, permanently—sacrificing a Pawn, does not seem to be justified.

WHITE	BLACK		WHITE	BLACK
1 P—K4	P—K4		2 P—KB4	P—Q4
	3 KPxP		P—K5	

17

(Position after 3 ... P—K5)

This is the position Black aims for with his key second move. Black hopes to use his King Pawn as a stumbling block to White's development. Hence White's reply.

4 P—Q3   N—KB3

After 4 ... PxP; 5 QxP, N—KB3; 6 N—QB3, B—QB4; 7 B—Q2, Castles; 8 Castles, Black has no compensation for the lost Pawn.

5 Q—K2!   ....

The pin on the King Pawn is very effective.

If instead 5 N—Q2 Black gets a good game with 5 ... PxP; 6 BxP, NxP etc.

5	QxP	9 PxP!	QxKP
6 N—QB3	B—QN5	10 QxQch	NxQ
7 B—Q2	BxN	11 BxP	R—N1
8 BxB	B—N5	12 B—K5	N—QB3
	13 B—Q3	....	

White's extra Pawn gives him the advantage.

18
(Position after 13 B—Q3)

Black has no compensation for the Pawn minus.

GRECO COUNTER GAMBIT

There is another counter gambit—an early attempt by Black to wrest the initiative from White. As such, it is suspect. What makes this counter gambit all the more dubious is that it is foolishly adopted as a reply to what is undoubtedly White's strongest *developing* move, 2 N—KB3.

WHITE	BLACK		WHITE	BLACK
1 P—K4	P—K4		2 N—KB3	P—KB4

19

(Position after 2 . . . P—KB4)

Black's advance of the King Bishop Pawn is premature. It weakens Black's King's position and allows White to gain time with a formidable threat.

3 NxP		. . . .	

Threatening 4 Q—R5ch and if 4 . . . P—KN3; 5 NxNP. Hence Black's reply.

3	Q—B3		5 N—B4	PxP
4 P—Q4	P—Q3		6 N—B3	Q—N3

The tricky 6 . . . P—B3 does not work because of 7 NxP, Q—K3; 8 Q—K2, P—Q4; 9 N/K4—Q6ch, K—Q2; 10 N—B7!!

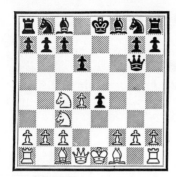

20

(Position after 6 . . ∴ Q—N3)

White is well ahead in development and Black's forces are split. His Queen will be sadly missed from the Queen-side.

| 7 B—B4 | N—KB3 | 8 N—K3 | B—K2 |

After 8 . . . B—K3; 9 P—Q5 followed by 10 Q—Q4, Black's game is disorganized and his King Pawn is weak.

| 9 B—B4 | P—B3 | 10 P—Q5! | . . . . |

White has definitely the better game because of his superior development. Black's King Pawn lacks the natural support of . . . P—Q4 and the prospects for development of his Queenside forces remain bleak.

532

PHILIDOR'S DEFENSE

Black's passive second move immediately puts him on the defensive with a cramped and passive game. White has the initiative and much more freedom no matter how Black proceeds.

(a) 3 . . . PxP Variation

WHITE	BLACK		WHITE	BLACK
1 P—K4	P—K4		2 N—KB3	P—Q3

The characteristic move of this defense. Note that it hems in Black's King Bishop.

	3 P—Q4	PxP

Black surrenders the center, giving White the opportunity to develop his Queen aggressively.

4 QxP!	N—QB3		7 N—B3	N—B3
5 B—QN5!	B—Q2		8 B—N5	B—K2
6 BxN	BxB		9 Castles QR	....

21

(Position after 9 Castles QR)

White has a splendid initiative with a marked lead in development and plenty of room for his pieces.

533

(b) 3 . . . N—Q2 Variation

	WHITE	BLACK		WHITE	BLACK
1	P—K4	P—K4	3	P—Q4	N—Q2
2	N—KB3	P—Q3	4	B—QB4!	....

By playing 3 . . . N—Q2 Black has announced his policy of not giving up the center as in the previous variation. However, his position is badly constricted.

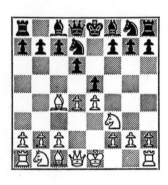

22

(Position after 4 B—QB4!)

Black is in trouble. If now 4 . . . B—K2?; 5 PxP!, NxP; 6 NxN, PxN; 7 Q—R5 — or 5 . . . PxP?; 6 Q—Q5. In either case White wins material.

4	P—QB3	6 Castles	KN—B3
5 N—B3	B—K2	7 P—QR4!	....

Prevents Black from making some room for his pieces on the Queen-side with . . . P—QN4 etc.

White has distinctly the better game because his pieces have far more mobility. A likely continuation is 7 . . . Q—B2; 8 Q—K2, Castles; 9 B—R2 followed by B—K3 and White maintains a noticeably freer position.

534

PETROFF'S DEFENSE

On the surface this is an aggressive defense, as Black counterattacks on the second move. Actually White has several simplifying drawish possibilities. Consequently Black should avoid the Petroff *if he is out to win.* On the other hand, if White strives for the initiative, Black has just enough resources to hold the position.

WHITE	BLACK	WHITE	BLACK
1 P—K4	P—K4	2 N—KB3	N—KB3

The key move. If now 3 P—Q4, PxP!; 4 P—K5, N—K5; 5 QxP, P—Q4; 6 PxP e.p., NxQP with even chances.

3 NxP   . . . .

23

(Position after 3 NxP)

This position is not as harmless as it looks. If now 3 . . . NxP??; 4 Q— K2! and White forces the win of some material—for example 4 . . . N— KB3???; 5 N—B6 dis ch.

3	P—Q3!	4 N—KB3	NxP

Here White has a colorless line which spoils the Petroff for aggressive players: 5 Q—K2, Q—K2; 6 P—Q3, N— KB3; 7 B—N5 etc.

5 P—Q4	P—Q4	6 B—Q3	. . . .

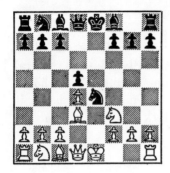

24

(Position after 6 B—Q3)

Momentarily it seems as if White may succeed in getting a slight initiative, say 6 . . . B—Q3; 7 Castles, Castles; 8 P—B4!, P—QB3; 9 N—B3 etc.

| 6 .... | B—K2 | 7 Castles | N—QB3 |
| | 8 P—B4 | .... | |

Again White seems to be making headway, for example 8 . . . N—B3; 9 P—B5! and Black's game is cramped.

| 8 .... | N—QN5! | 10 QxN | QxP |
| 9 PxP | NxB | 11 R—K1 | B—KB4 |

Even game. A plausible follow-up is 12 N—B3, NxN; 13 QxN, P—QB3; 14 R—K5, Q—Q2; 15 P—Q5!, Castles KR!; 16 PxP, PxP. In that case Black's Queen-side Pawns have been weakened, but he has good Bishops.

With his third and fourth moves, White violates the principles of rapid development. At move 4, Black is able to develop with gain of time and is thus assured of equality.

(a) 4 . . . B—B4 Variation

WHITE	BLACK		WHITE	BLACK
1 P—K4	P—K4		3 P—Q4	PxP
2 N—KB3	N—QB3		4 NxP	. . . .

A possibility here is 4 B—QB4. After 4 . . . N—B3 White can lead into the Two Knights' Defense with 5 Castles or 5 P—K5 (pages 46-49), or he can continue the gambit proper with 5 P—B3, PxP; 6 NxP. This gives him an active development as partial compensation for his Pawn.

4 . . . .   B—B4

25

(Position after 4 . . . B—B4)

Black develops with attack—pure gain of time. The following struggle for control of the center squares is very interesting and certainly offers Black no difficulty.

5 B—K3	Q—B3		8 NxB	Castles
6 P—QB3	KN—K2		9 B—K2	P—Q3
7 N—B2	BxB		10 Castles	B—K3
	11 N—Q2	P—Q4!		

The classic equalizing move. The game is perfectly even.

(b) 4 . . . N—B3 Variation

	WHITE	BLACK		WHITE	BLACK
1	P—K4	P—K4	5	N—QB3	B—N5
2	N—KB3	N—QB3	6	NxN	NPxN
3	P—Q4	PxP	7	B—Q3	P—Q4
4	NxP	N—B3	8	PxP	. . . .

After 8 P—K5, Black gets a good game with 8 . . . N—N5 or 8 . . . N—K5.

26

(Position after 8 PxP)

Black's simplest equalizing method is 8 . . . Q—K2ch; 9 Q—K2, NxP; 10 QxQch, KxQ etc.

	WHITE	BLACK		WHITE	BLACK
8	. . . .	PxP	10	B—KN5	B—K3
9	Castles	Castles	11	Q—B3	B—K2

Even game. White's position is more aggressive, but Black has ample resources.

PONZIANI OPENING

Whereas in the Scotch Game White advances too rapidly in the center to achieve any lasting effect, in the Ponziani Opening he advances too slowly. So Black equalizes without any trouble.

WHITE	BLACK		WHITE	BLACK
1 P—K4	P—K4		2 N—KB3	N—QB3
	3 P—B3		N—B3!	

27

(Position after 3 . . . N—B3!)

White's third move holds up his development and takes away his Queen Knight's best square.

4 P—Q4	P—Q4!

Much better than 4 . . . NxKP?; 5 P—Q5, N—N1; 6 B—Q3!, N—B4; 7 NxP when Black has an unpromising position.

5 B—QN5!	. . . .

White wisely takes the prudent course. If 5 KPxP, QxP; 6 B—K2, P—K5; 7 KN—Q2, P—K6!; 8 PxP, QxNP Black has the initiative.

Meanwhile White hopes for some such continuation as 5 . . . QPxP; 6 NxP, which gives him fair prospects of initiative. In addition, even after 6 . . . B—Q2 White would permanently spoil Black's Queen-side Pawn position with 7 BxN etc.

5	KPxP	8 BxBch	QxB
6 NxP	B—Q2	9 QxN	QxP
7 PxP	NxN	10 Q—K3ch	B—K2

Black has a slight lead in development, but the position may be considered even.

HUNGARIAN DEFENSE

Black sometimes adopts this defense to evade the Giuoco Piano or Evans Gambit (pages 38, 44). However, the result is a cramped game for him. Therefore this defense is not recommended for Black.

WHITE	BLACK	WHITE	BLACK
1 P—K4	P—K4	2 N—KB3	N—QB3
3 B—B4	B—K2		

Black's last move is the characteristic move of this defense.

4 P—Q4!   . . . .

28

(Position after 4 P—Q4!)

If Black plays 4 . . . PxP the sequel might be 5 NxP, P—Q3; 6 Castles, N—B3; 7 N—QB3, Castles; 8 P—KR3 when Black has a cramped position reminiscent of Philidor's Defense (page 28).

4 . . . .   P—Q3   5 P—Q5!   . . . .

The key move of White's plan: Black is to be permanently tied up.

5 . . . .   N—N1   6 B—Q3!   . . . .

White must prevent Black's only way of seeking freedom —by . . . P—KB4.

541

| 6 .... | N—KB3 | 7 P—B4 | Castles |

Or 7 ... QN—Q2; 8 N—B3, Castles; 9 P—KR3, N—B4;
10 B—B2, P—QR4; 11 B—K3 and Black's position is
crowded just as badly as in the text line.

8 P—KR3!	P—B3	10 B—K3	N—B2
9 N—B3	N—R3	11 Castles	KN—K1
	12 Q—B2!	....	

*White has much the better game. Black's position is sadly
constricted.*

This is the first opening in our survey which is based on strictly logical ideas. White strives for the initiative with his second move (2 N—KB3), and continues with 3 B—B4. Thus he gives his King Bishop an aggressive diagonal and attempts to restrain the liberating . . . P—Q4. Then he proceeds to construct a strong Pawn center.

All this sounds formidable, and it is. Black can easily go wrong if he does not know the safest lines.

(a) 4 . . . N—B3 Variation

WHITE	BLACK		WHITE	BLACK
1 P—K4	P—K4		3 B—B4	B—B4
2 N—KB3	N—QB3		4 P—B3	N—B3

The classic counterattacking move. Black intends to give up the center with his next move.

5 P—Q4	PxP	6 PxP	. . . .

Note that although 6 P—K5 looks impressive, Black has a perfect answer in 6 . . . P—Q4!

6	B—N5ch

29

(Position after 6 . . . B—N5ch)

The simple and safe course is now 7 B—Q2, BxBch; 8 QNxB, P—Q4!; 9 PxP, KNxP; 10 Q—N3, QN—K2; 11 Castles, Castles with equality.

543

The alternative 6 . . . B—N3? leaves Black with a miserable game after 7 P—K5, N—KN1; 8 P—Q5 etc.

7 N—B3?!   NxKP!?

Another way is 7 . . . P—Q4! and if 8 PxP, KNxP; 9 Castles, B—K3!; 10 B—KN5, B—K2; 11 BxN, QBxB; 12 NxB, QxN; 13 BxB, NxB; 14 R—K1, P—KB3!; 15 Q—K2, Q—Q2; 16 QR—B1, K—B2! and Black is safe after 17 . . . KR—K1 and 18 . . . K—N1.

Note that White's last move is a wild attempt to create dangerous complications at the cost of a Pawn or even more material.

8 Castles   . . . .

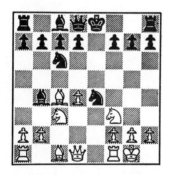

30

(Position after 8 Castles)

Black must proceed with great care.

Now 8 . . . NxN can lead to a lot of trouble for Black after 9 PxN, P—Q4; 10 PxB, PxB; 11 R—K1ch, N—K2 (if 11 . . . B—K3?; 12 P—Q5 wins a piece); 12 Q—K2, B—K3; 13 B—N5, Q—Q4; 14 BxN, KxB; 15 Q—B2!, P—KB3; 16 N—N5!, PxN (if 16 . . . QxN; 17 Q—K4 with a winning attack); 17 R—K5, QxQP; 18 QR—K1 and White wins back his piece with advantage.

Another dangerous line for Black is 8 . . . NxN; 9 PxN, BxP?; 10 B—R3!! and wins. Thus, after 10 . . . BxR??; 11 R—K1ch Black can resign.

544

And if 10 . . . P—Q4; 11 B—N5!, BxR; 12 R—K1ch, B—K3; 13 Q—R4! and Black is lost.

Or take this possibility: 10 . . . P—Q3; 11 R—B1, B—R4; 12 Q—R4, P—QR3; 13 B—Q5, B—N3; 14 RxN!, B—Q2; 15 R—K1ch, K—B1; 16 RxQP!! and wins.

| 8 .... | BxN! | 9 P—Q5 | .... |

31

(Position after 9 P—Q5)

This position is full of bewildering possibilities. Black's safest is 9 . . . N—K4!

| 9 .... | N—K4! | 10 PxB | NxB |
| | 11 Q—Q4 | .... | |

A famous trap here is 11 . . . N/B5—Q3?; 12 QxNP, Q—B3; 13 QxQ, NxQ; 14 R—K1ch. If now 14 . . . K—Q1??; 15 B—N5! wins. If 14 . . . K—B1??; 15 B—R6ch, K—N1; 16 R—K5! and Black is lost, for example 16 . . . N/Q3—K5; 17 N—Q2, NxN; 18 R—KN5 mate or 17 . . . P—Q3; 18 NxN, PxR; 19 NxN mate.

Finally, if 14 . . . N/B3—K5; 15 N—Q2, P—B4; 16 P—B3 with a winning game for White.

| 11 .... | P—KB4 | 12 QxN/B4 | .... |

Not 12 QxNP?, Q—B3 and White has no compensation for the lost piece.

12	P—Q3

Black has the advantage: his position is safe and he is a Pawn to the good.

(b) 4 . . . Q—K2 Variation

WHITE	BLACK	WHITE	BLACK
1 P—K4	P—K4	3 B—B4	B—B4
2 N—KB3	N—QB3	4 P—B3	Q—K2
	5 P—Q4	B—N3	

32

(Position after 5 . . . B—N3)

Black avoids exchanging Pawns in order to hold the center. The result is a very cramped game for him.

6 Castles	N—B3	7 R—K1	P—Q3
	8 P—KR3!	....	

Preventing the pin . . . B—N5. Thus White strengthens his Pawn center and deprives Black's Queen Bishop of its best square.

8	Castles	10 B—Q3!	P—B3
9 N—R3!	N—Q1	11 N—B4	B—B2

White has distinctly the better game because of his greater freedom. He can play 12 P—QN3! threatening 13 B—R3 with annoying possibilities.

(c) 4 P—Q3 Variation

WHITE	BLACK		WHITE	BLACK
1 P—K4	P—K4		3 B—B4	B—B4
2 N—KB3	N—QB3		4 P—Q3	....

This leads to a slow game which gives Black very little trouble.

4	N—B3		5 N—B3	P—Q3
	6 B—K3		....	

After 6 B—KN5, P—KR3 (6 . . . N—QR4 is also playable); 7 BxN, QxB; 8 N—Q5, Q—Q1; 9 P—B3, P—R3!; 10 P—Q4, PxP; 11 PxP, B—R2 Black's game is slightly preferable because of his two Bishops.

	6	B—N3

Better than 6 . . . BxB; 7 PxB, which gives White an open King Bishop file.

7 Q—Q2	B—K3		8 B—N3	....

White is confronted with the same problem that Black encountered at move 6. That is to say, White is unwilling to play BxB, for that would open the King Bishop file for Black. However, now that White has retreated B—N3, Black in turn has to meet the same problem. If Black now plays 8 . . . BxB, White replies 9 RPxB, acquiring an open Queen Rook file.

This reasoning about the desirability or undesirability of exchanging the Bishops is an important feature of the variation. Obtaining an open file is often the imperceptible beginning of a strong initiative.

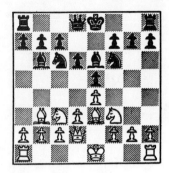

33

(Position after 8 B—N3)

This is a good variation for inexperienced players, as the position offers little scope for complications.

Even game; the symmetrical position of the Bishops and Pawns offers little to either side.

The Evans is a brilliant offshoot of the Giuoco Piano, wherein White sacrifices a Pawn in order to obtain open lines and gain time to form a strong Pawn center. The attack can become extremely vehement and calls for really resourceful play on the defender's part.

(a) Evans Gambit Accepted

WHITE	BLACK		WHITE	BLACK
1 P—K4	P—K4		3 B—B4	B—B4
2 N—KB3	N—QB3		4 P—QN4	. . . .

34

(Position after 4 P—QN4)

White offers a Pawn sacrifice which may involve many pitfalls, prepared variations, and tricky analysis. Black does well to choose a simple defense.

4	BxNP		5 P—B3	B—K2!

The old defense 5 . . . B—B4; 6 P—Q4, PxP; 7 PxP, B—N3; 8 Castles, P—Q3 leaves White with a strong lead in development after 9 N—B3.

6 P—Q4   N—QR4!

Guarding against 7 Q—N3.

7 B—Q3   . . . .

Or 7 NxP, NxB; 8 NxN, P—Q4; 9 PxP, QxP with a pleasant game for Black.

549

| 7 .... | PxP | 8 PxP | P—Q4 |

If now 9 PxP, N—KB3; 10 Q—R4ch, P—B3 and Black's game is very comfortable.

| 9 N—B3 | PxP | 11 NxNch | BxN |
| 10 NxP | N—KB3 | 12 Q—R4ch | N—B3 |

Black has an easy game after 13 B—R3, B—K2; 14 B—N5, Castles! returning the gambit Pawn. Note Black's emphasis on quick development—even at the cost of returning the gambit Pawn.

(b) Evans Gambit Declined

WHITE	BLACK		WHITE	BLACK
1 P—K4	P—K4		3 B—B4	B—B4
2 N—KB3	N—QB3		4 P—QN4	B—N3!
	5 P—QR4		....	

35

(Position after 5 P—QR4)

By declining the gambit Black gets a perfectly safe and satisfactory position. Thus he avoids all the complications of the gambit accepted.

5	P—QR3	9 BxR	N—Q5!
6 B—N2	P—Q3	10 NxN	PxN
7 P—N5	PxP	11 P—QB3	N—B3
8 PxP	RxR	12 Castles	Castles

Even game, with this possibility: 13 P—Q3, P—B3!; 14 NPxP, NPxP; 15 PxP, P—Q4!; 16 PxP, NxP and White's extra Pawn is worthless.

550

TWO KNIGHTS' DEFENSE

This is a line of play frequently selected by those who wish to evade the Guioco Piano or Evans Gambit. This defense calls for enterprising play, as many variations necessitate a Pawn sacrifice on Black's part.

(a) 4 N—N5 Variation

WHITE	BLACK
1 P—K4	P—K4
2 N—KB3	N—QB3
5 PxP	

WHITE	BLACK
3 B—B4	N—B3
4 N—N5	P—Q4
....	

36

(Position after 5 PxP)

Black's best is 5 . . . NxP!, for if 6 NxBP?! (the Fried Liver Attack), KxN; 7 Q—B3ch, K—K3; 8 N—B3, QN—N5!; 9 Q—K4, P—B3; 10 P—Q4, K—Q2! and Black is safe.

5	N—QR4	6 B—N5ch	....

After 6 P—Q3, P—KR3; 7 N—KB3, P—K5 Black has the initiative in return for his sacrificed Pawn; for example 8 Q—K2, NxB; 9 PxN, B—QB4; 10 KN—Q2, Castles; 11 N—N3, B—KN5! etc.

6	P—B3	7 PxP	PxP
8 B—K2		....	

On 8 Q—B3 Black can try the venturesome 8 . . . PxB!; 9 QxR, Q—Q2! with a notable lead in development against White's disorganized forces.

8	P—KR3	12 Castles!	BxN
9 N—KB3	P—K5	13 PxB	Q—Q5ch
10 N—K5	B—Q3	14 K—R1	QxKP
11 P—KB4!	Castles	15 P—Q4!	....

37

(Position after 15 P—Q4!)

White has benefited considerably by returning the Pawn at move 12.

White has the better game whether Black retreats his Queen or captures his Queen Pawn in passing. White's positional advantages are well-defined: he has an open King Bishop file, two aggressive Bishops, the Queen-side majority of Pawns. Black's Queen-side Pawns are split and his Queen Knight is sadly out of play.

(b) 4 P—Q4 Variation

WHITE	BLACK	WHITE	BLACK
1 P—K4	P—K4	3 B—B4	N—B3
2 N—KB3	N—QB3	4 P—Q4	PxP
	5 Castles	NxP	

The alternative 5 ... B—B4; 6 P—K5, P—Q4 may lead to the Max Lange Attack (page 48).

6 R—K1	P—Q4	7 BxP	QxB
	8 N—B3	....	

552

38

(Position after 8 N—B3)

White makes use of a piquant double pin to win back the sacrificed material.

8	Q—KR4
9 NxN	B—K3

10 B—N5	B—QN5
11 NxP	....

White has regained his Pawn with an even game. The continuation might be: 11 . . . QxQ; 12 KRxQ, NxN; 13 RxN, B—K2.

(c) Max Lange Attack

	WHITE	BLACK
1	P—K4	P—K4
2	N—KB3	N—QB3
3	B—B4	N—B3
4	P—Q4	PxP

	WHITE	BLACK
5	Castles	B—B4
6	P—K5	P—Q4!
7	PxN	PxB
8	R—K1ch	....

White should play for equality with 8 PxP, KR—N1; 9 B—N5 etc.

8	B—K3

9 N—N5	....

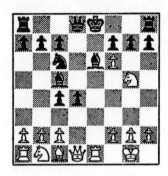

39

(Position after 9 N—N5)

White's threat is 10 NxB, PxN; 11 Q—R5ch winning the Bishop.

9 ....   Q—Q4   10 N—QB3!   Q—B4
               11 QN—K4   ....

If now 11 . . . B—KB1; 12 NxBP!, KxN; 13 N—N5ch and White regains the piece with a winning attack.

11 ....   Castles QR!   13 P—KN4   Q—K4
12 N/N5xB   PxN   14 PxP   KR—N1

In this wide-open position Black has the initiative, for example 15 B—R6, B—N5!; 16 R—K2, P—Q6! etc.

FOUR KNIGHTS' GAME
(including Three Knights' Game)

This stolid line of play is generally good for a draw, but unpromising if White wants to play for a win. Black has many equalizing methods, and numerous possibilities of simplifying exchanges.

(a) 6 . . . BxN Variation

WHITE	BLACK	WHITE	BLACK
1 P—K4	P—K4	4 B—N5	B—N5
2 N—KB3	N—QB3	5 Castles	Castles
3 N—B3	N—B3	6 P—Q3	....

A lifeless, drawish alternative is 6 BxN, NPxB; 7 NxP, R—K1; 8 N—Q3, BxN; 9 QPxB, NxP etc.

6	BxN	7 PxB	P—Q3
	8 B—N5	Q—K2	

After 8 . . . N—K2?; 9 BxN, PxB; 10 N—R4, P—B3; 11 B—B4, P—Q4; 12 B—N3, N—N3; 13 NxN, RPxN; 14 P—KB4! White has a decided initiative.

9 R—K1   N—Q1

40

(Position after 9 . . . N—Q1)

Black rearranges his pieces to get more maneuvering freedom.

10 P—Q4   N—K3   11 B—QB1   P—B4!

Black does not fear 12 PxP, PxP; 13 NxP?? for then 13 ... N—B2! wins a piece.

                12 P—N3   Q—B2

Black has a slight advantage because of his superior Pawn position. A plausible possibility is 13 Q—K2, P—QR3; 14 B—Q3, P—QN4; 15 P—Q5, P—B5!; 16 PxN, BxP! and Black regains the piece favorably.

(b) 6 ... P—Q3 Variation

WHITE	BLACK		WHITE	BLACK
1 P—K4	P—K4		4 B—N5	B—N5
2 N—KB3	N—QB3		5 Castles	Castles
3 N—B3	N—B3		6 P—Q3	P—Q3

41

(Position after 6 ... P—Q3)

Black intends to hold on to the two Bishops. If now 7 N—K2 Black replies 7 ... N—K2 with a symmetrical, drawish position.

                7 B—N5   N—K2

And not 7 ... B—N5 because of 8 N—Q5 intensifying the pin on Black's King Knight.

556

8 BxN	PxB	11 P—B4	B—B4ch
9 N—KR4	N—N3	12 K—R1	K—N2
10 NxN	RPxN	13 P—B5	....

After 13 . . . P—B3; 14 B—B4, P—Q4! Black's Bishop-pair and compact Pawn center promise well for him despite the somewhat barricaded character of the position.

(c) 4 . . . N—Q5 Variation

WHITE	BLACK	WHITE	BLACK
1 P—K4	P—K4	3 N—B3	N—B3
2 N—KB3	N—QB3	4 B—N5	N—Q5
	5 NxP	Q—K2	

42

(Position after 5 . . . Q—K2)

Black has violated the rules of good development, but how is he to be punished? If 6 N—B3, NxB; 7 NxN, QxPch; 8 Q—K2, QxQch; 9 KxQ, N—Q4; 10 P—B4, P—QR3! and White has nothing.

6 P—B4!	NxB	9 K—B2	N—N5ch
7 NxN	P—Q3	10 K—N1!	K—Q1
8 N—KB3	QxPch	11 P—Q3	Q—B3

After 12 QN—Q4, Q—N3; 13 P—KR3, N—B3;'14 K—R2 White has the better game. Black's King is insecure, his development disorganized.

(d) Three Knights' Game

WHITE	BLACK		WHITE	BLACK
1 P—K4	P—K4		2 N—KB3	N—QB3
	3 N—B3		B—N5	

43

(Position after 3 . . . B—N5)

Black's last move is the key to this opening. If instead 3 . . . N—B3 we have the Four Knights' Game.

4 N—Q5	N—B3		5 NxB	NxN

If now 6 P—Q4, P—Q4! — or 6 B—B4, P—Q4!; 7 PxP, P—K5! with equality in either event.

6 NxP	Q—K2		9 NxN	QPxN
7 P—Q4	NxKP		10 B—K2	Castles
8 P—QB3	N—QB3		11 Castles	B—K3

Even game. Neither side can accomplish much in this colorless position.

RUY LOPEZ

In the whole realm of the King Pawn openings, this is White's most serious attempt to seize the initiative. There are many lines of play in which White maintains a lasting pressure on Black's position. Undoubtedly Black's best defense is some form of the "Strong-point" Variation, for this gives him his best chance of freedom.

(a)   Morphy Defense with 5 . . . B—K2

WHITE	BLACK	WHITE	BLACK
1 P—K4	P—K4	2 N—KB3	N—QB3
	3 B—N5	. . . .	

This move exercises unmistakable pressure on Black's game. Sooner or later White will be threatening to win a Pawn by BxN followed by NxP.

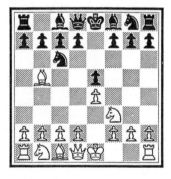

44

(Position after 3 B—N5)

Black can play 3 . . . P—QR3 for if 4 BxN, QPxB; 5 NxP, Black recovers his Pawn with 5 . . . Q—N4 or . . . Q—Q5.

    3 . . . .   P—QR3

This (known as the Morphy Defense) is Black's best. By driving off White's King Bishop with an eventual . . . P—QN4, Black rids himself of White's potential threat to win the King Pawn and gives his forces more playing room.

A possibility here for White is the Exchange Variation,

559

which does not have much sting: 4 BxN, QPxB. This may continue 5 P—Q4, PxP; 6 QxP, QxQ; 7 NxQ, B—Q2; 8 B—K3, Castles; 9 N—Q2, N—K2; 10 Castles QR, R—K1; 11 KR—K1, N—N3. Black's Bishops give him an excellent game.

4 B—R4   N—B3

A good developing move which gains time by attacking White's King Pawn.

5 Castles   ....

Momentarily White can leave his King Pawn in the lurch, as he has threats on Black's King Pawn himself.

5 ....   B—K2

Black can also play 5 . . . NxP, as in Variation *(c)*.

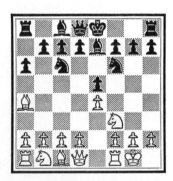

45

(Position after 5 . . . B—K2)

White can now choose between defending his King Pawn and advancing in the center by P—Q4.

If White advances 6 P—Q4, Black's best reply is 6 . . . PxP. In that event White should not pause for 7 R—K1, as he may fall into the Noah's Ark Trap: 7 . . . P—QN4; 8 B—N3, P—Q3; 9 NxP??, NxN; 10 QxN, P—B4 followed by . . . P—B5 winning White's King Bishop!

560

In reply to 6 . . . PxP White's best course is 7 P—K5. Then, after 7 . . . N—K5; 8 NxP, NxN (not 8 . . . NxKP??; 9 R—K1); 9 QxN, N—B4 the position is fairly level: White gets a lead in development, while Black has the two Bishops.

Coming back to the position of Diagram 45, White can also stop to defend his King Pawn with 6 Q—K2. Then if 6 . . . Castles? there follows 7 BxN, QPxB; 8 NxP, Q—Q5; 9 N—KB3, QxKP; 10 QxQ, NxQ; 11 R—K1 and White wins a piece.

Consequently, after 6 Q—K2 Black plays 6 . . . P—Q3, although after 7 P—B3, Castles; 8 P—Q4 his game is somewhat constricted.

6 R—K1   . . . .

This is the usual move. Now that White has protected his own King Pawn, he threatens to win a Pawn by 7 BxN and 8 NxP.

6 . . . .   P—QN4

Driving off the Bishop in order to safeguard his King Pawn.

7 B—N3   P—Q3

The safe and sane course, which avoids the premature counterattack 7 . . . Castles; 8 P—B3, P—Q4?!

In that event there may follow 9 PxP, NxP; 10 NxP, NxN; 11 RxN, P—QB3; 12 P—Q4!, B—Q3; 13 R—K1, Q—R5; 14 P—N3, Q—R6; 15 R—K4!

Although Black still has some attacking prospects, White has a satisfactory defense. His extra Pawn should tell in his favor.

8 P—B3   Castles   9 P—KR3!   . . . .

More precise than the immediate 9 P—Q4, which would allow the pin 9 . . . B—N5. By advancing his King Rook Pawn, White deprives Black's Queen Bishop of his best square.

9 . . . .   N—QR4!   10 B—B2   P—B4
                11 P—Q4   Q—B2

46

(Position after 11 . . . Q—B2)

Black has established a "strong point" at King 4. By advancing his Queen-side Pawns (beginning with 3 . . . P—QR3) he has established ample maneuvering space for his forces.

12 QN—Q2   N—B3

A plausible alternative is 12 . . . BPxP; 13 PxP, N—B3; 14 P—Q5, N—QN5; 15 B—N1, P—QR4; 16 P—R3, N—R3. Black's Queen Knight will come to Queen Bishop 4, but White's game is slightly freer.

13 P—Q5   N—Q1   14 P—QR4!   R—N1

But not 14 . . . P—N5, which allows White to post his Queen Knight magnificently at Bishop 4.

15 P—B4!   P—N5   17 P—KN4   P—N3
16 N—B1   .N—K1   18 B—R6   N—KN2

The position is approximately even. White has more maneuvering space, but Black's game is very compact and hard to get at.

(b) Morphy Defense with 4 . . . P—Q3

WHITE	BLACK		WHITE	BLACK
1 P—K4	P—K4		3 B—N5	P—QR3
2 N—KB3	N—QB3		4 B—R4	P—Q3

47

(Position after 4 . . . P—Q3)

Black has delayed playing out his King Knight as he has in mind variations in which this piece may play to King 2 or King Rook 3; he may also want to advance his King Bishop Pawn.

If now 5 BxNch, PxB; 6 P—Q4 Black holds the center with 6 . . . P—B3! and after 7 B—K3, N—K2; 8 N—B3, N—N3; 9 Q—Q2, B—K2 his position is satisfactory.

Another possibility is 5 P—Q4, P—QN4; 6 B—N3, NxP; 7 NxN, PxN. Now 8 B—Q5 is satisfactory for White, whereas 8 QxP??, P—QB4; 9 Q—Q5, B—K3; 10 Q—B6ch, B—Q2; 11 Q—Q5, P—B5 gives us another version of the Noah's Ark Trap.

	5 P—B3	B—Q2

Here 5 . . . P—B4 is premature: 6 PxP, BxP; 7 P—Q4!, P—K5; 8 N—N5, P—Q4; 9 P—B3! forcing line-opening which is distinctly in White's favor.

6 P—Q4	P—KN3		10 P—KR3	N—B2
7 B—KN5	P—B3		11 QN—Q2	Castles
8 B—K3	N—R3!		12 PxP	QPxP
9 Castles	B—N2		13 B—B5	R—K1

The position is approximately even. White's apparent pressure is neutralized by Black's solid position.

563

(c) Morphy Defense with 5 . . . NxP

WHITE	BLACK		WHITE	BLACK
1 P—K4	P—K4		4 B—R4	N—B3
2 N—KB3	N—QB3		5 Castles	NxP
3 B—N5	P—QR3		6 P—Q4!	....

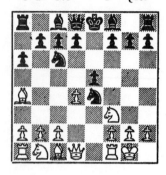

48

(Position after 6 P—Q4!)

Winning a second Pawn leads to trouble for Black, for example: 6 . . . PxP; 7 R—K1, P—Q4; 8 B—KN5!, Q—Q3; 9 P—B4!, PxP e.p.; 10 NxP, B—K3; 11 NxN, PxN; 12 N—Q4, P—N4; 13 RxP!, PxB; 14 QxP, Q—Q4; 15 R—K5!! and wins.

6	P—QN4		8 PxP	B—K3
7 B—N3	P—Q4		9 P—B3	....

An interesting possibility is 9 Q—K2, for example 9 . . . N—B4; 10 R—Q1, NxB; 11 RPxN, Q—B1; 12 P—B4!, QPxP; 13 PxP, BxP; 14 Q—K4 and White has a winning attack.

49

(Position after 9 P—B3)

Here 9 . . . B—QB4 gives Black an aggressive development but leaves him with a vulnerable Pawn position —for example 10 Q—Q3, Castles; 11 B—K3, BxB; 12 QxB, N—K2; 13 B—B2, P—KB4; 14 PxP e.p., RxP; 15 N—Q4!

| 9 .... | B—K2 | | 10 P—QR4! | .... |

Now White gets a strong initiative.

| 10 .... | P—N5 | 12 P—KB4 | B—N5 |
| 11 N—Q4! | NxKP | 13 Q—B2 | P—QB4 |

Not 13 . . . N—N3; 14 PxP, BxP?; 15 N—B6.

| 14 PxN | PxN | 15 PxQP | Castles |

White has a clear advantage because of his greater mobility, attacking chances, prospects of creating weaknesses in Blacks' King-side.

(d) Berlin Defense

WHITE	BLACK	WHITE	BLACK
1 P—K4	P—K4	2 N—KB3	N—QB3
	3 B—N5	N—B3	

5.0
(Position after 3 . . . N—B3)

The drawback of this once-popular defense is that it leads to a weak Pawn position for Black.

| 4 Castles | NxP | 5 P—Q4 | B—K2 |

Note that 5 . . . PxP?? will not do because of 6 R—K1.

6 Q—K2	N—Q3	10 N—Q4	B—B4
7 BxN	NPxB	11 R—Q1	BxN
8 PxP	N—N2	12 RxB	P—Q4
9 N—B3	Castles	13 PxP e.p.	PxP

The position is decidedly in White's favor. Black's game

is very difficult because of his weak Pawns and the bad position of his Knight.

(e) Steinitz Defense

WHITE	BLACK		WHITE	BLACK
1 P—K4	P—K4		2 N—KB3	N—QB3
	3 B—N5	P—Q3		

This defense gives Black a cramped game.

4 P—Q4!	B—Q2	5 N—B3	N—B3

If instead 5 . . . PxP; 6 NxP, N—B3; 7 BxN!, PxB; 8 Q—B3! and White has the better of it, for example 8 . . . B—K2; 9 P—K5!, PxP; 10 NxP etc.

6 Castles   B—K2

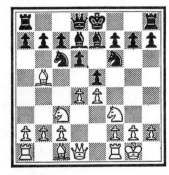

51
(Position after 6 . . . B—K2)

A likely continuation is 7 B—N5!, PxP; 8 NxP, Castles; 9 BxQN, PxB; 10 Q—Q3, N—N5; 11 BxB, QxB; 12 P—B4!, P—KB4; 13 QR—K1!

White has the better game. His aggressive development gives him much greater freedom of action.

(f) Classical Defense

WHITE	BLACK		WHITE	BLACK
1 P—K4	P—K4		2 N—KB3	N—QB3
	3 B—N5	B—B4		

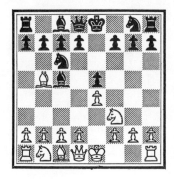

52

(Position after 3 . . . B—B4)

The drawback to this defense is that Black's King Bishop becomes a target for attack.

4	Castles	KN—K2		
5	P—B3	B—N3		
6	P—Q4	PxP		
7	PxP	P—Q4		
8	PxP	KNxP		

9 R—K1ch	B—K3
10 BxNch!	PxB
11 Q—R4	Q—Q3
12 B—N5	Castles
13 N—B3	

Thanks to Black's shattered Pawn position, White has a strategically won game.

(g) Bird's Defense

WHITE	BLACK		WHITE	BLACK
1 P—K4	P—K4		2 N—KB3	N—QB3
	3 B—N5		N—Q5	

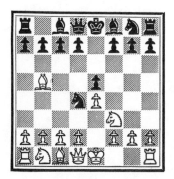

53

(Position after 3 . . . N—Q5)

This defense lacks punch. The offered exchange wastes time and allows White to get a clear initiative on the King-side.

4 NxN	PxN	9 N—B3	P—QB3
5 Castles	P—KN3	10 B—QR4	P—Q3
6 P—Q3	B—N2	11 B—K3!	B—N2
7 P—QB3!	N—K2	12 Q—B3	Castles
8 PxP	BxP	13 B—N3	K—R1
	14 Q—N3	....	

White is clearly forcing the pace, while Black has a difficult defensive game.

(h) Schliemann's Defense

WHITE	BLACK	WHITE	BLACK
1 P—K4	P—K4	2 N—KB3	N—QB3
	3 B—N5	P—B4	

54
(Position after 3 . . . P—B4)

Black's counterattack is risky and invites a brisk reaction by White.

4 N—B3!	PxP	8 BxPch	B—Q2
5 QNxP	P—Q4	9 Q—R5ch	K—K2
6 NxP!	PxN	10 Q—K5ch	B—K3
7 NxN	PxN	11 BxR	QxB

White is ahead in material and Black's King is exposed to attack.

FRENCH DEFENSE

From this point on, we no longer consider openings in which Black answers 1 P—K4 with 1 . . . P—K4. Instead, he tries to fight for control of the center in a different way.

In this opening, for example, he answers 1 P—K4 with 1 . . . P—K3, and then, after 2 P—Q4, he continues 2 . . . P—Q4. This is a defense with many solid defensive virtues, with the notable drawback that in many lines Black's Queen Bishop has little scope.

This explains why the simplifying course 3 PxP, PxP is rarely seen in modern play. The Pawn position is symmetrical and drawish, and Black's Queen Bishop has been liberated. Most variations in which White gets the initiative involve the move P—K5. This keeps Black's Queen Bishop tied up and also offers prospects of King-side attack.

(a) McCutcheon Variation

WHITE	BLACK		WHITE	BLACK
1 P—K4	P—K3		3 N—QB3	N—KB3
2 P—Q4	P—Q4		4 B—KN5	B—N5

Black fights vigorously for control of the center. If now 5 PxP, QxP; 6 BxN, BxNch; 7 PxB, PxB; 8 N—KB3, N—Q2; 9 P—N3, P—N3; 10 B—N2 and Black can play 10 . . . B—R3!, for if 11 N—R4, Q—QR4!; 12 BxR, QxBPch and wins.

| | 5 P—K5 | P—KR3 |

Forced. If now 6 PxN, PxB; 7 PxP, R—N1 regaining the Pawn with equality.

6 B—Q2	BxN	7 PxB	N—K5
	8 Q—N4	P—KN3	

569

55
(Position after 8 . . . P—KN3)

Now White tries a speculative sacrifice to preserve his valuable Queen Bishop, for if 9 B—Q3, NxB; 10 KxN, P—QB4 with a good game for Black.

9 B—B1!?	NxQBP	11 PxP	Q—B2
10 B—Q3	P—QB4	12 B—K3	N—Q2

With 13 Q—Q4! White maintains the initiative, and his two powerful Bishops assure him substantial attacking chances.

(b) 4 . . . B—K2 Variation

WHITE	BLACK	WHITE	BLACK
1 P—K4	P—K3	3 N—QB3	N—KB3
2 P—Q4	P—Q4	4 B—KN5	B—K2

Another way of fighting for the center. White can hit back with 5 BxN, BxB; 6 P—K5, but after 6 . . . B—K2; 7 Q—N4, Castles; 8 Castles, P—QB4! Black has good counterplay. For example: 9 PxP, N—B3; 10 P—B4, P—B4; 11 Q—R3, Q—R4!; 12 KN—K2, BxP; 13 P—KN4, P—Q5; 14 N—QN1, N—QN5 and Black has the initiative.

WHITE	BLACK	WHITE	BLACK
5 P—K5	KN—Q2	7 Q—Q2	Castles
6 BxB	QxB	8 P—B4	P—QB4
	9 N—B3	N—QB3	

570

56

(Position after 9 . . . N—QB3)

Black has attacked White's Pawn center with . . . P—QB4 and intends to intensify the attack with . . . P—B3.

If now 10 P—KN3, P—B3; 11 KPxP, NPxP! as in the main line, with a promising game for Black.

10 Castles	P—B3
11 KPxP	NPxP!

12 P—KN3	PxP
13 KNxP	N—N3

Even game. White may have the better development, but Black has open lines and a powerful Pawn mass in the center.

(c) Alekhine's Attack

WHITE	BLACK
1 P—K4	P—K3
2 P—Q4	P—Q4
3 N—QB3	N—KB3

WHITE	BLACK
4 B—KN5	B—K2
5 P—K5	KN—Q2
6 P—KR4!	....

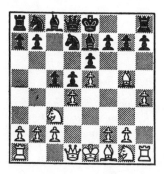

57

(Position after 6 P—KR4!)

Black cannot very well accept White's enterprising Pawn offer. After 6 . . . BxB; 7 PxB, QxP; 8 N—R3, Q—K2; 9 N—B4, N—B1; 10 Q—N4 White has a murderous lead in development.

If now 6 . . . P—KB3; 7 Q—R5ch!, P—KN3; 8 PxP!, PxQ; 9 PxB winning back the Queen with a very superior endgame for White; or 8 . . . NxP; 9 Q—K2! with strong pressure on Black's backward King Pawn.

| 6 .... | P—QB4! | 7 BxB | KxB! |

After 7 . . . QxB; 8 N—N5! Black has a difficult game.

| 8 Q—N4 | K—B1 | 10 QxQP | Q—N3! |
| 9 N—B3 | PxP! | 11 QxQ | PxQ |

Black has satisfactorily undermined White's center.

| 12 Castles | N—QB3 | 13 R—K1 | P—Q5! |

Black has an excellent game, for after the attacked Knight moves he can play . . . RxP.

(d) 4 . . . PxP Variation

WHITE	BLACK	WHITE	BLACK
1 P—K4	P—K3	2 P—Q4	P—Q4
	3 N—QB3	N—KB3	

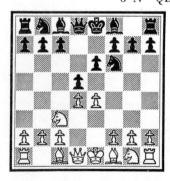

58

(Position after 3 . . . N—KB3)

If White ends the tension in the center with 4 P—K5, there follows 4 . . . KN—Q2; 5 P—B4 and now Black counters with 5 . . . P—QB4! liquidating White's valuable Queen Pawn.

4 B—KN5	PxP		

This colorless continuation leaves White with a more aggressive position.

5 NxP	B—K2	6 BxN	BxB

Likewise after 6 . . . PxB White has the more promising development: 7 N—KB3, P—N3; 8 B—B4!, B—N2; 9 Q—K2, P—B3; 10 Castles QR, Q—B2; 11 K—N1, N—Q2; 12 B—R6!, Castles QR; 13 BxBch, KxB; 14 P—B4! Black's Pawn position is weakened and he is exposed to attack.

7 N—KB3	N—Q2	8 P—B3!	Q—K2

Or 8 . . . Castles; 9 Q—B2, P—K4; 10 Castles!, PxP; 11 NxP, BxN; 12 RxB, Q—K2; 13 P—KB4, N—B4; 14 NxN, QxN; 15 B—Q3 when White has a splendid development and good attacking chances.

9 Q—B2	P—B4	12 BxBch	NxB
10 PxP	NxP	13 Castles QR	Castles QR
11 B—N5ch	B—Q2	14 Q—R4	K—N1

White's game is more comfortable and he has an advantage for the endgame in his Queen-side majority of Pawns.

(e) 3 . . . B—N5 Variation

WHITE	BLACK	WHITE	BLACK
1 P—K4	P—K3	2 P—Q4	P—Q4
	3 N—QB3	B—N5	

59

(Position after 3 . . . B—N5)

By pinning White's Knight Black counterattacks and thus maintains the fight for control of the center. 4 PxP would be a colorless reply as 4 . . . PxP frees Black's Queen Bishop.

White can ignore Black's threat, but the results are not particularly attractive, for example 4 P—QR3, BxNch; 5 PxB, PxP; 6 Q—N4, N—KB3; 7 QxNP, R—N1; 8 Q—R6, P—B4—or 4 Q—N4, N—KB3; 5 QxNP, R—N1; 6 Q—R6, P—B4. In either case Black has strong counterplay.

| 4 P—K5 | P—QB4 | 5 P—QR3! | .... |

The best reply to Black's logical counterattack in the center.

| 5 .... | BxNch | 6 PxB | .... |

Whereas Black's remaining Bishop has very little scope, White's Bishops are very powerful—as in the variation 6 . . . N—K2; 7 Q—N4, N—B4; 8 B—Q3, P—KR4; 9 Q—R3, PxP; 10 PxP, Q—R5; 11 QxQ, NxQ; 12 P—N3 etc.

| 6 .... | Q—B2 | 7 N—B3 | .... |

After Black's last move, he can answer 7 Q—N4 with 7 . . . P—B4.

| 7 .... | N—K2 | 8 P—KR4! | B—Q2 |

Striving for counterplay. If instead 8 . . . P—QN3; 9 P—
R5!, P—KR3; 10 P—R4!, B—R3; 11 B—N5ch!, BxB;
12 PxB and White has the initiative on both wings.

9 P—R5   P—KR3

White was threatening 10 P—R6 practically forcing . . .
P—KN3 and leaving Black dangerously weak on the black
squares.

10 P—N4!	B—R5	12 P—N5	QR—B1
11 B—Q3	N—Q2	13 R—QR2!	. . . .

*White has a strong initiative on the King-side, where he
will be able to open a file before or after R—N1. Black has
pressure on White's Pawn at Queen Bishop 2, but White has
adequate defense. White's greater command of the Board,
supported by the potential power of his Bishops, gives him
the better game.*

(f)   3 N—Q2 Variation

WHITE	BLACK		WHITE	BLACK
1 P—K4	P—K3		2 P—Q4	P—Q4
	3 N—Q2		. . . .	

60

(Position after 3 N—Q2)

*White's extraordinary third move is
playable despite the fact that it blocks
his Queen Bishop. The point of this
development is that it avoids 3 . . .
B—N5, as seen in Variation (e).*

The classic freeing move. The alternatives give Black a cramped game, for example 3 . . . N—KB3; 4 P—K5, KN—Q2; 5 B—Q3, P—QB4; 6 P—QB3, N—QB3; 7 N—K2, PxP; 8 PxP etc. Or 3 . . . N—QB3; 4 KN—B3!, N—B3; 5 P—K5, N—Q2; 6 N—N3, P—B3; 7 PxP!, KNxP; 8 B—QN5 etc.

4 KN—B3   P—QR3!

This gives Black a much more comfortable game than 4 . . . N—QB3, for example 5 KPxP, KPxP; 6 B—N5!, B—Q3; 7 Castles, N—K2; 8 PxP!, BxBP; 9 N—N3, B—N3; 10 B—K3!, BxB; 11 BxNch!, PxB; 12 PxB and White has strong pressure on the black squares.

5 KPxP	KPxP	6 PxP	BxP

Black has an isolated Queen Pawn, but he can develop his pieces rapidly and the diagonal of his Queen Bishop has been opened.

7 N—N3	B—R2!	10 B—K2	Q—Q3
8 B—KN5	N—KB3	11 Castles	N—B3!
9 QN—Q4	Castles	12 B—K3	B—N1!

Black has real attacking chances and a fine initiative. His admirable development outweighs the disadvantage of the isolated Queen Pawn.

(g) 3 P—K5 Variation

WHITE	BLACK	WHITE	BLACK
1 P—K4	P—K3	2 P—Q4	P—Q4
	3 P—K5!?	P—QB4!	

This is an extremely trying variation for both players. By advancing his Pawn to King 5, White creates a wedge in the King-side which among other things prevents Black's Knight from reaching its best square at Black's King Bishop 3. In general, White's intention when he advances the King Pawn is to leave Black with a permanently constricted position.

Naturally Black is not going to resign himself to being smothered to death. He intends to fight back, and the method he chooses is to try to undermine White's advanced King Pawn by removing its support (White's Queen Pawn).

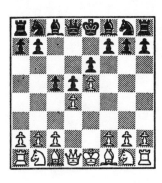

61

(Position after 3 . . . P—QB4!)

By playing . . . P—QB4 — always the logical counterattack to P—K5 — Black strives for counterplay on the Queen-side and in the center in order to neutralize White's constricting pressure on the King-side.

4 P—QB3	N—QB3	5 N—KB3	Q—N3

Superficially 6 B—Q3 looks like a good reply, for if 6 . . . PxP; 7 PxP, NxQP???; 8 NxN, QxN; 9 B—QN5ch winning the Queen. But Black plays 6 . . . PxP; 7 PxP, B—Q2! leaving White nothing better than 8 B—K2.

| 6 B—K2 | PxP | 8 P—QN3 | N—B4 |
| 7 PxP | KN—K2 | 9 B—N2 | B—N5ch |

Black's pressure on the Queen Pawn is so strong that White cannot interpose to this check.

| 10 K—B1 | Castles | 11 P—N4 | N—R3 |

After 12 R—N1 Black plays 12 . . . P—B3 when the fight for control of the center will rage on. Prospects are even, with chances for both sides.

SICILIAN DEFENSE

Like the French Defense, the Sicilian Defense immediately puts a veto on White's intended choice of opening. The characteristic 1 . . . P—QB4 is more aggressive than the French, and also riskier. If you like a complicated game with chances for both sides, the Sicilian is an ideal defense.

An important point to remember is this: White generally plays an early P—Q4 in order to get more space for his pieces in the center. After Black captures White's Queen Pawn with his Queen Bishop Pawn, the Queen Bishop file is half open (from Black's side). By playing his Queen Rook— and sometimes his Queen as well—to the Queen Bishop file, Black can often exert considerable pressure along the file.

On the other hand, White has an important attacking motif in advancing his King Bishop Pawn: P—KB4. This often gives him a powerful position in the middle game, when he threatens P—K5 or P—B5.

(*a*) Dragon Variation

WHITE	BLACK		WHITE	BLACK
1 P—K4	P—QB4		4 NxP	N—B3
2 N—KB3	N—QB3		5 N—QB3	P—Q3
3 P—Q4	PxP		6 B—K2	. . . .

If 6 B—K3, P—KN3; 7 Q—Q2, B—N2; 8 Castles, Castles; 9 B—K2 intending a Pawn-storming attack on the King-side. However, after 9 . . . NxN; 10 BxN, Q—R4 Black has good counterplay.

6	P—KN3		7 B—K3	B—N2
	8 Castles		Castles	

579

Here the simplifying move 8 . . . N—KN5? looks tempting, for if 9 BxN, BxB; 10 QxB?, NxN and Black holds his own. But instead White plays 10 NxN! and no matter how Black replies, he loses a piece.

9 N—N3   B—K3   10 P—B4   Q—B1!

Chiefly played to prevent P—B5, which may lead to troublesome complications. Thus after the alternative 10 . . . N—QR4 there might follow 11 P—B5, B—B5; 12 NxN, BxB; 13 QxB, QxN; 14 P—KN4!, N—Q2; 15 N—Q5! and White has a strong initiative.

62

(Position after 10 . . . Q—B1!)

If White plays 11 P—KR3 (intending P—KN4 and P—B5), Black counters energetically with 11 . . . R—Q1! Then if 12 P—N4, P—Q4! or 12 B—B3, B—B5!

Black has a solid position with good prospects for the middle game. Note that his fianchettoed Bishop exerts strong pressure along the long diagonal.

(b) Scheveningen Variation

	WHITE	BLACK		WHITE	BLACK
1	P—K4	P—QB4	4	NxP	N—B3
2	N—KB3	N—QB3	5	N—QB3	P—Q3
3	P—Q4	PxP	6	B—K2	P—K3
	7	Castles	P—QR3		

63

(Position after 7 . . . P—QR3)

Compare this Pawn formation with the one in Diagram 62. Black's Bishops have very little scope.

Aside from the following line, White can also proceed with 8 B—K3, Q—B2; 9 P—B4, B—K2; 10 N—N3, P—QN4; 11 B—B3, B—N2; 12 Q—K1! followed by Q—N3 with a strong attacking formation.

8	K—R1	Q—B2	11	P—KN4!	B—Q2
9	P—B4	B—K2	12	P—N5	N—K1
10	B—B3	Castles	13	P—QR4	N—R4

White continues 14 P—B5! with a powerful initiative, thanks to the advance of his King-side Pawns. Black's position is constricted and limited to purely passive defense.

(c) 2 ... P—K3 Variation

	WHITE	BLACK		WHITE	BLACK
1	P—K4	P—QB4	3	P—Q4	PxP
2	N—KB3	P—K3	4	NxP	N—KB3
	5	N—QB3	. . . .		

581

64

(Position after 5 N—QB3)

Black's position is difficult. If he plays 5 . . . B—N5 there follows 6 P—K5!, N—Q4; 7 B—Q2, NxN; 8 PxN, B—K2; 9 Q—N4 with an aggressive position for White.

| 5 .... | N—B3 | 6 N/Q4—N5 | .... |

Black's game remains difficult because of the early advance of his King Pawn. If Black tries to prevent N—Q6ch with 6 . . . P—Q3, the reply 7 B—KB4 is embarrassing: note that 7 . . . N—K4? is wrong because of 8 Q—Q4! winning a Pawn, while if 7 . . .. P—K4; 8 B—N5 and Black has a bad "hole" at his Queen 4 square.

6	B—N5	9 PxP	PxP
7 P—QR3	BxNch	10 B—Q3	Castles
8 NxB	P—Q4	11 Castles	....

White's position is definitely more promising. His two Bishops are a distinct asset for the endgame, and Black's isolated Queen Pawn is just as distinct a liability in an ending.

(*d*) 2 ... N—KB3 Variation

WHITE	BLACK	WHITE	BLACK
1 P—K4	P—QB4	2 N—KB3	N—KB3
	3 P—K5	N—Q4	

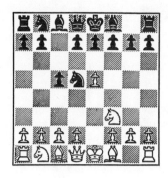

65

(Position after 3 . . . N—Q4)

This line of play is a forerunner of Alekhine's Defense—see page 86. Black allows his King Knight to be driven away in the hope that White's King Pawn will be weakened by advancing—a futile hope.

| 4 P—Q4! | PxP | 6 B—QB4! | N—QB3 |
| 5 QxP! | P—K3 | 7 Q—K4 | N—N3 |

This is one opening line in which an early development of the Queen does no harm, as White's Queen has a commanding position and Black's development is backward.

| 8 B—N3 | N—R4 | 10 RPxN | P—Q4 |
| 9 N—B3 | NxB | 11 PxP e.p. | BxP |

White has superior development and open lines. Here is one likely way for him to gain the initiative: 12 Castles, Castles; 13 R—Q1, Q—K2; 14 N—QN5!, B—N1; 15 B—K3 and White must win a Pawn (his chief threat is 16 BxN).

(e) 2 N—QB3 Variation

WHITE	BLACK	WHITE	BLACK
1 P—K4	P—QB4	3 P—KN3	P—KN3
2 N—QB3	N—QB3	4 B—N2	B—N2

66

(Position after 4 . . . B—N2)

White deliberately keeps the game closed, avoiding P—Q4. He trusts to superior maneuvering ability to obtain an advantage. However, with careful play Black maintains equality.

5 P—Q3	P—K3!		6 B—K3	Q—R4!

More promising than 6 . . . N—Q5; 7 QN—K2! with a view to dislodging the advanced Knight by P—QB3. (If 7 . . . NxN; 8 NxN, BxP; 9 QR—N1, Q—R4ch; 10 B—Q2, QxP; 11 RxB!, QxR; 12 B—QB3!)

7 KN—K2	N—Q5		9 N—B1	Castles
8 Q—Q2	N—K2		10 Castles	P—Q3

Even game. Black has done well to centralize his powerful Queen Knight, supported directly by the fianchettoed Bishop. White must play for King-side attack by P—B4 etc.

(*f*) Wing Gambit

WHITE	BLACK		WHITE	BLACK
1 P—K4	P—QB4		2 P—QN4	....

This is the Wing Gambit, played with the idea of getting a big lead in development and a powerful Pawn center (through the removal of Black's Queen Bishop Pawn).

| 2 .... | PxP | | 3 P—QR3 | P—Q4! |

Energetic counterplay in the center is the key to Black's policy against the gambit. White's reply is virtually forced, for after 4 P—K5?, N—QB3; 5 P—Q4, Q—B2; 6 N—KB3, B—N5 Black has a positional as well as material advantage.

| 4 KPxP | QxP | | 5 N—KB3 | .... |

Black was threatening 5 . . . Q—K4ch.

| 5 .... | P—K4 | | 6 PxP | BxP |

67

(Position after 6 . . . BxP)

The gambit has turned out to be a miserable failure, for Black is ahead in development as well as material!

Black is well prepared for complications, for example 7 N—R3, B—Q2!; 8 N—B4, N—QB3!, 9 N—N6, Q—K5ch; 10 B—K2, R—Q1 with a very good game. Or 7 N—R3, B—Q2!; 8 B—N2, N—QB3; 9 N—QN5, R—B1!; 10 NxRP, NxN; 11 RxN, P—K5!; 12 BxP, PxN; 13 PxP, B—QB4! with a winning attack.

7 P—B3	B—QB4	9 N—QN5	Castles!
8 N—R3	N—KB3	10 B—K2	....

Note that 10 N—B7 is answered by 10 . . . BxPch!

10	P—K5!	12 N—B7	Q—N4
11 KN—Q4	N—B3	13 NxR	....

Or 13 NxN, QxP; 14 R—B1, PxN; 15 NxR, N—N5 and Black must win.

13	QxP	14 R—B1	N—K4

Black has a winning attack, for example 15 P—Q3, B—KR6; 16 PxP, NxP etc.

586

CARO-KANN DEFENSE

Like the French Defense, the Caro-Kann Defense (1 P—
K4, P—QB3) allows White to build a broad Pawn center
and then challenges that center with 2 . . . P—Q4. But, since
Black plays 1 . . . P—QB3 instead of 1 . . . P—K3, it follows
that in most variations his Queen Bishop is not imprisoned.

This is definitely a defense for players who want a solid,
even position with little chance of complications. A player
who wants to avoid risks and who is satisfied with a draw,
should favor this defense.

(a)   3 N—QB3 Variation with 4 . . . B—B4.

WHITE	BLACK	WHITE	BLACK
1 P—K4	P—QB3	2 P—Q4	P—Q4

Note that White has little to gain from 3 P—K5, B—B4!
for example 4 B—Q3, BxB; 5 QxB, P—K3; 6 N—KB3,
Q—N3; 7 Castles, P—QB4 etc.

3 N—QB3	PxP	6 N—B3	N—Q2
4 NxP	B—B4	7 P—KR4	P—KR3
5 N—N3	B—N3	8 B—Q3	. . . .

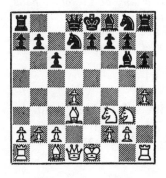

68

(Position after 8 B—Q3)

*White has decided to exchange Bish-
ops, as Black's Queen Bishop was too
well posted. The exchange increases
White's lead in development and gains
time for castling on the Queen-side.*

8	BxB	11 Castles QR	Q—B2
9 QxB	P—K3	12 K—N1	Castles
10 B—Q2	KN—B3	13 P—B4!	P—B4

White continues 14 B—B3! with distinctly more freedom for his pieces and strong pressure on the center. However, Black has no weak points and is well equipped for careful defense.

(b)   3 N—QB3 Variation with 4 . . . N—B3

WHITE	BLACK	WHITE	BLACK
1 P—K4	P—QB3	3 N—QB3	PxP
2 P—Q4	P—Q4	4 NxP	N—B3
	5 NxNch	. . . .	

69
(Position after 5 NxNch)

Whichever way Black captures he remains with a theoretical disadvantage, as his doubled Pawn is a positional weakness. White, on the other hand, has a clear majority of Pawns on the Queen-side, which will eventually be converted into a passed Pawn.

5 ....   KPxN

Or 5 . . . NPxN; 6 N—K2! with a favorable setup for White, for example 6 . . . B—B4; 7 N—N3, B—N3; 8 P—KR4, P—KR3; 9 P—R5, B—R2; 10 P—QB3, Q—N3; 11 B—QB4 etc.

6 N—B3	B—KN5	10 R—K1	N—Q2
7 B—K2	B—Q3	11 B—Q2	Q—B2
8 Castles	Castles	12 P—KR3!	B—R4
9 P—B4!	R—K1	13 B—B3!	....

White has greater command of the board and his potential passed Pawn (after an eventual P—Q5) gives him a marked positional advantage.

(*c*)   3 N—QB3 Variation with 4 . . . N—Q2

WHITE	BLACK	WHITE	BLACK
1 P—K4	P—QB3	4 NxP	N—Q2
2 P—Q4	P—Q4	5 N—KB3	KN—B3
3 N—QB3	PxP	6 N—N3	P—K3

70

(Position after 6 . . . P—K3)

By avoiding 4 . . . N—B3 Black has eliminated the possibility of getting a doubled Pawn. However, his position shows signs of becoming unpleasantly constricted. (His Queen Bishop has no move!)

| 7 B—Q3 | B—Q3 | 9 Q—K2 | Q—B2 |
| 8 Castles | Castles | 10 N—K4 | B—B5 |

White's development has been more efficient and he has more room for his pieces.

(d)   4 P—QB4 Variation

WHITE	BLACK		WHITE	BLACK
1 P—K4	P—QB3		3 PxP	PxP
2 P—Q4	P—Q4		4 P—QB4	....

Note that 4 B—Q3, N—QB3; 5 P—QB3, N—B3; 6 B—KB4, P—KN3; 7 N—B3, B—N2 gives Black an easy game.

| 4 .... | N—KB3 | | 5 N—QB3 | N—B3 |

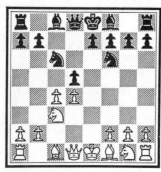

71

(Position after 5 . . . N—B3)

White's only hope for initiative is to put more pressure on the center—hence 6 B—N5 — but Black can parry adequately.

6 B—N5	P—K3		9 R—B1	N—K5!
7 N—B3	B—K2		10 BxB	QxB
8 P—B5	Castles		11 B—K2	R—Q1!

Black has equal prospects, as he is able to free himself after 12 Castles with 12 . . . P—K4!

ALEKHINE'S DEFENSE

This vehement counterattack is considered premature, as it leads to a difficult game for Black. After 1 P—K4, Black plays the dashing 1 . . . N—KB3. The idea is to provoke the advance of White's center Pawns to the point where they become weak. Actual practice has not borne out this attractive theory, and therefore this defense is best avoided in favor of some more solid line of play.

(*a*)   Four Pawns' Variation

WHITE	BLACK		WHITE	BLACK
1 P—K4	N—KB3		3 P—QB4	N—N3
2 P—K5	N—Q4		4 P—Q4	P—Q3
	5 P—B4		PxP	

Black hopes to undermine White's broad Pawn center. The attempt is destined to fail.

WHITE	BLACK		WHITE	BLACK
6 BPxP	N—B3		9 N—B3	Q—Q2
7 B—K3	B—B4		10 B—K2	Castles
8 N—QB3	P—K3		11 Castles	....

72

(Position after 11 Castles)

The indicated Pawn push 12 P—Q5 has tremendous power, for example 11 . . . B—K2; 12 P—Q5!, PxP; 13 BxN, RPxB; 14 PxP, N—N5; 15 N—Q4!, P—N3; 16 NxB, PxN; 17 RxP!, NxQP (if 17 . . . QxR; 18 B—N4); 18 P—K6!!, PxP; 19 RxN!, PxR; 20 B—N4 winning.

591

11	P—B3	14 BxN	NxNch
12 PxP	PxP	15 BxN!	RPxB
13 P—Q5!	N—K4	16 N—N5	....

White has a winning attack with Q—R4. He has taken energetic advantage of the poor position of Black's pieces.

(*b*)   Three Pawns' Variation

WHITE	BLACK		WHITE	BLACK
1 P—K4	N—KB3		3 P—QB4	N—N3
2 P—K5	N—Q4		4 P—Q4	P—Q3

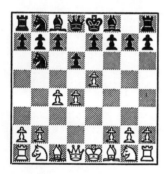

73

(Position after 4 . . . P—Q3)

Now White decides to exchange Pawns—a less aggressive but safer course than the one he followed in the previous variation.

5 PxP   KPxP

Here 5 . . . BPxP is definitely inferior: 6 P—Q5!, P—KN3; 7 B—K3!, B—N2; 8 B—Q4! and the removal of the valuable fianchettoed Bishop breaks the spine of Black's position.

592

6 N—QB3	N—B3	9 KN—K2!	B—N5
7 B—K3	B—K2	10 Castles	R—K1
8 B—Q3	Castles	11 P—KR3	B—R4

White continues 12 Q—Q2, remaining with a freer and more promising position.

(c) 4 N—KB3 Variation

WHITE	BLACK	WHITE	BLACK
1 P—K4	N—KB3	3 P—Q4	P—Q3
2 P—K5	N—Q4	4 N—KB3	....

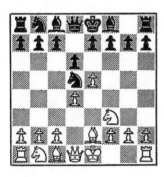

74
(Position after 4 N—KB3)

In this variation, White concentrates on quiet development. However, here too Black's King Knight ends up poorly posted at Queen Knight 3. This placement is definitely one of the drawbacks of the defense.

4	B—N5	8 PxP	PxP
5 B—K2	N—QB3	9 P—QN3	B—K2
6 Castles	P—K3	10 B—K3	Castles
7 P—B4	N—N3	11 N—B3	P—Q4

Otherwise P—Q5 drives the Queen Knight away.

| 12 P—B5 | N—Q2 | 13 P—QN4! | .... |

With his Queen-side majority of Pawns White has a decided positional advantage. If Black tries 13 . . . NxNP then 14 R—N1 recovers the Pawn and leaves White with an even greater advantage—a passed Queen Bishop Pawn.

CENTER COUNTER DEFENSE

This is definitely an inferior defense. The early moves of Black's Queen lose time, with further loss of time indicated. This comes about because after 1 P—K4, Black replies 1 . . . P—Q4 instead of preparing this Pawn move with 1 . . . P—K3 (French Defense) or with 1 . . . P—QB3 (Caro-Kann Defense).

WHITE	BLACK		WHITE	BLACK
1 P—K4	P—Q4		2 PxP	QxP
	3 N—QB3	Q—QR4		

75

(Position after 3 . . . Q—QR4)

Black's faulty development of the Queen has allowed White to gain time for his own development. Later on, White will gain more time by further attacks on the Black Queen.

4 P—Q4	N—KB3

Another possibility is 4 . . . P—K4; 5 PxP, QxKPch; 6 B—K2 followed by 7 N—B3 driving away the Black Queen with gain of time.

5 N—B3	B—N5	6 P—KR3!	B—R4

Or 6 . . . BxN; 7 QxB and White remains ahead in development and also has the positional advantage of two Bishops against Bishop and Knight.

595

7 P—KN4!   B—N3   8 N—K5!   P—B3

Preparing a retreat for his Queen in view of the threat of
N—B4.

9 P—KR4!   N—K5   10 B—Q2   Q—N3

Even worse is 10 . . . NxB; 11 QxN (threatening to win a
piece with P—R5), P—B3; 12 NxB, PxN; 13 B—Q3 when
Black's King-side Pawn formation has been damaged irre-
parably.

11 NxB   NxN   13 Q—Q2   P—K3
12 BxN   RPxN   14 Castles   . . . .

*White continues 15 B—N2, and with his greater freedom
of action and his two Bishops against Bishop and Knight,
has a clear positional advantage. Black's game has no com-
pensating features.*

NIMZOVICH DEFENSE

This is another mediocre defense that has little to recommend it. The immediate development of Black's Queen Knight (1 ... N—QB3 in answer to 1 P—K4) is untimely, and generally leaves White with a substantial lead in development.

(a) 2 ... P—Q4 Variation

WHITE	BLACK		WHITE	BLACK
1 P—K4	N—QB3		2 P—Q4	P—Q4

76

(Position after 2 ... P—Q4)

White can now push by with 3 P—K5, but this allows Black to develop comfortably with 3 ... B—B4. Hence White prefers to try a different way.

3 N—QB3	P—K3

After 3 . . . PxP, White disrupts his opponent's position with 4 P—Q5! Then on 4 . . . N—K4 he can either stop to regain his Pawn, or else play a gambit for rapid development with 5 P—B3!

4 N—B3	B—N5	5 P—K5	BxNch
6 PxB	N—R4		

Now White has excellent attacking prospects.

7 P—QR4	N—K2	10 Q—N4	P—B5
8 B—Q3	P—QN3	11 B—K2	N—B4
9 N—Q2!	P—QB4	12 N—B3	....

White has all the play and a clear initiative. His Queen Bishop can take up a strong position at Queen Rook 3.

(*b*) 2 ... P—K4 Variation

WHITE	BLACK	WHITE	BLACK
1 P—K4	N—QB3	3 PxP	NxP
2 P—Q4	P—K4	4 N—QB3	B—B4

Another way is 4 ... N—KB3, after which White gets the upper hand with 5 P—B4, N—B3; 6 P—K5, N—KN1; 7 N—B3, P—Q3; 8 B—N5 etc.

5 P—B4	N—N3	8 Q—K2	BxB
6 N—B3	P—Q3	9 QxB	Q—Q2
7 B—B4	B—K3	10 P—B5	....

White's pieces are actively posted and his position holds out great promise. Black's forces are scattered and no good plan of development is available.

YUGOSLAV DEFENSE

This line of play (1 . . . P—Q3 in reply to 1 P—K4) is as timid as Alekhine's Defense is brash. White maintains clear superiority by virtue of his better development and greater command of the board.

WHITE	BLACK		WHITE	BLACK
1 P—K4	P—Q3		2 P—Q4	N—KB3

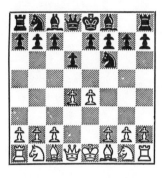

77

(Position after 2 . . . N—KB3)

Black counterattacks against White's King Pawn, which cannot very well advance. Consequently White protects the menaced Pawn.

3 N—QB3	P—KN3		5 N—B3	Castles
4 P—B4!	B—N2		6 B—Q3	P—B4

Black makes a flank thrust against White's formidable Pawn center.

7 P—Q5	P—K3		9 P—B5!	B—B1
8 PxP	BxP		10 Castles	N—B3

White's development is much more active and aggressive. Particularly troublesome is his threat to obtain a lasting bind with B—KN5 followed by N—Q5. Black is limited to passive play.

How
to Play
the Queen Pawn
Openings

Book Eight

Since the turn of the century this opening, beginning with 1 P—Q4, has been the favorite line of play used by the masters. It is much less popular among average players, who have some psychological difficulties with it. When they have White, they do not care to play 1 P—Q4. Yet when they have Black, they are exceedingly uncomfortable when their opponent starts with 1 P—Q4.

Consequently the Queen's Gambit is a formidable weapon, both technically and psychologically. The player who is reasonably familiar with its fine points has a marked advantage over his rivals.

What makes the Queen's Gambit such a dreaded weapon is that White often obtains much greater freedom of action for his pieces. As a result, he gets a frequently decisive command of the board. Sometimes this takes the form of slow strangulation of Black's forces; sometimes, through his superior mobility, White is able to win by extraordinarily brilliant play.

This explains why most players are afraid to play Black against the gambit. They either know from dreadful experience or from the reputation of this opening that they are about to confront a very trying ordeal. Yet, as has been explained, these same players, when they have White, will avoid playing the Queen's Gambit! Rightly or wrongly, they feel they do not know enough about it.

The Queen's Gambit starts with these moves:

1 P—Q4   P—Q4   2 P—QB4   . . . .

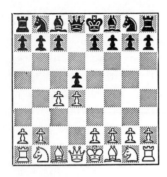

1

(Position after 2 P—QB4)

White threatens to obtain an over-whelming Pawn center with PxP. If Black plays 2 . . . PxP, White may still very well obtain the overwhelming Pawn center.

White's offer of a Pawn by 2 P—QB4 constitutes the Queen's Gambit. A gambit, as you know, is an opening in which material is offered speculatively for the purpose of gaining development or other advantages. The King Pawn opening gambits, such as the King's Gambit or the Evans Gambit, have a highly speculative character. The Queen's Gambit, in most forms, is less of a gamble, as White can generally recover the Pawn with ease. (For example, if Black plays 2 . . . PxP, White can recover the Pawn immediately with 3 Q—R4ch if he wants to.)

Thus we see that there is little about this gambit that can be called speculative. On the other hand, 2 P—QB4 embodies a definite threat. *White is momentarily threatening to remove Black's center Pawn.* If he gets rid of Black's Queen Pawn, White can soon continue with P—K4, obtaining a broad Pawn center and leaving Black with a hopeless inferiority in space. (White, in the position of Diagram 1, threatens 3 PxP, QxP; 4 N—QB3 followed by 5 P—K4 with an overwhelming position.)

Our main problem is: *how is Black to maintain a firm*

604

foothold in the center? To maintain a hold in the center is essential for Black. If he loses out in the center, he will be faced with the danger of White's getting overwhelming control of the board. (This is exactly what happens when Black is not familiar with the pitfalls of this opening.)

The object of our treatment of this vital opening is to familiarize you with the basic schemes that must be followed by White and Black. You will see what White aims for, and how Black parries the dangers involved. After you read this section, you should be able to play the Queen's Gambit Declined for either side, with a fair amount of confidence.

QUEEN'S GAMBIT DECLINED

2 . . . P—K3 Defense

To ensure his hold on the center, Black must support his Queen Pawn *with a Pawn move*. Then, if White plays PxP, Black replies . . . PxP. In this way he keeps a Pawn at his Queen 4 square and maintains a solid foothold in the center.

Black has two supporting Pawn moves that will answer the purpose: 2 . . . P—K3 (treated in this section) and 2 . . . P—QB3 (see page 27).

So let us see the consequences of 2 . . . P—K3.

2 ....   P—K3

2

(Position after 2 . . . P—K3)

Black now has a firm foothold in the center, but a new problem has arisen for him: how is he to develop his Queen Bishop?

By playing . . . P—K3, Black has blocked the diagonal of his Queen Bishop. This piece is solidly hemmed in by the Black Pawn at King 3, which is why the Bishop is sometimes known as "the problem child of the Queen's Gambit."

It is this serious loss of mobility which often leads to defeat for Black. If he fails to bring out the Bishop, his development remains inadequate for the rest of the game, giving White an advantage which often reaches right down into the ending. Worse yet, many a player of the Black pieces is not even aware of this danger!

However, since we do see the problem, how are we to solve it? There are two possible ways: (a) to strive for . . . P—K4, which will open the Queen Bishop's diagonal, or (b) to fianchetto this Bishop by playing . . . P—QN3 or . . . P—QN4. These, then, are generally Black's objectives. Where he fails to achieve them, his Queen Bishop's lack of mobility may often lose the game for him.

Diagram 3 shows the consequences of Black's failing to solve the problem of the Queen Bishop.

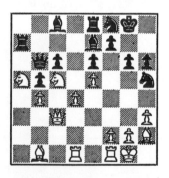

3

No matter how Black turns and squirms, he cannot develop his Queen Bishop. It is hemmed in in all directions by Black Pawns on white squares (his King Pawn, Queen Bishop Pawn, Queen Knight Pawn).

When we turn to specific variations, we find that they revolve to a considerable extent about this problem. But White has other trumps that Black must watch out for.

Thus, White can often post his King Knight on his King 5

square very effectively. Here the Knight has a magnificent center outpost, radiating power in all directions. An example of this is seen in Diagram 4. White's Queen, Knight, and Bishop aim powerfully at the King-side, while his Rook on Queen Bishop 3 is poised for R—KR3 or R—KN3.

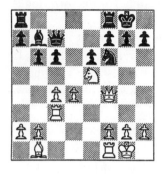

4

If Black tries 1 . . . N—Q2 (to get rid of White's Knight), the sequel might be 2 R—KR3, P—KR3; 3 RxP!!, PxR; 4 Q—N3ch, K—R1; 5 N—N6ch!, PxN; 6 QxQ. Or 3 . . . P—B3; 4 R—R8ch!!, KxR; 5 Q—R4ch, K—N1; 6 Q—R7 mate.

Another danger (partly illustrated in the play arising from Diagram 4) is that White's King Bishop can operate formidably on the diagonal Queen Knight 1 to King Rook 7, leading to the heart of Black's castled position. This menace becomes even more drastic if White's Queen is on the same diagonal, as in Diagram 5.

5

White plays 1 B—N1 (with the threat of 2 BxN, BxB; 3 QxP mate). Black stops this with 1 . . . P—N3, but there follows 2 BxN, BxB; 3 N—K4!, B—K2; 4 P—QN4! and White wins a piece.

Finally, you must remember that White's second move

in the Queen's Gambit Declined (2 P—QB4) often allows him to open the Queen Bishop file and post his Queen Rook powerfully on it. (An example of this appears on page 15.) Black must be in a position to neutralize this pressure, and the best way for him to do it is to aim for a fairly early . . . P—QB4, assuring himself counterplay for his own Rooks on the Queen Bishop file.

Thus you see that the dangers Black must meet are many, varied, and formidable. Yet there is no reason to despair. If Black is unaware of the dangers, there is a strong likelihood that he will succumb to them. If he is aware of them, however, he can take countermeasures in good time.

(a) Orthodox Defense

1 P—Q4   P—Q4   2 P—QB4   P—K3

Now White has the choice of bringing out his Queen Knight or King Knight. 3 N—KB3 is less exact, as it may lead to Variations (e), (f), or (g), which give Black an easier game than after 3 N—QB3.

3 N—QB3   N—KB3   4 B—N5   . . . .

6

(Position after 4 B—N5)

By now playing 4 . . . QN—Q2, Black sets one of the most popular traps in the whole range of the openings: 5 PxP, PxP; 6 NxP??, NxN!!; 7 BxQ, B—N5ch; 8 Q—Q2, BxQch; 9 KxB, KxB and Black has won a piece!

4 ....   QN—Q2

It doesn't matter whether Black plays 4 . . . QN—Q2 or 4 . . . B—K2. But if he wishes to adopt the Cambridge Springs Defense—Variation (c), he must play . . . QN—Q2.

5 P—K3   B—K2   6 N—B3   Castles
              7 R—B1!   ....

The Rook move exercises a powerful restraining grip on Black's game. It sets up the potential pressure of the Rook on the Queen Bishop file.

7 ....   P—B3

Temporarily neutralizing the pressure of White's Rook along the Queen Bishop file. Of course, Black still means to play . . . P—B4 at a suitable moment later on.

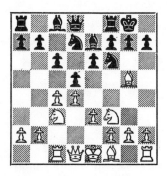

7

(Position after 7 . . . P—B3)

Black must think hard about the problem of developing his Queen Bishop. Note that at this moment the Bishop does not have a single move!

8 B—Q3   ....

This is a crucial position, and Black can easily go wrong. In one game, for example, the play was 8 . . . P—QN3?; 9 PxP, NxP; 10 NxN, BPxN; 11 BxB, QxB; 12 R—B7!, Q—N5ch; 13 Q—Q2, QxQch; 14 KxQ, P—QR3; 15 KR—QB1 and White has a strategically won game.

Nor is the preparation for fianchettoing Black's Queen Bishop fully successful: 8 . . . P—KR3; 9 B—R4, PxP; 10 BxP, P—QN4; 11 B—Q3, P—R3; 12 Castles, P—B4; 13 P—R4! (this forces a weakening of Black's Queen-side Pawns), P—B5; 14 B—N1, N—Q4; 15 BxB, QxB; 16 P—QN3! and Black ends up with a weak Pawn on the Queen-side.

8 ....   PxP   9 BxBP   N—Q4

Black has surrendered the center in order to free his constricted position by several exchanges—and also in the hope of freeing his imprisoned Bishop.

10 BxB   QxB   11 Castles   ....

White can avoid the exchange of Knights with 11 N—K4, but after 11 . . . KN—B3; 12 N—N3, P—K4! (freedom for the Bishop!) Black stands well enough.

11 ....   NxN   12 RxN   P—K4

8

(Position after 12 . . . P—K4)

At last Black has made the liberating move . . . P—K4, which means that the development of his Bishop is assured.

In the event of 13 PxP, NxP; 14 NxN, QxN; 15 P—B4 Black can hold his own with 15 . . . Q—K5!; 16 B—N3, B—B4!; 17 Q—R5, P—KN3; 18 Q—R6, QR—Q1 etc.

With this move White continues to maintain some advantage in space. If now 13 . . . P—K5; 14 N—Q2, N—B3; 15 P—QN4!, P—QR3; 16 KR—B1, B—N5; 17 P—QR4 and White has strong play on the Queen Bishop file with the coming P—N5 etc.

Probably best for Black is 13 . . . PxP; 14 PxP, N—N3; 15 B—N3, Q—B3; 16 R—K1, B—K3; 17 BxB, PxB; 18 R/B3—K3, QR—K1. *White still has more space for his pieces, but Black has completed his development and has a strong point for his Knight at Queen 4.*

(b) Exchange Variation

1 P—Q4	P—Q4	4 B—N5	QN—Q2
2 P—QB4	P—K3	5 P—K3	P—B3
3 N—QB3	N—KB3	6 PxP	KPxP

It will become clear later on that White is pursuing a definite policy with this exchange of Pawns, despite the fact that the swap allows Black to open the diagonal for his Queen Bishop.

7 B—Q3   B—K2

Planning to free his game with 8 . . . N—K5!

8 Q—B2!   ....

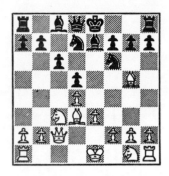

9

(Position after 8 Q—B2!)

White's last move has prevented 8 . . . N—K5? which would now be answered by 9 BxB winning a Pawn. So Black must find some other way to free himself.

White plans to play QR—N1 in due course, followed by P—QN4 and P—N5. If Black then exchanges Pawns (. . . BPxNP) he is left with a weak Queen Pawn and Queen Knight Pawn; aside from which, White has the mastery of the open Queen Bishop file.

On the other hand, if Black stands pat against this "minority attack" and allows White to play NPxBP, then Black is left with a backward Queen Bishop Pawn on the open Queen Bishop file. Such a Pawn remains a lasting weakness right into the endgame stage.

Here are some typical possibilities: 8 . . . N—R4; 9 BxB, QxB; 10 KN—K2, P—KN3; 11 Castles KR, P—KB4; 12 QR—N1, Castles; 13 P—QN4!, P—QR3; 14 P—QR4, P—B5! (counterplay on the King-side); 15 NxBP, NxN; 16 PxN, RxP; 17 N—K2, R—B3; 18 P—N5, RPxP; 19 PxP, N—B1; 20 PxP, PxP. Black is left with the backward Queen Bishop Pawn.

Or 8 . . . N—B1; 9 N—B3, N—K3; 10 B—R4, P—KN3; 11 Castles KR, Castles; 12 QR—N1, N—N2; 13 P—QN4!, B—B4 (getting rid of the problem child); 14 P—N5, BxB; 15 QxB, N—B4; 16 PxP, NxB; 17 NxN, PxP. Again Black is left with the backward Queen Bishop Pawn.

612

| 8 .... | Castles | 9 N—B3 | R—K1 |
| | 10 Castles KR | .... | |

Now it is still too soon for 10 . . . N—K5? for then 11 BxN! wins a Pawn. (Black's King Rook Pawn is unprotected.)

| 10 .... | N—B1 | 11 QR—N1 | N—K5 |

If now 12 BxN, BxB and Black is safe. (His King Rook Pawn is protected.)

| 12 BxB | QxB |

10

(Position after 12 . . . QxB)

Again White is in a position to carry out the minority attack: 13 P—QN4!, P—QR3; 14 P—QR4, NxN; 15 QxN followed eventually by P—N5 with a strong initiative.

(c) Cambridge Springs Defense

| 1 P—Q4 | P—Q4 | 3 N—QB3 | N—KB3 |
| 2 P—QB4 | P—K3 | 4 B—N5 | QN—Q2 |

A good alternative is 4 . . . B—N5, with ideas akin to those of the Nimzoindian Defense (page 46).

After 4 . . . QN—Q2, White can, if he wishes, transpose into the Exchange Variation with 5 or 6 PxP.

| 5 P—K3 | P—B3 | 6 N—B3 | Q—R4 |

(Position after 6 . . . Q—R4)

With his last move Black pins White's Queen Knight, exploiting the absence of White's Queen Bishop. Note that 7 PxP is not so good now, as Black has 7 . . . NxP, intensifying the pin.

7 N—Q2   ....

Taking measures against the pin. Black can now get equality with 7 . . . B—N5; 8 Q—B2, PxP (attacking White's Queen Bishop); 9 BxN, NxB; 10 NxP, BxNch; 11 QxB, QxQch; 12 PxQ, K—K2; 13 P—B3, B—Q2; 14 QR—N1, P—QN3; 15 N—K5, KR—QB1 followed by . . . P—B4. However, the main line is even simpler and more promising.

7	PxP	10 R—B1	N—Q4!
8 BxN	NxB	11 B—Q3	NxN
9 NxP	Q—B2	12 PxN	....

Not 12 RxN?, B—N5 winning the Exchange.

| 12 .... | B—K2 | 14 P—B4 | P—KN3 |
| 13 Castles | Castles | 15 N—K5 | P—QB4 |

The position is approximately even. White has a freer game, but Black's Bishop-pair has great potential power.

1 P—Q4	P—Q4		5 P—K3	Castles
2 P—QB4	P—K3		6 N—B3	P—KR3
3 N—QB3	N—KB3		7 B—R4	N—K5!
4 B—N5	B—K2		8 BxB	QxB

12

(Position after 8 . . . QxB)

Black's emphasis is on exchanging and simplifying so as to liberate his remaining forces.

Black has already achieved a satisfactory position, for example 9 NxN, PxN; 10 N—Q2, P—K4! Then if 11 NxP?, PxP; 12 QxP??, R—Q1 and Black wins a piece.

Or if 9 Q—B2, NxN; 10 QxN, PxP!; 11 BxP, P—QN3!; 12 Castles KR, B—N2; 13 B—K2, R—B1!; 14 KR—Q1, P—QB4! and Black stands well.

| 9 PxP | NxN | | 10 PxN | PxP |

Black's Bishop is liberated at last.

| 11 Q—N3 | R—Q1 | | 13 BxP | N—B3 |
| 12 P—B4 | PxP | | 14 Q—B3 | B—N5 |

615

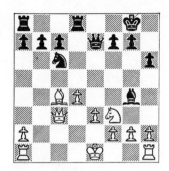

13

(Position after 14 . . . B—N5)

Black's Bishop has developed with a threat of 15 . . . BxN; 16 PxB, NxP (or 16 . . . RxP).

15 Castles KR	BxN	16 PxB	Q—B3

Black has a thoroughly satisfactory position. All his pieces are in good play.

(e) Prague Variation

1 P—Q4	P—Q4	3 N—QB3	N—KB3
2 P—QB4	P—K3	4 N—B3	P—B4

Thanks to the fact that White's fourth move here is less energetic than 4 B—N5, Black can hit back vigorously in the center.

14

(Position after 4 . . . P—B4)

If now 5 B—N5, BPxP; 6 KNxP, P—K4; 7 N—B3, P—Q5; 8 N—Q5, B—K2; 9 NxB, QxN with a good game for Black.

5 BPxP	NxP!

616

After 5 . . . KPxP Black would be faced with the later possibility of PxP, leaving him with an isolated Queen Pawn as in Variation (h).

6 P—K4	NxN	8 PxP	B—N5ch
7 PxN	PxP	9 B—Q2	BxBch

As in the previous variation, Black frees his game by exchanging pieces.

10 QxB	Castles	12 Castles KR	P—QN3
11 B—B4	N—B3	13 KR—Q1	B—N2

Black has developed his Queen Bishop satisfactorily. After 14 Q—B4, R—B1 he has a good game. White has a powerful-looking Pawn center, but Black has the Queen-side majority of Pawns. Both sides have good prospects for the middle game.

(f) Duras Variation

1 P—Q4	P—Q4	3 N—KB3	N—KB3
2 P—QB4	P—K3	4 B—N5	P—KR3!

This takes advantage of the fact that White's third move is not quite so strong as 3 N—QB3.

White's next move is practically forced, for if 5 B—R4, B—N5ch!; 6 N—B3, PxP! and Black can hold the gambit Pawn in all variations.

Proof: if 7 P—K4? P—KN4!, winning White's King Pawn (this is the point of 4 . . . P—KR3!). If 7 P—K3, P—QN4! (this is the point of 5 . . . B—N5ch!). Finally, if 7 Q—R4ch, N—B3; 8 P—QR3, BxNch; 9 PxB, Q—Q4!; 10 P—K3, P—QN4 and again Black keeps the Pawn.

5 BxN	QxB

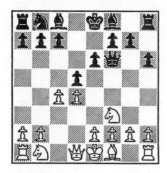

15

(Position after 5 . . . QxB)

Black has the positional advantage of two Bishops against Bishop and Knight; but his position is somewhat constricted.

6 Q—N3	P—B3	10 B—Q3	N—B3
7 QN—Q2	N—Q2	11 NxNch	QxN
8 P—K4	PxKP	12 Castles KR	B—Q3
9 NxP	Q—B5	13 KR—K1	Castles

Equal game. White has a freer position, but Black's forces have considerable potential power, especially if he can free his Queen Bishop.

(g) Vienna Variation

1 P—Q4	P—Q4	4 B—N5	B—N5ch
2 P—QB4	P—K3	5 N—B3	PxP
3 N—KB3	N—KB3	6 P—K4	P—B4 .

This counterthrust in the center leads to very exciting play. Here again Black has taken advantage of the fact that 3 N—KB3 is less energetic than 3 N—QB3.

An extremely complicated game can now arise from 7 P—K5, but it appears that Black can hold his own, for example 7 . . . PxP; 8 PxN, PxP; 9 Q—R4ch, N—B3; 10 Castles,

PxB; 11 NxQP, BxN!; 12 PxB, B—Q2!; 13 NxN, Q—B2!
etc. Or 7 . . . PxP; 8 Q—R4ch, N—B3; 9 Castles, B—Q2!;
10 N—K4, B—K2; 11 PxN, PxP; 12 B—R4, QR—B1!;
13 K—N1, N—R4; 14 Q—B2, P—K4! and Black has compensation for the piece down. (His Pawns are powerful.)

7 BxP   . . . .

Black can now play 7 . . . PxP; 8 NxP, BxNch; 9 PxB,
QN—Q2 with a perfectly safe game. However, 7 . . . PxP;
8 NxP, Q—R4 seems much too risky: 9 BxN!, BxNch; 10
PxB, QxBPch; 11 K—B1, QxBch; 12 K—N1, N—Q2 (not
12 . . . PxB?; 13 R—B1 winning); 13 R—B1!, Q—R3;
14 BxNP and White has a terrific initiative.

7 . . . .   BxNch!   8 PxB   Q—R4!

16

(Position after 8 . . . Q—R4!)

*Black must win a Pawn, for example
9 Q—B2 (or 9 Q—Q3), NxP! etc.
Or 9 BxN, QxBPch; 10 N—Q2, PxB;
11 PxP, N—Q2 etc.*

*This line of play is unsatisfactory for White, as Black wins
material.*

(h) Tarrasch Defense

| 1 P—Q4 | P—Q4 | 3 N—QB3 | P—QB4 |
| 2 P—QB4 | P—K3 | 4 BPxP! | KPxP |

White intends to burden Black with an isolated Queen Pawn (see White's ninth move).

5 N—B3   N—QB3   6 P—KN3!   . . . .

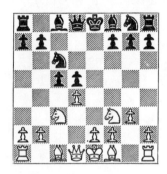

17

(Position after 6 P—KN3!)

White will fianchetto his King Bishop in order to exert powerful pressure on Black's weak Queen Pawn.

| 6 . . . . | N—B3 | 8 Castles | Castles |
| 7 B—N2 | B—K2 | 9 PxP! | . . . . |

This is the move that sets off White's advantage. The counter gambit 9 . . . P—Q5 simply leaves Black a Pawn down after 10 N—QR4, B—B4; 11 B—B4, N—K5; 12 P—QN4!, B—B3; 13 P—N5, N—K2; 14 B—K5.

| 9 . . . . | BxP | 11 B—K3 | N—K5 |
| 10 N—QR4 | B—K2 | 12 R—B1 | . . . . |

White has a marked positional advantage, thanks to Black's isolated Queen Pawn.

Summary: After 3 N—QB3, Black's most promising defenses appear to be the Cambridge Springs Defense, Lasker's Defense, and the Prague Variation.

After 3 N—KB3, Black does well with the Duras Variation or Vienna Variation.

QUEEN'S GAMBIT DECLINED

Slav Defense (2 . . . P—QB3)

By propping up his Queen Pawn with 2 . . . P—QB3 Black takes up the fight for the center in the same way as when playing 2 . . . P—K3. However, 2 . . . P—QB3 does not block his Queen Bishop, and, as we would expect, we often see the Black Bishop developed to King Bishop 4 (or even to King Knight 5) in this line of play.

After 2 . . . P—QB3 Black frequently accepts the gambit on move 4, on the theory that he can fight for the center by playing his Queen Bishop to King Bishop 4. White generally gets the better of it, however, by angling for P—K4, or trying to control the center in some other fashion.

Despite the early . . . P—QB3, Black will generally try to free his game in the late opening or early middle game by playing . . . P—QB4.

The so-called "Semi-Slav" defenses involve Black's playing . . . P—K3 after . . . P—QB3. As this hems in his Queen Bishop, he will generally try to fianchetto his problem Bishop.

(a) Deferred Acceptance of the Gambit

1 P—Q4	P—Q4	3 N—KB3	N—B3
2 P—QB4	P—QB3	4 N—B3	PxP

Here 4 . . . B—B4 looks *logical*, but after 5 PxP!, PxP; 6 Q—N3! Black is in trouble because of the twofold attack on his Queen Knight Pawn and Queen Pawn.

After 4 . . . PxP White can play to recover the gambit Pawn directly by 5 P—K3, P—QN4; 6 P—QR4, P—N5 (if 6 . . . P—QR3; 7 PxP, BPxP; 8 NxP etc.); 7 N—R2, P—K3;

8 BxP etc. But as this leaves his Queen Knight out of the game, White chooses a different way.

5 P—QR4   B—B4

18

(Position after 5 . . . B—B4)

Black has achieved his heart's desire —development of the Queen Bishop.

6 N—K5   . . . .

The alternative is 6 P—K3, P—K3; 7 BxP, B—QN5 (to restrain an eventual P—K4); 8 Castles, Castles; 9 Q—K2. Now Black can try to stop P—K4 or accept it as inevitable.

Thus: 9 . . . N—K5; 10 B—Q3! (an interesting Pawn sacrifice), BxN (if 10 . . . NxN; 11 PxN, BxP; 12 R—N1 and White regains the Pawn); 11 PxB!, NxQBP; 12 Q—B2, BxB; 13 QxB, N—Q4; 14 B—R3 with a magnificent development in return for the Pawn.

Or 9 . . . B—N5; 10 P—R3, BxN; 11 QxB, QN—Q2; 12 R—Q1 (not P—K4 at once because of . . . N—N3), P—K4!; 13 P—Q5! (if 13 PxP, NxP!), BxN!; 14 PxP!, P—K5!; 15 Q—B5, B—K4!; 16 PxN, Q—B2! and Black can just about hold his own.

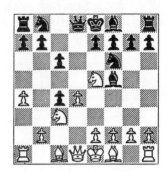

19

(Position after 6 N—K5)

White intends to fianchetto his King Bishop. He will recover the gambit Pawn by capturing it with his King Knight.

6 ....   QN—Q2

Here 6 . . . P—K3 looks plausible, but after 7 P—B3! Black's Queen Bishop can run into trouble, for example 7 . . . B—QN5; 8 NxP/B4, Castles; 9 B—N5!, P—B4; 10 PxP, QxQch; 11 KxQ, BxP; 12 P—K4!, B—KN3; 13 N—K5. White will play NxB obtaining the positional advantage of two Bishops against Bishop and Knight.

7 NxP/B4	Q—B2	9 PxP	NxP
8 P—KN3!	P—K4	10 B—B4	N/B3—Q2
	11 B—N2	....	

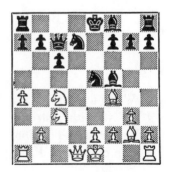

20

(Position after 11 B—N2)

Black has developed freely and rapidly, but the pin on his King Knight promises to be troublesome.

11	P—B3	13 Q—B1!	B—K3
12 Castles	R—Q1	14 N—K4!	....

The point is that after 14 . . . BxN; 15 QxB, NxQ; 16 BxQ White has a very favorable endgame with his two Bishops against Bishop and Knight.

14	B—QN5	15 P—R5!	....

White has a very strong position. If now 15 . . . BxN; 16 QxB, BxP??; 17 Q—K6ch, K—B1; 18 KR—Q1! and White's pressure must be decisive. Or 15 . . . Castles; 16 NxN, NxN; 17 N—B5 with powerful pressure.

(b) Semi-Slav: Classical Variation

1 P—Q4	P—Q4	3 N—KB3	N—B3
2 P—QB4	P—QB3	4 N—B3	P—K3
	5 P—K3	QN—Q2	

Against the "Stonewall" set-up of 5 . . . N—K5; 6 B—Q3, P—KB4 White has the vigorous 7 P—KN4!!

6 B—Q3	B—Q3

The conservative 6 . . . B—K2 allows White to play 7 Castles, Castles; 8 P—QN3!, P—QN3; 9 B—N2 with a strong White initiative because his King Bishop's aggressive position contrasts favorably with the passive position of Black's King Bishop.

7 Castles	Castles	8 P—K4!	....

21

(Position after 8 P—K4!)

White opens up the game advantageously, for if 8 . . . PxBP; 9 BxP, P—K4; 10 B—KN5! with a more aggressive development.

8	PxKP	9 NxP	NxN
	10 BxN	N—B3	

Not 10 . . . P—K4?; 11 PxP, NxP; 12 NxN, BxN; 13 BxPch!, KxB; 14 Q—R5ch winning a Pawn.

11 B—B2	....

White has distinctly the freer game. Note that Black's Queen Bishop is still hemmed in.

(c) Semi-Slav: Meran Variation

1 P—Q4	P—Q4	5 P—K3	QN—Q2
2 P—QB4	P—QB3	6 B—Q3	PxP
3 N—KB3	N—B3	7 BxBP	P—QN4
4 N—B3	P—K3	8 B—Q3	....

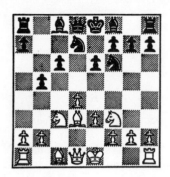

22

(Position after 8 B—Q3)

Black can avoid the intricacies of the following play by continuing 8 . . . B—N2; 9 P—K4, P—N5!; 10 N—QR4, P—B4; 11 P—K5, N—Q4 etc.

| 8 .... | P—QR3 | 9 P—K4 | .... |

After the colorless 9 Castles, P—B4; 10 P—QR4, P—N5; 11 N—K4, B—N2 Black has an easy game (generally true whenever he succeeds in developing the Queen Bishop).

| 9 .... | P—B4! | 10 P—K5 | PxP! |
| | 11 NxNP! | NxP! | |

If instead 11 . . . PxN; 12 PxN, Q—N3; 13 PxP, BxP; 14 Castles, B—N2; 15 B—KB4, Castles KR and Black's King is somewhat exposed because of the missing King Knight Pawn.

| 12 NxN | PxN | 13 Q—B3 | .... |

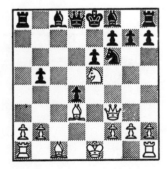

23

(Position after 13 Q—B3)

To all appearances Black is in serious trouble, but he has ingenious resources.

626

13 ....   B—N5ch!   14 K—K2   QR—N1

Calmly ignoring 15 N—B6, which he can answer with
15 . . . B—N2.

15 Q—N3	Q—Q3!	17 RPxQ	B—Q3
16 N—B3	QxQ	18 NxP	B—Q2

*White has regained his Pawn, and the position is even.
However, this variation is too complicated and dangerous for
the average player.*

(d) Semi-Slav: Anti-Meran Gambit

1 P—Q4	P—Q4	2 P—QB4	P—QB3
	3 N—KB3	N—B3	

After 3 . . . P—K3 White can calmly protect the gambit
Pawn with 4 P—K3—or he can go in for the complex alter-
native 4 N—B3!?, PxP; 5 P—K3, P—QN4; 6 P—QR4,
B—N5; 7 B—Q2, P—QR4; 8 PxP, BxN; 9 BxB, PxP; 10
P—QN3!, B—N2!; 11 PxP, P—N5; 12 B—N2, N—KB3
and White's powerful center is more or less balanced by
Black's bristling Queen-side passed Pawns.

4 N—B3   P—K3   5 B—N5!?   ....

Avoiding the Meran Variation which could arise after
5 P—K3, QN—Q2; 6 B—Q3, PxP; 7 BxP, P—QN4 etc.

5 ....   PxP!?

Leading to dangerous complications, whereas the sedate

alternative 5 . . . QN—Q2 would transpose into quieter lines like the Cambridge Springs Defense, Orthodox Defense, or Exchange Variation. After Black's last, 6 P—K3 is too slow because of 6 . . . P—N4. Therefore:

6 P—K4   P—N4   7 P—K5   P—KR3

This and Black's next move are forced.

8 B—R4   P—N4   9 NxKNP!   PxN

If 9 . . . N—Q4; 10 NxBP!, QxB; 11 NxR etc.

10 BxNP   QN—Q2

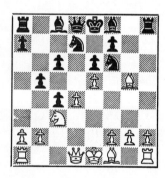

24

(Position after 10 . . . QN—Q2)

Though Black is temporarily a Pawn down and must lose back the extra piece, but he has excellent prospects. Thus, if 11 Q—B3, B—QN2; 12 B—K2, Q—N3!; 13 PxN, P—B4! with a splendid position.

11 P—KN3   Q—R4

A good alternative is 11 . . . B—QN2; 12 B—N2, Q—N3; 13 PxN, P—B4!; 14 PxP, BxP; 15 Castles, Castles.

12 PxN   P—N5   13 N—K4   B—QR3!

An exciting position in which both sides have weaknesses and attacking possibilities.

1 P—Q4	P—Q4	3 N—KB3	N—B3
2 P—QB4	P—QB3	4 P—K3	B—B4

Thus Black avoids the intricacies of the Meran Variation and develops his problem Bishop. But White manages to maintain the initiative.

5 B—Q3	BxB	7 N—B3	QN—Q2
6 QxB	P—K3	8 Castles	B—N5

Hoping—in vain—to stop P—K4. If instead 8 . . . B—Q3; 9 P—K4 with greater freedom of action for White.

9 B—Q2! . . . .

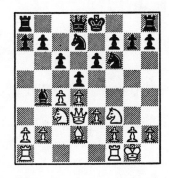

25

(Position after 9 B—Q2!)

White has set a trap: if Black castles now, then 10 NxP! wins a Pawn.

9	B—R4	10 P—QN4!	B—B2

Not 10 . . . BxP; 11 NxP!, NxN; 12 PxN, BxB; 13 PxBP!, PxP; 14 NxB and White has a substantial positional advantage.

11 P—K4	PxBP	12 QxBP	. . . .

White has a noticeably freer game.

1 P—Q4	P—Q4	4 N—QB3	N—KB3
2 P—QB4	P—QB3	5 N—B3	N—B3
3 PxP	PxP	6 B—B4	....

26

(Position after 6 B—B4)

White's exchange at move 3 gives the variation its name. If now 6 . . . P—K3; 7 P—K3, B—K2 and Black's conservative development has the drawback of blocking his Queen Bishop's diagonal.

6 ....   B—B4!

Black develops the problem Bishop, although he sees difficulties ahead.

| 7 P—K3 | P—K3 | 8 Q—N3 | B—QN5! |

So that if 9 N—K5, Q—R4! counterattacking vigorously.

9 B—QN5   Castles!

Black is not afraid of 10 BxN, for then 10 . . . BxNch; 11 QxB, R—B1! is strong (12 Q—R3, RxB; 13 QxP, B—Q6!).

| 10 Castles | BxN | 12 BxNP | BxR |
| 11 BxN | BxNP | 13 RxB | .... |

White must regain the Exchange, with a perfectly even position resulting.

Summary: Black's best practical chances seem to arise from the Meran and Anti-Meran lines in the Semi-Slav form. The deferred acceptance of the gambit is less suitable for Black because it leaves White with too much freedom of action.

ALBIN COUNTER GAMBIT

Like all gambits played by Black, this one must be viewed with suspicion. Black gives up a Pawn very early in the hope of gaining time for rapid development. White's cue is to develop quickly without attaching too much importance to the extra Pawn. The result is either that White keeps the extra Pawn and the initiative to boot; or else that he returns the Pawn and maintains powerful pressure.

1 P—Q4	P—Q4	2 P—QB4	P—K4?!

Rarely does Black have the opportunity to indulge in such violent play. This is good policy only against a definitely weaker opponent.

3 QPxP	P—Q5

The gambit is in operation. Black hopes that his advanced Queen Pawn will prove a stumbling block for White's development. More often than not, it becomes a target for White's pieces.

4 N—KB3	N—QB3	5 QN—Q2	....

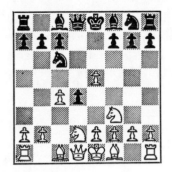

27

(Position after 5 QN—Q2)

In practically all variations White fianchettoes his King Bishop. This completes the mobilization of his King-side and gives the Bishop a powerful diagonal.

5	B—K3

After 5 . . . P—B3; 6 PxP, NxP (or 6 . . . QxP) Black has inadequate compensation for the sacrificed Pawn.

On 5 . . . B—QN5 White has no objection to returning the extra Pawn, thus: 6 P—QR3!, BxNch; 7 QxB!, B—N5; 8 P—N4!, BxN; 9 KPxB, NxKP. For after 10 B—N2, Q—K2; 11 Castles, Castles; 12 P—B4 White has a marked positional advantage—two Bishops against two Knights.

Against 5 . . . B—KN5 White proceeds favorably with 6 P—KN3 etc.

6 P—KN3	Q—Q2	7 B—N2	R—Q1

Black can also castle at this point, but this leaves his King exposed to a withering attack based on the White King Bishop's long diagonal.

8 Castles	KN—K2	9 Q—R4	N—N3

Black hopes to win the advanced King Pawn—but this would cost him his Queen-side Pawns—thanks to the powerful action of White's pieces.

10 P—QR3!	B—K2	11 P—QN4	Castles

White continues 12 B—N2 with a very powerful position. Black cannot recover his Pawn, and his position has no appeal in other respects.

QUEEN'S GAMBIT ACCEPTED

In order to evade the difficult problems which confront the defender in the Queen's Gambit Declined, some players prefer to accept the gambit by answering 2 P—QB4 with 2 . . . PxP. This clears the long diagonal which extends out from Black's Queen Rook 1 square, and Black hopes to fianchetto his Queen Bishop to exploit this long diagonal.

Theoretically, this is an excellent notion—but there are drawbacks. Black's immediate surrender of the center gives White more space, quicker development, and the makings of a powerful Pawn center.

Black may try a different approach after 2 . . . PxP by developing his Queen Bishop to King Knight 5. Aggressive though this seems, White knows how to hit back hard. Thus the acceptance of the gambit involves Black in thorny problems.

(a) 4 . . . P—K3 Variation

| 1 P—Q4 | P—Q4 | 3 N—KB3 | N—KB3 |
| 2 P—QB4 | PxP | 4 P—K3 | P—K3 |

It is instructive to observe that it would be futile for Black to try to hold on to the gambit Pawn. Thus, if 4 . . . P—QN4; 5 P—QR4!, P—QB3; 6 P—QN3! No matter how Black plays, he loses back the Pawn and remains with a weakened Queen-side Pawn structure.

5 BxP	P—B4

An important counterthrust. By engaging the Queen Pawn at once, Black takes much of the sting out of an eventual P—K4 by White.

6 Castles	P—QR3	7 Q—K2	N—B3

28

(Position after 7 . . . N—B3)

White has two advantageous ways to proceed: 8 PxP! in order to fian-chetto his Queen Bishop on a power-ful diagonal; or 8 R—Q1! in order to operate on the center files with his Rooks.

Proceeding with inexorable logic, White can get a clear-cut positional advantage with 8 PxP!, BxP; 9 P—QR3!, P—QN4; 10 B—R2, B—N2; 11 P—QN4, B—K2; 12 B—N2, Castles; 13 QN—Q2! The point of White's play is clearly revealed in his last move: his Queen Knight can occupy the Queen Bishop 5 square. As for Black, his Queen Knight, being developed differently, cannot imitate this convincing maneuver.

There follows: 13 . . . Q—N3; 14 N—N3, KR—Q1; 15 QR—B1, QR—B1; 16 N—B5 with a distinctly superior position for White.

8 R—Q1	P—QN4

In order to answer 9 B—Q3 (or 9 B—N3) with 9 . . . P—B5!; 10 B—B2, N—QN5! and . . . NxB assuring Black the

634

positional advantage of two Bishops against Bishop and Knight.

| 9 PxP | Q—B2 | 10 B—Q3 | BxP |

Not 10 ... N—QN5; 11 P—QR4!, NxB; 12 QxN, P—N5; 13 P—B6! with a stranglehold on Black's game, as he cannot play 13 ... QxBP?? because of 14 Q—Q8 mate.

| | 11 P—QR4! | P—N5 |

The alternative 11 . . . PxP; 12 RxP, N—QN5 is not appealing because of 13 B—N5ch!, B—Q2; 14 BxBch, NxB; 15 B—Q2 etc.

| 12 QN—Q2 | Castles | 12 N—N3 | B—K2 |

White now plays 13 P—K4 followed by B—KN5 and QR—B1 leaving Black with a cramped, difficult game.

(b) 4 . . . B—N5 Variation

| 1 P—Q4 | P—Q4 | 3 N—KB3 | P—QR3 |
| 2 P—QB4 | PxP | 4 P—K3 | B—N5 |

As we have already seen, it would be pointless for Black to play 4 ... P—QN4 because of 5 P—QR4, P—QB3; 6 P—QN3! etc. Instead, he develops his Queen Bishop, pinning White's King Knight.

| 5 P—KR3 | B—R4 | 6 BxP | P—K3 |
| | 7 Q—N3! | .... | |

29

(Position after 7 Q—N3!)

Protecting the Queen Knight Pawn poses an awkward problem for Black, as neither 7 . . . Q—B1 nor 7 . . . R—R2 looks inviting.

7	BxN	9 B—K2	P—QB4
8 PxB	P—QN4	10 P—QR4	P—N5
	11 PxP	BxP	

White has two Bishops against Bishop and Knight, and he can make good use of the open King Knight file. In addition, Black's Queen-side Pawn structure has been weakened. The position definitely favors White.

MISCELLANEOUS DOUBLE QUEEN PAWN OPENINGS

There are openings in which White plays 1 P—Q4 and Black replies 1 . . . P—Q4, whereupon White deliberately avoids playing the Queen's Gambit. The result is an absence of tension in the central Pawn position. This lack of tension makes it easy for Black to achieve equality.

(a) Colle System

1 P—Q4	P—Q4	3 P—K3	P—B4
2 N—KB3	N—KB3	4 P—B3	....

The characteristic move of this system. White's idea is to

support his Queen Bishop Pawn with a view to an eventual P—K4. This often gives him the initiative in the center. In turn such a preponderance, if met by indifferent moves, may lead to a powerful attack by White.

The alternative 4 P—QN3 has gone out of style because of the continuation 4 . . . P—K3; 5 B—N2, N—B3; 6 B—Q3, B—Q3; 7 Castles, Castles. Now if 8 QN—Q2, Q—K2!; 9 N—K5 (else Black frees himself at once with . . . P—K4), PxP; 10 PxP, B—R6 with an excellent game for Black. This applies also to 8 P—QR3, Q—B2 followed by . . . P—K4.

4 ....   QN—Q2!

An important finesse. After 4 . . . P—K3; 5 QN—Q2, N—B3; 6 B—Q3, B—Q3; 7 Castles, Castles; 8 PxP!, BxBP; 9 P—K4! White has the initiative in the center plus the Queen-side majority of Pawns. These advantages have led to some very impressive White victories with the Colle System.

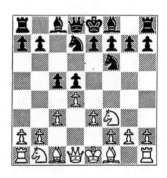

30

(Position after 4 . . . QN—Q2!)

If now 5 QN—Q2, P—K3; 6 B—Q3, B—Q3; 7 Castles, Castles; 8 P—K4, BPxP!; 9 BPxP (not 9 NxP?, N—B4!), PxP; 10 NxP and White is left with the positional disadvantage of an isolated Queen Pawn.

5 QN—Q2   P—KN3

As the caption to Diagram 30 indicates, 5 . . . P—K3 is a perfectly suitable alternative. However, 5 . . . P—KN3 is even more promising, as it breaks the diagonal of White's

King Bishop and thereby crushes White's hopes of King-side attack.

Note that Black's 5 . . . P—KN3 is made possible by his previous move, which guards his Queen Bishop Pawn and gives him freedom of action.

6 B—Q3	B—N2	7 Castles	Castles

If now 8 P—K4, QPxP; 9 NxP, PxP; 10 NxP (not 10 PxP? leaving White with an isolated Queen Pawn), N—K4; 11 NxNch, BxN; 12 B—K2, B—Q2 and Black has more freedom of action.

We arrive at the same conclusion after 8 P—QN4, PxNP; 9 PxP, N—K1!; 10 B—N2, N—Q3; 11 Q—N3, N—N3; 12 P—QR4, B—B4!; 13 BxB, PxB! when White's remaining Bishop is hemmed in by its own Pawns.

(b) Stonewall Variation

1 P—Q4	P—Q4	3 B—Q3	P—B4
2 P—K3	N—KB3	4 P—QB3	....

White intends to continue with P—KB4, establishing the Stonewall formation of his center Pawns. The force of this is best seen after the passive 4 . . . P—K3?; 5 P—KB4, QN—Q2; 6 N—B3, B—Q3; 7 QN—Q2, P—QN3; 8 N—K5, B—N2; 9 Q—B3, leaving White with a very powerful position in the center that often leads to an overwhelming attack.

4	N—B3

Black intends to proceed along different lines. He does not mind the possibility of 5 PxP, which gives him a tremendous Pawn center after 5 . . . P—K4. In any event, 5 PxP would be the negation of White's planned Stonewall set-up.

5 P—KB4	B—N5!		

Immediately solving the problem of the troublesome Bishop.

6 N—B3	P—K3	9 P—QN3	PxP
7 QN—Q2	B—Q3	10 BPxP	QR—B1
8 P—KR3	B—R4	11 Castles	B—N3

Black has somewhat the better of it after 12 BxB, RPxB, as his remaining Bishop has more freedom of action than the White Bishop.

(c) 2 B—B4 Variation

1 P—Q4	P—Q4	2 B—B4	....

This old-fashioned move is discredited nowadays for two reasons. In the first place, White gives Black the initiative in the center by permitting him to play . . . P—QB4. Secondly, White plays out his Queen Bishop before ascertaining what is the best square for that piece.

2	N—KB3	4 P—K3	N—B3
3 N—KB3	P—B4!	5 P—B3	Q—N3

Black is developing very comfortably.

6 Q—B1	B—B4	7 QN—Q2	P—K3

It is clear that White has frittered away the initiative. Black has a very promising game.

In the "Indian" Defenses Black answers 1 P—Q4 with
1 . . . N—KB3. Momentarily, then, Black is trying to control
the center by the Knight move (rather than the orthodox
. . . P—Q4). Later on, Black may intensify this policy of
controlling the center by using his pieces. On the other hand,
he may resort to Pawn moves.

All this sounds inconsistent, but it really isn't. It puts a
considerable burden on White, who must be prepared to contend with either policy on Black's part. Thus, in a psychological sense it may be said that 1 . . . N—KB3 is a subtle
attempt on Black's part to dictate the course of the game.

As in the Queen's Gambit, the opening struggle in the
Indian Defenses revolves about control of the center and
freedom of the pieces. Whoever achieves the advantage in
these respects will have the better game.

Now let us see how these theoretical concepts apply to the
specific problems of the Nimzoindian Defense. Here are
the opening moves:

1 P—Q4	N—KB3	2 P—QB4	P—K3
	3 N—QB3	....	

Now White is on the point of playing 4 P—K4, with a
Pawn center that would crush Black. Here is a crucial situation typical of the problems in this defense.

Of course, Black can solve the difficulty readily enough by
playing 3 . . . P—Q4, getting his fair share of the center by
transposing into the . . . P—K3 defense of the Queen's Gambit Declined. But Black is intent on playing the Nimzoindian
Defense. Therefore:

3	B—N5

31

(Position after 3 . . . B—N5)

By pinning White's Queen Knight, Black makes it impossible for White to advance P—K4. Meanwhile Black conceals his intentions: He may play . . . P—Q4 or . . . P—Q3 later on— or perhaps not move the Queen Pawn altogether!

White has a great variety of replies at his disposal. Before we consider them, we will have to reflect on the possible forms that the struggle for the center may take.

For example, Black may play . . . P—Q4 later in order to stop White's extreme expansion in the center with P—K4.

Or Black may allow White to play P—K4, and proceed to build up a "counter-center" with . . . P—Q3 and . . . P—K4.

Another possibility is that Black may try . . . P—QB4 by way of a flank thrust at White's center.

But there are also other aspects to be considered. Black's 3 . . . B—N5 leads most of the time to an exchange of this Bishop for White's Queen Knight. In that case White has two Bishops against Bishop and Knight. This is a decided point in White's favor *if he also has a strong development.*

On the other hand, if Black develops rapidly and favorably (as generally happens in this defense), he can neutralize the theoretical advantage of the two Bishops.

This must be appraised in the light of still another problem. It often happens that when Black plays . . . BxN, White retakes with his Queen Knight Pawn. This supports his Queen Pawn and is likely to give him the makings of a powerful Pawn center.

On the other hand, Black reasons that the doubled Queen

Bishop Pawn is a weakness, and he may elect to train his guns on the Pawn at White's Queen Bishop 4 square.

Who is right? It all depends on how the game continues. What we have here is a struggle of extreme tension, in which each player attempts to cash his own potential advantages and nullify those of his opponent. In the detailed analysis that follows, you will repeatedly observe the clash between the rival conceptions.

These comments explain the widespread popularity of the Nimzoindian Defense. It offers great rewards to an enterprising and inventive player.

(a) 4 Q—B2 Variation with 4 . . . P—Q4

| 1 P—Q4 | N—KB3 | 3 N—QB3 | B—N5 |
| 2 P—QB4 | P—K3 | 4 Q—B2 | .... |

Renewing the struggle for the center. White is on the point of playing P—K4.

4 . . . .   P—Q4

32

(Position after 4 . . . P—Q4)

By advancing his Queen Pawn to Queen 4 Black has adopted the simplest way to maintain a foothold in the center.

Now 5 P—QR3 looks obvious, in order to get rid of the pin, but after 5 . . . BxNch; 6 QxB, N—K5; 7 Q—B2, extremely wild play may result:

7 ... P—QB4; 8 QPxP, N—QB3; 9 N—B3, Q—R4ch; 10 N—Q2, N—Q5; 11 Q—Q3, P—K4!?; 12 P—QN4, Q—R5; 13 R—R2!

Or 7 ... N—QB3; 8 P—K3, P—K4!?; 9 BPxP, QxP; 10 B—B4, Q—R4ch; 11 P—QN4, NxNP; 12 QxN, N—B7 dbl ch; 13 K—K2, Q—K8ch; 14 K—B3, NxR; 15 B—N2.

In either case we have wild complications which the average player does well to steer clear of.

5 PxP   ....

33

(Position after 5 PxP)

Again Black must make a choice: to command the center with pieces (5 ... QxP) or the Queen Pawn (5 ... PxP).

The simplest method of recapture is 5 ... PxP. If then 6 B—N5, P—KR3; 7 BxN, QxB; 8 P—QR3, BxNch; 9 QxB, P—B3; 10 P—K3, Castles; 11 N—B3, B—B4 and Black stands well.

Note that after 6 B—N5, P—KR3; 7 B—R4 allows Black to counterattack vigorously with 7 ... P—B4!, for example 8 PxP, N—B3; 9 Castles, P—KN4!; 10 B—N3, Q—R4 etc.

5 ....   QxP   6 N—B3   P—B4

Operating against White's Pawn center.

7 B—Q2   BxN

In order to maintain the centralized position of his Queen.

| 8 BxB | PxP | 9 NxP | P—K4 |

A valuable freeing move. If now 10 N—B5, BxN; 11 QxB, N—B3; 12 P—K3, Castles; 13 B—K2, Q—K5! with equality.

| 10 N—B3 | N—B3 | 12 B—K2 | B—N5 |
| 11 P—K3 | Castles | 13 P—KR3 | .... |

Equal game. White has the two Bishops, but Black has freedom of action, for example 13 . . . B—R4; 14 Castles KR, KR—Q1; 15 P—R3, B—N3; 16 Q—B1, N—K5 etc.

(b) 4 Q—B2 Variation with 4 . . . N—B3

| 1 P—Q4 | N—KB3 | 3 N—QB3 | B—N5 |
| 2 P—QB4 | P—K3 | 4 Q—B2 | N—B3 |

Gaining time by attacking White's Queen Pawn and preparing to build up a center with . . . P—Q3 and . . . P—K4.

| 5 N—B3 | P—Q3 |

34

(Position after 5 . . . P—Q3)

Black is prepared to concede the two Bishops to White, as the forthcoming . . . P—K4 will maintain the balance of power in the center.

If now 6 P—QR3, BxNch; 7 QxB White has the two
Bishops and Black must play carefully to avoid a constricted
position. 7 . . . P—QR4! prevents too much White expan-
sion (by 8 P—QN4). Then, after 8 P QN3, Castles; 9 B—
N2 Black plays for . . . P—K4 with 9 . . . R—K1!; 10
R—Q1, Q—K2! etc.

| 6 B—Q2 | P—K4 | 8 BxB | Q—K2 |
| 7 P—QR3 | BxN | 9 PxP | .... |

Loosening up the position so that his Queen Bishop will
have more scope.

| 9 .... | PxP | 10 P—K3 | P—QR4! |

Again preventing White from expanding unduly with
P—QN4 (threatening P—N5).

| | | 11 P—R3! | .... |

Preventing the development of Black's Queen Bishop via
. . . B—N5. But Black has a resourceful continuation.

| 11 .... | Castles | 12 B—K2 | P—KN3! |

*Black maintains equality by preparing . . . B—B4. After
13 P—QN3, B—B4; 14 Q—N2, KR—K1; 15 Castles, N—
K5 the position is approximately even.*

(c) 4 Q—B2 Variation with 4 . . . P—B4

| 1 P—Q4 | N—KB3 | 3 N—QB3 | B—N5 |
| 2 P—QB4 | P—K3 | 4 Q—B2 | P—B4 |

This flank thrust is intended to demolish White's center by removing White's Queen Pawn. White generally gets pressure on the opened Queen file and on the opened long diagonal extending from his Queen Rook 1 to King Rook 8. However, Black can equalize by getting good play for his pieces in the center.

5 PxP   . . . .

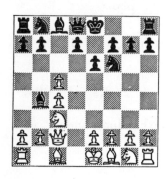

35

(Position after 5 PxP)

Black can hold his own with 5 . . . BxP; 6 N—B3, N—B3; 7 B—N5, B—K2 followed by . . . P—Q3. But this leads to a cramped position which is not to everyone's taste.

5 . . . .   Castles

And now the pinning move 6 B—N5 looks good. However, Black counterattacks effectively with 6 . . . N—R3!; 7 P—QR3, BxNch; 8 QxB, NxP. White has the two Bishops, but Black has a good grip on the center, for example 9 Q—B2 (to avoid . . . N/B4—K5), P—QR4!; 10 P—B3, P—R5; 11 R—Q1, N—N6; 12 P—K4, Q—R4ch; 13 B—Q2, NxB; 14 QxN, P—Q4 and Black has at least equality.

6 N—B3   N—R3!

Here too the Knight arrives rapidly at an influential post for controlling the center. If now 7 P—QR3, BxNch! 8 QxB, NxP; 9 P—QN4, N/B4—K5 and Black's commanding centralized position makes up for White's two Bishops.

646

7 B—Q2	NxP	8 P—QR3	BxN
	9 BxB	N/B4—K5	

As in the previous note, Black has equality, thanks to the fine position of his centralized Knight.

(d) 4 P—K3 Variation

1 P—Q4	N—KB3	3 N—QB3	B—N5
2 P—QB4	P—K3	4 P—K3	....

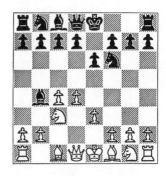

36

(Position after 4 P—K3)

White's last move is stronger than it looks. He prepares the development of his King Bishop and is ready to benefit by any advantages that may accrue from his having the Bishop-pair after . . . BxN.

If now 4 . . . Castles, the play may very likely transpose into one of the variations shown below. An independent possibility is 5 KN—K2, P—Q4; 6 P—QR3, B—K2; 7 PxP, PxP; 8 P—KN3 (much more promising than 8 N—N3, P—B4! and if 9 PxP, BxP; 10 P—N4, P—Q5!), QN—Q2; 9 B—N2, N—N3; 10 Q—Q3, P—QR4; 11 P—QR4, P—B3; 12 Castles, QN—Q2; 13 P—B3; with the idea of forming a powerful Pawn center with P—K4.

Against 4 . . . P—QN3 White can also proceed with 5 KN—K2 and if 5 . . . B—R3; 6 P—QR3, B—K2; 7 N—B4, P—Q4; 8 PxP, BxB; 9 KxB, PxP; 10 P—KN4! with a strong initiative.

647

Another way is 4 . . . P—QN3; 5 KN—K2, B—N2; 6 P—QR3, BxNch; 7 NxB, Castles; 8 B—Q3!, P—B4 (not 8 . . . BxP; 9 KR—N1, B—N2; 10 P—K4 followed by P—K5 with a withering attack); 9 P—Q5! cramping Black's game considerably. If then 9 . . . PxP; 10 PxP, NxP?; 11 NxN, BxN; 12 Q—R5—or 10 . . . BxP?; 11 NxB, NxN; 12 B—K4 and White wins in either event.

| 4 . . . . | P—Q4 | 5 B—Q3 | Castles |

If White now continues 6 N—B3, P—B4; 7 Castles, N—B3; 8 P—QR3, Black's simplest course is 8 . . . BxN; 9 PxB, P—QN3 with good prospects for Black despite White's two Bishops.

Or Black may try (after 8 P—QR3) 8 . . . QPxP; 9 BxBP, PxP; 10 PxP, B—K2. Then after 11 Q—Q3, P—QN3; 12 B—R2, B—N2; 13 B—N1, P—N3 White has a freer game and attacking chances, while Black has pressure on White's isolated Queen Pawn.

| 6 P—QR3 | BxNch | 7 PxB | . . . . |

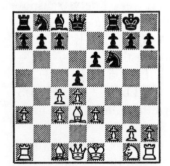

37

(Position after 7 PxB)

White's sturdy Pawn center and his possession of two Bishops give him many powerful attacking chances.

Black must handle the defense with great care. Thus, after

648

7 ... P—B4; 8 BPxP!, KPxP; 9 N—K2, P—QN3; 10 Castles, B—R3; 11 BxB, NxB; 12 Q—Q3 White has the makings of a powerful attack despite the disappearance of his attacking Bishop. The sequel might be 12 ... P—B5; 13 Q—B2, N—N1; 14 P—B3!, R—K1; 15 N—N3, N—B3; 16 Q—B2, Q—Q2; 17 B—N2, R—K3; 18 QR—K1, QR—K1 (Black strives in vain to prevent P—K4); 19 R—K2, P—N3; 20 KR—K1, N—QR4; 21 P—K4, Q—N2; 22 P—K5 followed by P—B4 with a formidable "Pawn-roller."

7	PxP!	10 Castles	Q—B2!
8 BxBP	P—B4	11 B—Q3	P—K4
9 N—B3	N—B3	12 Q—B2	....

An intensely interesting position. Black has freed himself admirably, but White hopes to open up the position and get his center Pawns moving so that he can demonstrate the power of his Bishops.

A possibility is 12 ... R—Q1; 13 R—K1, B—N5; 14 NxP, NxN; 15 PxN, QxP; 16 P—B3, B—K3; 17 R—N1, P—B5; 18 B—B1, N—Q4!; 19 B—Q2, Q—B2.

A wilder line of play is 12 ... R—K1 (threatens ... P—K5); 13 P—K4, KPxP; 14 PxP, B—N5!; 15 P—K5, BxN; 16 PxN, NxQP; 17 BxPch, K—R1; 18 PxPch, KxP; 19 B—N2!; QR—Q1!; 20 PxB, R—KR1!; 21 K—R1, RxB.

In both cases Black holds his own because the free play of his pieces compensates for White's Bishop-pair. This is often the verdict on Nimzoindian variations.

(e) 4 P—QR3 Variation

1 P—Q4	N—KB3	3 N—QB3	B—N5
2 P—QB4	P—K3	4 P—QR3	....

This leads to a very difficult game for both sides. After the following exchange White hopes to get a good attack, based on his two Bishops and his powerful-looking Pawn center. Black hopes for a close position where his Knights can maneuver skillfully; he also has prospects of turning White's Pawn at Queen Bishop 4 into a target.

| 4 .... | BxNch | 5 PxB | .... |

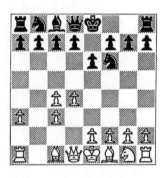

38

(Position after 5 PxB)

Note that White's Pawn at Queen Bishop 4 can no longer be protected by Pawns, and must be protected by pieces. Hence this Pawn is weak, and Black will try to train his guns on it.

| 5 .... | P—B4! |

This "fixes" White's theoretically weak Pawn at White's Queen Bishop 4. In addition, Black exerts pressure on White's Pawn center.

| 6 P—K3 | P—QN3 |

Black's Bishop will go to Queen Knight 2 (later to Queen Rook 3, to press against the weak Pawn).

On the other hand, playing for an early . . . P—K4 is doubtful policy, as it often allows White to open the King Bishop file with impressive effect, for example 6 . . . N—B3; 7 B—Q3, P—K4; 8 N—K2, P—Q3; 9 Castles, Q—K2; 10 P—K4!, N—Q2; 11 P—B4, P—QN3; 12 N—N3, P—N3;

13 BPxP, QPxP; 14 P—Q5, N—QR4; 15 R—R2!, N—N2;
16 QR—KB2, N—Q3; 17 B—R6 with considerable positional advantage for White.

| 7 B—Q3 | B—N2 | 9 N—K2 | Castles |
| 8 P—B3 | N—B3 | 10 P—K4 | N—K1! |

A star move. To allow the pinning maneuver B—N5 would be fatal to Black's freedom of action. The retreat of the Knight also prepares for the blockading move . . . P—B4.

| 11 B—K3 | P—Q3 | 12 Castles | N—R4! |

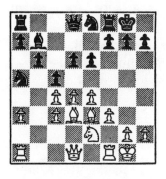

39

(Position after 12 . . . N—R4!)

Black begins the attack on the Queen Bishop Pawn.

Black has the initiative, as Black's threats against the Queen Bishop Pawn outweigh White's attacking possibilities on the other wing. For example: 13 N—N3, Q—Q2; 14 P—B4, P—B4; 15 Q—K2 (if 15 QPxP, QPxP; 16 PxP, R—Q1!), P—N3!; 16 KR—Q1, N—N2; 17 R—R2, Q—R5!; 18 B—B1, QR—B1! (note the mounting pressure on White's Queen Bishop Pawn); 19 Q—QB2, QxQ; 20 RxQ, B—R3! and Black wins the weak Queen Bishop Pawn.

In this defense Black fianchettoes his Queen Bishop very early, with a view to commanding the long diagonal, particularly his King 5 square. White does best to fianchetto his King Bishop, thus carrying on a long-range duel for control of the diagonal.

This duel often centers about a specific problem: White wants to enforce P—K4, Black wants to prevent this move. If White gets in P—K4, he will have an advantage in space, which explains the critical nature of the struggle. Bear in mind, though, that since White plays an early N—KB3 (instead of N—QB3 as in the Nimzoindian Defense), it will not be easy for him to enforce P—K4.

On the whole, White gets a freer game than Black in this opening. White's goal is to secure the initiative; Black's goal is to maintain an adequate defense.

(a) 5 . . . B—K2 Variation

1 P—Q4	N—KB3	4 P—KN3	B—N2
2 P—QB4	P—K3	5 B—N2	B—K2
3 N—KB3	P—QN3	6 Castles	Castles
	7 N—B3	. . . .	

Black can now get a firm foothold in the center with 7 . . . P—Q4 at the cost of condemning his Queen Bishop to inactivity after 8 N—K5!

| 7 . . . . | N—K5 | 8 Q—B2 | NxN |

White's next move is more or less forced, as 9 PxN would give him a doubled Queen Bishop Pawn with no tangible compensation.

9 QxN   . . . .

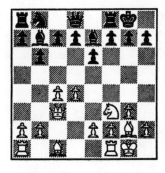

40

(Position after 9 QxN)

Black has a double goal: to retain control of his King 5 square, and also to form a center of his own by . . . P—Q3 and . . . P—K4.

White has good chances of getting the initiative: if for example 9 . . . P—KB4; 10 P—Q5!, PxP; 11 N—K1 *with lasting pressure on Black's game.*

Another possibility from Diagram 40 is 9 . . . B—K5; 10 B—B4!, P—Q3; 11 Q—K3!, B—N2; 12 KR—Q1, N—Q2; 13 P—QN4, N—B3; 14 P—QR4, P—QR4; 15 P—N5 *and White has considerably more freedom of action.*

(b) 5 . . . B—N5ch Variation

1 P—Q4	N—KB3	3 N—KB3	P—QN3
2 P—QB4	P—K3	4 P—KN3	B—N2
	5 B—N2	. . . .	

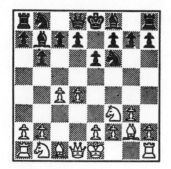

41

(Position after 5 B—N2)

Black decides on a simplifying exchange, which, however, still leaves him with difficult problems to solve.

5	B—N5ch	6 B—Q2	BxBch

The obvious reply is now 7 QNxB. But White's Queen Knight will be more aggressively posted at Queen Bishop 3 than at Queen 2. This explains White's next move:

7 QxB!	Castles	8 N—B3	P—Q3

After this White will be able to play P—K4, but if instead 8 . . . N—K5; 9 Q—B2!, NxN; 10 N—N5! winning the Exchange because of the mate threat.

9 Q—B2	Q—K2	10 Castles KR	P—B4

Black must forestall P—K4, which would permit White to answer a later . . . P—B4 with P—Q5, seriously constricting Black's game.

11 QR—Q1	PxP	12 NxP	BxB

After 13 KxB White is on the way to playing P—K4, which will give him a much greater command of the board. White has an unmistakable initiative.

KING'S INDIAN DEFENSE

This is generally considered the most complex and most interesting of all the Indian Defenses. As in other "Indian" lines, Black avoids answering 1 P—Q4 with 1 . . . P—Q4. Instead, he plays 1 . . . N—KB3 and continues with . . . P—KN3 and . . . B—N2.

Of course, he cannot wholly neglect the center. He almost invariably plays . . . P—Q3 followed in due course by . . . P—K4. After that, he has several possibilities. One is to play . . . KPxQP, opening up the long diagonal for his fianchettoed Bishop. This has the customary drawback of freeing White's position as well.

Or Black may stand pat after . . . P—K4, giving White the opportunity to push by with P—Q5, which leads to a rather locked position in which the advantage generally goes to the player who can first advance his King Bishop Pawn two squares.

Theoretically, White ought to have the advantage because his position is freer. But Black's position is solid and full of resource; a tenacious player can accomplish miracles with this defense.

(a) 3 P—KN3 Variation with . . . P—Q3

| 1 P—Q4 | N—KB3 | 3 P—KN3 | B—N2 |
| 2 P—QB4 | P—KN3 | 4 B—N2 | Castles |

Experience has shown that fianchettoing is an effective way to develop White's King Bishop.

| 5 P—K4 | P—Q3 | 6 N—K2 | . . . . |

All in all this is preferable to N—KB3. At King 2 this Knight does not stand in the way of P—B4.

6 ....   P—K4   7 QN—B3   ....

Also possible is 7 P—Q5, which on the whole seems to give White preferable chances. For he can strive to gain further terrain with P—B4, as well as P—QN4 followed by P—QB5. A likely sequel is 7 . . . P—QR4; 8 Castles, QN—Q2; 9 QN—B3, N—B4; 10 P—KR3, N—K1; 11 B—K3, P—B4; 12 PxP, PxP; 13 P—B4, and White's game is more promising.

7 ....   QN—Q2   8 Castles   P—B3

In order to be able to play : . . Q—B2 or . . . Q—N3. In some cases the move prepares for an eventual . . . P—Q4, which is, however, too ambitious a project.

9 P—KR3!   ....

White wants to play B—K3, but first he rules out the annoying . . . N—N5.

9 ....   PxP   10 NxP   ....

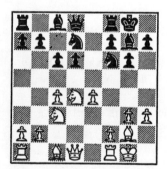

42

(Position after 10 NxP)

Black has obtained maneuvering freedom for his Knights and King Bishop. However, his weakened Queen Pawn is readily subject to pressure.

Black has numerous possibilities here, but White maintains the upper hand with accurate play. Thus, if 10 ... R—K1; 11 B—K3, N—N3; 12 P—N3, P—Q4?; 13 KPxP, PxP; 14 P—B5, QN—Q2; 15 KN—N5!, Q—R4; 16 P—R3!, N—K5?!; 17 P—QN4, NxN; 18 NxN, Q—Q1; 19 NxP!, BxR; 20 QxB and White has an overwhelming game in return for the sacrifice of the Exchange.

Another possibility is 10 ... R—K1; 11 B—K3 (also good is 11 R—K1, N—B4; 12 B—B4 with pressure on the Queen Pawn), N—B4; 12 Q—B2, P—QR4; 13 QR—Q1 (threatens 14 NxP!, PxN; 15 BxN), Q—K2; 14 KR—K1 and White has a fine game. (Note the trap 14 . . . KNxP?; 15 NxN, NxN; 16 BxN, QxB; 17 B—Q2! and White wins!)

The superior development of White's pieces assures him the better game with careful play.

(b) 3 . . . P—KN3 Variation with . . . P—Q4

1 P—Q4	N—KB3	3 P—KN3	B—N2
2 P—QB4	P—KN3	4 B—N2	P—Q4
	5 PxP	NxP	

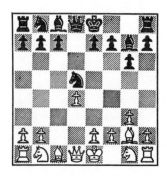

43

(Position after 5 . . . NxP)

White plans to get a powerful center Pawn position. Black hopes to prove that White's plans are too ambitious.

6 P—K4   N—N3

Though 6 . . . N—N5 is playable, it involves tactical finesses, for example 7 Q—R4ch, QN—B3; 8 P—Q5, P—QN4! (even 8 . . . Castles! is possible, for if 9 PxN, N—Q6ch and Black regains the piece); 9 QxNP (or 9 Q—N3?, N—Q5!), N—B7ch; 10 K—Q1, B—Q2 and White cannot play 11 KxN?? N—Q5ch nor 11 PxN??, BxP dis ch. And after 6 . . . N—N5; 7 P—Q5, P—QB3; 8 N—K2 (8 P—QR3 is best answered by 8 . . . Q—R4!), PxP; 9 PxP, B—KB4; 10 Q—R4ch, QN—B3!; 11 QN—B3! (not 11 PxN??, N—B7ch; 12 K—B1, Q—Q8 mate), B—B7! or . . . P—QN4! and Black can hold his own in the coming complications.

7 N—K2   . . . .

Immediate measures against White's center are futile, for example 7 . . . P—K4; 8 P—Q5, P—QB3; 9 QN—B3, PxP; 10 PxP and White's passed Pawn is a power for the endgame.

| 7 . . . . | Castles | 8 Castles | . . . . |

44

(Position after 8 Castles)

Black cannot make any headway against White's powerful center. For example 8 . . . P—QB4; 9 P—Q5 and Black's Knights have no prospects.

8	N—B3		12 PxP	N—B5
9 P—Q5	N—N1		13 R—K1	R—K1
10 KN—B3!	P—QB3		14 N—R3!	N—Q3
11 P—QR4!	PxP		15 QN—N5!	....

White's pressure is stifling. But the avoidance of this line (with 6 . . . N—N5) requires first-class tactical abilities.

(c) B—K2 Variation

1 P—Q4	N—KB3		4 P—K4	P—Q3
2 P—QB4	P—KN3		5 B—K2	Castles
3 N—QB3	B—N2		6 P—B4	....

A plausible-looking alternative is 6 B—N5, but Black can take advantage of the absence of White's Queen Bishop from the Queen-side in this fashion: 6 . . . P—B4!; 7 P—Q5, P—K3; 8 N—B3, PxP; 9 BPxP, P—KR3; 10 B—KB4, P—QN4!; 11 BxNP, NxKP!; 12 NxN, Q—R4ch; 13 Q—Q2, QxB; 14 NxQP, QxP; 15 QxQ, BxQ; 16 QR—N1, B—B6ch; 17 K—Q1, B—R3; 18 BxP, R—Q1; 19 B—B4, B—R4! and the threat of . . . B—B2 enables Black to regain his Pawn with a superior position, thanks to his two Bishops.

6 ....   P—K4

Black does not fear 7 PxP, PxP; 8 NxP which he can answer with 8 . . . NxP!

7 Castles   N—B3!

The old move was 7 . . . QN—Q2, which allowed Black to equalize after 8 R—K1, P—B3; 9 B—B1, R—K1; 10 P—QN3, PxP!; 11 NxP, P—Q4! or 10 R—N1, PxP; 11 NxP, P—Q4!

However, on 7 ... QN—Q2 White maintains the initiative with 8 P—Q5, N—B4; 9 Q—B2, P—QR4; 10 N—K1!, KN—Q2; 11 B—K3, P—B4; 12 PxP, PxP; 13 P—B4, P—K5; 14 Q—Q2, N—B3; 15 N—B2. White will eventually break through with P—KN4. Meanwhile he commands his vital Queen 4 square and more than adequately blockades Black's passed Pawn.

8 P—Q5	N—K2	10 B—K3	P—KB4
9 N—K1	N—Q2!	11 P—B3	P—B5
	12 B—B2	P—KN4	

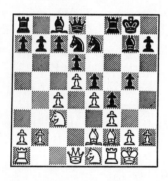

45

(Position after 12 ... P—KN4)

A very exciting position. White attacks on the Queen-side, intending to open lines there with P—B5. Black attacks on the King-side, intending to open lines there with ... P—N5.

13 N—Q3	N—KB3

Another way is ... R—B3 followed by ... R—N3 intending ... P—N5.

14 P—B5	N—N3	16 PxP	PxP
15 R—B1	R—B2	17 N—QN5	P—N5

Both sides have carried out their plans according to schedule, and a fierce fight is in progress.

1 P—Q4	N—KB3	4 P—K4	P—Q3
2 P—QB4	P—KN3	5 P—B3	Castles
3 N—QB3	B—N2	6 B—K3	P—K4
	7 P—Q5	....	

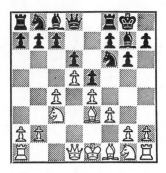

46

(Position after 7 P—Q5)

White's solid 5th move is the key to this variation. He delays somewhat the development of his King-side while he prepares to castle on the other wing and begin an attack with P—KN4 and P—KR4 etc.

7	P—B4	10 PxP	PxP
8 Q—Q2	N—R4	11 B—Q3	P—QR3
9 Castles	P—B4	12 KN—K2	P—N4?!

Black offers a Pawn in order to open attacking lines against the hostile King. But White is more interested in furthering his own attack.

13 QR—N1	PxP	14 B—N1!	....

Played in order to lend greater strength to White's coming P—KN4. *White's attack on the open file should then win for him.*

1 P—Q4	N—KB3		3 N—QB3	B—N2
2 P—QB4	P—KN3		4 P—K4	P—Q3
	5 P—B4		. . . .	

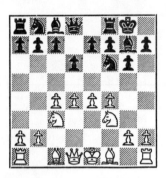

47

(Position after 5 P—B4)

White's last move is very aggressive and may leave Black with a very cramped game. On the other hand, the slightest inexactitude on White's part may grant Black a powerful counterattack.

5	P—B4		6 PxP!	. . . .

Best. After 6 P—Q5, Castles; 7 N—B3, P—K4! Black's game is quite solid (8 PxP, PxP; 9 NxP, NxP!).

After the text, 6 . . . PxP; 7 QxQch, KxQ; 8 P—K5 gives Black a poor game.

	6	Q—R4

Threatens . . . NxP.

7 B—Q3	QxBP		8 Q—K2	N—B3

White now continues 9 N—B3 followed by B—K3, after which his more harmonious development should tell in his favor.

Summary: On the whole, White's best chance of obtaining a solid positional advantage stems from the early fianchetto of his King Bishop—Variation (*a*).

662

GRUENFELD DEFENSE

In this Indian Defense, Black combines the fianchetto of his King Bishop with . . . P—Q4. As a rule, Black's Queen Pawn disappears quickly, allowing White to set up an impressive Pawn center.

To make up for White's advantage in this respect, Black must concentrate on agile maneuvers with his pieces. In some cases, he can hit back at White's center with . . . P—QB4. At all times Black must be prepared to put his King Bishop to good use on the long diagonal.

(a) Exchange Variation

| 1 P—Q4 | N—KB3 | 3 N—QB3 | P—Q4 |
| 2 P—QB4 | P—KN3 | 4 PxP | . . . . |

White sets out at once to build up a Pawn center. After the quiet alternative 4 P—K3, B—N2; 5 N—B3, Castles; 6 Q—N3, P—K3; 7 B—Q2, P—N3 Black fianchettoes his other Bishop with a good game.

| 4 . . . . | NxP | 5 P—K4 | NxN |
| | 6 PxN | P—QB4! | |

48

(Position after 6 . . . P—QB4!)

Black loses no time in hitting at White's powerful Pawn center. Black will immediately intensify the pressure with . . . B—N2.

| 7 B—QB4 | B—N2 | 8 N—K2! | .... |

The more aggressive-looking N—B3 allows a future pin
by . . . B—N5.

| 8 .... | Castles | 10 PxP | N—B3 |
| 9 Castles | PxP | 11 B—K3 | .... |

49

(Position after 11 B—K3)

*A crucial position, as Black must now
be prepared to demonstrate the effectiveness of his pressure on the center
Pawns.*

| 12 .... | N—R4! | 13 B—Q3 | N—B3! |

*Thus Black establishes equality. White must guard his
Queen Pawn, and if 14 B—QB4, N—R4 etc. threatens to
repeat moves indefinitely. If 14 B—B2, P—N3 intending
15 . . . N—N5; 16 B—N3, B—QR3 with an excellent game
for Black.*

(b) 5 Q—N3 Variation

1 P—Q4	N—KB3	3 N—QB3	P—Q4
2 P—QB4	P—KN3	4 N—B3	B—N2
	5 Q—N3	....	

50

(Position after 5 Q—N3)

White insists on clearing up the position in the center. As 5 . . . P—K3 or 5 . . . P—B3 would be rather passive, Black gives up the center in the hope of getting active play for his pieces.

5 . . . .   PxP   6 QxBP   Castles

As in the previous variation, White now creates an imposing Pawn center.

            7 P—K4   B—N5

Black attacks the Knight which guards White's Queen Pawn.

8 B—K3   KN—Q2   9 Q—N3   N—N3

51

(Position after 9 . . . N—N3)

White's Queen Pawn is under pressure, now that the Black King Knight has unmasked the diagonal of Black's King Bishop. However, White has ample resources.

10 R—Q1	N—B3	12 B—K2	NxNch
11 P—Q5	N—K4	13 PxN	B—R6

White has considerably more maneuvering space for his pieces, and after 14 KR—N1, Q—B1; 15 P—B4!, B—Q2; 16 P—B5! he has a formidable attack.

(c) 4 B—B4 Variation

1 P—Q4	N—KB3	3 N—QB3	P—Q4
2 P—QB4	P—KN3	4 B—B4	B—N2
	5 P—K3	Castles!	

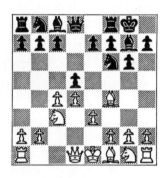

52

(Position after 5 . . . Castles!)

Black's last move amounts to a gambit, as White can now win a Pawn. However, Black's threats assure him adequate compensation.

After 6 PxP, NxP; 7 NxN, QxN; 8 BxP White has won a Pawn. However, Black gets a very strong game with 8 . . . N—R3! for example 9 B—N3, B—B4 (threatens . . . N—N5); 10 P—QR3, QR—B1 with a view to . . . R—B7. Also possible is 8 . . . N—R3!; 9 BxN, PxB when White's most prudent course is 10 N—B3 allowing Black to regain the Pawn with 10 . . . Q—N2. If instead 10 Q—B3, Q—QN4!! when 11 QxR will not do because of 11 . . . QxP; 12 R—Q1, Q—B6ch; 13 R—Q2, B—N5! and wins.

666

6 R—B1	P—B4!	7 QPxP	B—K3!

Black stands well despite the Pawn minus, for example
8 PxP, NxP; 9 NxN, BxN; 10 P—QN3, Q—R4ch; 11 Q—
Q2, QxQch; 12 KxQ, R—Q1 etc.

Summary: White should rely on his Pawn center, while Black should strive for utmost mobility. Variation (*b*) favors White, while the other two lines are satisfactory for Black.

BLUMENFELD COUNTER GAMBIT

As we have seen earlier, counter gambits, being attempts to wrest the initiative out of White's hands, have slight chance to succeed. This reasoning applies to the Blumenfeld line.

1 P—Q4	N—KB3	3 N—KB3	P—B4
2 P—QB4	P—K3	4 P—Q5	P—QN4?!

Risky—and unnecessary as well, as the simple 4 . . . PxP transposes into the Benoni line described on page 77. Black hopes for the speculative continuation 5 QPxP, BPxP; 6 PxP, P—Q4 which gives him a strong center and open lines for his pieces in return for a relatively unimportant wing Pawn.

5 B—N5!	KPxP	

Another way, just as disadvantageous, is 5 . . . Q—R4ch; 6 Q—Q2, QxQch; 7 QNxQ, KPxP; 8 BxN, PxB; 9 PxQP, B—QN2; 10 P—K4, P—QR3; 11 N—R4 with considerable positional advantage for White.

6 PxQP	P—KR3	9 P—K4	P—R3
7 BxN	QxB	10 P—QR4	P—N5
8 Q—B2	P—Q3	11 P—R3!	. . . .

With his last move, White has hemmed in Black's Queen Bishop. After 11 . . . B—K2; 12 QN—Q2, Castles; 13 B—K2, N—Q2; 14 N—B4 White has considerably greater freedom of action. Black's two Bishops can accomplish little.

BUDAPEST DEFENSE

This is also a counter gambit, but it has more positional justification than most defenses of its kind. If White clings slavishly to the gained material, he often gets into trouble. On the other hand, if he develops systematically, he is likely to get the better game. A too rapid advance, however, should be shunned, as it may enable Black to counterattack successfully.

(a) 4 B—B4 Variation

| 1 P—Q4 | N—KB3 | 2 P—QB4 | P—K4 |

This is the counter gambit.

| 3 PxP | . . . . |

53

(Position after 3 PxP)

If Black tries 3 . . . N—K5, White continues with simple development: 4 N—KB3, N—QB3; 5 QN—Q2, N—B4; 6 P—KN3, P—Q3; 7 PxP, QxP; 8 B—N2, B—B4; 9 P—QR3, P—QR4; 10 Castles, Castles; 11 P—QN4! returning the Pawn for a winning attack.

3 ....   N—N5

And now 4 P—B4? would be quite bad: 4 . . . B—B4;
5 N—R3, P—KB3 with an overwhelming game for Black.

4 B—B4   N—QB3   5 N—KB3   B—N5ch

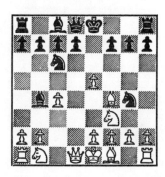

54

(Position after 5 . . . B—N5ch)

*If now 6 N—B3, Q—K2; 7 Q—Q5,
BxNch; 8 PxB, P—B3! and White's
extra Pawn, being doubled and isolated, is not worth much.*

6 QN—Q2   Q—K2   7 P—QR3   KNxKP

If now 8 PxB???, N—Q6 mate.

8 NxN   NxN   10 QxB   P—Q3
9 P—K3   BxNch   11 B—K2   N—N3

*After 12 B—N3, Castles; 13 Castles KR, White's two
Bishops and slightly greater freedom of action give him the
better prospects.*

(b) 4 P—K4 Variation

1 P—Q4   N—KB3   3 PxP   N—N5
2 P—QB4   P—K4   4 P—K4   ....

Here White's objective is to develop rapidly. But he must
be careful not to overextend himself.

669

| 4 .... | NxKP | 5 P—B4 | N—N3 |

Apparently better than 5 . . . KN—B3, which leaves White with a much freer game after 6 P—QR3, P—QR4; 7 B—K3, N—R3; 8 N—KB3, B—B4; 9 Q—Q2, P—Q3; 10 N—B3, Castles; 11 B—Q3, BxB; 12 QxB, N—B4; 13 Castles QR.

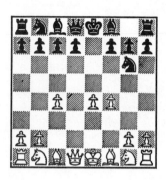

55

(Position after 5 . . . N—N3)

Black will attempt to prove that White's numerous Pawn moves have weakened his position.

| 6 B—K3 | .... |

If 6 N—KB3, B—N5ch; 7 N—B3, Q—B3!; 8 P—K5, Q—N3; 9 Q—Q3, P—Q3; 10 P—QR3, BxNch; 11 QxB, PxP; 12 NxP, NxN; 13 QxNch, Q—K3 with a level position.

| 6 .... | B—N5ch | 8 PxB | Q—K2 |
| 7 N—B3 | BxNch | 9 B—Q3 | P—KB4 |

White is hard put to it to defend the center.

| 10 Q—B2 | PxP | 12 BxN | P—Q4! |
| 11 BxP | NxP! | 13 PxP | B—B4 |

After 14 Castles, BxB; 15 Q—N3, N—Q2 Black's position seems somewhat exposed, but he just has time to castle and consolidate his position.

After 1 P—Q4, P—QB4 White can reply 2 PxP, but in that case Black recovers the Pawn comfortably with 2 . . . P—K3. The usual move against the counter gambit is therefore 2 P—Q5, which leads to a complex maneuvering game in which White has a greater command of the board.

1 P—Q4	P—QB4

An alternative line is 1 . . . N—KB3; 2 P—QB4, P—B4; 3 P—Q5, with this likely continuation: 3 . . . P—K3; 4 N—QB3, PxP; 5 PxP, P—Q3; 6 N—B3, P—KN3; 7 P—KN3, B—N2; 8 B—N2, Castles; 9 Castles, P—QR3 (in the hope of gaining space on the Queen-side with . . . P—QN4); 10 P—QR4!, QN—Q2; 11 N—Q2, KR—K1; 12 P—R5! with considerable pressure.

2 P—Q5	. . . .

56

(Position after 2 P—Q5)

A position which leaves both sides with scope for considerable maneuvering. As a rule White has the better prospects because Black's position is apt to become cramped.

2	P—K4	3 P—K4	P—Q3
	4 B—Q3	N—K2	

Black can also try 4 . . . P—QR3, but then 5 P—QR4! rules out the intended . . . P—QN4.

671

Here 5 . . . P—B4 opens up the game to White's advantage: 6 P—KB4!, BPxP; 7 BxP, N—Q2; 8 Castles, N—KB3; 9 QN—B3! and White's free, rapid development will tell in his favor.

On the other hand, 5 . . . P—QR3; 6 P—QR4!, N—N3; 7 N—R3!, B—K2; 8 N—QB4!, Castles; 9 Castles, N—Q2; 10 B—Q2, P—N3; 11 P—QB3, R—N1; 12 P—QN4! leaves White with a strong Queen-side initiative.

| 6 P—QB4 | B—N2 | 8 Castles | P—B4 |
| 7 QN—B3 | Castles | 9 P—B4! | QN—Q2 |

By now playing 10 N—N3! White maintains a strong initiative, for example 10 . . . KPxP; 11 BxP, N—K4; 12 PxP, NxB; 13 QxN, NxBP; 14 KN—K4! and White's lasting pressure on Black's weak Queen Pawn is embarrassing. White has two decisive threats in N—QN5 and P—KN4, leaving Black at a loss for a good continuation.

DUTCH DEFENSE

As in the Queen's Gambit Declined and the Queen's Indian Defense, Black fights for control of the King 5 square. In this defense he carries on the fight by playing an early . . . P—KB4. He can then continue the struggle with . . . P—Q4, or he can play . . . P—Q3 with a view to forming a counter-center with . . . P—K4.

Theorists are pretty well agreed that White's best course is to fianchetto his King Bishop, striking at the important center squares. The development of White's King Knight poses

672

an interesting problem—to develop it to King Bishop 3, where it bears down on the King 5 square; or to play N—KR3 followed by N—KB4, to bear down on the Queen 5 square. Both methods have their good points.

(a) P—KN3 Variation

1 P—Q4	P—KB4		2 P—KN3	N—KB3
3 B—N2	P—K3			

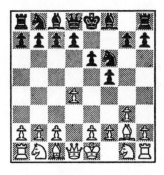

57

(Position after 3 . . . N—KB3)

White must choose between developing his King Knight at King Bishop 3 or King Rook 3.

4 N—KB3 . . . .

We may consider this the main line, although 4 N—KR3 is an excellent alternative: 4 . . . P—Q4 (Black has a "Stonewall" formation); 5 Castles, B—Q3; 6 P—QB4, P—QB3. Then after 7 N—B3, QN—Q2; 8 Q—Q3, N—K5; 9 P—B3!, NxN; 10 PxN, White is ready to smash the center with P—K4.

Another alternative is 4 N—KR3, B—K2; 5 Castles, Castles; 6 P—QB4, P—Q3; 7 N—B3, Q—K1; 8 P—K4, PxP; 9 N—B4!, P—B3; 10 N/B3xP with a fine game for White.

4	B—K2		5 Castles	Castles
6 P—B4	P—Q3			

673

If Black adopts the Stonewall formation with 6 . . . P—Q4, White can get a clear positional advantage in several ways. For example 7 P—N3, P—B3; 8 B—QR3! By exchanging the black-squared Bishops, White leaves Black with the white-squared Queen Bishop, which is hemmed in by the Black Pawns on white squares.

Another way after 6 . . . P—Q4 is 7 P—N3, P—B3; 8 N—B3, Q—K1; 9 Q—B2, Q—R4; 10 N—K5, QN—Q2; 11 N—Q3!, P—KN4; 12 P—B3! with a view to P—K4! with a powerful initiative in the center.

| 7 N—B3 | Q—K1 | 8 R—K1 | .... |

A good alternative for White is 8 Q—B2, Q—R4; 9 B—N5, P—K4; 10 PxP, PxP; 11 BxN!, PxB; 12 N—Q5, B—Q1; 13 QR—Q1, P—B3; 14 N—B3, B—K3; 15 N—KR4! and White has all the play.

| 8 .... | Q—R4 |

Even after 8 . . . Q—N3 White can play 9 P—K4!, for after 9 . . . PxP; 10 NxP, NxN; 11 RxN, QxR?; 12 N—R4, Black's Queen is trapped.

| 9 P—K4 | PxP | 10 NxP | NxN |
| 11 RxN | .... | | |

White, with his superior development, has lasting pressure on Black's position.

1 P—Q4   P—KB4   2 P—K4   ....

A gambit attack which can give Black a great deal of trouble unless he plays carefully.

2 ....   PxP   3 N—QB3   N—KB3

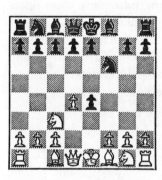

58

(Position after 3 . . . N—KB3)

After 4 B—KN5 Black must avoid the trap 4 . . . P—Q4? for after 5 BxN, KPxB; 6 Q—R5ch, P—KN3; 7 QxQP White comes out a Pawn ahead.

4 B—KN5   N—QB3!

Black can hold his own, for example 5 P—B3, P—K4!; 6 P—Q5, N—Q5; 7 PxP, B—K2; 8 B—QB4, P—Q3!; 9 KN—K2, N—N5!

Or 5 P—Q5, N—K4; 6 Q—Q4, N—B2; 7 BxN, KPxB; 8 NxP, P—KB4; 9 N—N3, P—KN3!; 10 P—KR4, B—R3!

These variations show how Black gets an excellent game by consistently developing and seeking counterplay.

and Related Systems

From here to the end of the book we shall consider close openings which are for the most part not characterized by the move 1 P—Q4. They are given here in order to complete our survey of the most important close openings.

Reti's Opening, starting with 1 N—KB3, has great flexibility and possibilities of transposing into many other openings. It involves, as a rule, the immediate fianchetto of White's King Bishop and the ensuing fianchetto of the remaining Bishop. White's strategy is to control the center squares from the flanks. Black generally counters with aggression in the center in order to obtain equality.

(a) London System

1 N—KB3	P—Q4

Black can fend off an immediate decision by first playing the flexible 1 . . . N—KB3, which may transpose into many other openings.

2 P—B4	P—QB3

Now White has the option of transposing into the Queen's Gambit Declined (Slav Defense, p. 27).

3 P—QN3	N—B3	4 P—N3	B—B4!

A good development for this Bishop, which now bears strongly on the center.

5 B—KN2	QN—Q2	6 B—N2	P—K3
7 Castles		. . . .	

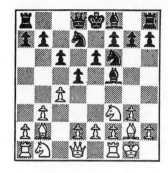

59

(Position after 7 Castles)

Black is well on the way to achieving a model development and need not fear the coming struggle for the center.

7	P—KR3

In order to create a haven for his Queen Bishop. He can also continue his development directly, for example 7 . . . B—Q3; 8 P—Q4, Castles; 9 N—B3, Q—K2; 10 P—QR3, P—QR4!; 11 N—KR4, B—KN5 with an excellent position for Black.

8 P—Q3	B—K2	9 QN—Q2	Castles

With Black's Queen Knight ready to go to Queen Bishop 4, he need not be afraid of White's P—K4, for example 10 Q—B2, B—R2; 11 P—K4, PxKP; 12 PxP, N—B4 with a good game for Black.

10 R—B1	P—QR4	12 R—B2	B—Q3
11 P—QR3	R—K1	13 Q—R1	Q—K2

Note how White bears down on the center from the wings. Black's game is playable.

(b) 2 . . . P—Q5 Variation

1 N—KB3	P—Q4	2 P—B4	P—Q5

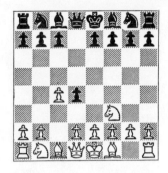

60

(Position after 2 ... P—Q5)

According to "hypermodern" theory, Black has compromised his position by advancing the Queen Pawn. In actual practice, the Pawn has a cramping effect on White's game.

| 3 P—K3 | N—QB3! | 5 NxN | QxN |
| 4 PxP | NxP | 6 N—B3 | B—N5! |

Black has seized the initiative.

| 7 Q—R4ch | B—Q2! | 9 B—K2 | B—B3 |
| 8 Q—N3 | Q—K4ch! | 10 Castles | Castles |

Black retains the initiative and has lasting pressure on White's backward Queen Pawn.

(c) King's Indian Reversed

| 1 N—KB3 | N—KB3 | 2 P—KN3 | P—KN3 |

White is playing the King's Indian Defense with a move in hand. If instead of the text Black plays 2 ... P—Q4, a likely continuation is 3 B—N2, P—K3; 4 Castles, B—K2; 5 P—Q3, Castles; 6 QN—Q2, P—B4; 7 P—K4 with an excellent game for White.

| 3 B—N2 | B—N2 | 4 Castles | Castles |
| | 5 P—Q3 | .... | |

678

61

(Position after 5 P—Q3)

Black can still choose between an eventual . . . P—Q3 or . . . P—Q4.

| | 5 . . . . | P—Q4 |

Also after 5 . . . P—B4; 6 P—K4, N—B3; 7 QN—Q2, P—Q3; 8 P—QR4 followed by N—B4 White has an excellent game.

| 6 QN—Q2 | P—B4 | 8 R—K1 | P—K4 |
| 7 P—K4 | N—B3 | 9 PxP | NxP |

Now White continues 10 N—B4 with a good game.

CATALAN SYSTEM

This opening features the fianchetto of White's King Bishop (as in the Reti Opening) and P—Q4 (as in the Queen's Gambit). It abounds in positional finesses that can prove fatal for Black if he plays carelessly.

| 1 P—Q4 | N—KB3 | 3 N—KB3 | P—Q4 |
| 2 P—QB4 | P—K3 | 4 P—KN3 | . . . . |

62

(Position after 4 P—KN3)

This position can be reached by many transpositions, as for example 1 N— KB3, P—Q4; 2 P—B4, P—K3; 3 P—KN3, N—KB3; 4 P—Q4 etc.

4	PxP

More interesting—and more complicated—is the alternative 4 . . . B—K2; 5 B—N2, Castles; 6 Castles, P—B4; 7 BPxP, NxP! (not 7 . . . KPxP leading into the inferior Tarrasch line—p. 25); 8 P—K4, N—N3; 9 N—B3, PxP; 10 NxP, N—B3; 11 NxN, PxN; 12 Q—K2, P—K4.

In this position White undoubtedly has possibilities of pressure against Black's weak Queen Bishop Pawn. On the other hand, Black's excellent development gives him ample resources.

5 Q—R4ch	B—Q2!

Simpler than 5 . . . QN—Q2; 6 QxBP, P—QR3; 7 B— N2, P—QN4; 8 Q—B6, QR—N1; 9 Castles, B—N2; 10 Q—B2, P—B4; 11 P—QR4, Q—N3 with a difficult position that gives both sides fighting chances.

6 QxBP	B—B3	7 B—N2	B—Q4

Black has countered White's fianchetto without weakening his position in any way. After 8 Q—B2, N—B3; 9 Q—Q1, B—N5ch—or 8 Q—Q3, P—B4; 9 N—B3, B—B3; 10 Castles, QN—Q2; 11 R—Q1, Q—N3 the position is even.

After 1 P—QB4, Black has many replies, such as 1 . . . N—KB3 or 1 . . . P—K3, which are likely to transpose into other openings. Generally speaking, it is only 1 . . . P—K4 which gives this opening independent status. In the ensuing play it is White's object to utilize 1 P—QB4 to control the Queen 5 square. The logical way to do this is to fianchetto the King Bishop, which is consequently one of the most popular positional motifs of this openings. Black must fight energetically for control of the center in order to maintain equality.

(a) King Fianchetto Variation with . . . P—Q4

1 P—QB4	P—K4	3 P—KN3	P—Q4
2 N—QB3	N—KB3	4 PxP	NxP
	5 B—N2	. . . .	

63

(Position after 5 B—N2)

Note how powerfully White's fianchettoed King Bishop bears down on the long diagonal, particularly on the vital center square Queen 5. Black must come to a decision about the future of his attacked Knight.

Black can maintain the Knight at his centralized post with 5 . . . B—K3, but after 6 N—B3, N—QB3; 7 Castles, B—K2 White forces Black to give way with the dynamic 8 P—Q4! Then, after 8 . . . PxP; 9 NxP, N/Q4xN; 10 PxN, NxN;

11 PxN, P—QB3; 12 R—N1! White still maintains his pressure on Black's game.

| 5 .... | N—N3 | 7 N—R3! | Castles |
| 6 P—Q3 | B—K2 | 8 Castles | N—B3 |

White's 7 N—R3 is a notable exception to the rule that it is poor play to develop a Knight to the side of the board. On King Rook 3 this Knight allows the Bishop to exert full sway on the long diagonal, and also permits the early line-clearing advance P—B4! (Both objectives would be blocked by the orthodox N—KB3.)

| 9 P—B4! | R—N1 | 10 PxP | NxP |
| | 11 N—B4! | .... | |

White's position is distinctly superior. His fianchettoed Bishop and both Knights control the crucial center square Queen 5; he has an open King Bishop file; and his center Pawns have great potential power in case of an eventual advance.

(b) King Fianchetto Variation with . . . P—Q3

| 1 P—QB4 | P—K4 | 3 P—KN3 | P—KN3 |
| 2 N—QB3 | N—QB3 | 4 B—N2 | B—N2 |

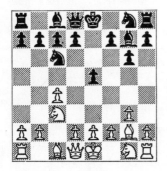

64

(Position after 4 . . . B—N2)

White has the best of both worlds: he not only controls the important Queen 5 square, but he can also control his own Queen 4 square with P—K3 and utilize this Pawn move to build a Pawn center.

5 P—K3!	P—Q3	8 NxP	NxN
6 KN—K2	KN—K2	9 PxN	Castles
7 P—Q4	PxP	10 Castles	N—B4

After 11 P—Q5, R—K1; 12 N—K4!, P—KR3; 13 Q— Q3! White has a very superior position, as he can increase his positional advantage with R—N1 and B—Q2 followed by B—QB3!

(c) Four Knights' Variation

1 P—QB4	P—K4	3 N—B3	N—B3
2 N—QB3	N—KB3	4 P—Q4	....

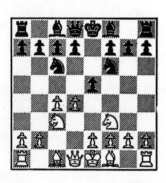

65

(Position after 4 P—Q4)

White immediately opens up the position on the theory that he can seize the initiative, for example 4 . . . P— K5; 5 N—Q2, NxP; 6 N/Q2xP, N— K3; 7 P—KN3 with a promising position for White.

4	PxP	7 B—R4	BxNch
5 NxP	B—N5	8 PxB	N—K4
6 B—N5	P—KR3	9 P—B4!	....

Much more vigorous than the routine 9 P—K3, N—N3; 10 B—N3, N—K5 with a good game for Black.

9 ....   N—N3

Not 9 . . . NxBP?; 10 P—K4!, N—K6; 11 Q—K2, NxB; 12 P—K5!, Castles; 13 N—B5! with a winning game.

| 10 BxN | QxB | 12 P—K4 | P—Q3 |
| 11 P—N3! | Castles | 13 B—N2 | P—B3 |

After 14 Castles, R—K1; 15 R—N1 White has considerably more mobility, while Black has vague possibilities of menacing White's weak Queen Bishop Pawns.

BIRD'S OPENING

A rare opening, as 1 P—KB4 contributes nothing to White's development. The idea of controlling the King 5 square often leads to a kind of Dutch Defense (p. 78) with colors reversed. Black has a number of ways to obtain an excellent game.

1 P—KB4   N—KB3

From's Gambit (1 . . . P—K4) is not quite satisfactory, for example 2 PxP, P—Q3; 3 PxP, BxP; 4 N—KB3, P—KN4; 5 P—Q4, P—N5; 6 N—N5!, P—KB4; 7 P—K4!, P—KR3; 8 P—K5, B—K2; 9 N—KR3, PxN; 10 Q—R5ch, K—B1; 11 B—QB4, Q—K1; 12 QxP/R3 with a decisive attack in return for the sacrificed piece.

2 P—K3   P—KN3   3 N—KB3   ....

Nor is the immediate Queen fianchetto very promising, for example 3 P—QN3, B—N2; 4 B—N2, P—Q3!; 5 Q—B1, Castles; 6 N—KB3, N—B3; 7 B—K2, B—N5; 8 Castles, P—K4! and Black has the better game.

3 ....   P—Q4

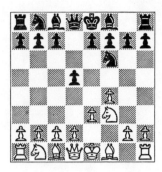

66

(Position after 3 . . . P—Q4)

White can now resort to a Stonewall formation, but after 4 P—Q4, B—N2; 5 B—Q3, Castles; 6 QN—Q2, P—B4; 7 P—B3, P—N3; 8 Q—K2, B—N2 Black has a fine game.

4 B—K2	B—N2		7 Q—K1	Castles
5 Castles	P—B4		8 Q—R4	Q—B2
6 P—Q3	N—B3		9 QN—Q2	P—K4

Black has an excellent game in this position (a Dutch Defense with colors reversed).

Index

L

M

N

O

P

V

W

Y

Z